AF521984

Cultural Politics in Colonial Tehuantepec

JUDITH FRANCIS ZEITLIN

Cultural Politics in Colonial Tehuantepec

Community and State among the Isthmus Zapotec, 1500–1750

STANFORD UNIVERSITY PRESS 2005
Stanford, California

Stanford University Press
Stanford, California

Library of Congress Cataloging-in-Publication Data

Zeitlin, Judith Francis.
Cultural politics in colonial Tehuantepec : community and state among the Isthmus Zapotec, 1500–1750 / Judith Francis Zeitlin.
p. cm.
Includes bibliographical references and index.
ISBN 0-8047-3388-0 (cloth : alk. paper)
1. Zapotec Indians—Mexico—Tehuantepec, Isthmus of—History. 2. Zapotec Indians—Mexico—Tehuantepec, Isthmus of—Politics and government. 3. Zapotec Indians—Mexico—Tehuantepec, Isthmus of—Antiquities. 4. Excavations (Archaeology)—Mexico—Tehuantepec, Isthmus of. 5. Tehuantepec, Isthmus of (Mexico)—Antiquities. I. Title.
F1219.8.Z37.Z45 2005
972.6004'9768 dc22 2005008178

Printed in the United States of America
Original Printing 2005
Last figure below indicates year of this printing:
14 13 12 11 10 09 08 07 06 05

Typeset at Stanford University Press in 10/13 Sabon

For ANDY *and* JEREMY,

who bore it all with filial patience and good humor and, in the end, have found their own paths to the heart of Mexico

Contents

Maps, Figures, and Table

Maps

Figures

Table

Preface

The subject of this book is an historical and archaeological examination of the late prehispanic Isthmus Zapotec state, established at Tehuantepec through a campaign of conquest and colonization, and of the responses that its descendant populations made to the complex political, economic, and cultural changes introduced by Spanish colonialism. Exploring these familiar ethnohistorical themes in the particular regional context of the southern Isthmus is an obvious research choice for an anthropologist interested in Mexico's native people and their cultural persistence. No one who has visited the hot, wind-swept towns of Tehuantepec or Juchitán and stepped into the busy markets with their brassy *tehuana* and *teca* merchants or witnessed the lavish *velas* that mark community religiosity can fail to be impressed by the vitality of Isthmus Zapotec culture and the unusual mix of indigenous and European traits that distinguishes it. Long before the Zapatista movement surfaced in Chiapas, the rise of COCEI (the Coalición Obrera Estudiantil del Istmo) in the early 1980s and the political commotion that this radical social movement caused within Mexico and across its northern border have only underscored the role of politics in the maintenance of Isthmus Zapotec society. Yet unlike many more isolated regions of Mesoamerica, where it might be argued that vestiges of the indigenous past remain because of the native population's ability to isolate itself from the Hispanic world, the southern Isthmus has long played a central role in the economic schemes of outsiders. To solve the puzzle of how these fiercely independent people have managed to perpetuate a distinctive ethnic identity in the context of an ongoing historical confrontation with nonnative society requires us to look more closely at the earliest stages of this engagement.

For me personally, the journey into the Isthmus colonial past came by a circuitous route. As students of the eminent Mesoamerican archaeologist Michael Coe, my husband Robert Zeitlin and I conducted doctoral dissertation projects in the southern Isthmus for ten months in 1972. Our programs of archaeological test excavation and surface survey were designed to begin filling a significant gap in regional prehistory by linking the settlements of the Pacific coastal plain with the Olmec phenomenon centered on the northern Isthmus, the developing Zapotec civilization of the Oaxaca highlands, and the nearby populations of Chiapas and Guatemala. My own research focused on changing settlement patterns during the Classic and Postclassic periods (AD 300–1500), which interested me for the interrelationships they revealed between subsistence, population growth, and changes in the social and natural environments. Like most Mesoamerican archaeologists, my concerns at the time were with the precontact, autochthonous developments in this region, even as the life we lived in the town of Juchitán drew both Bob and me into the warm embrace of the modern Zapotec community. I remarked to many of my fellow students that the work of an archaeologist was a terrific ruse for a closet ethnographer like myself, fascinated by the everyday realities of other lives, but uncomfortable asking questions that offered few tangible benefits for their answering.

When I began looking at the Spanish historical accounts of the region and the sixteenth-century Zapotecs during the last stages of my thesis, it was in order to flesh out the dry facts of the material record with more colorful descriptions of the native population before a great deal had changed under colonialism. Privileged to do much of that research ensconced in Coe's extensive private library, I was captivated by the record of cultural confrontation and change that could be glimpsed in published documentary compendia of Spain's business in Mesoamerica. Why, I asked myself, was I arbitrarily ending my study of social change on the eve of the most significant social and environmental upheaval witnessed in the Isthmus? Sensibly, I waited until after finally submitting my doctoral dissertation in 1978 to begin probing these new questions in earnest, for the startup costs of my new research venture were great and it took considerable time to acquire the most basic skills of a more properly trained historian.

The next decade of archival research led me more deeply into Tehuantepec's colonial past. For a time I thought I had packed up my trowel and spade permanently, so rich was the documentary residue of Spain's bureaucratic obsessions. Gradually, however, my frustrations over what was missing from this record grew. With but one colonial Spanish observer interested in describing Oaxaca's native communities in any detail, the bulk of the written record focused on occasions of conflict—disputes between native communities, struggles between communities and Spanish landowners and administrators, and occasional confrontations between communities and native elites. Massive court records typically presented Indian communities as undifferentiated social entities and rarely afforded a look at the inner workings of native sociopolitical organizations or cultural practices not sanctioned by colonial authorities. It was difficult to glimpse everyday life within Zapotec towns and villages from papers drawn up to meet the expectations of the Spanish courts, yet there were at the time few known colonial documents produced by Isthmus communities or individuals for their own purposes without the intermediary voices of translators or attorneys. The consequent portrayal of these towns and villages as beleaguered victims of the economic pressures put upon them by the colonial state was difficult to reconcile with the vibrancy of modern Isthmus Zapotec society and culture.

To get a closer look at the nature of colonial community life, I returned to the Isthmus in 1990 searching for historic-period archaeological sites. Small-scale excavations within the town of Tehuantepec and at one of its abandoned subject hamlets yielded new evidence for household consumption and settlement patterns. In the intervening years, I have been able to analyze and publish portions of this new research, while continuing to investigate archival records in Mexico and Spain. A fellowship at the John Carter Brown Library gave me access to the extensive colonial era literature documenting the Dominican effort to proselytize the Zapotecs. The dictionaries, catechisms, sermons, and moral polemics that dominate this literature have been important resources for understanding the conflicting systems of meaning and views of the world that continued to separate pastor and flock.

It is the intent of the present monograph to bring these disparate sources of information together in an effort to chart the course of colonial sociopolitical change in the Tehuantepec province. Rather than treat each class of evidence separately, the book draws upon whatever combination of textual, semantic, or material information best illustrates the particular historical or structural questions at hand, contrasting different data sets when they suggest different interpretations. If archaeological data are relatively poor at discriminating individual actors or distinguishing brief periods of time, they excel at documenting the practical realities of daily living and longer-term adaptive patterns. The fact that the detritus of material culture represents all sectors of society helps compensate for the limitations that partial preservation and burdensome retrieval problems impose. With sufficient time and financial resources for its full recovery, the archaeological record would be a useful independent source of information about native sociopolitical structure and enduring values in the colonial era. That is, unfortunately, a still distant goal for Tehuantepec, like most of Mesoamerica, but these preliminary data help bridge significant gaps in the archival record.

Even for the prehispanic past, written documents play an important role in elucidating structural arrangements in this study. Oaxaca archaeologists have relied extensively on published colonial period sources to illuminate late Zapotec political and economic networks and to detail the religious ideas behind ritual objects, art, and architecture, "upstreaming" these historical accounts to illuminate the 2,500-year-old foundation of Zapotec civilization. These same sources contribute to the present analysis, but additional archival material from the mid-sixteenth century specific to the establishment of the Isthmus Zapotec conquest state further refines this portrait of its sociopolitical integration. Where I differ in my use of the written record from many of my archaeologist colleagues is my interest in understanding the historical context in which these records appeared, finding the questions of whose voice is represented and what audience is framing the presentation of facts to be essential parts of the story.

The story I am telling concerns the aftermath of a dramatic cultural confrontation between the Isthmus Zapotec and Spanish empires. Although the Zapotec conquest of the Isthmus probably began a half-century earlier, my focus is the mature polity seen at the onset of the sixteenth century, when many of the individuals who gave testimony in Tehuantepec's earliest colonial litigation were witness to its operations. This examination of the process of cultural change and adaptation concludes in the mid-eighteenth century, just before the wave of Bourbon reforms began to make a significant impact on the colonial political economy and just before the dramatic native population rebound accelerated internal pressures on land and resources. During that 250-year period, I distinguish three phases of cultural transition for the Isthmus Zapotecs. A protracted initial period of adjustment to the political realities of Spanish hegemony concluded with the death of the last native king and the

1563 removal of the province from Hernán Cortés's seignorial domain, the Marquesado del Valle. The next one hundred years saw the province fully engaged with the imposed political, economic, and religious structures of the colonial enterprise, and documentary and archaeological sources are used here to chart the nature of the developing native adaptation. The final period of study represents not a qualitatively different challenge for Isthmus Zapotec communities, but rather the maturation of structural arrangements that framed how recovering native populations would maintain their cultural and political identity.

The study uses the year 1660 to divide these two last phases of colonial accommodation because of a signal event in Tehuantepec's history that occurred that year, the much studied and much remembered Tehuantepec rebellion. This and other instances of political crisis play an important role in my analysis of cultural change. One obvious reason for that role is the importance such crises were given by the Spanish authorities and the consequent flurry of probing documentation that followed these events, in marked contrast to the intermittent and superficial nature of much routine record-keeping for the province. But there is a deeper reason for focusing analytical attention on moments of crisis. As the social anthropologist Victor Turner observed some years ago in his book, *Dramas, Fields, and Metaphors*, "conflict seems to bring fundamental aspects of society, normally overlaid by the customs and habits of daily intercourse, into frightening prominence" (p. 35). By observing the unfolding social drama that conflict engenders, Turner suggested, it is possible to glimpse the underlying structures and symbolic values that orient society's members.

Turner's own interests in social change make it clear that he regarded these structures and values as dynamic and responsive to historical circumstances. One advantage to incorporating the archaeological record in the present study is that we are provided with a separate class of temporally sensitive data concerning the "customs and habits of daily intercourse" that may be used to chronicle cultural shifts. These customs and habits, or "durable dispositions," to use the terminology of Pierre Bourdieu, reflect the unselfconscious precepts governing how individuals engage in the world around them. While no two individuals necessarily present the same set of dispositions or "habitus," similar lived experiences and the mutual ability to predict the outcome of social interactions result in a similar "logic of practice" for the actors. Not surprisingly, many archaeologists have found Bourdieu's framework helpful in articulating the relationship between material culture patterns and the individuals whose actions created them, since his model avoids the presumption of fixed cultural rules that cannot be observed directly. Indeed, Bourdieu argues that such rules are components of theoretical models constructed by scientific observers and cannot be equated with the axioms or rules articulated by society's participants. Even in moments of crisis, when individuals are pressed to articulate their own goals and concerns, his model cautions us to recognize that these subjective understandings are not the same as the systemic underpinnings of the social framework.

This brief digression sketches a theoretical rationale for combining two imperfect data sets in my endeavor to understand the apparent paradox of Isthmus Zapotec society's ability to persist through change. The archaeological record demonstrates substantial change through time in Isthmian material culture, mirroring the changing customs and habits of daily life that were to become second-nature for the province's native inhabitants. As Bourdieu reminds us, the very fact that habitus reflects the lived experiences of individuals makes it responsive to the changed conditions of life, even as it shapes and limits the nature of that response. The broken pottery, discarded animal bones, and other residue of former habitations are used in this study in conjunction with historical and architectural data on settlement and population shifts to get closer to the experience of daily life for the province's native people and to see the ways in which that life changed over time. But the mere ability to carry on in such a dramatically different colonial environment does not address questions of why this society was so resilient and how it achieved its success at resisting Spanish hegemony. Following Turner's advice, I look to the historical confrontations between the Isthmus Zapotec and the colonial state for clues as to the fundamental values of the colonial community that marked it as a distinctive cultural entity and the structural framework that facilitated its perpetuation.

The eclectic and protracted nature of this study has left me with a longer list of personal and intellectual debts to acknowledge than might otherwise be the case. My first debt is to the people of the Isthmus, whose innate curiosity about the world and proud pleasure in their own way of life made this work such an easy compulsion. Many people welcomed us into their lives during our long seasons of archaeological fieldwork, but my greatest appreciation is due the Nicolás and Orozco families of Juchitán, who took Bob and me under their wings in 1972, patiently instructed us like small children in proper behavior, and rewarded us with a deep and abiding friendship that transcends cultural barriers and lengthy separations. My special thanks go to our dear friends Manuel and his sister Rosa, Rosa's daughter Teresa and her husband Arturo, and their now grown-up children, Aracele, Selene, and Arturo.

During my 1990 fieldwork in Tehuantepec, I was fortunate to have the advice and friendship of Fernando Santos Gutiérrez and his father Antonio Santos Cisneros of the Santa María Reloteca barrio, whose shared passion about the history of the Isthmus Zapotec and warm companionship facilitated my efforts to trace its archaeological clues. To Cont. Cesar Rojas Pétriz, then director of the Casa de la Cultura, I am grateful for the opportunity to photograph ceramic collections from the restoration of Tehuantepec's Dominican convent and for his generous permission to conduct preliminary excavations in the newly planted kitchen courtyard. I wish also to extend my appreciation to Sr. Francisco Barrera Valdivieso of the Santa Cruz Tagolaba barrio and Sr. José Santos Ibaños of the Rancho Santa Cruz, who indulged my request to excavate on their lands. Salomón Jiménez of Chihuitán and Luís Martínez Hinojosa, director of the Casa de la Cultura of Ixtepec, offered many leads in my search for colonial period archaeological remains, and Sr. Fernando A. Lavin Mier was extremely generous in allowing me to view his family's documentation for Rancho Santa Cruz.

The 1990 archaeological field research was conducted under a grant from the Wenner-Gren Foundation for Anthropological Research, whose support made the project's advancement possible. Lillian Thomas served as my field assistant and her energy, good sense, and good humor provided crucial sustenance throughout many long hot days. Mexico's Consejo de Arqueología, under the leadership of Lorena Mirambell, permitted me to undertake this fieldwork, and Ernesto González Licón, then director of the Instituto Nacional de Antropología e Historia's Centro Regional de Oaxaca, and Marcus Winter, staff archaeologist, facilitated the work's progress at more than one critical juncture. The Centro Regional directorate has continued to provide storage facilities for the archaeological collection and permitted me all needed access to the materials for analytical purposes. Elizabeth Wing, whose zooarchaeological analysis was vital to my doctoral dissertation research, kindly took in the faunal remains from the 1990 excavations at the Florida Museum of Natural History and supervised their initial classification by Abaco Robinson. Elizabeth Newman, who is launching her own career in

Mesoamerican historical archaeology, completed this project at Yale's Peabody Museum.

My initial archival research in Mexico was facilitated by a grant from Brandeis University's Mazer Fund for Faculty Research. A 1993 National Endowment for the Humanities fellowship supported further documentary research in Mexico and Spain and, most importantly, gave me the gift of time with which to launch the book's composition. The courteous and professional staffs at Mexico's Archivo General de la Nación and Spain's Archivo General de las Indias have provided ready access to the documentary resources on which this study depends. Grants from the University of Massachusetts Boston faculty development fund have provided timely support for database construction and illustration of materials, and I am grateful to Desiree Zymroz, John Kelly, and Paul Mohler for their assistance in these disparate efforts. Carol Obrion of Falmouth, Maine, skillfully rendered new maps from my vague instructions.

No such project develops in intellectual isolation, and I have been particularly privileged to be sustained by more than one formal academic community and by a large network of scholar-friends. Let me mention the special debt I have to the Institute of Latin American Studies at the University of Texas Austin, where in 1991 I spent a happy fall semester as a Rockefeller Fellow; my understanding of the Isthmus Zapotecs has been deepened by discussions with my co-participants in the Ethnic Studies Working Group and in particular with my co-fellows, Alcida Ramos and Jeffrey Gould. Moving the following term to the John Carter Brown Library, where I was a National Endowment for the Humanities Fellow, was an extraordinary privilege, and I am indebted to the library's director, Dr. Norman Fiering, and the scholarly community he and his staff have forged around the library's unique resources. At Brown University I was fortunate to have the continued support of the Center for Latin American Studies and the intellectual companionship of Thomas Skidmore, Shepherd Krech, Douglas Cope, Julio Ortega, and José Amor y Vásquez.

To my fellow Mesoamericanists, I have incurred debts too numerous to attempt more than a partial list. Michael Coe was responsible for my initial focus on the Isthmus, and his singular example gave me the courage to follow my own nose wherever it might lead. As a path breaker in the seamless integration of archaeological and historical resources, Ronald Spores has been both a role model and a timely mentor during the evolution of this study. I have benefited immensely from the scholarly advice and support of my colleague María de los Angeles Romero Frizzi. Her generous spirit is shared by a broad circle of Oaxaca ethnohistorians and ethnologists whose insights I have drawn upon, including John Chance, Victor de la Cruz, Héctor Díaz-Polanco, Manuel Esparza, Nancy Farriss, Laura Machuca, Carlos Manzo, Vicente Marcial, Guido Münch, Leticia Reina, and David Tavárez. In this group I would like to acknowledge the special collaboration I have enjoyed with Michel Oudijk, whose selfless dedication to uncovering Zapotec history is unrivaled. Pedro Carrasco guided me through Nahuatl word lists and saved me from numerous interpretative errors along the way. With few practicing historical archaeologists in Mesoamerica, I have had the good fortune to be able to rely on Janine Gasco as a regional neighbor, friend, and problem-solver. George Cowgill, Arthur Joyce, Louise Paradis, Joyce Marcus, Michael Smith, and Javier Urcid have provided counsel on archaeological and interpretative matters often far removed from their own interests.

Thanks to the insightful comments of Stephen Silliman, Matthew Restall, and an anonymous reviewer for Stanford University Press, all of whom reviewed the draft manuscript in its entirety, the present work has what I hope will be found to be a clearer and more compelling argument. I am grateful to the press's senior editors, Norris Pope and Muriel Bell, for seeing promise in this project at an early date and for having patience with its prolonged development. John Feneron and Mary Bearden brought the manuscript into print with a light but careful editorial hand. Most of all I am indebted to my husband, Robert Zeitlin, whose critical eye and ear have helped me keep this work on track and whose forbearance and understanding in this shared life have made it all possible. Although I have taken the suggestions of these scholar-friends and professionals to heart, I alone am responsible for any inadvertent errors and stubborn interpretations that remain.

Cultural Politics in Colonial Tehuantepec

CHAPTER ONE

Tales of the *binni gulasa*

Native History and the Zapotec Conquest of Tehuantepec

> All the natives of this province were newcomers, originally from the Valley of Oaxaca, and they came to conquer the Guazontec [Huave]-speaking people who were here, whom the grandparents and ancestors of this Don Juan conquered and threw out and destroyed in such a manner that everything went to their side. And the grandfather and ancestor of this Don Juan Cortés, seeing that the land remained vacant of the people that had possessed it, populated all this province and settled it with his people.
>
> From the 1571 testimony of Don Alonso de Toribio, son-in-law of Don Juan Cortés, hereditary ruler of Tehuantepec.[1]

As they gazed across the broad band of hot coastal plain stretching for 100 km before them, the army of mostly Zapotec-speaking soldiers gathered on the mountain ridge saw a land little like the intensively cultivated highland valley they called home. Vast stretches of deciduous tropical forest spread from the piedmont slopes nearly to the edge of the network of shallow lagoons and barrier beaches separating the mainland from the Pacific Ocean. While small fishing hamlets lined the lagoon shore, larger villages were confined to the mesquite-covered banks of the rivers draining the southern slopes of the Sierra Atravesada. These settlements, divided between the agriculturalist Zoque and their more recent fisher-folk neighbors, the Huave, were too small or too weakly organized to present a formidable defense against the disciplined Zapotec army. Ruthlessly, the invaders swept down from the mountains in a "fire and blood" campaign that destroyed the coastal plain villages between the Tehuantepec and Perros rivers.

When did these destructive events take place and what precipitated the war and ensuing Zapotec colonization that was to change forever the Isthmus's sociocultural landscape? Narrations of the *binni gulasa,* or an-

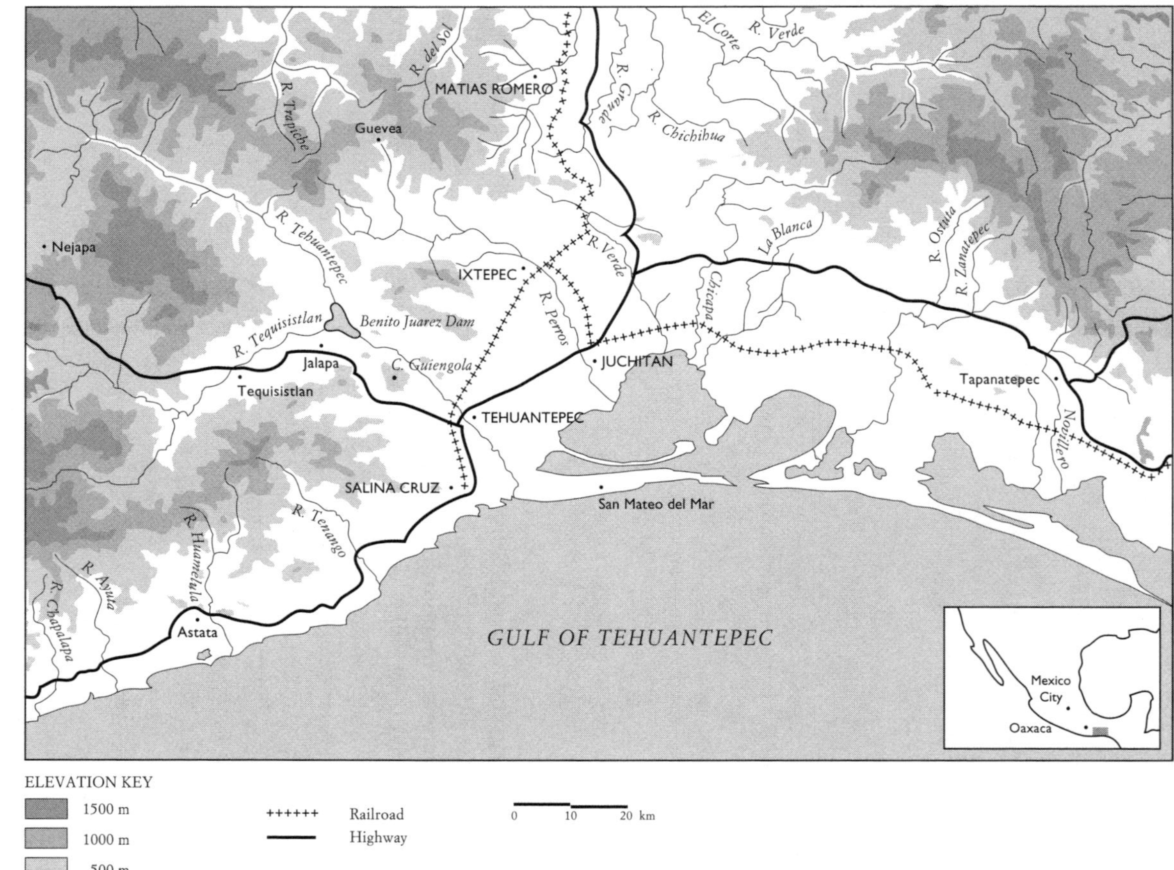

MAP 1.1. The Southern Isthmus.

cestors, were kept alive by the conquerors' descendants in Tehuantepec, but definitive answers to these questions are not to be found in the vague chronologies and ethnocentric biases that permeated oral history. As retold by the seventeenth-century Dominican chronicler Fr. Francisco de Burgoa, the Zapotec accounts claimed that the king of Zaachila took offense at the ease of passage which local Huaves had given the powerful Mexica armies en route to the cacao groves of Soconusco and resolved to take the province for himself.[2] Other stories recounted by their Mixtec rivals intimated that the Zapotec invaders needed to find a new arena from which to assert their political ambitions, thwarted as they were at home by Mixtec encroachments into the very heart of the Oaxaca Valley.[3] In the tangled web of late prehistoric cultural politics in Mesoamerica, such shifts in power among towns and ethnic groups were commonplace, and the ignominy of subordination was assuaged only by the successful conquest of other peoples.

A Zapotec ruler's chief political ambition was to be recognized as a lord conqueror or *coquitao huezaquiqueche*, literally a great lord, maker of vanquished communities.[4] The act of conquest (or often its mere threat) had longer-term rewards than just the goods pillaged in the heat of battle. Conquered towns could be made to provide tribute at regular intervals. This tribute was assessed in rich sumptuary items such as gold, colorful feathers, precious stones, and rare animal skins, along with foodstuffs and other goods of more utilitarian value. Thin copper axes, cacao beans, and lengths of woven cotton cloth, all standard Mesoamerican monetary equivalents, were regular tribute obligations of conquered provinces as well. Prime lands might be appropriated by the conqueror for his own use, or like the tribute he received, be redistributed among his high-ranking captains, who were installed as governors in the defeated towns. Finally, for the commoners who risked themselves in battle, each life taken was regarded as a gift to the gods, with many captives offered as human sacrifices on all sides. Seen more pragmatically, battlefield valor was an important vehicle for gaining personal prestige and social advancement.[5]

Such notions of war and conquest were widely shared among later Mesoamerican societies, and they are best known from early colonial writers familiar with Aztec narrative history. Typical of this historical genre among the Nahuas is the beginning tale of migration from some distant place of origin, followed by battles with local populations that culminated in the establishment of the victorious polity's *altepetl* or ethnic state.[6] Whereas the majority of these foundation tales are situated in the remote past and provide few details of either the place of origin or the early history of the *altepetl*, Tehuantepec's foundation emerges out of this legendary fog into the realm of concrete events and social processes that can be traced historically and archaeologically.

As such, the Zapotec triumph in Tehuantepec presents us with an uncommon empirical example of the wholesale displacement of a conquered population by a highly organized force of invaders. Transplanting themselves to a new land, the colonists had the opportunity to re-create Zapotec society both in the sense of replicating familiar institutions and in the sense of making those institutions anew. In the course of just two or three generations, they built a remarkably adaptable Isthmian culture, at once linked to the traditions of the past while exhibiting a fluidity that was to serve the Isthmus Zapotecs well under the yoke of later invaders. Before this accomplishment is examined in greater depth, some fundamental issues surrounding the timing and nature of the Zapotec conquest must first be disentangled.

Historiography of the Tehuantepec Invasion

Like their Aztec contemporaries, the Tehuantepec kings promulgated an official account of their historic conquest and migration, one which emphasized the kings' instrumental role in establishing suzerainty and validated royal claims to legitimate political authority. The public retelling of past events in lavish ceremonies marked by dancing, music, and the ruler's display of gold jewelry gained by his conquering ancestor was one important vehicle for transmitting this story in prehispanic times.[7]

Not surprisingly, especially for a culture in which elite literacy had endured nearly two thousand years, this official account was preserved in written form as well. No certain precolumbian Zapotec codices or *lienzos* have survived to the present day, but recent scholarly searches have added to the small collection of colonial-period examples and may yet uncover late prehistoric texts. The resemblance of later sixteenth-century Zapotec texts to the better known corpus of Mixtec and Central Mexican writings makes it possible to reconstruct their preconquest antecedents. Single large sheets and folded screen books of either prepared animal skin or paper made from fibrous plants or tree bark were the primary media for writing in late prehistoric times, largely replacing the better-preserved stone carvings that grace Oaxaca's earlier archaeological sites. In addition to calendrical texts consulted for ritual observances, a large portion of these writings would have been of a genealogical-historical nature, tracing the births, marriages, and political accomplishments, principally territorial conquests, of the ruling family associated with a particular polity. Conventionalized representations of these events painted in several colors on a lime-sized background were further specified by hieroglyphic notations. These glyphs indicated the names of people and places and the dates within the fifty-two-year Mesoamerican calendrical cycle when certain events occurred.[8]

Juan Bautista de Avendaño, the former Spanish *alcalde mayor* or administrator of Antequera, remembered having been shown ancient written texts called *pinturas*, or paintings, by the Spaniards, in 1552 by Don Juan Cortés, the last prehispanic Zapotec ruler of Tehuantepec. These texts portrayed the history of Don Juan's family and its political domination of the province. Writing over a hundred years later, Fr. Francisco de Burgoa made mention of "history and paintings" he consulted that recounted preconquest events in Tehuantepec unmentioned by authors utilizing Aztec historical sources.[9] How these native writings largely disappeared over the ensuing centuries remains a mystery, although there are several possible causes, from a fire in the house of books (*lichi quichi*) where they were stored, to their piecemeal loss among scattered inheritors or, perhaps more likely, their purposeful destruction by overzealous Spanish missionaries or administrators.

Besides Burgoa, no other known colonial-period author undertook the task of preserving Isthmus Zapotec history in the introduced Latin script. An early capitulation by the Tehuantepec king to the forces of Hernán Cortés left the province barely mentioned by either the conqueror or his lieutenants in their battlefield accounts of meritorious service to the Spanish monarch.[10] Distant from any major colonial population center, the province later attracted a mixed lot of entrepreneurial settlers, who were more concerned with making a living in ranching and long-distance commerce than in accounting for indigenous culture history.

Few of their Dominican missionary compatriots were so disposed either. With the notable exception of Fr. Diego Durán, who examined many native Mexican sources to compose his late sixteenth-century *Historia de las indias de Nueva España y islas de tierra firme*, Burgoa's predecessors among the religious brethren of the Order of Preachers did not exhibit much ethnographic curiosity in the populations whose souls they sought to save. Establishing their first convent in Antequera in 1529 (*conventos* were the church and living quarter complexes established throughout New Spain by Catholic missionary orders), the Dominicans were the custodians of the evangelizing process in what was to become the state of Oaxaca, yet their earliest chroniclers made specific note of indigenous customs or historical traditions only when these presented obstacles to the saintly efforts of the missionaries.[11]

Although many were gifted linguists, mastering native dialects and composing vocabularies, grammars, catechisms, and sermons in indigenous languages, such works were intended primarily for European readers committed to advancing the careful dissemination of Catholic orthodoxy. Despite their reputation as early supporters of human rights in the Americas, Dominicans in New Spain were wary from the outset of the indigenous population's capacity to achieve the pure understanding of Christianity they considered essential to a religious vocation. The Mexican chapter's early vicar general and uncompromising ascetic, Fr. Domingo de Betanzos, fought against the inclusion of natives in the priesthood and discouraged the establishment of schools of higher learning which might have advanced religious or cultural education.[12]

As was typical for the other missionary orders, the Dominicans brought large numbers of native children, primarily the sons of members of the nobility, into the convent for instruction in catechism and the basics of reading and writing.[13] Such training accounts for the frequency with which we find sixteenth-century Tehuantepec *principales* or nobles able to sign their own names to legal documents. Left unexposed to Latin-based models from the classics of humanistic education, the post-conquest Zapotec aristocracy, once the guardians of native writing and its intellectual foundations, paradoxically became less erudite under early Spanish rule. Many were at least modestly functional in the Latin alphabet; some composed letters and formal documents in Spanish by the seventeenth century, and the extent to which they used alphabetic writing within their own communities is reflected in the growing corpus of Zapotec-language colonial texts. Still no indigenous Zapotec writer emerged during colonial times who was sufficiently familiar with European-style histories to put into writing a parallel account of the past, as did Ixtlilxóchitl, Tezozomoc, Chimalpahin, and other sixteenth- and seventeenth-century Nahua and mixed-blood Mexican chroniclers.

The oral tradition of Zapotec history persisted long after Western literacy supplanted indigenous writing systems and may even have gained a new populist vigor. Despite losing its most formal, ceremonial settings, as both the institution of rulership and its ritual celebrations were suppressed under Spanish control, Zapotec history could now be retold in a manner that served its audience's needs rather than the needs of rulers promulgating a single version of past events. The heroic battles waged by famous political leaders continued to fascinate Zapotec listeners long after their own defeat by the Spaniards, but the details of when these battles were waged, why they were instigated, and by whom were all subject to the memory and discretion of the narrator.

That these stories were widely circulated in colonial-period Oaxaca is evidenced by a rare recorded example from the early eighteenth century. In 1730 the heirs to the Tehuantepec ruler's lagoon-shore salt pans brought suit before the General Indian Court against a man who called himself "Don Antonio de Velasco y Montesuma de Austria, cacique of the city of Antequera, offspring of the head town of Teozapotlan and of the *villa* of Guadalcazar [Tehuantepec]." Despite his claim to be a descendant of the contact-period Zapotec rulers of Zaachila and Tehuantepec and in possession of certain of their most important personal papers, the Tehuantepec heirs alleged that "Don Antonio" was in fact an imposter and a mixed race, *mulato* pretender to the royal patrimony. They rejected his fancy titles and referred to him by what they said was his real name, Antonio de Aguero.

Irrespective of the dubious merits of this genealogical claim, the story the illiterate Antonio presented to the court gives a firsthand version of what contemporary popular accounts of the conquest of the Isthmus were like. According to Antonio's testimony, the king of Zaachila or Teozapotlan

> named in his language in pagan times Cosijoeza, which means Lightning Bolt of Steel, left this *cabecera* of Teozapotlan and went to establish the Zapotec nation in the *villa* of Tehuantepec, and there it was that the emperor Moctezuma of this court, having received news of the Zapotec king's advance into Tehuantepec, tried to eject him, but the emperor was overcome in that contest, and for that reason had to reach an accord and make peaceful overtures to the Zapotec king, the principal of which was [Cosijoeza's] marriage to one of the emperor's daughters, called for her beauty Cotton Puff [Copo de Algodón]. And once the king Cosijoeza was settled in Tehuantepec, the couple produced Cosijopii, which means Lightning Bolt of Wind, as he was called in his language in pagan times, and finding him to be capable, Cosijopii stayed in

> the *villa* of Tehuantepec, while his father returned to his throne in Teozapotlan. Cosijopii married a Huave woman, who was called Billosicahi in pagan times, and thus was the state of the two kings when Don Fernando Cortés del Castillo came to take these lands.[14]

Antonio went on to describe how both kings and their wives had been converted to Christianity by Cortés and assumed new baptismal names. The names he attributed to these individuals, however, were at least partly a product of narrative invention. They embellished the story with a tone of specificity meant to give his own claims greater authenticity and to repudiate the legitimacy of the titles currently held by Tehuantepec's Zúñiga Cortés family, whose members were in fact caciques of the Huave village of San Francisco del Mar.

Although lacking this subplot of a Huave marital alliance, a similar version of the Isthmus conquest was heard by Burgoa over fifty years earlier. The verbose Dominican lamented not doing full justice in the final chapters of his 1674 *Geográfica descripción* to the rich stories he had been told regarding the history of this celebrated province, but both the broad territorial sweep of his work and his fragile health, not to mention his penchant for turgid pious digressions, forced him to write an abbreviated version.[15]

According to Burgoa, the Zapotec armies of the king of Teozapotlan or Zaachila, allied with the Mixtecs under twenty-four captains, conquered the Isthmus some three hundred years earlier in a brutal campaign that subjugated or exterminated all the mountain communities in their path and pushed the Huaves out of Tehuantepec to the margins of the Pacific coastal lagoons. When the Aztec ruler learned what had happened to his own weakly defended soldiers in the province, he planned a retaliatory campaign to win back his former conquest. The Zapotecs, freshly stocked with provisions for a long siege, picked away at the Mexica army for seven months from their fortified location atop a steep mountain overlooking the Tehuantepec River, until at last the powerful ruler chose to negotiate a peace settlement. Under the terms of this settlement, the Zapotec king, Cosijoeza, would receive as his bride a daughter of Moctezuma himself, the beautiful princess Copo de Algodón. Her magical prenuptial appearance before the bathing Cosijoeza kindled a great passion, one that proved stronger than filial loyalty when her father conspired again to reconquer the province. Their son, Cosijopii, who was Cosijoeza's third child, became lord of Tehuantepec not long before the arrival of the Spaniards in Mexico, while Cosijoeza returned to Zaachila.[16]

Burgoa's overview of the Zaachila dynasty's tenure at Tehuantepec was to become the critical source for all Oaxaca's later historians, particularly during the nineteenth century, when local pride coupled with emerging national consciousness fostered a serious regional narrative tradition. That few other materials were available was noted in frustration by José María Murguía y Galardi in his 1827 survey of the state's towns. Speaking of Zaachila, he apologized: "I have not been able to find anything concerning this village as the seat of the Zapotec nation, and it should not be taken as a defect of that which I write, for it should speak of the royal palace, its courtesans, government, etc. If it does not, it is because neither documents nor traces have remained."[17]

Like Murguía y Galardi, Juan Bautista Carriedo relied heavily on Burgoa in his 1847 *Estudios históricos y estadísticos del estado libre de Oajaca*. Although he saw other Dominican manuscripts, principally Zapotec catechisms, in the Oaxaca convent library, virtually all Carriedo's information on Isthmus preconquest and colonial history came from Burgoa.[18] Not until the last decades of the nineteenth century were there renewed efforts to compose modern histories in the works of the scholarly Catholic priest José Antonio Gay and his secular contemporary Manuel Martínez Gracida. Both authors attempted to find factual verification and amplification for Burgoa's stories in the Aztec narratives transcribed by such early colonial chroniclers as Durán, Sahagún, Alvarado Tezózomoc, Torquemada, and Alva Ixtlilxóchitl. At best these sources helped to bring some chronological order to late Oaxaca prehistory by correlating battles between certain Oaxaca towns and the Mexica army with the reign of particular Tenochtitlan kings.

In the case of Father Gay, the more careful and self-conscious historian of the two men, weaving disparate narrative threads into a seamless culture history called for a large measure of editorial license. Attempting to give the Zaachila dynasty greater chronological depth than that known from Burgoa's accounts of the Tehuantepec kings, Cosijoeza and Cosijopii, Gay assembled other stories interspersed in Burgoa's *Geográfica descripción* or gleaned from a careful study of colonial Nahua sources to construct the affairs of still earlier kings of Zaachila, whom he called Zaachila I, II, and III. Martínez Gracida accepted Gay's reconstruction and elaborated the Zaachila dynastic story further with colorful details from traditional tales and poetic renditions in his more romantic account of the Zapotec kings, modestly subtitled a "historical and legendary summary of the last rulers of Zaachila."[19]

Each of these writers repeated and embellished the facts as known to him, inspired by his personal proclivities and constrained by the historiographic and literary standards of his day. It may be easy to recognize the extent to which nineteenth-century literary conventions legitimized the invented dialogue of Martínez Gracida's account, but even the more painstaking and original account by Father Gay is strongly shaped by his efforts to make the available data conform to a linear narrative of real events, as dictated by the canons of Western historiography.

In the course of the last half-century, the writing of history has been subjected to vigorous debate at all points of its construction, from the nature of evidence to the standards of analysis and the logic and ideology of explanation. Judged in the light of modern scholarship, the works of these late nineteenth-century historians may seem dated by their romanticism or indiscriminate use of sources, yet the weight of their realistic narrative chronology still presses heavily on contemporary views of the Zapotecs. For it is fundamentally this canon of chronologically based narrative realism that has been the standard against which all stories about the precolumbian past in New Spain and throughout the Americas have been measured. Whether written by Spaniards, natives, or mestizos, these narrations are judged reliable or authentic insofar as they conform to Western historiography's essential standards of temporal lineality, factual consistency, and the realistic portrayal of both actors and events.[20]

In recent years the convergence of structuralist history and hermeneutical literary criticism has opened up entirely new approaches to prehispanic and colonial-period indigenous history, as the search for narrative accuracy has given way to text-based analyses which emphasize the agency of the narrator or the culture-historical context of the narration. Not only have such approaches revalidated the texts of "confused" indigenous authors like the Andean Guaman Poma de Ayala, but by looking beyond the "factual" chronicling of events, these newer studies have explained essential concepts of prehistoric Aztec rulership, illuminated persistent patterns of Maya-*ladino* ethnic conflict, or highlighted changing ideas about the path to power in the colonial Mexican highlands.[21]

It is in this light that I intend to reexamine the traditional narrative history upon which our understanding of the preconquest Isthmus Zapotecs has been based. To do so, I will avoid tackling the role of literary critic in order to offer a deeper reading of either Burgoa's text or those of his nineteenth-century successors. Instead I mean to bring to the discussion of the Isthmus conquest a series of other kinds of "texts," largely originating in the sixteenth century or even earlier, some new and already familiar in the published literature, some written or painted, some left on the landscape as artifactual remains, but none of them conforming to conventional narrative history. What I propose to do here is not to establish some corrected chronology, although I believe this evidence will undermine the assumed factual veracity of the established later works. Rather I hope to demonstrate that these stories are all contingent versions of the past, each with its own determinative context, and that variability among the stories may be used both to better understand the sociocultural setting in which they were created and to highlight the processes by which the Zapotecs reinterpreted their own past.

Beyond Burgoa

Part I: Dynastic history in the Lienzo de Guevea

One colonial-period source providing an authentic Zapotec perspective on the establishment of the Tehuantepec dynasty has long been the focus of international scholarly interest. Ever since the 1906 publication of the Lienzo de Guevea by the celebrated German archaeologist, Eduard Seler, this painted manuscript from the Isthmian mountain community of Santiago Guevea has held unique authority as an indigenous affidavit recording protohistoric events. That status has been compromised, however, by the fact that both versions of the *lienzo* published by Seler (which he designated Copy A and Copy B) were acknowledged to be distinctive later copies of an original *pintura* that had long disappeared from public view. In 1978 photos of a third version were discovered in the Genaro García collection at the University of Texas, a version subsequently identified by John Paddock and later confirmed by Joseph Whitecotton as the original manuscript itself. In 1997 Michel Oudijk located a fourth version of the *lienzo* in the community of Santo Domingo Petapa, a version that he identifies as the prototype for Seler's Copy A.[22]

As is typical of midsixteenth-century historical-cartographic documents, the original *lienzo* is a painting on a long strip of coarsely woven cotton cloth that documents the territorial boundaries and political history of Santiago Guevea, a community that was subordinate to Tehuantepec at the time of the Spanish conquest. The top half of the García *pintura* comprises a map of the village's physical boundaries, with eighteen

FIG. 1.1. García version of the Lienzo de Guevea. *Above:* upper portion of the *lienzo*. *Facing page:* lower portion of the *lienzo*. Photos courtesy of the Benson Latin American Collection, University of Texas at Austin.

hieroglyphic toponyms, accompanied by glosses in Zapotec, Nahuatl, and Spanish, all arranged in a numbered sequence around a central image that places the Guevea toponym behind a seated lord identified as Don Pedro Santiago. A dedicatory inscription in Nahuatl and Spanish states that the manuscript is based on a boundary survey conducted by order of the king of Spain on June 1, 1540. I have argued on the basis of stylistic and documentary evidence that the original *pintura* may actually have been executed several years later, perhaps in the late 1550s.[23]

As a map of the geographic and symbolic space claimed by the Guevea community, the top half of the *lienzo* has been the focus of studies by Seler, Joyce Marcus, and other students of Zapotec calendrical ritual.[24] It is the document's lower half, however, which has attracted even wider attention, largely because of the genealogical information it provides for the Zaachila dynasty and its transfer to Tehuantepec. To the left a column of eight men, each attired like the lord of Santiago Guevea and individually identified by his hieroglyphic personal name, is placed opposite another column of eight figures representing the Zaachila-Tehuantepec rulers, seven of whom are identified by hieroglyphic calendrical names. The first of these rulers sits on a jaguar-cushion throne above the stepped-platform hill glyph for Zaachila. A footpath, originating at the base of this hill and extending to the Guevea toponym in the upper half of the document, divides the rulers from the column of Guevea lords and indicates a separate, earlier colonization of this community by people from Zaachila.[25]

A second footpath connects the fifth Zaachila ruler with a figure identified in Latin letters as "Cociyobii" as well as by his hieroglyphic name. Placed to his right is the toponym for Tehuantepec, a hill with a jaguar head at its summit. Pictured above him is "Coziyohueze—Montesuma," seated next to a gold-bedecked temple. At the top of the column, attired in Spanish dress and seated on a Spanish chair, is "Don Juan Cortes," who alone has no hieroglyphic name, nor does he have the array of tribute goods spread before him of the previous Tehuantepec rulers.

Only the Tehuantepec rulers have Latin letter glosses for their names in either the García version (referred to by Oudijk as Guevea I) or in Seler's Copy B (Guevea II), which follows the original García text closely. The nineteenth-century artist of the Copy A version, however, followed the earlier Petapa copy of the *lienzo* (Oudijk's Petapa I) in supplying names for the Zaachila kings as well as for the lords of Guevea in the lower half of the manuscript. The Guevea lords were given appellations that in the main approximated the pictographic sense of their personal glyphs, but for the Zaachila kings, the Petapa I artist took familiar figures from local history and attributed their names or descriptive titles to the ancient rulers. Although it is not possible to say precisely when the first Petapa copy was made, its historical referents have strong parallels with a late seventeenth-century collection of Zapotec-language historical documents known as the Probanza de Petapa, and Oudijk suggests that it may have been composed as part of the same effort to document the community's political and territorial legitimacy.[26]

Since it appears that they were based on roughly contemporary oral histories, it is not surprising then that the Petapa I artist reproduced the same royal genealogy recorded by Burgoa. The Dominican's 1674 *Geográfica descripción* identified only five members of the Tehuantepec royal family: the aforementioned father and son rulers, Cosijoeza and Cosijopii; the latter's beloved sister, Pinopiaa; and two unnamed older brothers of Cosijopii, who was the third-born son.[27] Accordingly, the Petapa artist also supplied five names: Peñobiya (although a male figure is represented); Coçijhueça; Coçijobij; Rinijcoxij Chalequeça; and Yobicoxij Chalachi. As Seler noted, the names of the last two "kings" include Zapotec terms for second- and firstborn sons, respectively, and Oudijk finds the honorific term, "brave man," as well as calendrical names embedded in these designations.[28]

Such was the power of late colonial oral history that these familiar figures were equated with the copied document's kings, even though this identification violated some transparent meanings conveyed by the original drawing. One obvious breach is the repetition of the names of the Tehuantepec kings Cosijopii and Cosijoeza for the third and fourth rulers of Zaachila, even though these figures are identified by different hieroglyphic names than those given for the presumably same individuals as rulers of Tehuantepec. The glyphs, although they lack accompanying numbers (a trait shared with colonial Nahua name glyphs), are clearly calendrical names; they are straightforward representations of day signs from the late Mesoamerican ritual calendar, unlike the composite personal names given to the Guevea chiefs opposite them. Following longstanding Mesoamerican tradition, individuals were known both by their astrologically fateful day of birth and by a more descriptive personal name. Rulers and other politically prominent persons were identified first by their birthday name in many historical codices.

Seen more readily in the García version of the *lienzo* than in any of the

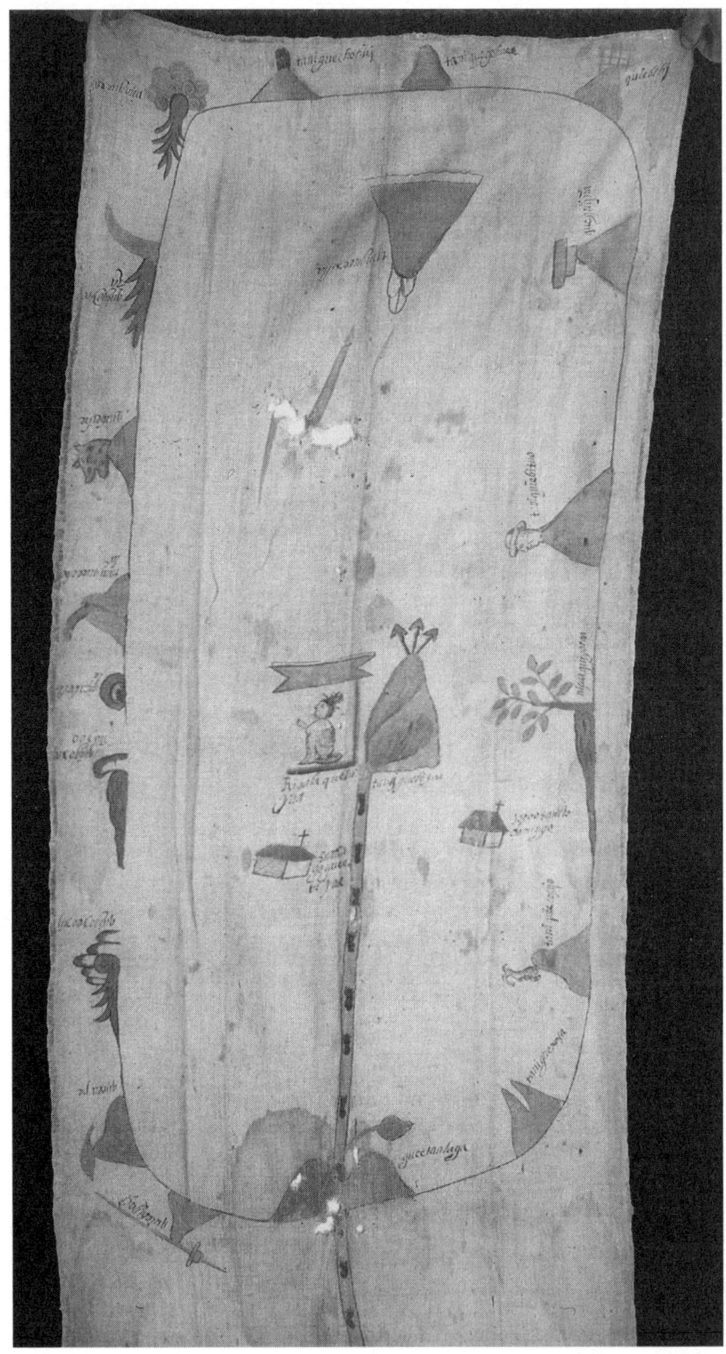

FIG. 1.2. Petapa I version of the Lienzo de Guevea. *Above:* upper portion. *Facing page:* lower portion. Document archived in the community of Santo Domingo Petapa. Photos courtesy of Michel Oudijk.

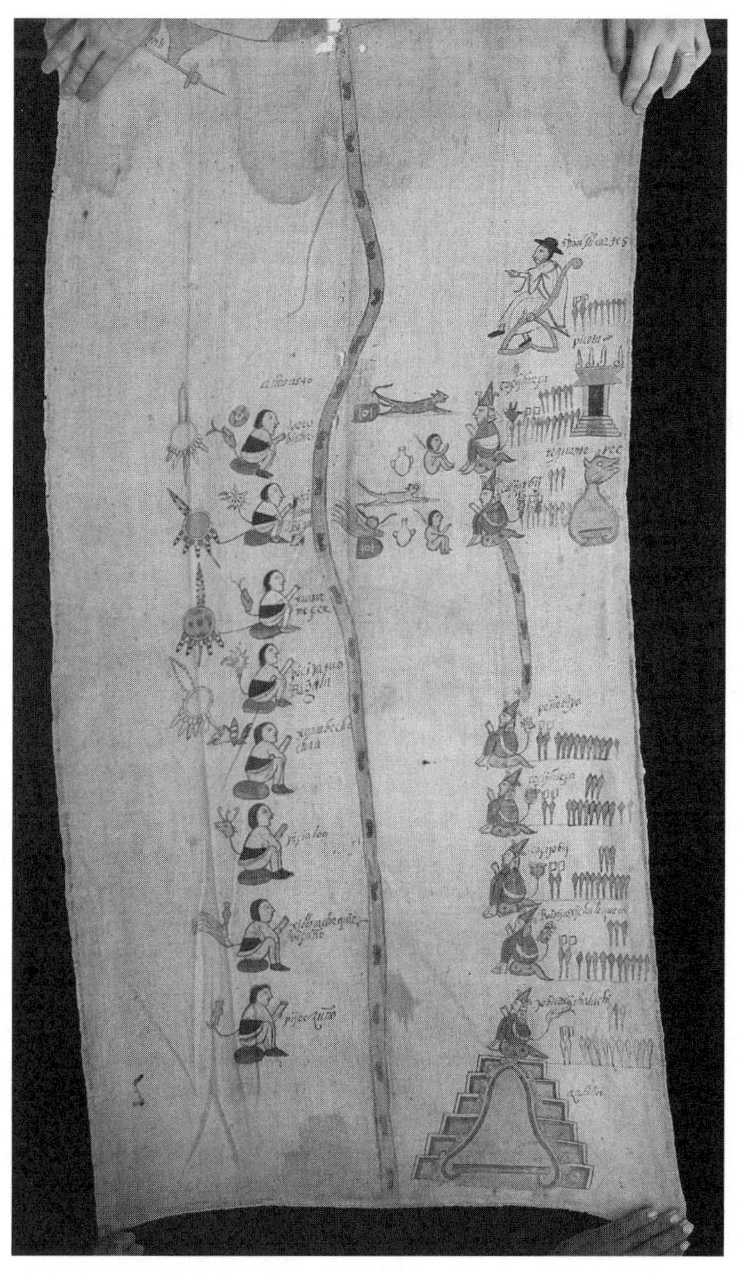

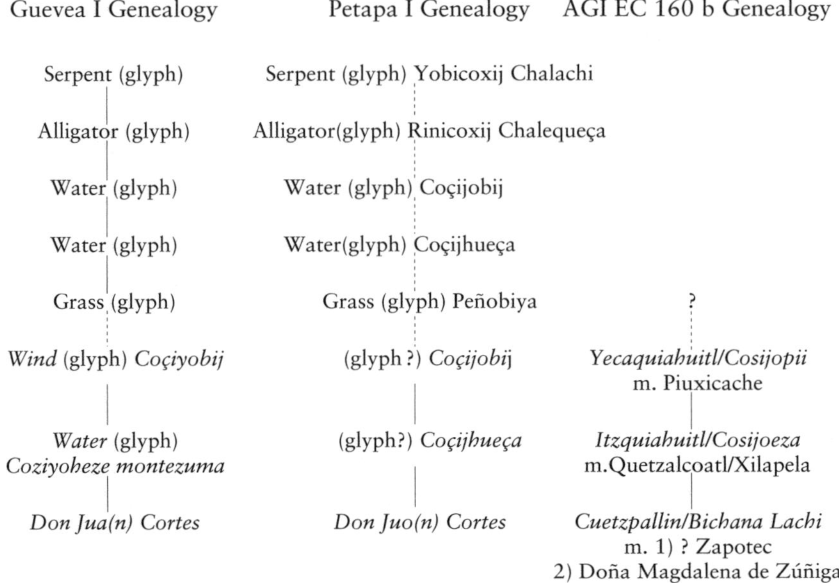

FIG. 1.3. Guevea I and Petapa I royal genealogies for the Zaachila and Tehuantepec kings compared with the testimony presented in Don Juan Cortés's and Doña Magdalena de Zúñiga's dispute with the royal *fiscal*, Archivo General de las Indias Escribanía de Cámara, 160b. Males in italic type ruled at Tehuantepec.

later copies, the hieroglyphs denoting the calendrical names of the Zaachila kings read from bottom to top in the following order: Serpent, Alligator, Water, Water, and Grass.[29] As Maarten Jansen first noted and Paddock subsequently affirmed, the Guevea sequence overlaps in large part with one sequence of royal kings depicted in the precolumbian Mixtec book, the Codex Nuttall. The Nuttall shows 9 Serpent, 5 Flower, 3 Alligator, 11 Water, and 6 Water wearing dynastic insignia or seated on jaguar thrones as successive heirs to a dynasty founded at the foot of "Great and Famous Hill," as the Mixtecs referred to Monte Albán. The long abandoned site of Monte Albán, with its many stepped temple platforms, is surely the "Great Platform Hill" represented in the Lienzo de Guevea as a prominent feature of the hieroglyphic toponym for nearby Zaachila.[30] Only two individuals among these Zaachila rulers are listed on one of the two documents and not the other: the Nuttall's 5 Flower, who may not have assumed the throne at Zaachila, and the Guevea document's ruler Grass, who may be the individual 1 Grass shown seated on a jaguar throne behind his brother 11 Water.

Several distinctive costume elements are associated with these Codex Nuttall rulers that Paddock, like Caso before him, considered to be markers for the Xipe dynasty that ruled at Zaachila. They include a conical or cylindrical headdress with right-angle elements at the corners and a long drape of alternating red-and-white rectangles.[31] Both headdress elements are carefully detailed for the Tehuantepec-Zaachila kings in the García version of the Lienzo de Guevea. Doubtlessly, the conical crown is the same as the one which the Nahua chronicler Hernando Alvarado Tezózomoc recounted being bestowed on the Aztec king Ahuitzotl in tribute by the Tehuantepec *principales:* "they then put on his lordship that which they called *teocuitla Ixcuaamatl*, which was a half miter made of paper studded with very rich jewels."[32] An even greater symbol of kingly authority than the jaguar-skin thrones on which the rulers sit, the Xipe dynasty headdress was used by the original Guevea artist to convey the legitimacy of the Zaachila kings and their Tehuantepec descendants. That this legitimacy was so prominently displayed over a century earlier in royal genealogies maintained by the kings' supposed Mixtec rivals would seem to be a perplexing development.

The basis for kingly authority resided in widely shared Mesoamerican principles of political inheritance favoring purity of royal lineage and bilateral royal heritage. As an alternative to warfare, marital alliances between the hereditary ruling families of competing city-states were a common means of consolidating political ambitions. As a matter of practice, the marriage of a defeated lord to a royal woman from a more powerful polity was a formula for ensuring the loyalty of subsequent heirs to their maternal kinsmen. Given the culturally diverse landscape of late highland Mesoamerica, the strategic practice of royal exogamy would often result in the ethnic mixing of ruling families, even as the people they governed remained segmented by the language communities into which they were born.

In this light the intertwining of Zapotec and Mixtec royalty was a predictable consequence of their competition for Oaxaca Valley lands and tributary subjects. The offspring of strategic marital alliances were identified with the places they ruled, regardless of their mixed ethnic heritage. Oudijk has compared the Teozacualco-based Nuttall document genealogy with that presented in the Tlaxiaco-based Codex Bodley to add fur-

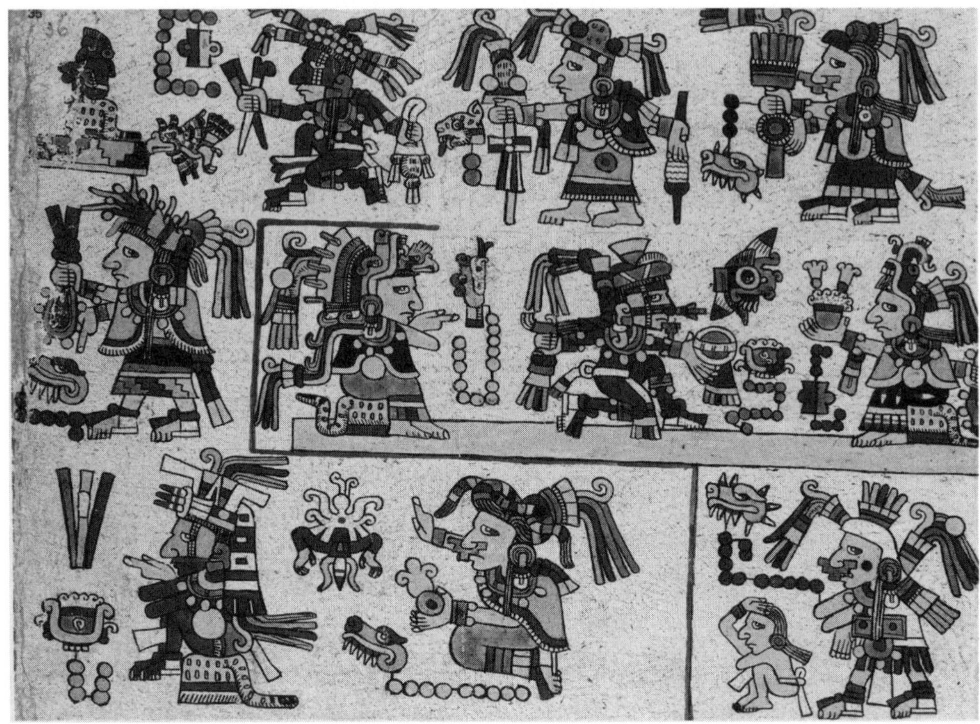

FIG. 1.4. Representation of 11 Water, "Obsidian Knife Rain Storm," Xipe dynasty ruler of Zaachila, and his son 6 Water, "Colored Strips," in the precolumbian Mixtec manuscript, the Codex Zouche Nuttall, p. 35, British Museum Ethnology Add. Mss. 39671. Facsimile edition by Akademische Druck-u. Verlagsanstalt, Graz/Austria 1987. The central male figure on this page is 11 Water, who is offered a cup of frothy chocolate beverage by his second wife 8 Movement, while his wife 13 Snake looks on; Rain God Obsidian Knife appears as his personal name glyph. His son 6 Water is shown on the lower left, seated on a jaguar-skin throne and wearing the Xipe dynasty headdress.

ther details of the marriage alliances forged between the Zaachila royal family and the rulers of these and other prominent Mixtec towns. He believes that the brief succession of the elderly 1 Grass to the Zaachila throne following the death of his childless nephew 6 Water triggered competition for the rulership among contending royal factions, with the Tlaxiaco-based lord 8 Deer claiming the throne in the mid-fifteenth century on the basis of his maternal connections. It was this competition for the Zaachila throne that may have prompted the defeated 1 Grass faction to launch its Tehuantepec campaign.[33]

For the artist who composed the Lienzo de Guevea, this long succession of Zaachila's Xipe dynasty kings was an affirmation of the legitimate political authority of the Tehuantepec rulers. By the late sixteenth and seventeenth centuries, however, when indigenous rulers no longer exercised significant political authority in either town, such genealogical details may no longer have held the same importance to informants from Zaachila and Tehuantepec, whose historical memories were preoccupied with stories of Mixtec-Zapotec hostilities. Whether we should attribute these omissions from the Relaciones Geográficas and Burgoa's synthesis to a resurgence of nativism, as Paddock suggested, is a question I will turn to later.[34] What is clear is that the demise of royal authority under Spanish colonial rule and the appearance of European writing as a vehicle for chronicling popular history gave new voice to opinions about political history that would not have been recorded in prehispanic times.

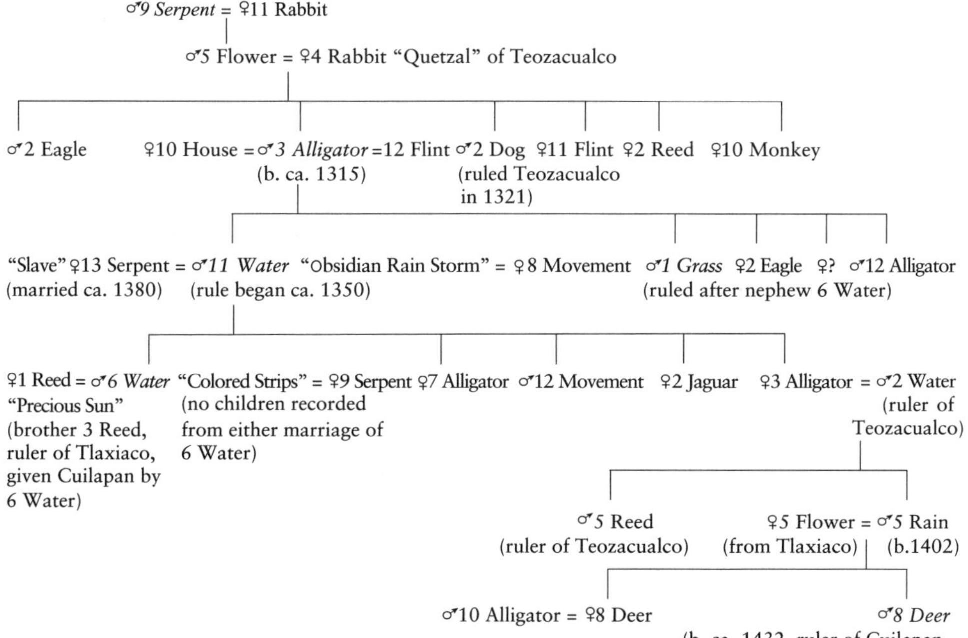

FIG. 1.5. Genealogy of the Xipe Dynasty royal family at Zaachila. Males in italic type ruled at Zaachila. Source: Oudijk, *Historiography of the Bènizàa*, pp. 100–183, based on Codex Nuttall and Codex Bodley genealogies.

Part II: A contested royal legacy

Another conspicuous error committed by the Petapa I artist in his identification of popular historical figures with the Zaachila kings is the violation of the *lienzo*'s intended succession order for the Oaxaca Valley royal family. Although the dynasty's founder should have been placed at the bottom of the column, the late seventeenth-century artist scattered the names of people from two generations randomly among the five Zaachila rulers. We might attribute this "error" to one individual's misinformed exuberance, but it is harder to explain away a further genealogical discrepancy common to all versions of the Lienzo de Guevea, including the sixteenth-century García original. In that earliest *lienzo*, only the Tehuantepec kings are identified by Latin-letter personal names, but their order is inverted from what seventeenth-century popular history recounted it to be, placing the name "Cociyobii" next to the first Tehuantepec ruler and the name of the man identified in colonial popular history as Cosijopii's father, "Coziyohueze," in the son's generational position. Joseph Whitecotton, reexamining the Lienzo de Guevea versions in his study of Zapotec elite genealogies, speculated that this apparent generational reversal might not be another copyist's error after all, but the true order of succession somehow forgotten by later colonial informants. By the late seventeenth century, when Fr. Francisco de Burgoa reinterpreted existing *pinturas* and oral histories in his *Geográfica descripción,* what was known about the Zapotec royal family was essentially the same story familiar to the Petapa I artist.[35]

In fact a different story was preserved in the protracted litigation that developed between the widow of Don Juan Cortés, which was the baptismal name of the Tehuantepec cacique, and the colonial government's chief prosecutor. The dispute, initiated by the *fiscal* in 1567, concerned Doña Magdalena de Zúñiga's assertion of her children's inherited rights to the province's productive salt beds, as well as certain *estancias* populated by *indios terrazgueros* or native serfs that were claimed to be part of her late husband's patrimonial estate.[36] The thick transcript of five years of legal claims and counterclaims received by the Council of the Indies includes earlier court records as well, most notably an examination of witnesses initiated by Don Juan Cortés himself in 1554. Nearly one hundred individuals were called to give testimony in the combined proceedings, and unlike much litigation from the Tehuantepec province, in these two cases all but a handful were natives.

Caciques, *principales,* commoners, and even one former slave were represented among the indigenous witnesses, many of whom had been alive before the Spanish conquest, some of whom had known Don Juan's father personally. The formality of the judicial proceedings and the filter imposed by the use of translators were, of course, barriers to the free expression of witnesses, but the multivocality of the testimony recorded here is unique for the sixteenth-century Isthmus, making it an invaluable resource. Both the 1554 and 1567–72 interrogatories include specific questions about the genealogy of the Tehuantepec kings and early history of the Zapotec conquest of the province. The statements of witnesses responding to these questions provide important information that clarifies the Lienzo de Guevea genealogy and undermines our traditional understanding of Tehuantepec history derived from Burgoa.

Both the interrogatories of Don Juan and his widow Doña Magdalena identify by name Don Juan's father and grandfather, referring in Nahuatl to the father as Itzquiahuitl and to the grandfather as Yecaquiahuitl. Although their Zapotec names are not indicated, the Nahuatl root *quiahuitl* or rainstorm, an alternative name for the Mexican god Tlaloc, is clearly a gloss for the Zapotec *cociyo.* Itzquiahuitl (the Nahuatl equivalent of "Obsidian Knife Rainstorm") can be equated with the personal name Cosijoeza, and Yecaquiahuitl (the Nahuatl equivalent of "Wind God Rainstorm") corresponds to Cosijopii.[37] Thus the generational succession of Tehuantepec rulers implied by their order, from bottom to top, in the Guevea document is corroborated by the testimony given by Don Juan and his contemporaries (see Fig. 1.3).

The sixteenth-century Nahuatl translation also lays to rest etymological questions about the personal name Cosijoeza.[38] "Obsidian Knife Rainstorm" appears to have been an esteemed royal name in late precolumbian Oaxaca, whether spoken in Zapotec, Nahuatl, or Mixtec. The Codex Nuttall shows an earlier ancestor of the Tehuantepec Cosijoeza, 11 Water, who was the penultimate ruler of Cuilapan-Zaachila at the time the codex was painted, with a composite glyph representing the very same personal name—a *cociyo* or Rain God mask combined with an obsidian or flint knife (see Fig. 1.4). Were it not sufficiently confusing that the Tehuantepec ruler shared a personal name with his ancestor 11 Water, the hieroglyphic name depicted on the Guevea original for Tehuantepec's Cosijoeza appears to be an alternative version of the calendrical glyph for Water as well.

There are further generational ambiguities surrounding the Tehuantepec ruler's spouse. Although not mentioned in her son's interrogatory, Itzquiahuitl/Cosijoeza's wife was named voluntarily by several witnesses in 1554 as Xilabela (later known as Pelaxílla), a sister of Moctezuma. Pelaxílla can be translated as Cotton Puff (Copo de Algodón), the name by which Burgoa identified Cosijoeza's wife, but in Doña Magdalena's interrogatory her Nahuatl name is given as Quetzalcoatl, not Coyolicatzin, the Nahuatl equivalent of Cotton Puff.[39] Quetzalcoatl, or Feathered Serpent, appears to be an unusual woman's name, yet it fits the Zapotec translation well, since Xilabela combines *xilla*, meaning "rich green feather," and *péla,* meaning "snake" in sixteenth-century Zapotec. Oudijk notes that one of 11 Water's wives, Lady 13 Serpent, is identified on another Mixtec document, the Codex Bodley, by the personal name "Feathered Serpent." He suggests that the Tehuantepec ruler went to great lengths in assuming the aura and power of this famous ancestral couple, adopting their personal names both for himself and for his own wife.[40]

Might a similar, deliberate transposition not account for the puzzle surrounding Don Juan's identification with his own grandfather? If so, there should be further corroboration of this identification from the sixteenth-century interrogatories. According to the testimony of various witnesses, Yecaquiahuitl was the first conqueror of the Tehuantepec province. Here the likely derivation of the Nahuatl affix *yeca-* from *ehecatl*, signifying breeze, wind, or ghost, supports the traditional reading of Cosijopii as "Lightning Wind" or "Rainstorm Wind" (*pij* or *pii* referring to wind or spirit).[41] "Wind" was also the calendrical name of this first Tehuantepec ruler, for the day glyph associated with him in the original Guevea document has the fringed beard, protruding snout, and bulging eye connected with the Wind God. Although the grandfather was clearly referred to as Cosijopii by Don Juan's Zapotec contemporaries, there is no indication that Don Juan himself bore this personal name. His widow identified her husband's pagan name as Quetzpal, most likely a rendering for *cuetzpallin* or "Lizard," the fourth day in the Aztec ritual calendar, and local witnesses in her suit similarly referred to him by the Zapotec calendar equivalent day name "Lachi."[42] If Don Juan acquired the personal name of Cosijopii in addition to this calendrical name, it may have been some time after his death, for no known sixteenth-century document refers to him thus.

It appears then that the glosses for the kings of Tehuantepec found on all four versions of the Lienzo de Guevea do reflect, from bottom to top, the dynastic sequence for the Isthmus capital as it was generally understood by people in the late sixteenth century, both those who had lived before the conquest and those who had only heard about Don Juan Cortés's ancestors from their own parents. According to these witnesses, neither Cosijopii nor Cosijoeza was alive when Hernán Cortés first landed in Veracruz, contradicting the claims of later historical sources that Cosijoeza had turned over the Tehuantepec throne to his young son and was himself reigning in Zaachila at the time of the conquest. One witness in this suit placed the death of the grandfather Yecaquiahuitl/Cosijopii in the year 1498, although he may have relinquished the throne many years before. Other witnesses testified that the father Itzquiahuitl/Cosijoeza died in about 1504, when Don Juan was still a child, after summoning all the caciques and *principales* of the region to his deathbed to inform them of his choice for successor and demand their allegiance to his young son.[43]

With this genealogical history still so clearly remembered in testimony given as late as 1570, how can it be that Burgoa heard something quite different just a century later? It would be easy to attribute the confusion to a terrible error on the part of the Dominican chronicler, but, as discussed earlier, another tale much like Burgoa's was elaborated upon by the pretender to the Zaachila-Tehuantepec *cacicazgo*, Antonio de Aguero, less than a half-century after Burgoa's *Geográfica descripción* was published.[44] Rather than simply repeating a story he might have heard indirectly from the earlier published account, Aguero appears to have presented his version of the same popular tale told to Burgoa. One interesting new detail he provided was the name of Cosijopii's wife, Billosicahi, whom Aguero claimed was a Huave. Adjusting for orthographic inconsistencies in the transcription of indigenous names, it seems that this is the same Piuxicache named in Doña Magdalena's 1567 interrogatory as the wife of her husband's grandfather Yecaquiahuitl/Cosijopii. It would have been standard Mesoamerican practice for the victorious Cosijopii, as conqueror of the Isthmus Huave, to take a wife among the vanquished former rulers.[45] If so, her generational position had been displaced by late colonial times in the popular inversion of the Tehuantepec dynasty which equated Don Juan Cortés with his ancestor Cosijopii.[46]

Comparing these complicated genealogical and historical details brings us a little closer to a determination of the date of the Zapotec conquest and colonization of the Isthmus. If Cosijopii's own ancestor, 6 Water, reigned in the late 1430s, the date proposed by Alfonso Caso for the composition of the Codex Nuttall, and he was at least one generation removed from that Zaachila-Cuilapan king, it may have been as late as the early 1450s or 1460s that Cosijopii launched his successful attack on the unprepared Guazontecas and their neighbors. It would be compatible as well with Oudijk's reconstruction of the usurpation of the Zaachila throne by Tlaxiaco's 8 Deer. Several witnesses gave testimony in both Don Juan's 1554 interrogatory and in the suit by his widow nearly twenty years later as to the decisiveness of the Zapotec victory under Yecaquiahuitl, which sent the Guazontecas fleeing and compelled all the lords of the province from a distance of 12 to 15 leagues to recognize Yecaquiahuitl as a great lord.[47]

Although the Nahua witness Baltasar García did not arrive in the province until after the Spanish Conquest, serving first as a translator for Cortés and later being installed as governor of Xalapa del Marqués, his testimony provided many colorful details of the conquest told him by people of the province. That he assigned the conquest events to Don Juan's father in one set of answers, while later referring to the grandfather as the founder of the Tehuantepec dynasty, indicates how easily identities might be transposed in the oral accounts of historic events that a century later were recorded by Burgoa:

> Itzquiahuitl [sic] came to this province with only six hundred men from the Valley of Oaxaca and conquered the province which had belonged to the Guazontec-speaking Indians, and once all the land had been conquered by his side, Itzquiahuitl [sic] distributed it among the Indian soldiers that he brought. And in this manner among the villages and places which he partitioned and gave away were the barrios and pueblos and *estancias* of Totonilco, Tlacotepec, Chiltepec, Xochitlan and Amatitlan. Left there by the Guazontec Indians were orchards of *zapotes* and other trees and fruits, and Don Juan and his parents always enjoyed the use of these orchards and fruits. And when he had finished, Itzquiahuitl [sic] sent certain Indians back to the Valley of Oaxaca where they were *naturales* to give notice of the land that he had conquered and to plead with the lords there that they send him people to populate the land and so they sent him 300 men with whom he finished populating this province.[48]

Part III: Archaeology of the Zapotec conquest

Victorious parties may extol their heroic triumphs in words long remembered, but the actual events are often less easily discerned in the material record recovered by archaeologists. Once buried by time's sediments, prehistoric battlefields littered with broken weapons or unclaimed corpses may have too little surface visibility to attract the kind of scientific attention that long-settled habitation sites and monumental constructions arouse. And while the conquest of another group may have important political and economic significance for both conqueror and conquered, it may be a significance difficult to distinguish in the house forms, burial customs, and domestic refuse that are the mainstay of the archaeological record. Even when a population's decline or material impoverishment over time are empirically observed archaeological phenomena, their historical explanation can stir rancorous debate.

In the case of the Tehuantepec province, the as-yet incompletely investigated archaeological record bears remarkably close resemblance to the events chronicled in both Burgoa's work and this sixteenth-century litigation testimony. Archaeological sites spanning the last few centuries before the Spanish Conquest exhibit profound changes in community size and distribution and in their inventory of cultural materials and practices, changes that can only be correlated with tremendous social dislocation. Taken together these data argue strongly for the destruction of indigenous seats of power by an outside force, one which displaced most of the native population and established its own administrative centers and cultural norms. The next chapter will consider more fully how the archaeological record contributes substantively to understanding the nature of the imposed Zapotec political system. At this time I will limit my review to archaeological evidence for the timing and impact of Zapotec colonization.

From the onset of the Classic period at about AD 300, prehistoric inhabitants of the Tehuantepec province enjoyed a millennium of stable growth and cultural continuity. The floodplain of the Río de los Perros, thus far the only intensively investigated section of the Pacific coastal plain, was the focus of an expanding network of communities, whose economies were based on fishing, hunting, and the rainy season cultivation of maize and other crops in its deep alluvial soils. Trade outside the region is presumed to have been based on the province's historically desirable resources—salt, salted fish and shrimp, ornamental marine shells, precious feathers, and animal skins. That trade contributed to the growth and prosperity of the floodplain's primary center near modern Juchitán and to the proliferation of smaller villages and hamlets subordinate to it. At the onset of the Classic period, this settlement covered an area of 68 ha; ten additional smaller settlements were located within a 100 km^2 area

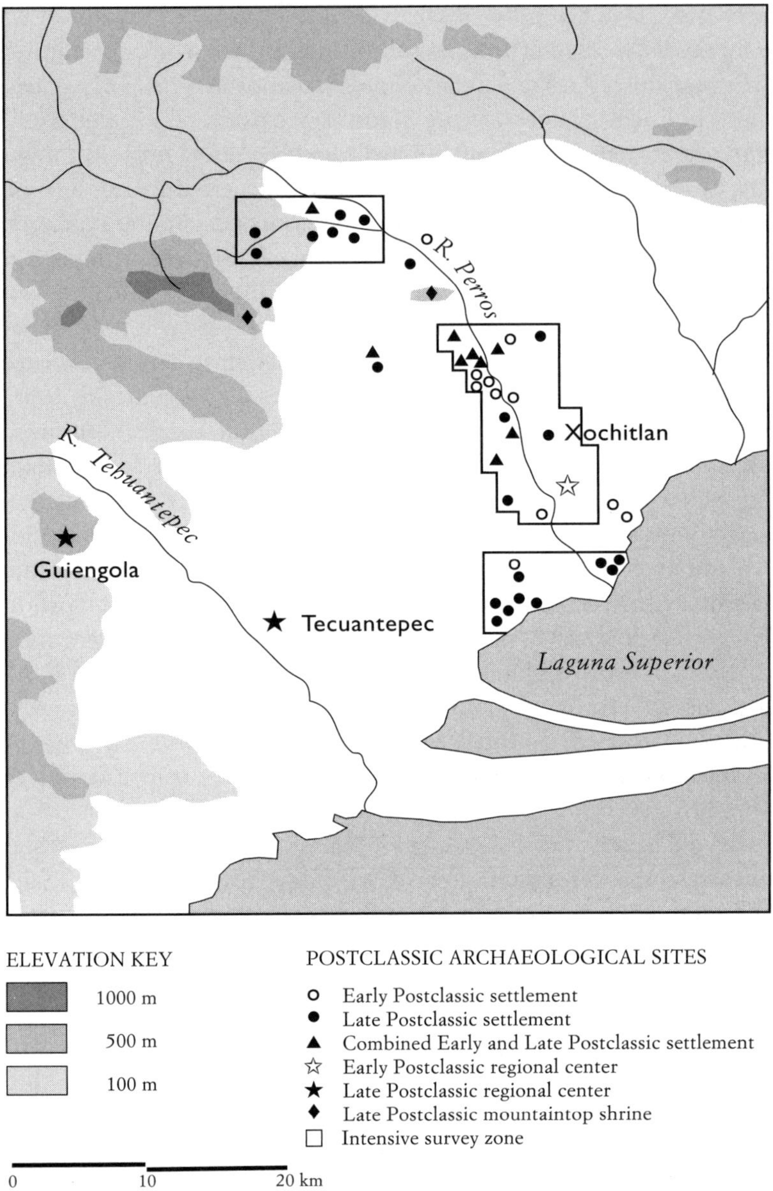

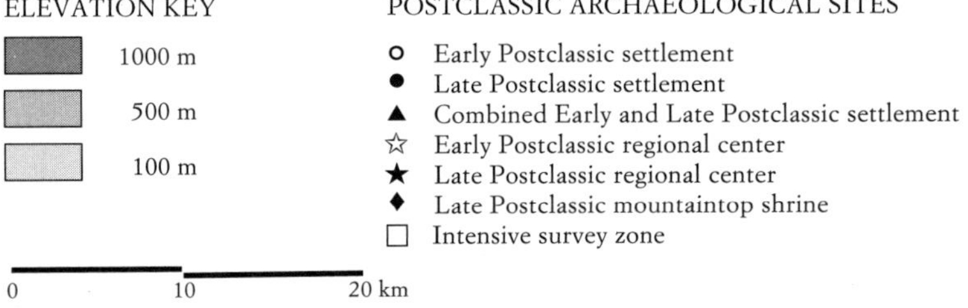

MAP 1.2. Early and Late Postclassic site distributions.

of intensive archaeological investigation. During the Early Postclassic (AD 900 –1300/1400), seventeen rural sites were occupied and the expanding regional center now covered an area of 267 ha.[49]

This lengthy period of protracted growth came to a precipitous halt sometime in the fourteenth or fifteenth century; there are no radiocarbon dates from the study area which might allow a more precise determination for this cultural shift. The regional center was abandoned abruptly and while some of its population may have moved to a more consolidated site now buried by the modern city of Juchitán, sixteenth-century records indicate that the native community at Xochitlan was just one of many small villages on the coastal plain. Rural settlements did increase in number, with twenty-nine identified in the intensive survey zone, but most of these were quite small, under 2 ha in area. As a consequence, the total area of occupied land along the banks of the Río de los Perros fell sharply, from a calculated high of 294 ha in the Early Postclassic to a low of 46 ha in the Late Postclassic. The small population that remained was distributed in dramatically different ways. Nearly two-thirds of the late settlements were located at sites not occupied during the Early Postclassic. Many of these new communities were located in two zones that evidenced little sign of previous habitation in the nearly three thousand years since village life was first established on the southern Isthmus. Both zones offered decided economic advantages: the lagoon shore-estuarine zone at the mouth of the river presented rich fishing and shellfish-collecting opportunities, and the piedmont zone at the edge of the coastal plain held several small streams feeding into the Río de los Perros that might be tapped for canal irrigation.

As striking as the settlement reorientation appears, even further social dislocation is indicated by the artifacts found at these sites. Earlier in the Classic period, the Río de los Perros communities popularized the use of a fine paste kaolin clay in the manufacture of pottery for serving and ritual vessels. When new vessel forms and decoration motifs came into style during the Early Postclassic, these changes were part of the evolution of white ware pottery that had been manufactured locally and dominated household kitchens for several hundred years. Strong cultural affiliations throughout this period link the southern and northern sides of the Isthmus of Tehuantepec, which many historical linguists see as the homeland of the Mixe-Zoque language family.[50]

In the Late Postclassic, however, these trans-Isthmian ties were broken. Late sites often have little or no kaolin pottery, but their surfaces are lit-

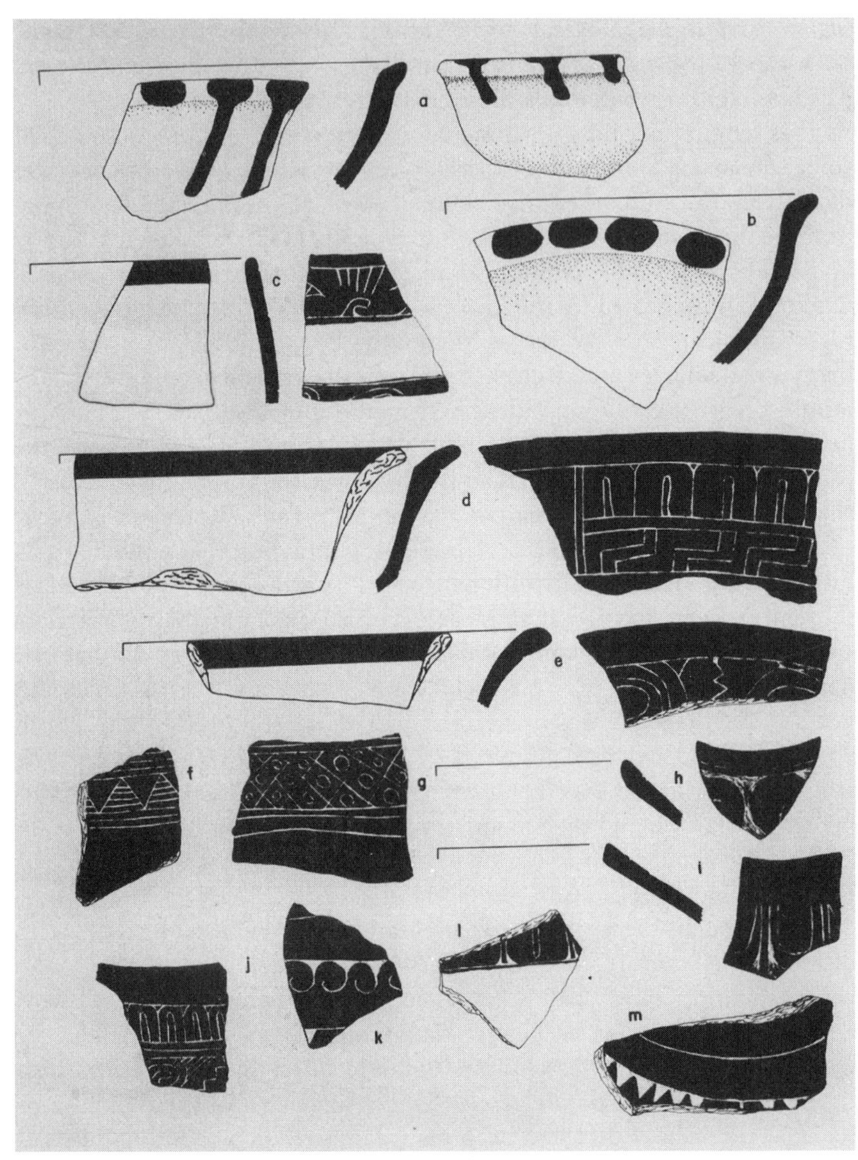

FIG. 1.6. Early Postclassic pottery styles; red painted decoration on white ware pottery (c–m have additional *sgraffito* incised decoration).

FIG. 1.7. Late Postclassic gray ware pottery; bowls with serpent head feet from private collection in Tehuantepec.

tered with broken sherds of fine paste gray pottery of a type common in the protohistoric Oaxaca Valley. Some of the gray ware pottery is found in the new lagoon-shore sites, helping to confirm their contemporaneity with those of the coastal plain and piedmont zones. Despite these common elements, the sand-tempered orange ware plates and jars that predominate in collections from the lagoon-shore sites are so distinctive that they have been grouped into a separate ceramic complex. Another unique characteristic of the shoreline sites is the high concentration of imported obsidian found on their surfaces. This valuable volcanic glass, seen only in small quantities as preformed blades elsewhere on the coastal plain, here was worked into large flakes and finished artifacts from heavy cores brought to the shoreline zone. The distribution pattern suggests that the lagoon-shore communities had preferential access to this material, which Robert Zeitlin has traced spectrochemically to obsidian mines that were under Aztec control.[51]

Differences in the kinds of pottery used by individual communities can have many explanations. Communities may play specialized economic roles within a cultural system that assigns different ceramic utensils to specific tasks. Social class distinctions among communities may be reflected in pottery usage, when cost or sumptuary privileges restrict access to certain wares to members of the social elite. Arguing that ceramic styles are markers of ethnic identity or that sudden shifts of pottery popularity reflect ethnic change does not today have the persuasive appeal to archaeologists that it did thirty years ago, before the widespread recognition that cultural systems are not homogenous and that cultural artifacts do not have necessary linguistic or ethnic identities. Nonetheless, given the historical record of late prehispanic cultural dislocation in the Tehuantepec province, a compelling case can be made for explaining the unusual settlement and artifact patterns seen in the Río de los Perros archaeological sequence in terms of known ethnic groups.

The lagoon-shore habitat traditionally occupied by the Huave makes that group one likely candidate for the prehistoric population scattered among the small archaeological sites lining the river mouth estuaries, even though no sixteenth-century Huave settlements were recorded near the Río de los Perros. With their own narrative histories portraying them as recent migrants to the Isthmus from lands to the south, a distinctive ceramic complex would be a likely archaeological correlate, one which might be demonstrated through controlled excavations at established Huave communities. The special relationship between Huave settlements and Aztec merchants which the Zapotecs cited as their motivation for conquering the province appears to have supplied the lagoon-shore settlers with abundant quantities of the valued obsidian widely traded by the Aztecs. Alternatively, these estuarine sites might be the remnants of Aztec encampments, with the paucity of artifact debris reflecting the temporary nature of Aztec military and trading sojourns.[52]

As to the decapitation of the regional settlement system and widespread community dislocation that took place along the river floodplain, here the archaeological record mirrors Zapotec accounts of their invasion with striking fidelity. In the early colonial period, the Río de los Perros served as a boundary zone between the largely Zapotec-speaking communities that inhabited the western coastal plain and the Zoque-speaking villages to the east. The Late Postclassic period settlement dislocation evidenced in the Río de los Perros investigation is strong archaeological confirmation for a Zapotec invasion in which existing Zoque settlements were destroyed and any survivors were either pushed farther east or resettled in small hamlets administered by Oaxaca Valley colonists. The persistence of local Isthmus ceramics at some late sites, while others have a purer assemblage of Oaxaca Valley pottery styles, does suggest that pockets of Zoque-speakers continued to live in the midst of the Zapotec invaders, contrary to the colonists' recollections, but their increasing acculturation to Zapotec patterns may not have been entirely voluntary. New settlements in the irrigable piedmont zone could be the archaeological manifestation of the private estates owned by the Zapotec royal family and other Tehuantepec nobles, where orchards of cacao and other tropical fruits were tended by slaves and *terrazgueros* or serfs.[53]

The main focus of Zapotec settlement, however, was farther west along the Tehuantepec River, where the patterns of late prehistoric sociocultural change have yet to be as fully documented archaeologically. With modern urban growth obscuring the prehispanic foundations of Tehuantepec itself, only the mountaintop fortress of Guiengola, immortalized in Burgoa's account as the site of Cosijoeza's successful defense against a seven-month-long siege by the Aztec army,[54] still stands in silent tribute to the Zapotec king. Although the prominence of the site, with its exposed complex of pyramid mounds, ball court, tombs, and elite residential zones, has attracted the attention of local collectors and visiting archaeologists since the early nineteenth century, systematic investigations have been few. The brief mapping operations conducted by the Institute of Oaxaca Studies in 1970 and 1972 have provided the most comprehensive data on the construction, chronology, and probable function of the site's architectural features. As reported by David Peterson, an intensive surface collection of the site conducted during the mapping survey produced only a relatively small collection of 742 potsherds, 92 percent of which matched the fine paste gray ware category that distinguished the Río de los Perros settlements during the Late Postclassic, a pottery type originating in the Oaxaca Valley. With few sherds from the Isthmian white ware tradition encountered here, Guiengola should be seen as a purely Zapotec occupation.[55]

Before recent breakthroughs in refining the Oaxaca Valley's Late Postclassic ceramic chronology, it was not possible to use these long-lived gray wares to pinpoint Guiengola's foundation within a several-hundred-year period. More promising options came from Isthmus archaeological or ethnohistorical sources. Burgoa's account suggests that the site's thick defensive walls were erected quickly in anticipation of the advancing Aztec army, but the enormous investment of human labor underlying the construction of the hilltop ceremonial and residential complex clearly demanded both a coherent plan for the site and the political authority to effect its execution. Such requirements would not, however, necessitate sev-

FIG. 1.8. View of the ruins of Guiengola by Miguel Covarrubias. From *Mexico South: The Isthmus of Tehuantepec* by Miguel Covarrubias, copyright 1946 by Alfred A. Knopf, Inc. Used by permission of Alfred A. Knopf, a division of Random House, Inc.

eral lifetimes to complete. In fact, the relative scarcity of potsherds and other artifactual debris indicates that occupation must have been brief or perhaps just intermittent at Guiengola. Similar hilltop fortress complexes were a common component of the Late Postclassic settlement system in the Oaxaca Valley, where they served as a fortified and sanctified retreat for the nobility, while year-round settlement was concentrated on the valley floor. For Guiengola's builders, permanent residence was located about 15 km away at Tehuantepec itself.

Nearly five hundred years of postconquest settlement and rebuilding have demolished once-standing Postclassic structures and covered up most traces of the population that inhabited them, but archaeological materials can still be found widely dispersed around Tehuantepec and its numerous barrios. Private collections of intact gray ware and, more rarely, polychrome funerary offerings, are frequently amassed from homeowner excavations, but seldom does an archaeologist have the opportunity to examine the context in which such finds are made. Salvage operations conducted by archaeologists from the Instituto Nacional de Antropología e Historia's (INAH) regional center in Oaxaca have on occasion temporarily stalled construction activities in and around the city

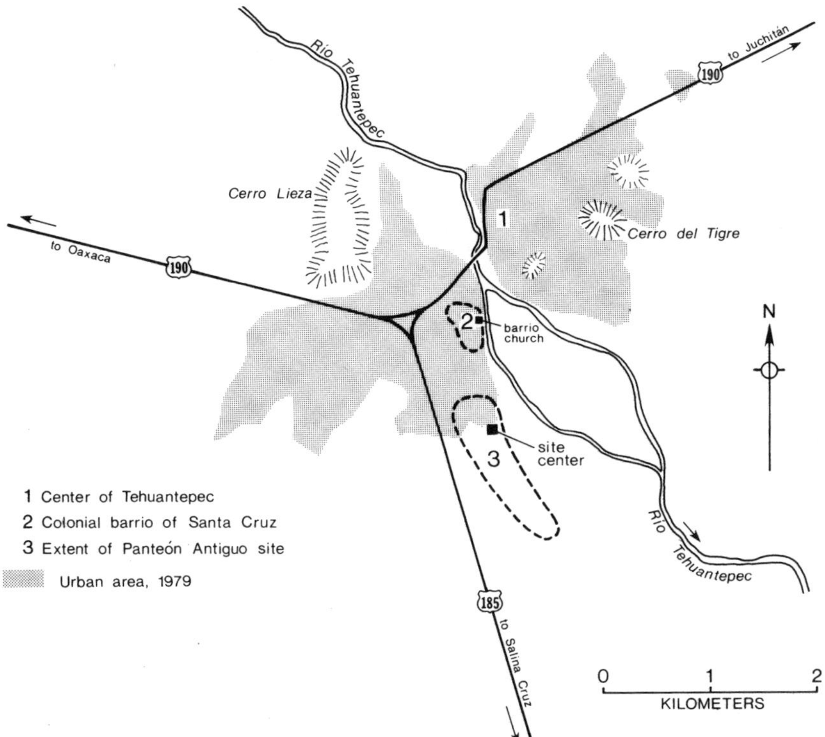

MAP 1.3. Relationship of the Panteón Antiguo archaeological site and the colonial Santa Cruz Tagolaba barrio.

long enough to record fast-disappearing archaeological features. At Cerro Padre López, for example, only traces of plaster-floored buildings were left for the salvage team to map before continued house construction destroyed the last remains of this important site overlooking the center of town, where carved stone friezes once decorated a substantial building.[56]

At least one area of prehispanic settlement at Tehuantepec managed to withstand the onslaught of postcolonial urban growth, protected by the very policies of colonial-period resettlement that led to its abandonment. Across the Tehuantepec River, on the southern limits of the urban barrio of Santa Cruz Tagolaba, a small artificial mound and partially exposed plaster floor indicate the presence of a late prehispanic administrative center at the site known locally as the Panteón Antiguo or "ancient cemetery." My preliminary excavations and surface survey of this site in 1990 confirmed that the two-room temple mound and columned public building were the political and ceremonial focus of the barrio on the eve of the Spanish Conquest, when the associated settlement covered an area of about 0.5 km^2.[57]

These colonists re-created at Tehuantepec the same kind of settlement unit favored in Zapotec-speaking areas of the Oaxaca Valley, one in which the "basic building blocks" of the settlement system consisted of clusters of houses surrounding small ceremonial-administrative complexes, with stretches of unoccupied land separating such units from one another.[58] Such a pattern is observed archaeologically at ancient Santa Cruz Tagolaba, where there may have been some two hundred houses loosely aggregated around the ceremonial and administrative center. The social organization behind this settlement pattern will be considered more fully in the next chapter, but for now let us consider the implications of the archaeological data for the timing and nature of Tehuantepec's Zapotec colonization. I have estimated a substantial population of 1,000–1,200 for the barrio, but the shallow surface scatters of predominantly gray ware sherds marking ancient house lots do not evidence much time depth. Although the public buildings underwent repeated refurbishing of their plaster floors, such attentiveness to these structures is not inconsistent with an estimate of less than one hundred years of occupation at this site prior to the Spanish Conquest.

According to the 1571 testimony of Baltasar García quoted previously, the Zapotec king colonized Tehuantepec and its subject communities with just six hundred soldiers and another three hundred colonists and their families enlisted from the Oaxaca Valley lords. In fact a much larger immigrant population must have been drawn to the expanding Isthmus capital to account for its likely population of at least 25,000 by the early 1500s, an estimate derived from the spatial extent of residential barrios like the ancient Tagolaba settlement and from sixteenth-century census data.

Based on settlement pattern evidence, the dynastic capital of Zaachila appears not to have held enough of a population base itself to have supplied Tehuantepec's colonists. The Tlacolula arm of the Oaxaca Valley is a much more likely source, since archaeological survey data suggest a precariously high population of about 72,000 in this relatively poor agricultural zone during the Late Postclassic. A disproportionate demographic crash by the mid-sixteenth century, when just 12 percent of that population remained, represents a loss too big to be accounted for by even the most radical estimates of postconquest indigenous mortality. My own interpretation of the Tlacolula peak and subsequent decline is that Zapotec-speaking populations displaced from other valley zones by intruding Mixtecs settled temporarily in the Tlacolula area sometime during the Late Postclassic, perhaps in the late thirteenth or early fourteenth century, only to move again with the promise of a vast territory opened up on the Tehuantepec coastal plain.[59]

Reconciling the Narrative and Archaeological Sources

Although archaeology cannot tell us precisely when or why, it does provide strong confirmation for the Zapotec conquest of Tehuantepec's western coastal plain sometime within the last few centuries prior to Cortés's arrival. If anything, the prehistoric material record evidences an even more profound impact of that conquest on the region's human landscape, because, unlike the Zapotec historical sources, it gives equal representation to the experiences of the conquered peoples. Long-established settlement hierarchies were overturned and the remaining local population was driven from its farms and homes or pressed into service on lands now under Zapotec control. Whether the colonists left Oaxaca motivated by individual social and economic pressures or as part of a politically organized exodus that transplanted larger social units to the Isthmus, their numerical strength in the newly established city was the foundation upon which the Tehuantepec king's political power rested.

To find out when that polity was inaugurated, we must return to the narrative sources. Burgoa claimed that the Zapotec migration to the Isthmus took place some three hundred years before the time of his writing, but a mid- to late fourteenth-century date is even more at odds with the foreshortened dynastic sequence familiar to him, which identified Cosijoeza as the conquering king. It is possible that some small colony of Zapotec speakers had been established on the coastal plain before Cosijopii launched his decisive campaign. The Isthmus *sierra* Zapotecs, who are linguistically distinct from their coastal cousins, apparently arrived at their present homeland in just such a migration depicted in the Lienzo de Guevea, where a separate path leads from Zaachila to Santiago Guevea parallel to the path connecting the Tehuantepec rulers to their Zaachila ancestors. If a similar founding coastal colony did exist, its influence over the surrounding population would appear to have been slight. Archaeologically, Postclassic Oaxaca Valley pottery styles are associated with sites evidencing the kind of sweeping cultural dislocation that is better attributed to a well-orchestrated, highly centralized program of conquest.

To the right of each of the Zaachila-Tehuantepec rulers, the Lienzo de Guevea shows a numerical tally signifying the individual's years of life or years of rule. In the original García version, the number is the same, fifty-three, for all the kings but two: Cosijoeza, who is shown with the number fifty-six, and Don Juan Cortés, presumably still alive at the time the document was painted, who has forty-eight. In arguments justifying his claim to the disputed Isthmus *salinas* and *estancias*, Don Juan asserted in 1554 that he had held possession of these lands for fifty years, like his grandfather and father before him, who had held the lands for a period of fifty years each. Clearly more of a rhetorical device indicating the longevity of possession of lands or titles than a calculation of the number of years each individual held actual control, the Hispanicized "fifty" appears to have functioned like the precolumbian "fifty-three," which was one year more than the fifty-two years of the basic Mesoamerican calendrical cycle, indicating a very long period of time. Accepting this improbable duration of rule would situate Cosijopii's conquest in the first decade of the fifteenth century, but a mid-century date seems more likely.[60]

Either scenario places the political transformation of the southern Isthmus squarely within the fifteenth century AD, a tumultuous time that also witnessed the rise to power of the New World's more famous empires, the Aztecs of Mexico and the Incas of Peru. It was a century in which ambitious elites throughout Mesoamerica pursued dreams of greatness through warfare and fragile political alliances, dreams that were barely realized before the intrusion of strangers seeking a different kind of renown cut them short. Why the remembrance of the Isthmus triumph underwent such a profound revision by natives living under Spanish colonial rule is a story I will return to later. Before looking at the conquest of the Zapotec colonizers, however, let us examine more closely the kind of society these descendants of the Xipe kings created in their lowland realm.

CHAPTER TWO

King and Community in Prehispanic Tehuantepec

To understand what kind of society the prehispanic Zapotec colonizers forged in their new Isthmus home requires a synthesis of disparate historical, linguistic, and archaeological sources. However sketchy or narrow the picture provided by any one document or any one class of material remain, layering these sources together helps reinforce a multidimensional view of the Tehuantepec state and its organizational structure. Key elements of that portrait are the size and spatial configuration of the Zapotec population, its division into wards or barrios imbued with corporate functions, and the nature of social classes with their specific political and economic characteristics. A focus on the architecture of the precolumbian polity alone, however, does not reveal much about the framework of cultural values and social needs that bound it internally and made the polity resilient in the face of outside attack. Zapotec religious ideas and rituals provide an important window on these shared principles and will be touched on here as well. Last to be addressed are the ways in which the Tehuantepec polity interacted with its neighbors and with another major conquest state of the Late Postclassic era, that of the Aztecs or Mexica.

Urbanism in the Tehuantepec City-State

The earliest Spanish description of Tehuantepec does not come from the pen of the conqueror Hernán Cortés or from that of his lieutenant Pedro de Alvarado, whose report from a stay in the province prior to embarking on the brutal conquest of Guatemala has been lost. Rather it is an account of harrowing adventure by the cleric Juan de Areyzaga, who

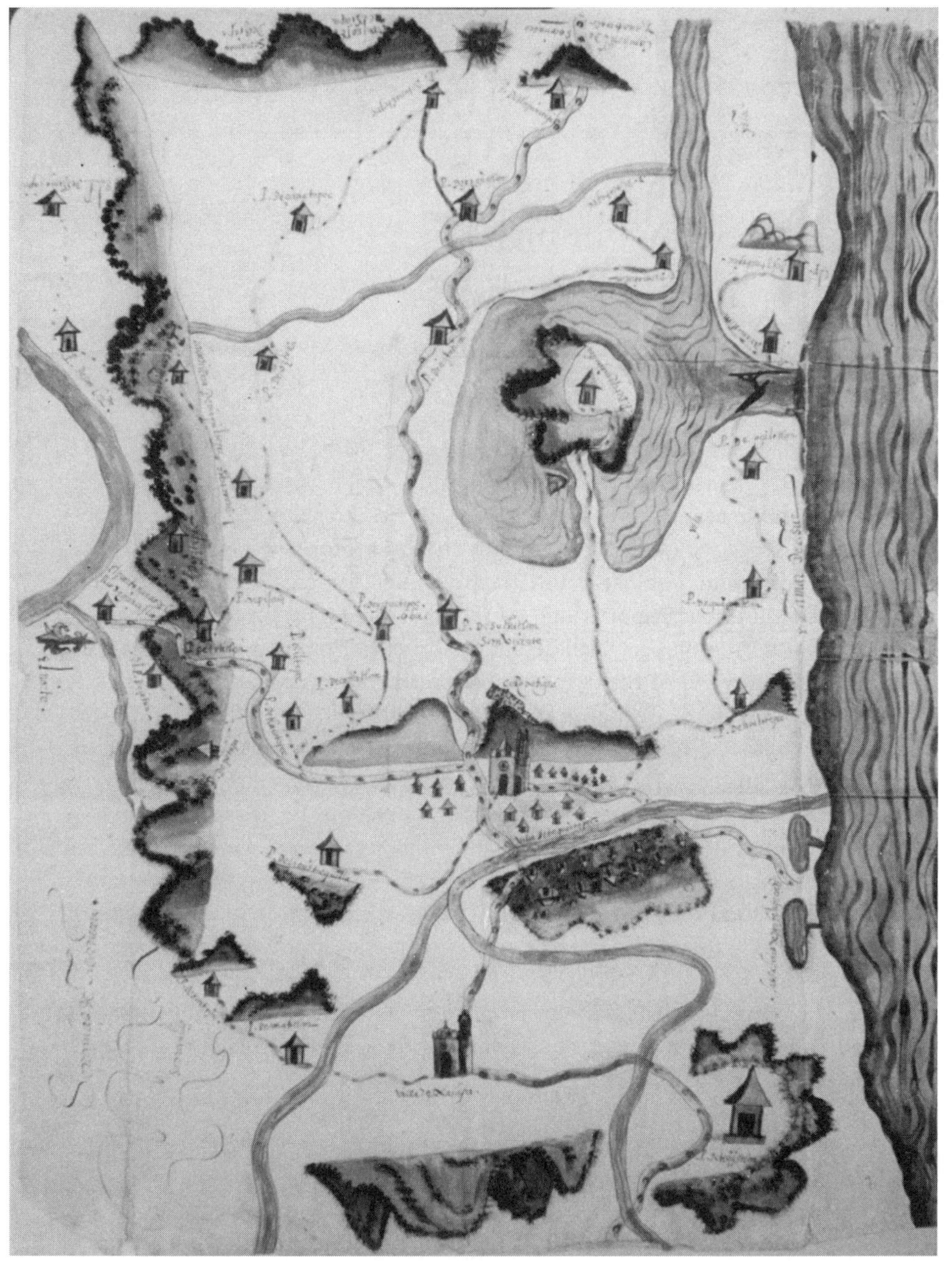

FIG. 2.1. 1580 Relación Geográfica map of the Tehuantepec province (JGI XXV-4). Photo courtesy of the Benson Latin American Collection, University of Texas at Austin.

was among the fortunate crew making landfall near Tehuantepec in 1526, after their boat became separated from the other ships in the ill-fated Loaysa expedition to the Spice Islands. As related by the chronicler of the Indies, Gonzalo Fernández de Oviedo, the party sailed alone after passing through the Straits of Magellan for 2,000 leagues without adequate supplies of food and water until coming aground on July 25 on a sand bar off Mazatlan. Following a friendly reception by the cacique of this populous town, messengers were sent to Cortés's administrator in nearby Tehuantepec, who arrived to welcome them several days later carried in a hammock by twelve men. At the direction of the governor and the ship's captain, the latter too ill to make the trip himself, Areyzaga departed Tehuantepec on July 31 for Mexico City to meet with Cortés, who reported receiving word of the ship's landing in his fifth letter to Charles V.[1] Both coastal towns were very large; Areyzaga gave one estimate of about 100,000, which Oviedo did not find surprising: "because those communities or populations are composed of wards, like the populations in the valleys of some provinces of Spain, such as Vizcaya and Guipúzcoa and in the mountains, and it all appeared to this clergyman and to the others that it was one community, even though it really was large populations close to one another."[2]

Improbably high as Areyzaga's impressionistic estimate might be, Tehuantepec was one of the largest communities in southern New Spain and considerably more populous than any of its Oaxaca Valley neighbors on the eve of the Spanish Conquest. The fairly conservative figure of about 25,000 for the prehispanic city that I have projected from archaeological data at the Santa Cruz Tagolaba site and from widespread early colonial depopulation rates is nearly twice the population estimated for any of the three largest Late Postclassic sites in the Oaxaca Valley.[3] Although ancient Tehuantepec was certainly large enough to be considered a city, at the same time it is clear that, as Oviedo maintained, it was in essence an aggregate of separate wards or barrio communities.

This aggregate character is graphically underscored in the indigenous-style map of the province that accompanied the 1580 Relación Geográfica mandated by Philip II, King of Spain. While all other Isthmus villages are represented on the map by a single peaked-roof house, Tehuantepec has thirty-one such structures surrounding the Catholic convent and church, each of which must have corresponded to a distinct barrio. Even this large number is a reduction from the forty-nine barrios counted twenty-five years before in Baltasar de San Miguel's mid-century census.

By the early seventeenth century, the number of Tehuantepec barrios diminished further as Dominican missionaries regrouped the decimated population that remained into more tightly nucleated parishes clustered around the center of town, one of many early colonial attempts to aggregate native populations into more manageable units, following the policy of *congregación* or forced relocation.

However much battering by colonial political and demographic forces the Isthmus population would suffer in the years ahead, the indigenous barrio community endured as the primary corporate unit beyond the extended family and the focus of social and religious life for Tehuantepec's citizens through the close of the twentieth century. Given the barrio's similarly high archaeological visibility in prehispanic Oaxaca, it is clear that this core community had been the heart of Zapotec social structure for hundreds of years before the Isthmus colonization. Far from being some petrified relic of ancient tradition, the barrio's capacity for meeting social needs over the long run depended on its ability to adjust to the surrounding economic and political context. No new context presented a greater challenge to Zapotec social institutions than did the advent of Spanish colonialism. In order to measure the extent of those colonial adjustments, it is important to first understand the barrio's role in the immigrant nation that was the Tehuantepec city-state.

Function and organization of the Zapotec barrio

Both archaeological data and documentary evidence prior to the late sixteenth- and early seventeenth-century *congregaciones* provide useful information on the structure and organization of the Tehuantepec barrios, but each source brings with it certain limitations that must be considered as well. Although the material record alone can provide direct evidence for the late fifteenth-century city, it is difficult to recover under the sprawl of continuous urban occupation. At present the only Tehuantepec barrio for which there is more information than isolated archaeological traces is the Santa Cruz Tagolaba community. Sharing core features with long-standing settlement forms from Zapotec-speaking parts of the Oaxaca Valley, this archaeological community is an appropriate starting point for exploring Tehuantepec's prehispanic barrio community. Architectural and artifactual evidence from the site is used here to provide a core framework for understanding how community life was structured in late Zapotec towns and villages, a framework that will be filled in with sixteenth-century linguistic and documentary data. Turning to these colonial written sources to reconstruct prehispanic patterns, I have taken care to focus on those documents that reflect native understandings of Zapotec social organization and that derive primarily from the testimony of informants born prior to the Spanish Conquest.

Fundamental to the Zapotec barrio was a ceremonial and administrative complex that in the prehistoric Santa Cruz Tagolaba barrio was centered at the Panteón Antiguo archaeological complex. A single, two-roomed temple raised on a small platform mound dominated this complex, facing slightly north of east toward the Tehuantepec River. Flanking it on either side of a wide earthen plaza were at least two plaster-floored buildings, only one of which is sufficiently well preserved to permit a reconstruction of its floor plan. This building, which our archaeological team initially dubbed the "palacio" because its elaborate architectural details suggested a fancy elite residence, in fact appears to have played an important public role. Only one long room, measuring over 24 m by 5 m, was contained within its plastered adobe walls. Some well-preserved sections on the south side of the building indicate that a broad porch or veranda ran along the exterior walls underneath the roof eaves. The most impressive architectural feature is the porticoed entrance, where four plaster-faced adobe columns, each measuring roughly 1 m in diameter, made for dramatic access to the building from the adjoining plaza. Directly opposite the portico, traces of an adobe platform or bench measuring 49 cm wide were found against the interior wall.

No hearths or evidence of domestic activity were located within the building proper, although test pits dug in one of several areas of exposed reddish brown subfloor did indicate food preparation activities 25 m to the north. What was particularly striking about the pattern of remains associated with the building itself was the unusual frequency of potsherds pertaining to an otherwise rare, cylindrical incense burner. These sherds were found along with high concentrations of obsidian blades and pointed bladelets in excavation units placed at the porch and plaza area just outside the portico. Their contextual association indicates that the building's entrance was the scene of repeated acts of ritualized bloodletting. Rather than serving primarily as a private home for the barrio chief, whose actual residential quarters may have been located behind this building, the "palacio" appears to have functioned more publicly as a ceremonially consecrated hall.

The majority of the community's population resided in a 0.5 km^2 zone surrounding this precinct, where Late Postclassic artifacts are scattered

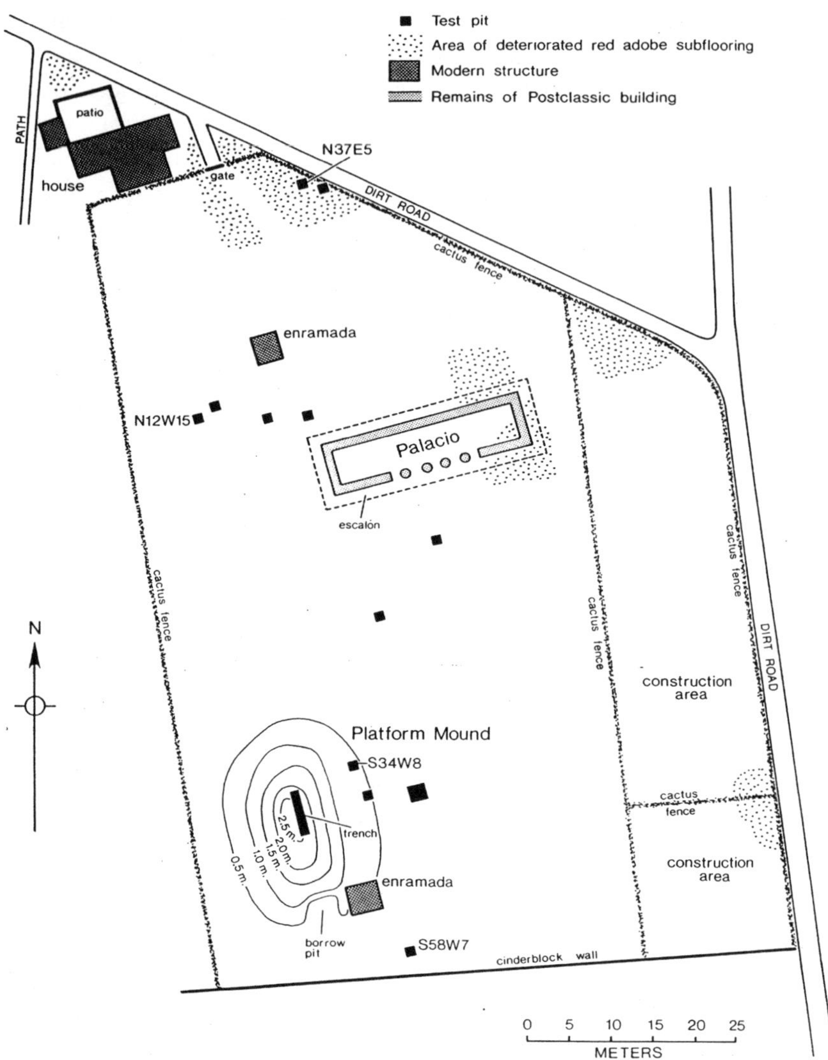

MAP 2.1. Panteón Antiguo site administrative center, Santa Cruz Tagolaba barrio.

widely on the ground and in exposed subsurface deposits. A marked fall-off in surface artifacts separates the Santa Cruz Tagolaba site from its nearest prehispanic neighbor. One fortuitously cleared lot just south of the ceremonial center evidenced a pattern of artifact distribution that may be typical for the settlement as a whole. Although no plaster floors or adobe walls remained to indicate the location of actual buildings, surface artifact concentrations were clustered in units probably corresponding to individual households about 10 m in diameter; similar clusters were separated by a distance of about 40 m. If this pattern is representative of the site as a whole, then about two hundred houses comprised the ancient barrio community.

No clear artifactual or architectural remains in these preliminary data indicate major socioeconomic differences among the constituent households. Most of the surface pottery corresponds to the ubiquitous Postclassic gray ware or its coarse utilitarian contemporary. While some worked jade from this part of the city appears in local private collections, it is without meaningful archaeological context. Even a more complete picture of the material record from this site would likely miss subtleties of barrio social structure that could be confirmed by good documentary data. Analyzing just such a set of detailed early colonial Nahuatl census records from several smaller towns in Morelos, Pedro Carrasco found that Nahua barrio units known as *calpolli* exhibited great disparities among households in the amount of agricultural land they farmed and that wealth as well as social class were powerful determinants of social relationships within the community.[4]

No comparable written source has been found for Tehuantepec, but several documents from the first few decades of Spanish rule hint at a more complex barrio social structure than can be discerned from the prehistoric material record alone. Although these turbulent years were filled with political and cultural disruption, basic patterns of indigenous social organization are less likely to have been the object of colonial interference, and the ingrained practices of a generation born prior to the arrival of Cortés may still be seen underneath the surface of the colonial contexts which these documents served. First among the documents to be considered is Baltasar de San Miguel's remarkably comprehensive, mid-sixteenth century census, which separates the town of Tehuantepec and the province's rural communities in its enumeration of age groups and households. These data indicate that a different kind of household structure predominated in Tehuantepec than that found among rural communities in the province, where the typical house sheltered six people. Unlike the rural pattern of nuclear family-based households, the average Tehuantepec house of just under fifteen people must have comprised some form of joint family, such as the children and spouses of grown siblings, or perhaps a nonkin group, such as an elite household that included a number of attached retainers.[5]

At about the same time as San Miguel's *visita*, an important complaint

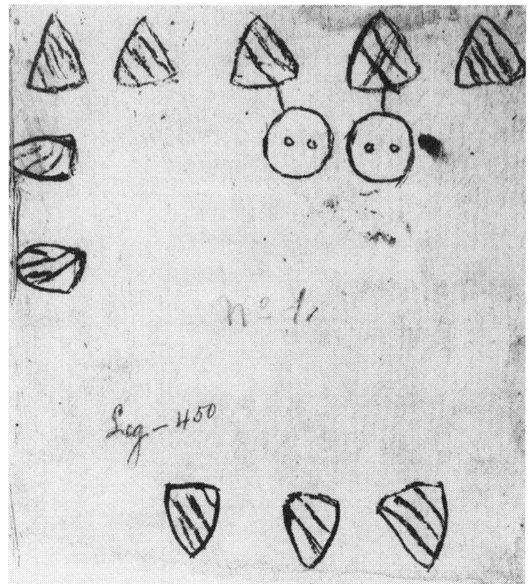

FIG. 2.2. Tribute record sheets from the 1553 criminal complaint against Don Juan Cortés, governor of Tehuantepec; Archivo General de la Nación, Hospital de Jesús, leg. 450, papeles sueltos, exp. 1, catalog nos. 3122, 3123, and 3124. Reproduced by permission of the Archivo General de la Nación. The three sheets of maguey paper were originally glued to others to form a longer, scroll-like document (known in Spanish as a *tira*) recording community tribute records. The button-like symbols on all three pages represent the Spanish two-tomín coin; other symbols are taken from the native pictographic tradition. The hatched triangles on the left represent an extended family household and the tribute obligations of its two full tribute-payers

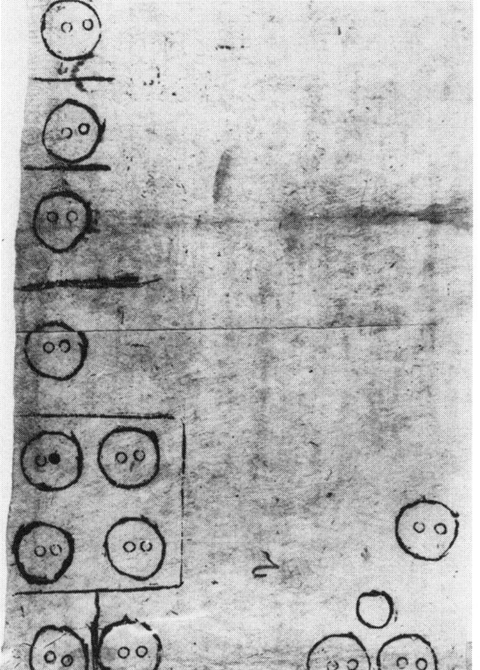

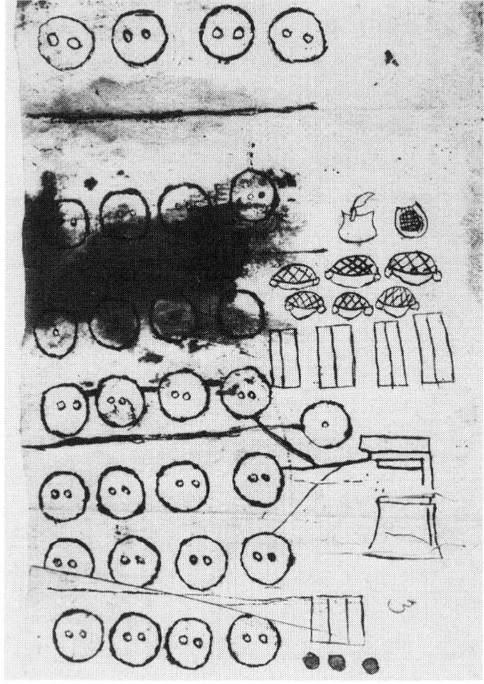

was brought before the Spanish administrator of the province by Zapotec commoners from one of Tehuantepec's barrios. Four men, Andrés Tine, Domingo Tio, Alonso Pica, and Bernardino Gualopa, charged that a barrio leader, Domingo Goma, had exacted excessive tribute from them, which the ruler and his associates then diverted to their own purposes. Arguing in his own defense, Domingo Goma claimed that one particular household, "Andrés Tine and the other two Indians of his house," had improperly hoarded a large sum of cacao for four years that was supposed to be paid in tribute.[6] Although it is clear that the other natives referred to in the statement were, like Andrés Tine, adult male, tribute-paying commoners, no further details were given about the relationships within this multitributary household. That such households were common within the barrio is indicated by another form of documentation presented in this case.

The Zapotec complainants offered maguey-paper drawings to support their charges of excessive tribute demands and physical abuses suffered at the agency of the cacique Don Juan and Goma, their barrio tribute collector or *tequitlato*. One is a narrative scene showing different kinds of corporal punishment, while the other three sheets that have survived appear to have been part of a longer *tira* or glued scroll similar to those used in Central Mexico as tribute records. These similarities suggest plausible interpretations for the different icons and their patterning in the more crudely drawn *tira* pages of this complaint, which have no Latin letter glosses. Horizontal lines and boxes, seen on sheets two and three, demarcated social units from which tribute was collected, largely in the form of two-*tomín* gold pieces. The first sheet, with one coin connected to each of two hatched triangles from a group of ten, has a different format from that of the others, and it appears to represent the tribute paid by a single joint household of ten people, symbolized by the triangles. On sheet three, nonmonetary tribute goods are included as well: strips of cotton cloth or *mantas*, a possible honeycomb, baskets representing some dry commodity like maize or beans, and a pot representing another liquid. Quantities of each item are indicated either by repetition of the item or by use of symbols from the indigenous notational system, with dots for single digits and a feather representing twenty items. Unfortunately, the interpreters who testified as to the meaning of these *pinturas* mentioned only unspecified tribute demands in money and *mantas* and sometimes cacao beans.[7]

Although the monetary tribute paid in Spanish coins, like the layer of colonial administration now supported by tribute exactions, was obviously a postconquest introduction, at mid-century Indian communities far from Mexico City still retained control over the structures by which tribute obligations were met, and I suggest that this set of 1553 *pinturas* may evidence prehispanic practices. Some joint households represented on the Zapotec complainants' drawings paid more tribute than others on the same page. Colonial tribute reforms that were not regulated very strictly in Tehuantepec until 1555 did set standard rates of tribute paid per married household head, and it is possible that the higher tribute payments made by some of these households reflected the presence of more tributaries.[8] An alternative scenario suggests that these rules were not yet adhered to in Tehuantepec and that the tribute disparities among households reflect an indigenous taxation system based on property values. One Central Mexican tribute list dated shortly before this Tehuantepec complaint, the 1549 Codex Mariano Jiménez, has a long explanatory page which details a system by which natives were obligated to pay monetary tribute according to a precise schedule based on the amount of land they farmed. Rebecca Horn has examined a large sample of Coyoacan household properties recorded in similar mid-sixteenth-century census and cadastral records and found that Nahua tribute was assessed on the basis of a standard agricultural plot of 20 by 20 measuring units known as *quahuitl*.[9] Without a more detailed early tribute schedule for Tehuantepec, it is not possible to determine with certainty whether some commoner families had access to more land or better quality lands than their barrio neighbors.

Whatever the system by which agricultural lands were distributed among community members in Tehuantepec, the barrio appears to have functioned as the principal corporate landholding unit. That authority was central to the role of the Nahua *calpolli* or *tlaxilacalli*, as it was more commonly referred to in native documents, and there are important semantic clues to parallel functions among the Zapotecs. The sixteenth-century Dominican linguist Fr. Juan de Córdova gave several Zapotec glosses for "barrio" in his *Vocabulario*, two of which reflect this landholding function: *quiñaqueche* or *naaqueche*, signifying a unit of community agricultural fields; *collaba* was a third term for a "ranch or barrio of a community." Other corporate functions associated with the barrio included its collective participation in public works projects ("unit of people in a pueblo for community works, or like a squadron"): *to-*

biquiña, *tobicollaba*, *tobicozaana* (*tobi*: one unit). This last term indicates that there was a kinship component to barrio composition, because *cozaana* referred to a group of collateral kinsmen. Such a grouping would also be mobilized for war: *tobiquiñapeni*, *tobicollaba* ("squadron of people together or as in for a war").[10] The persistence of Zapotec terms associated with war a generation or two after the imposition of the *pax hispanica* underscores the usefulness of this 1587 dictionary as a source of indigenous concepts and values, despite its compiler's cultural biases.

Given the overlapping roles played by the barrio, it is likely that barrio-based squadrons of citizen-soldiers comprised the founding core of many of Tehuantepec's constituent communities. They would have been mustered as a unit from their home communities in the Oaxaca Valley and, following a successful routing of the indigenous Isthmus population, settled as a unit on lands apportioned to them by the victorious Yecaquiahuitl/Cosijopii. Others were established after the conquest was secured, as the victor recruited colonists from allied communities. According to testimony presented in Doña Magdalena de Zúñiga's 1567–72 dispute over *cacicazgo* properties in the province, her late husband's grandfather populated the province by appealing to the lords of the Oaxaca Valley to send him settlers, a request which must have been satisfied in large part by mobilizing traditional barrio structures.[11] Whether arriving in peace or in war, these barrio-based units had an organic coherence that would have made them the natural unit by which Zapotec society was replicated in this foreign land.

A long list of Zapotec witnesses identified by their village or barrio affiliations in Doña Magdalena's lawsuit mentions sixteen of Tehuantepec's urban barrios, the majority of which had Nahuatl place names. These names give few clues as to how or where most individual barrio communities originated, although many have survived to the present day. Two of the barrios, Izquiapa and Atotonica, were said to have been organized as patrimonial communities of the king, rather than as subject dependencies of the polity, a distinction I will return to shortly. Santa Cruz Tagolaba, the location of the Panteón Antiguo archaeological site, was represented as Tecolapa or "charcoal river," and several other recognizable modern barrio names minus their patron saints appear in the witness identifications: Atempa ("at the shore of the water"), Xalisco ("in front of the sand"), Atotonica ("hot place"). Names including the word for "palace" might suggest some special social role for these barrio inhabitants:[12] Tecpanquiahuat ("entrance to the palace"), Tecpantlacatl ("palace attendant"), Nahuitelpa ("four palaces"). A referent to the Oaxaca Valley is present in the barrio name Teozapotlan. Some of Tehuantepec's most prominent sixteenth-century elites came from the barrio of Teozapotlan, the Nahuatl name for Zaachila, and the community's identification with the ancestral capital suggests its special political importance.[13] One barrio name stands apart in this list, identified by witnesses not by a Nahuatl place name but as the "barrio of Domingo Goma." Domingo Goma is the same individual against whom barrio commoners complained twenty years earlier during Don Juan Cortés's *residencia secreta*. At that time, however, Goma served as *tequitlato* or tribute collector for the barrio, which in 1553 was referred to as the barrio of another man, Miguel Copilo. The first issue posed by this unusual naming practice is one of barrio formation. Does the naming of the barrio after living individuals suggest that these men were personally responsible for the recruitment of barrio households to Tehuantepec, or did the barrio namesake enjoy a different kind of patronage relationship with its commoner residents than that found elsewhere? John Chance and others have demonstrated that many late prehispanic communities in Central Mexico were organized primarily by stratified noble houses, with commoner families bound to their elite leaders by patronage relationships rather than kinship or other corporate structures traditionally associated with the Aztec *calpolli*.[14] This one example suggests that Tehuantepec's barrio organization may also have been more diverse originally than most sixteenth-century testimony indicates, but it appears that the larger and more resilient barrios conformed to the corporate residential model.

Although current data cannot resolve any questions concerning the particular history and status of the Miguel Copilo/Domingo Goma barrio, the barrio's name change over time hints at what may be a broader organizational pattern among Tehuantepec's communities. The Miguel Copilo/Domingo Goma barrio recognized at least two official positions in its leadership. One of these positions, that of *tequitlato*, a Hispanicized Nahuatl term, or *collabachiña,* as it was called in Zapotec, with *collaba* referring to barrio and *chiña* meaning "tribute" or "work," is widely documented in sixteenth-century records; ten of the witnesses in Doña Magdalena's suit were identified as barrio or village *tequitlatos*. In addition to his duties of collecting tribute in money or goods, the *collabachiña* was responsible for the requisition and supervision of barrio workers in public works projects. A typical project for which such service was required was the construction and maintenance of Tehuantepec's irrigation canals, in which work parties from several barrios were assembled, with one of the *tequitlatos* serving as overseer for the project, assigning tasks and ensuring their completion.[15]

The existence of yet another barrio office, corresponding to that of barrio headman, is implicit in Goma's transition from barrio *tequitlato* in 1553 to barrio namesake by 1570. What this official position may have been called both in Goma's barrio and in more conventionally named barrios, where it surely was found as well, is unspecified in the Spanish litigation records that are my principal sources of information concerning social practice. Goma himself held office on the 1570 Tehuantepec *cabildo* as one of two designated *mayordomos de la comunidad,* but this seems to have been an office separate from, but probably related to his status as barrio headman. Córdova provided the Zapotec *copeeche* as a universal term for "officeholder" or "official," and gave the related term *cólào copéeche* for the highest official in a community ("principal oficial el mayor or mejor"). Since urban barrios and rural subject villages or *estancias* were organized similarly, this may be an indigenous Zapotec term for barrio headman that went unrecognized by Spanish authorities more interested in the tribute-collecting role of the *tequitlato* or *collabachiña.* Most of the native witnesses in Doña Magdalena's suit who were not identified as nobles by the title of "don" were either *tequitlato* or *principal* of their barrios or villages, the latter term translated into Zapotec by Córdova as *nitácaláo.* Much later in the colonial period, Tehuantepec barrios recognized as their spokesmen a single *principal* or *primero principal* for each barrio, who functioned outside the Spanish-introduced, citywide *cabildo* offices.[16] It is quite possible that these colonial period roles derived from prehispanic chief-like offices in each barrio, whose occupant was the community's most distinguished elder. If Domingo Goma's history reflects common practice, younger men served as *tequitlato* before achieving the position of barrio headman or *primero principal* in later life. Whatever the precise nature of the barrio's administrative structure, the range of ceremonial and civic functions that would have taken place at barrio administrative centers like the one excavated at Santa Cruz Tagolaba calls for more positions of authority than that of single *tequitlato.*

Although sixteenth-century records for some Oaxaca Valley towns suggest that the *tequitlato* was appointed by the cacique, testimony presented in Doña Magdalena's suit makes it clear that these individuals were ranking members or *principales* of the particular barrios in which they served.[17] That such offices may have been inherited or elected only within certain families is embedded within the terms associated with the

Zapotec minor nobility. Córdova tells us that such lesser lords (members of the "hidalguía," as contrasted with the "caballería") also formed lineages, which he identified as the *tijajoánahuini* or *tijacollàba* (*collaba* being one term for barrio), that were further contrasted with the commoner lineages ("de populares o labradores"), known as the *tijapèniquéche* (*peniqueche* referring to commoners or *macehuales*, the commonly used Nahuatl-derived term). The ruler's authority to appoint *tequitlatos* then may in reality have been a confirmation of individuals already qualified for such positions by virtue of their inherited rank within the barrio or village community.

Other kinds of communities

All the organizational features described thus far for the urban barrio applied to most rural communities in Zapotec-speaking parts of the province as well. These corporate land-holding entities had their own *tequitlatos* under whom they fulfilled communal obligations to the city-state and its ruler. Their physical layout appears to have been similar, whether the community stood alone in the countryside or as one of the many aggregated communities composing the city. Indeed, the small size of most late prehispanic archaeological sites suggests that rural villages were seldom as large as the ancient Santa Cruz Tagolaba barrio. The inhabitants of such communities were known as *peniqueche* or village people, whether they resided in an urban barrio or in a rural village.

According to Córdova's *Vocabulario*, the Zapotecs recognized two kinds of communities. The type of village or barrio community discussed thus far was considered to be subject to a head town ("pueblo estancia de otro o tequitlato"), and a subject village or *sujeto* was distinguished from a foreign community ("pueblo de estranjeros o advenidizos"), which the sixteenth-century cleric translated as *quéchepezáa, quéchequizàa, quèchepénicozága*. On the Isthmus, where ethnically distinct communities persisted long after the Zapotec invasion, it is certain that the cultural landscape included many non-Zapotec speaking (*quizàa*) villages, but the term *quèchepénicozága* may have implied more political "otherness" than just ethnic or linguistic separation. *Pénicozága* ("people collected from diverse lands") were not only people with a separate origin, but with a separate political history that implied a different relationship with the Zapotec lord. That these terms conveyed real sociopolitical distinctions is further demonstrated in the sixteenth-century litigation records involving Don Juan Cortés and his widow, which highlight two types of communities that were not subject *estancias* or barrios of Tehuantepec.

Since this litigation was specifically concerned with establishing the nature of traditional political and economic obligations to the ruler among distinct classes of communities, it is an authoritative, if not always unambiguous source for understanding prehispanic practice.

One kind of non-*sujeto* pueblo was the autonomous community, which based its political independence and authority on a history of settlement in the region independent of Yecaquiahuitl's conquest of the province. Such communities typically were also subordinate to the powerful Tehuantepec ruler. According to indigenous testimony offered in 1554 on behalf of Don Juan, all the villages and all their lords for a distance of 12 to 15 leagues from the city recognized the Tehuantepec king as "great lord" and came to his summons and gave him tribute and other things for which he asked.[18] But despite their subservience to the king, the leaders of these communities were recognized as natural lords in their own right; Don Juan Cortés himself referred to two of his witnesses, Don Gaspar of Astatla and Don Juan of Nanacatepec (Santiago Guevea), as "caciques." No *tequitlatos* are mentioned for these communities, and it would appear that this omission reflects their internal political autonomy.

Astatla was a non-Zapotec community located farther west along the Oaxaca coast, outside the Isthmus proper but allied through marriage to the Tehuantepec royal family, as Don Gaspar's status as a son-in-law of Don Juan indicates. We know considerably more about the Zapotec-speaking community of Nanacatepec or Guevea, which occupied the slopes and narrow valleys of the Sierra Atravesada, just north of Tehuantepec. Nanacatepec lords, as the Lienzo de Guevea indicates, acknowledged the authority of the Tehuantepec kings, but claimed to have arrived in the Isthmus earlier and independently from Zaachila, a claim bolstered by the linguistic differences between the Zapotec spoken in Guevea and other mountain villages and that of Zapotec-speaking villages of the coastal plain. The more numerous class of coastal-plain Zapotec pueblos mentioned as *sujeto* communities of Tehuantepec in this litigation recognized no individuals with the title of "cacique" during Don Juan Cortés's lifetime or during his widow's legal battles. By the close of the sixteenth century, however, many of them were professing their political autonomy and claiming the title of cacique for themselves, a colonial-period change that will be returned to later.

At the core of Don Juan's suit to reclaim his *cacicazgo* estates and privileges was his assertion that yet another kind of community existed on the Isthmus, one which he claimed possession of "as my own patrimonial properties." These were a group of named *estancias* and barrios of

Tehuantepec—Atotonica, Sustla (Xustlan or Xochitlan), Tlacotepec, Amatitlan, Cuizcatepec, Chiltepec, Yzquiapa, Sutepec (also known as Nintepec or Nectepec), and Pantlaca (possibly Tecpantlaca, or "palace people")—to which he claimed patrimonial rights "with all the Indians and natives that live on these ranches, enjoying the lands and harvesting them and enjoying their tributes as their natural and nearest lord."[19] These communities, he maintained, paid him tribute not as the natural lord of the city-state to which they were subject, but as residents of private lands which he had inherited from his father and grandfather.

The distinction between these patrimonial communities and the communities of tribute-paying commoners was one not always acknowledged by the Spanish administrators, as the suits brought by Don Juan in 1554 and subsequently by his widow indicate. Their special status was conceded during the early years of colonial rule under the Marquesado del Valle, since only one of the patrimonial communities, the often problematic *estancia* of Chiltepec, appears on a 1542 tribute list for the province, in which twenty-seven barrios and estancias (in addition to the *villa* of Tehuantepec) were cited as owing either gold or goods and services to the Marqués.[20] Testifying against Doña Magdalena as a witness for the royal prosecutor, Pedro de Alcala remembered disputing this special status with Don Juan when he served as the Marquesado's *alcalde mayor* for the province in the early 1550s. The cacique, however, tried to persuade him that they had always paid him separate tribute as patrimonial Indians: "and so he [Don Juan] brought food and other things of little value several times to this witness, saying that was what these *estancias* gave for tribute, and that a little later Diego Ramírez was sent as *visitador* by the lord Viceroy Don Antonio de Mendoza and this *visitador* turned all the *estancias* over to Don Juan, and this witness does not know why he returned them."[21]

What Alcala did not know (or chose not to remember in his testimony) was the apparently persuasive case that the cacique presented before these investigators in 1554. As a result, Mendoza's successor, Don Luís de Velasco, issued a decree the following year confirming Don Juan's rights to appoint tribute collectors and *mayordomos* for the cattle ranches, salt pans, and "some *estancias* of Indians and orchards of cacao and *zapotes* and other properties" which the cacique owned.[22] After Don Juan's death and the transfer of the province from the Marquesado to the Crown in 1563, the new *alcalde mayor*, Juan de Salinas, finally implemented Valderrama's regulations freeing all Tehuantepec's indigenous slaves and *terrazgueros*. In so doing he abolished the special status of the patrimonial estates and salt beds inherited by the cacique's children, on whose behalf the widow Doña Magdalena sought redress, culminating in the litigation analyzed here.

In testimony offered by witnesses speaking both on behalf of the cacique in 1554 and on behalf of his widow nearly 20 years later, the following facts were presented as evidence of the distinctions between the patrimonial *estancias* and the other barrios and subject villages of Tehuantepec. Unlike the city-state's component communities, the patrimonial *estancias* were not administered by officials drawn from their own communities, but instead had "collectors and *tequitlatos* and *calpixques*" assigned to them from Tehuantepec. Indians from the *estancias* did not participate in public works projects, nor did they provide tribute or services to the town, but they did supply certain goods and services for the cacique personally. All the fruits of these lands were considered to belong to the cacique, and each *estancia* was responsible for delivering to him in person the maize cultivated in his fields, the fruits and cacao grown in his orchards, as well as the foods that were gathered or hunted or fished on these lands. Indians from the patrimonial *estancias* supplied domestic servants and construction workers for the king as well, making, repairing, and maintaining his houses, and bringing water and firewood to meet his household needs.[23]

Sebastian Niza, *principal* of Macuiltepec, testified in 1554 that he personally had seen how the patrimonial Indians paid tribute to Itzquiahuitl, Don Juan's father, and served him "as if they were his slaves."[24] However the dispute that emerged in this litigation over the precise status and origin of the patrimonial Indians makes it clear that these people were not in fact slaves but belonged to another social category. Don Juan's detractors did not deny that the lands in question were part of his private estate, but some asserted that their only inhabitants prior to the arrival of the Marqués del Valle were a few slaves, and that the postconquest population swelled when Don Juan forced many free Indians to leave their home villages and take up residence on the patrimonial lands. Fr. Bernardo de Santa María, who had learned of these events when he served as vicar of the Dominican monastery in Tehuantepec, explained on behalf of Don Juan's widow that many Indians from these *estancias* had fled:

> because of the many tributes that the Spaniards asked of them and for other causes. Later this same Don Juan Cortés went looking for them as his patrimonial vassals and he went to look in the neighboring villages, and he spoke to them and he said that because he had always treated them as his children and they [treated] him as their father and lord, he pleaded with them to return

to his *estancias* where they would cultivate and work the lands as they used to before. And from then on they began to pay him tribute anew as they used to, and [he stated that] they only paid tribute to Don Juan Cortés and not to the Marqués and that these *estancias* and the lands on them always belonged to the grandparents and parents of Don Juan and, after his days, to his patrimony.[25]

Exactly what the ancient Zapotec would have called this category of people is difficult to say with certainty, but some kind of serf-like social status seems to be implied by the testimony. According to Córdova's *Vocabulario*, both Zapotec and Spanish distinguished "vassal" in the feudal sense (*vasallaje*), *xopàci* or *copàci,* and in the sense applied to commoner citizens ("vasallos gente plebeya, vide popular"), *càni pèniquèche*. The first kind of vassal might work as a day laborer, *pènicopàci,* while the *pèniquèche,* as we saw earlier, had usufruct rights to community agricultural lands. Those who hired themselves to others out of poverty ("alquilado por pobreza"), *peniconeto,* were also distinguished from the vassal, who might be hired for any kind of service ("alquilado para todo servicio"), *penicopácitáho,* with *táho* appearing in many different terms for kinds of hiring or hired goods.[26] Whether this or some other Zapotec name was favored, the fact that such people, who lived in socially segregated communities like the named urban barrios of Atotonica and Yzquiapa or the rural villages of Xochitlan and Tlacotepec, did not participate in public works, underscores their status apart from that of commoner citizens in the Zapotec city-state.[27]

By the late sixteenth century, Don Juan's patrimonial Indians were referred to as "indios terrazgueros," for thus was translated the Zapotec term used by Don Francisco Vásquez de Coronado, a thirty-six-year-old Zapotec nobleman from Tehuantepec who had personally traveled to Mexico City to present Doña Magdalena's case to the Audiencia. Testifying before the Tehuantepec court that the *cabildo* officials and *principales* of the town had pleaded with Juan de Salinas to keep the patrimonial Indians of Doña Magdalena and her children separate from the tribute count, Vásquez revealed that a large number of *terrazgueros* were held by the town's *principales,* including himself, but that their pleas fell on unsympathetic ears.[28]

To summarize the historical and archaeological evidence presented above, it appears that the late prehispanic Tehuantepec empire embraced several kinds of communities with differing political, social, and economic relationships to the city-state. At its periphery were the independently formed polities that were allied to the Tehuantepec kings, alliances sealed through marriage alliances, as in the case of Aztatla, or perhaps through military cooperation, as the warrior shields accompanying two local lords on the Lienzo de Guevea may suggest. These communities provided "gifts" to the Tehuantepec king and came to his summons for military and other ventures. At the core of the city-state was a large number of urban and rural barrios or *estancias*, populated by commoner subjects of the king and governed by leaders drawn from the minor nobility within their own corporate communities. Obliged to perform military services and to provide taxes in specie or labor for the polity, barrio households in turn received landholding privileges as members of their residential communities. At least some of the smaller barrios may have been formed as noble houses, with patronage relationships rather than corporate affiliations providing the glue that bound their members together. To the extent that such noble houses permeated Tehuantepec's social organization, they may have resembled more closely the patrimonial communities better documented for the royal family but implied by the broader presence of *terrazgueros* among the high nobility. The serf-like residents of these communities worked land belonging to the king and provided the royal household with the bulk of the land's produce and their personal labor services; they had no obligations to the polity itself and thus did not participate in the city-state's labor drafts.

Nobility and Royalty in the Zapotec State

Don Francisco Vásquez de Coronado, like four of the five other *principales* he named as possessors of *terrazgueros*, bore the Spanish honorific title of "don." The title evidently had restricted use within the Tehuantepec elite, for these five men alone were referred to as "don" among the thirty-two witnesses identified as *principales* or officeholders from the *villa* in Doña Magdalena's suit. Three other titled individuals were cited as officers in the Tehuantepec *cabildo* in 1570 and 1571, but were not called to testify in these proceedings; another individual of this rank was named by a Spanish witness. The colonial native government or *cabildo* offices filled by such men were limited to the higher-ranking positions of *gobernador, alcalde,* and *regidor*, although other men without this title might also serve in these offices. It is a pattern confirmed even in the rare earlier reference to Tehuantepec *cabildo* officials. They did not serve as *escribano*, as *mayordomos de la comunidad*, or as barrio-based *tequitlatos*. Barrio affiliation, in fact, was not a primary means of social identification for these nobles. Unlike other *principales* whose barrio was routinely identified in court, Doña Magdalena's litigation revealed the barrio affiliation of only one of these highest status witnesses, the aforementioned Don Francisco Vásquez de Coronado, who lived in Atempa.

If we assume that Spanish titles and offices during the first decades following the conquest were apportioned among the Zapotec nobility according to indigenous principles of rank and entitlement, then linguistic evidence may help extrapolate the prehispanic foundations of these early colonial social practices. Of the three Zapotec high-status ranks identified by Córdova, the title of "don" seems to have been bestowed only on the small number of individuals who were members of the *tijacoqui* or "linaje de señores grandes." We know enough about the lives of four of the titled men named in Doña Magdalena's suit to be reasonably confident that the honorific was restricted to the class-endogamous highest nobility. One individual was the cacique's own son, though as his *hijo natural*, Don Francisco de Figueroa's birth did not conform to Spanish criteria of legitimacy; another claimed to be the cacique's cousin; two others were sons-in-law of the ruler, having married, like Don Gaspar, cacique of Aztatla, daughters of Don Juan Cortés never identified by name in the Spanish documents. The adoption of Spanish titles in early colonial Tehuantepec by members of the ruling class alone conforms to a pattern seen widely within Mesoamerican society and well documented among the Nahua, Maya, and Mixtec.[29]

Lords who were not members of the ruling class were recognized as *joána,* a title that persists among the Isthmus Zapotec today as a term of respect for barrio elders (*xuaana*'). Córdova usually distinguished two grades of *joána* in his *Vocabulario*, the *joána* proper, whom he equated with the Spanish rank of *caballero*, and the *joanahuini*, or little nobility, whom the cleric likened to the *hidalgo* rank in Spain. That these were discrete inherited statuses is indicated by his listing four specific classes of lineages among the Zapotec: that of the great lords, the *tijacoquij*; that of lesser lords like *caballeros*, the *tijajoàna*; the lower lineage of *hidalgo* status, the *tijajoánahuíni* or *tijacollàba*; and the lineage of commoners or workers, the *tijapèniquéche*.[30] I discussed earlier how these last two classes may have operated within the barrio organization, but the *tijajoàna* remains a kind of residual category whose social role is only weakly reflected in the documents.

From the fact that individual members of the nobility who were not referred to as "don" did hold high office in the early colonial Tehuantepec *cabildo*, we might infer that *caballero*-rank lords also held positions of political importance in the precolumbian city-state. What those offices may have been is still an unanswered question, but it is not likely that the Zapotec conceived of political authority in terms of the same discrete powers attributed to the Spanish offices of *gobernador*, *alcalde*, and *regidor*. Indeed, all three terms could be translated into Zapotec by Córdova as *huetògoticha*, as were the Spanish offices of *juez*, *condenador*, *difinidor*, *sentenciador*, and *estimidor* or *tasador*, with *ticha* meaning "speech" or "words" and *huetogo* standing for "one who cuts" (*cortador*), or "one who shears" (*tresquilador*). Similar conceptually to the Nahua *tlatoani* or speaker (lit. "One who issues proclamations and commands"[31]), the Zapotec "Shearer of Words" was a person of authority whose judgment helped define a course of action for the polity and administer justice to its citizens. Córdova gave one meaning of "authority" (*autoridad de persona vide honor*) as a "property of the lords" (*quelajoàna*). For the *huetògoticha,* it was an authority so fundamental to Zapotec concepts of governance that it was natural to extend it to the Christian God ("Dios regidor governador con todos los atributos que a esto se ayuntan") in the title *huetògotichatào* (*-tào* meaning supreme or great).[32]

Was the status of *huetògoticha* conceptualized as a formal office, perhaps one restricted to just a select number of *joàna* or individuals of noble birth chosen by the ruler? Spanish political organization limited the number of *cabildo* offices, with which Córdova equated the term, but Tehuantepec practice during the early years of its imposition among the Isthmus Zapotec suggests that a wider assembly of the male nobility deliberated issues of importance to the polity and its citizens. Don Francisco Vásquez de Coronado testified that such an assembly of *alcaldes, regidores*, and *principales* met after Juan de Salinas was installed as Spanish administrator in 1563 to decide upon their collective response to Salinas's plan for including *terrazgueros* in the tributary count.[33] Such a body may have corresponded to the *huexija* or *huexijaticha* that Córdova incorporated into his translations for royal court, council, *cabildo,* and *audiencia.*

In addition to the deliberative role they played, the early colonial record suggests that middle-level nobles as well as persons of royal caste were responsible for administering public works. In one well-documented example of how commoner labor was organized, the irrigation canal project referred to earlier, the *alcalde* Francisco Pima was present to supervise the project, although both Don Juan Cortés and Don Luís de Velasco appeared for a time at the work site. Direct involvement with the laborers, however, rested in the hands of the *tequitlatos* who recruited the work parties from their barrios.[34]

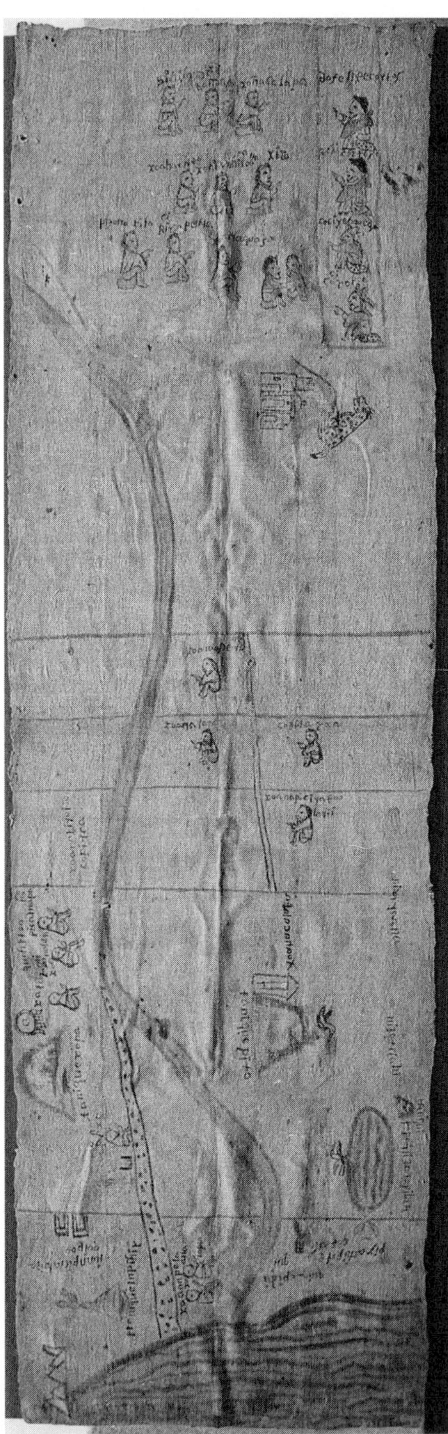

FIG. 2.3. The Mapa de Huilotepec, a late sixteenth-century cotton cloth *lienzo*. Archivo Histórico de la Secretaría de la Reforma Agraria; photo courtesy of Michel Oudijk.

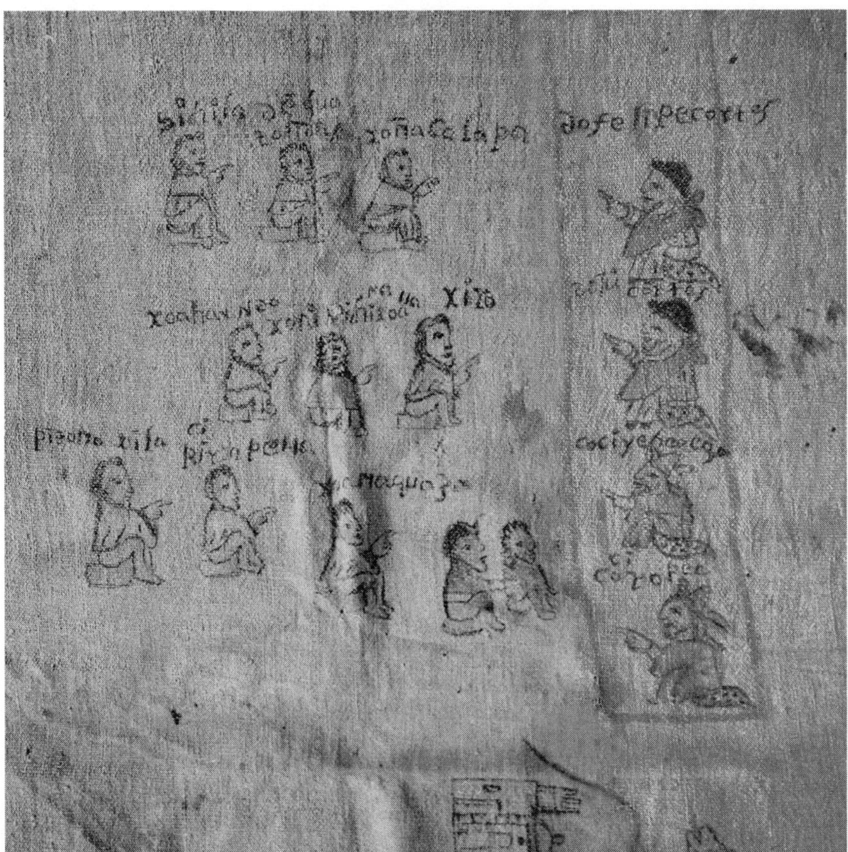

FIG. 2.4. The Mapa de Huilotepec, detail of the upper register showing the Tehuantepec kings and their advisors. Archivo Histórico de la Secretaría de la Reforma Agraria; photo courtesy of Michel Oudijk.

During each ruler's lifetime, a smaller group of close advisors, drawn primarily if not exclusively from the higher nobility, assisted him in routine matters of governance. The late sixteenth-century Mapa de Huilotepec depicts what I suggest may be the members of such a high-level council. Michel Oudijk has made the first detailed analysis of this unusual cadastral *lienzo*, including its crudely lettered Zapotec glosses identifying people and toponyms positioned in an area extending from Tehuantepec south to the Pacific Ocean. Three named men wearing short capes are shown seated on cushions opposite both Don Juan Cortés, his father Cosijoeza, and his heir, Don Felipe Cortés, in a genealogical history of

Tehuantepec that fills the upper section of the map. Two additional, unnamed figures clad only in loin cloths sit before Cosijoeza, but no men are depicted directly opposite Don Juan's grandfather, Cosijopii, at the bottom of the column. Only one of the cloaked men in the top row bears a difficult-to-decipher Christian name, along with the title "don," but five of the remaining eight men have the Zapotec title "xoana" (cf. Córdova "joàna"). Oudijk suggests that the cloaked figures represent noblemen from Huilotepec participating in a ceremonial ceding of community lands by the ruler to the village's noblemen, whose territorial jurisdictions are marked in the lower section of the map. My own view is that the distinctive clothing worn by the upper register figures and their grouping in three rows of three are a better fit with the council of royal advisors documented elsewhere for Tehuantepec.[35]

The ruler's advisors are not the only persons named in the Mapa de Huilotepec. Ten other seated individuals wearing hip-cloths were placed at selected points along the coastline, near the Tehuantepec River, or on either side of a road passing from Tehuantepec to Huilotepec, eight of whom appear to have the title *joàna*. Three additional names are not associated with any figure, and one of these is the only name that is repeated from the group of cloaked men in the upper register. The positioning of these lords near well-labeled estuaries, corrals, and other topographic features and the use of red horizontal lines to further delineate territorial parcels in the absence of such distinctive features suggest an alternative explanation for the document than that offered by Oudijk, namely that it was formulated to clarify the titles of private lands that the Tehuantepec kings had ceded to the named nobles. The fact that it was later used by the Huilotepec community to assert community territorial boundaries and political autonomy, much as the Lienzo de Guevea did, represents a changed function for the map. Indeed this surviving *pintura* appears to be a late sixteenth-century copy of a now lost original that was probably executed by a skilled native scribe not many years before. This artist's poor facility with Latin letters caused him to make a number of copying mistakes, leading to his frequent insertion of missed letters above a glossed word and, in one curious instance, his writing a mirror-image version of the name.[36]

While the livestock corrals pictured on the map were clearly of European introduction, the concept of private property had deep roots within Zapotec society. Of course the extensive private holdings of the Tehuantepec cacique in agricultural properties and his monopoly of the coastal salt beds were at the heart of Don Juan and his widow's dispute with the Crown, so there is ample evidence that rulers enjoyed the products of personally held, heritable properties, as well as the tribute payments and services of their subjects. Don Francisco Vásquez de Coronado's statement in that same suit that he and other *principales* also had *terrazgueros* (and, by implication, the lands for them to work) provides direct support for the kind of extensive elite landholdings reflected in the later Huilotepec map. It seems that the eagerness of the Tehuantepec nobility to enter ranching in the latter half of the sixteenth century drew on traditional concepts of elite property.[37]

The only direct testimony as to how such properties were acquired came from Don Baltasar García, who was governor of Xalapa in 1571, when he appeared as a witness for the *fiscal.* As a non-Zapotec who arrived on the Isthmus with the Spaniards, serving Hernán Cortés as *nahuatlato*, Don Baltasar was neither fond of the Tehuantepec cacique and his family nor always clear about names and events. He does seem to have learned many stories about the Zapotec conquest and been more comfortable reiterating their details in this formal setting than were most of his Zapotec contemporaries, however. According to Don Baltasar, the Zapotec conqueror dispossessed the Guazonteca of their villages and lands and distributed them among the soldiers who accompanied him.[38]

Whether or not all the early colonial period private holdings of the Tehuantepec *jòana* originated at this time, the principle that such lands were bestowed on individuals as a gift from the ruler in return for services to the king and polity would follow what is known from better documented Mesoamerican political systems. Like the Aztecs, the ancient Zapotecs may also have used military distinction or other forms of special service as a mechanism of social mobility within an otherwise rigidly stratified society. One of the individuals whose lands are marked on the Mapa de Huilotepec has a warrior shield by his name. The title of *jòana*, once earned, would, like the lands or privileges associated with it, have been passed down through the recipient's family from generation to generation, thus creating the *tijajòana* or noble lineage.

As was the case with the ruler's private *estancias*, the fruits of such holdings would primarily have served the household needs of the *jòana* himself, which could be considerable. Dependent on a lord's income were one or more wives and their children as well as numerous *criados,* as the Spaniards referred to the household servants or slaves, known in Zapotec as *xillàni* or *hueyana.* While the *criados* lived in a separate structure

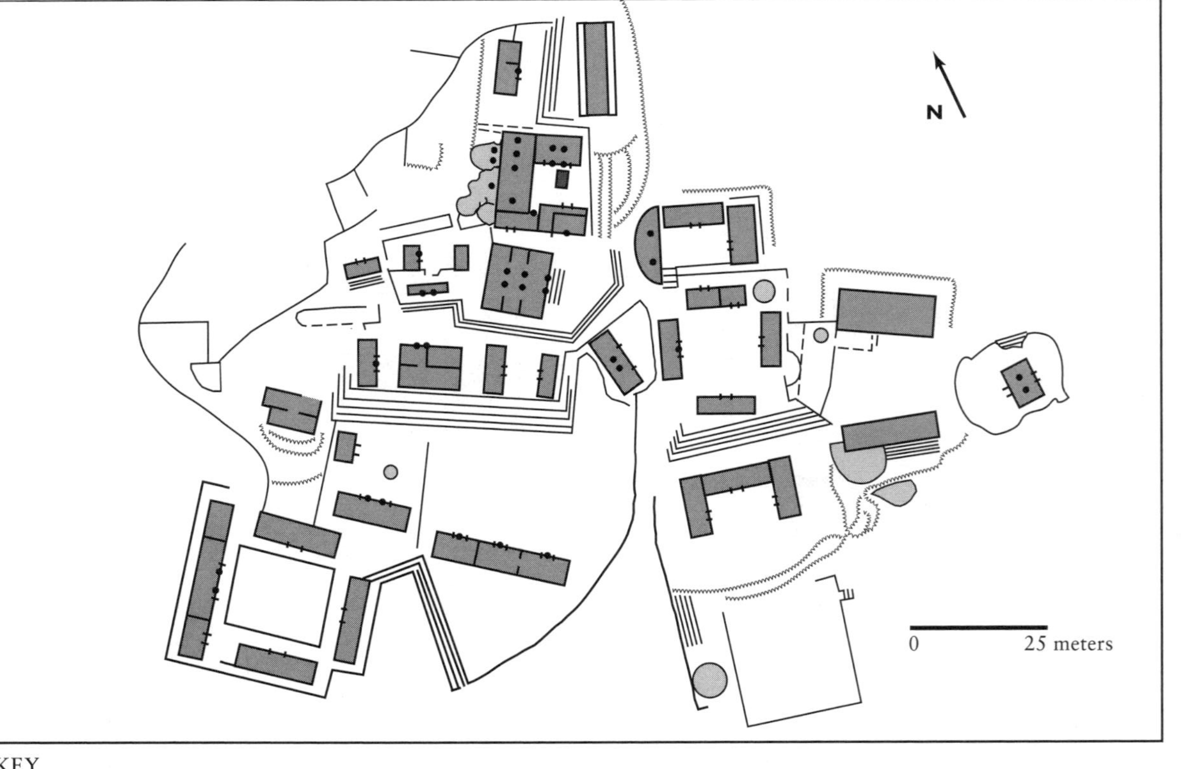

MAP 2.2. The palace complex at Guiengola. Based on David Peterson and Thomas B. MacDougall, *Guiengola: A Fortified Site in the Isthmus of Tehuantepec*, figure 9. Vanderbilt University Publications in Anthropology, no. 10 (Nashville: Department of Anthropology, Vanderbilt University, 1974).

(*yyni*) that probably resembled the commoner dwellings of pole and thatch construction, the *joàna* house was a substantial flat-roofed structure of "cal y canto," as the Spaniards referred to plaster-faced stone or adobe buildings, which the Zapotec called "*yòhoquie*" or "*yòhoyaòo*."

Surviving examples of elite housing in Tehuantepec today are limited to Guiengola, where Peterson mapped an extensive complex of patios, temples, and living quarters in an area he called the Elite Residential Area, located in the southeast sector of the walled mountaintop site. There over thirty-five masonry-walled rooms, most with columned entrances, stand alone or are arranged in groups around one of eleven patios. The difficulty of access to some rooms and the interconnectedness of the patio groups argue for this fortified area serving as the ruler's palace (*yòhoquèhui* or *quíhuitáo*), rather than a more generalized elite residential zone. In addition, more than thirty other unmapped single rooms or room-and-patio structures have been found at the site, and these simpler buildings may have been the special residences of the Tehuantepec nobility, who, like the ruler himself, lived most of the year in the town below.[39]

The largest of the limestone-block and clay-mortar rooms in the Elite Residential Area is less than 15 m in length, with just two round stone columns at its entrance, but its layout is similar to that of the much larger public building excavated at the ancient barrio of Santa Cruz Tagolaba. There may have been an ideal floor plan for the *yòhoyaòo* or beamed building, for which the size and number of columns could be varied according to the structure's intended function or relationship to other buildings. The adobe walls of the Panteón Antiguo building are likely to have prevailed in elite house construction as well in Tehuantepec proper, where suitable stone would have been more difficult to find than it was at Guiengola. Once plastered on the exterior and interior surfaces and ornamented with painting or the kind of limestone frieze from which fragments have been collected in modern times at Cerro Padre López, fine houses belonging to the nobility would have been readily distinguished from those that served the barrio or community as a whole.

Besides housing, many other sumptuary privileges set the Zapotec elite apart from the commoner *peniqueche* and distinguished various grades of the nobility from one another. Certain foods like cacao and hunted game may have been consumed exclusively by the Zapotec elite, as was the case in some Nahuatl-speaking communities within the Oaxaca archbishopric, like Teotitlán del Camino.[40] Intricately decorated polychrome pottery may also have been restricted to elite consumption, for it is not found in commoner burials or in domestic refuse in Tehuantepec's barrios, though it has been collected from high status tombs. Even the manner of speaking is likely to have distinguished noble and commoner; Córdova's *Vocabulario* lists special terms for courtly speech ("habla cortés polida travada palaciega"), *ticha quihui, ticha gòla, ticha natàa* ("palace, ancestral, or delicate speech"), a type of reverential speech similar to that in use by Mixtec nobles in the sixteenth century. Unfortunately, few Zapotec songs or prose from the early colonial period have survived to provide examples of this courtly dialogue for comparison with that found in the well-established corpus of Nahua *cuicatl* and *tlahtolli*.[41]

Clothing was also a primary status marker in this status-conscious society. Tehuantepec elders informed the Spanish *alcalde mayor* in 1580 that the following distinctions of dress were observed in Precolumbian times:

> The clothing that the natives of this province wore in ancient times was in the style of a sleeveless, collarless cloak of cotton cloth, painted in the customary fashion and this costume reached to the knee and the *principales* wore it to the ground and others walked naked with only a loincloth to cover their private parts. And they did not wear hats and they let their hair grow to the length that today women wear and they braided it and gathered it [in a knot]. And their wives dressed in a length of cloth and shirt that they called *huipil* and *naguas* and all this clothing was of cotton.[42]

Some confirmation for these patterns can be seen in the Isthmus and Oaxaca Valley pictorial documents of the sixteenth century. The ruler is always shown wearing either a long, Aztec-style cape tied at the neck or a long robe or full-body garment with a hip-cloth like that depicted earlier on Oaxaca Valley genealogical registers and on several Mixtec codices, where elite women are always attired in skirt and *huipil*. On the Mapa de Huilotepec, however, only the ruler's advisors are shown wearing short capes of the sort described in the Relación Geográfica as being in general use in Tehuantepec, even though both documents were composed at approximately the same time, while the other *jòana* appear to be attired more simply in hip-cloths. *Peniqueche* dress is featured in the *pintura* presented by the Zapotec commoners in their suit against Don Juan Córtes, where the simple loincloth worn by most figures in the drawing corresponds well to the 1580 description. Although the Relación Geográfica suggests that all clothing was made from cotton cloth and painted, Cordóva's *Vocabulario* lists many other distinctive kinds of cloth and clothing, some of which must have been status markers. Besides having different kinds of textures (coarse, silk-like, etc.), cloth was distinguished by the manner and degree to which it was elaborated (from simple to striped or painted or made out of small feathers).

Ideology as an Integrative Force in Zapotec Society

Like its organization into numerous barrios, Spanish observers saw many parallels between the Tehuantepec city-state's rigid social distinctions, with its array of class-specific economic privileges, and their own nation's division into separate estates. Social and political hierarchies in the European world were regarded as part of the divinely mandated natural order. In Mesoamerica, where stratified society had prevailed among widespread regional traditions at least since the founding of Monte Albán in 500 BC, distinctions of social class were part of a similarly ingrained perception of the natural order, one that likewise had deep cosmological foundations. Because Zapotec understandings of the supernatural were so different from those on which the humanistic Catholic traditions of the conqueror rested, it is important to characterize them briefly here and to point to the ways in which they helped shape the day-to-day lives of individuals and their relationships with others as members of the social communities in which they were born. Like the beliefs of all people, these ideas both helped integrate and regulate social behavior and, in some cases, exacerbated social tensions by underscoring the contrast between expectations and practical realities.

Early Dominican chroniclers were not, for the most part, interested in the nature of the ancient Zapotec cosmovision and belief system. More often indigenous religiosity and morality inspired only disgust in the Dominican preacher, for whom any aberration from Christian convention was seen as Beelzebub-inspired perversion among the natives. However elusive the substance of the indigenous world may be in the historical record, however, it is still clear several centuries later that religiosity permeated Zapotec life. When the specific beliefs being acted upon cannot be read from Spanish sources, the context and organization of ancient religious devotion can often be inferred from the archaeology of sacred places, from ethnographic tidbits presented in Córdova's *Vocabulario* and his Zapotec grammar or *Arte*, and, of course, from the circumstances of idolatrous acts exposed in early colonial times. Although this discussion draws from primary sources and scholarly studies of Zapotec culture, highlighting specific evidence for Tehuantepec when possible, it should be emphasized that these religious beliefs were not unique to the Zapotecs or to the people of present-day Oaxaca. Rather they were part of a widespread complex of ideas and practices shared among Mesoamerican peoples since remote times.

Time and cosmology

The Zapotecs, like other Mesoamerican peoples, viewed the world in which they lived as one closely constrained by the passage of time. The rhythm of daily life in this agricultural society conformed to the 365-day solar calendar and was measured in eighteen months or moons of twenty days length, with a five-day period known as *quicholla* at the end of the solar year. The fate associated with each day, however, was controlled by a separate, 260-day ritual calendar that ran concurrently, allowing the two cycles to return to the same starting date only after a period of fifty-two solar years. Shared by all Mesoamerican cultures, this distinctive ritual calendar was based on the intercycling of thirteen numbers with a series of twenty day names. It was a system of great antiquity among the Zapotecs, who inscribed calendrical dates on stone monuments in their Oaxaca Valley homeland as early as the seventh century BC.[43]

Although the practice of writing on stone declined precipitously after the abandonment of Monte Albán, the complex calendars continued to be sustained through other media and were in active use when the Dominicans settled in Oaxaca. Many aspects of the Zapotec calendrical system were described in some detail by Fr. Juan de Córdova in his *Arte en lengua zapoteca*.[44] The 260-day calendar was subdivided into four principal periods of sixty-five days length known by the "signs" or "planets" which governed them. Each of the four periods was composed of five numbered intervals of thirteen days each, which the Spaniards called *trecenas*. In Zapotec, Córdova referred to the sixty-five-day periods either as *pitào*, the generic term he cited in the *Vocabulario* for "pagan god," or as *cociyo*, the word for lightning and the name associated with the Rain God; he referred to the thirteen-day periods as *cocii*. The *cociyos* were thought to control the fate of all things on earth and as such they were propitiated with blood sacrifices:

> And the Indians said that these four planets caused all the things on the earth and so they held them to be gods, and they called them *cociyos* or *pitaos*. And that means "great ones," and to these they offered their sacrifices, and they

> drew their blood from diverse parts of their bodies, such as the ears, the tip of the tongue, from the muscles and other parts. And the order which they held was that, while the 65 days of one planet ran, they sacrificed to it, and when that period was complete, to another, which began in the same fashion, and so on in order until it returned to the first one, etc. And to these [planets] they asked for all that they needed for their sustenance.[45]

Besides their correlation with the major divisions of the ritual calendar, the four *cociyos* were associated as well with the four world directions. This quadripartite space-time division was universal among Mesoamerican cultures, whose shared rain-god imagery underscores their common cosmological roots; a fifth spatial dimension identified with the principal rain or lightning deity may also be represented to demarcate the earth's center. A few examples will suffice to show the pervasiveness of this imagery. In the Late Formative and Classic period Oaxaca Valley, effigy urns accompanying deceased royalty frequently depicted imagery associated with lightning. Alfonso Caso and Ignacio Bernal's study of Oaxaca Valley effigy urns includes two Classic-period examples of an anthropomorphic *cociyo* figure bearing five open ceramic vessels on his back, which they identify with these five directions and compare to depictions in the Borgia Codex of the Central Mexican rain gods pouring water from ceramic containers. Surviving Zapotec folktales include stories of Cociyo keeping the elements clouds, rain, hail, and wind shut up inside four immense ceramic jars, each attended by a lesser *cociyo*. Among the Yucatec Maya, rain gods known as *chacs* were depicted pouring vessels of water on the earth in the Postclassic Dresden Codex. This theme has persisted in stories that attribute the gathering rain clouds at the approach of the Yucatán rainy season to the movement of the four *chacs* summoned by the principal rain god, Kunku Chac as together they ride across the sky to the world directions, bearing their water jars.[46]

Córdova affirms that the four *cociyos* that partitioned the ritual year were believed to hold special power over the natural world, but there were other deified supernatural forces connected to calendrical rituals as well. Scholars have long relied upon the names of pagan gods listed in Córdova's *Vocabulario* and those identified in seventeenth-century and eighteenth-century anti-idolatry campaigns in Oaxaca to delineate these connections. Recent research by Thomas Smith Stark has clarified the semantic associations of Córdova's deity names, as well as other sixteenth-century linguistic data pertaining to Zapotec religious organization and ritual, and, where possible, I have cross-checked my own derivations against his more comprehensive analysis. Studies by José Alcina Franch and Javier Urcid have examined in detail how the gods named in these colonial accounts functioned in the ritual calendar as patrons of the twenty *trecenas* or as thirteen Lords of the Day, in which roles they controlled the supernatural forces that impinged on daily life.[47]

At the apex of the supernatural hierarchy was a deity identified in seventeenth-century San Miguel Sola as the god of the Thirteen Gods. Both Alcina and Urcid equate this god with the supreme deity Córdova identified for the Zapotecs ("dios infinito y sin principio; criador de todo y el increado"), who was called, among other names, *coquixee* or *xeetao* or *piyetao*. *Xee* was the Zapotec word for eternal, and like *piye*, the word for "time" and "calendar," could be combined with *-tao*, meaning "great," to name the supreme being. The Dominicans took care not to apply this name to the Christian God, whom they left untranslated as "Dios," but some of its components appeared among the authorized terms for "heaven" ("cielo la gloria donde estan los sanctos, el qual es ciudad real, eternal, sempiterna, resplandeciente, bienaventurada"): *quèchequihuiquiepaa* ("heavenly community"), *quèchexèe* ("eternal community"), and *quèchechiño*. This last term, meaning "thirteenth community," suggests that the Zapotecs, like the Nahua, may have visualized the heavens as being organized into thirteen levels, with the supreme deity occupying the thirteenth or uppermost level.

Marcus has rightfully cautioned against a too literal reading of various Zapotec deity lists, arguing that the essentially animistic Zapotec view of the world cannot readily be squeezed into a discrete pantheon of gods and that several so-called "gods" in colonial-period Spanish accounts were in fact deceased mortals.[48] Still, the central role played by the ritual calendar in Zapotec cosmology, giving meaning to the lives of mortals by relating the passage of time and the occurrence of human events to the most fundamental conceptions of how the universe was organized, argues strongly for this being the arena of supernatural belief that was the most systematically conceived and elaborated upon by the ancient Zapotecs, as it was for other Mesoamerican people. Whether the *trecena* deities or the four *cociyos* or the twenty day-name "planets" were all fully anthropomorphized gods or not, they embodied the transcendental powers that impinged directly on each individual and required propitiation from the community.

Zapotec ritual specialists and the structure of religious ritual

The intercycling of the thirteen days of the *trecena* with the twenty day names produced in each sixty-five-day period a confluence of supernatural forces controlling the outcome of human endeavor on any given day. The job of interpreting the ritual calendar to understand what the predetermined fortune of a day might be was the domain of the *colanij,* who could determine what the calendrical name of a newborn would be, whether a proposed marriage would be felicitous, what the best day would be to undertake a given action, or what the outcome would be of an illness.[49] Córdova called this specialist a "maker of celebrations or someone expert in them" ("echador de las fiestas o docto en ellas"), but the Zapotec term appears to have referred particularly to a calendrical specialist. The root *lanij* was glossed in his *Vocabulario* for "week" (*semana*) and is the same term used in a corpus of early eighteenth-century calendars from the Villa Alta region of the Sierra Zapoteca for the *trecena.* Other aids used by the *colanij* to divine the future were dreams, omens, the stars, the earth, fire, air and water, and auguries made by sorting piles of beans and by sacrificing small animals.[50]

While these calendrical specialists or diviners would cater to the needs of individuals by interpreting a fate that lay before them, the community at large was served as well by a more highly trained hierarchy of noble-born priests, about whose activities we have information from various colonial period sources.[51] They alone were charged with attending the temples dedicated to the gods and performing the rites of human sacrifice and bloodletting required for their nourishment. Explaining ancient practice, Córdova described the role of the high priest (*huiatao* or *vuijatao*), saying that he alone could enter the inner room of the two-room temple to offer sacrifices to the images of the deities.[52] The *huezàyèche* was the second rank priest ("sacerdote otro menor").

In the context of translating terms for the Catholic priesthood into Zapotec, Córdova provided other words for "sacerdote": *copapitòo* (or *copapitao,* a specialist in things relating to god); *peni napana* (holy man or person who is in a special caste); *xipigaana* (his servant). Both *copa pitao* and *bigaña* or *pixana* were used by colonial period Spanish writers as titles for the ancient Zapotec priests and the idolators caught performing pagan rituals. Writing a century after Córdova, Burgoa refered to the minor priests as *copa vitoo*, while reserving the term *huipatoo* for the highest-ranking religious specialist; he dubbed *vijanas* the young boys who were being trained for the priesthood. The late sixteenth-century Dominican chronicler Fr. Agustín Dávila Padilla called all the Zapotec religious specialists *vigana*, which he said meant guardian of the gods.[53]

Archaeologically, there is ample evidence for the temples served by the Zapotec priesthood. In the Oaxaca Valley, two-room buildings sitting atop platform mounds had been a prominent feature of public architecture since 150 BC, and the inner room of these structures conforms well to the description of the inner sanctuary where Córdova claimed sacrifices were offered to the idols.[54] In Tehuantepec late prehispanic temple mounds of this type were located both in barrio administrative centers, like that of Santa Cruz Tagolaba, and in more prominent public locations. Any ceremonial structures that once graced the center of the city were destroyed in the early sixteenth century, but they must have mirrored the kinds of buildings still standing at the mountaintop fortress of Guiengola. There, what appear to be small temples are scattered in several different sectors of the site, but two much larger temple platforms dominate the site center. The building that once stood on the east platform has fallen; traces of the walls of a two-room temple on the west platform can still be seen (see Fig. 1.8).[55]

Córdova's description of the *huiatao*'s role as one of offering sacrifices to the gods whose images were kept in the inner room of these sanctuaries calls into question what manner of deities or supernatural forces were venerated in public temples. Few traces of ritual activity have been found in archaeological excavations of the cleanly swept floors of prehispanic temples, let alone any images of the deities being worshiped. At San José Mogote, an offering box underlying the floor of a Late Formative inner temple room held a composed scene suggestive of the way in which temples were thought to channel supernatural forces. Marcus and Flannery interpret the small box of upended adobe bricks, covered with a stone slab, as representing a miniature tomb. Inside a quail offering flanked a bowl with a kneeling human "companion" figurine, a type frequently found in royal tombs. Lying above the stone box cover was a *cociyo* figure with a long cape stretched out over his prone body; behind him were four apparently female figures wearing *cociyo* masks, whose heads were hollow receptacles. The excavators propose that the scene depicts the supernatural metamorphosis of a deceased Zapotec lord represented by the "companion" figure.[56] Whether or not this interpretation is correct, it seems clear that the dedicatory offering was intended to concentrate within the sacred confines of the temple the supernatural forces represented by the *cociyo* complex, forces that encompassed time, space, and the rain that ensured agricultural fertility.

Colonial-period accounts confirm that not all temple idols represented unearthly spirits and that the Zapotecs regarded deceased royalty as having special supernatural powers. The Dominican chronicler Burgoa recounted one early seventeenth-century instance of idol-worship among Zapotec speakers in nearby Xalapa in which the object of veneration was an ancestor of the Tehuantepec royal family. This idol, a shapeless white stone marked only by a thick drill hole, was said to have been an image of the daughter of Cosijoeza. Known by her calendrical name Pinopiaa or 12 Grass, she was said to have died in Xalapa en route to join her brother in Tehuantepec, and her body was transformed into the stone still being attended by an elderly devotee in 1609.

> She was the maiden queen, daughter of the Zapotec king of Zaachila or Teozapotlán named Cosijoeza, and when he conquered this land, sending his third son Cosijopii, he ceded much of it to the sister named Pinopiaa so that he [Cosijopii] would have her with him in his kingdom, in which he governed Tehuantepec and Soconusco, because she was a very holy woman according to their custom, very honest, devoted to the gods and unwilling to marry, and that arriving in the lands of Xalapa, she fell mortally ill, and gathering together all the lords and captains to weep over her, like the Hebrews, and preparing to bury her, they found that the body had disappeared. And with the sky making a great uproar, the body was transformed into that stone so that they would serve it and adore it, making it useful for all their needs and works, and that it had been punishing them greatly, because after arriving in that parish they had not accorded it much veneration.[57]

The idol had come to the attention of the vicar of the Xalapa convent through a shepherd working for the Dominicans, who, while searching for stray sheep in his charge, came upon the curious stone that had been placed in the midst of an offering of pottery and flowers. The mountain summit where the shepherd found the well-swept little ceremonial plaza is but one example of the many caves, springs, and other prominent natural features where colonial-period Zapotecs throughout Oaxaca continued to honor familiar supernatural forces long after the Dominicans had banished them from public view. Archaeological evidence of this kind of sacred place is still encountered in the Isthmus at remote rock shelters and mountain promontories, where petroglyphs and broken pots that must once have contained offerings are found.[58] Burgoa described in more detail one particular sacred cave important to the Tehuantepec royal family. Located on the island-like tip of the barrier beach connecting the Huave village of San Dionisio with the mainland, the cave housed Tehuantepec's principal idol, known in Spanish as "Corazón del Reino," or "Heart of the Realm." When the son of Cosijoeza, known to Burgoa as Cosjopii, was coronated, the young king made a pilgrimage to this cave, performed solitary sacrifices to the idol, and through some oracular communication, received dire prognostications about the fate that would befall his people after the arrival of white men from the east.[59]

The cave was visited in the mid-sixteenth century by Fr. Bernardo de Santa María, whose scandalized description of the chamber, surrounded by altars covered with incense burners and blood-spattered offerings of cloth, feathers, and gold jewelry, was recalled a century later by Burgoa.[60] A more complete firsthand Spanish account of ritual patterns associated with another sacred site in the Oaxaca Valley gives us a better view of what may have been inside the San Dionisio cave. As recently summarized by Ángeles Romero, the local curate of Mitla went on a campaign to uncover pagan idolatry and discovered a cave seven leagues from the town in 1565. There a huge idol, similarly known as "Corazón del Pueblo" or "Heart of the Community," had been worshiped by all the surrounding villages. In this case the idol was adorned with a stone-encrusted human skull, and the cave itself held other masks, more than three hundred sacred bundles (presumably containing relics or objects associated with the dead), many idols, feathers, and signs of other recent sacrifices. That the human skull was said to belong to a Spaniard is, as Romero points out, a curious commentary on Zapotec perceptions of these powerful foreigners. Whether or not that was the case, rare archaeological examples of mosaic-decorated human skulls indicate that such treatment was accorded only the most powerful of ancestors.[61]

Marcus emphasizes that much Precolumbian Zapotec religious ritual and imagery was focused on these powerful deceased royal ancestors.[62] Burgoa's account of the physical transformation of Pinopiaa is a striking description of the process by which members of the royal family acquired supernatural powers in death. While the circumstances of that death seem to have departed from patterns by which Zapotec lords and ladies were said to be entombed along with their sacrificed servants within the community, the story of Pinopiaa suggests that the royal tombs discovered archaeologically represent only the beginning of the deceased's journey into immortality. Perhaps the corporeal remains themselves (or some portion of them) were later removed to the site of a sacred cave or, as in the case of Pinopiaa, an unusual stone object was later interpreted as embodying the spirit of the deceased and placed in a sacred spot.[63]

Pinopiaa was held to have special supernatural powers that, with careful attention to her image's ritual requirements, could be invoked to bring good fortune to the community. Conversely, failure to honor this royal ancestor with sacrifices and other offerings brought her anger down upon the community, and the suffering that ensued was interpreted as a direct punishment from Pinopiaa. For, while the great supernatural forces embodied in the calendrical deities were perceived as exerting an almost mechanical control over the world of humans, the royal ancestors were directly interested in the affairs of their descendants. Properly appealed to, they could mediate fate's outcome on behalf of the living community with which they were inextricably bound.

That community had a recognizable political identity: the conquest state, as implied in Tehuantepec's "Corazon del Reino;" the independent town, referred to in Mitla's "Corazon del Pueblo;" or even the barrio community, as Burgoa's tale of the Pinopiaa idol reveals. While the idol itself rested at its mountaintop shrine, the Xalapa barrio of Santa Catarina de Sena, from which the cult's guardians all hailed, so identified its abstemious Italian patroness with Pinopiaa that, when parishioners prayed to the saint in church, they were in reality worshiping the pagan "goddess." Since this kind of identification between specific Catholic saints and indigenous deities was widespread in New Spain, the Dominican chronicler was disingenuous when he called this practice an evil invention of the clever Hispanicized young man who was training to assume Pinopiaa's priesthood.[64]

Colonial-period sources paint a broad picture of the traditional Zapotec worldview as one in which individuals had little control over the course of their own lives. The cyclical intersection of powerful supernatural forces through time generated specific outcomes in the daily activities of mortal men and women. All that an individual might do to thwart disaster is consult with a calendrical specialist who could determine a propitious time for specific actions. As a member of a political community, however, the commoner citizen gained influence over a fate he or she shared with that community, an influence acquired through sacred rituals executed by religious specialists in honor of specific gods and deified royal ancestors. By performing these esoteric rites, the noble-born priests and the lords who supported them and engaged in rituals alongside them sustained the polity itself. Were they to fail to meet their ritual obligations, all members of the community would suffer.

Religious authority and political power

A belief that only the nobility was invested with sacred power provided the ideological basis for Zapotec class distinctions, but it was the physical enactment of the nobility's mediating rituals that integrated Tehuantepec's diverse social segments. By what schedule these rites took place within the barrio or at the city's central temples or in pilgrimages to sacred places is not known, but the regular spectacle of ceremonial performance would have given powerful psychological reinforcement to elite authority, justifying the harsh economic burden born by ordinary citizens with the greater mystery of ritual power. Within the nobility itself, however, ceremonial performance may have been judged more instrumentally and might itself exacerbate tensions among the *tijacoqui* and the *tijajoana*. Most male members of the higher nobility would themselves have had religious training. As discussed previously, the prebaptismal name of Tehuantepec's king Don Juan Cortés was Bichana Lachi, and the title *bichana* accompanying his calendrical name is one of the many names Spanish observers gave for religious specialists (cf. *bigaña*, *pixana*). Perhaps few noblemen were sufficiently trained to have entered the temple's inner sanctum and offer sacrifices directly to the idols, but all elite observers would have been able to appraise the sufficiency of ritual practice.

When that practice was deemed inadequate, either because of shortcomings in the ceremonies themselves or because the intended outcome of ritual performance went awry (e.g., when crops failed or battles were lost), perhaps the political authority behind the ritual may have also been challenged by the lord's own extended kinsmen. For, just as Zapotec principles of political authority placed one individual of royal blood on the jaguar-skin throne for life, they simultaneously disenfranchised the anointed king's brothers, as the brothers of kings before him had been. This large group of royal siblings and cousins, a group ever expanding through the practice of elite polygyny, would have been a weighty countercheck to the exercise of kingly authority. With a similar blood tie to the deceased royal ancestors on whom the fate of the polity depended, royal kinsmen were personally invested in the quality of their ritual invocation. Personal jealousies and political disagreements must have erupted from time to time, however unrecognized they may be in official histories of the Zaachila-Tehuantepec kings, and any perceived ritual laxity on the part of the ruler would serve to justify political challenges.

Such challenges were particularly likely to erupt over issues of royal succession when and if the normal Zapotec pattern of inheritance by the first-born son of the deceased ruler was bypassed. Comparing Mixtec royal genealogical and marital patterns with Oaxaca Valley narrative histories, Oudijk has concluded that the initial event precipitating the Isthmian campaign of Cosijopii was the death of Zaachila's king 6 Water, who had no surviving son. Rival claims for the throne made by followers of his elderly Zaachila-based uncle, 1 Grass, who succeeded him briefly, and by the Tlaxiaco-based descendant of 6 Water's half-sister ultimately led to the victory of the Mixtec faction from Tlaxiaco, leaving the supporters of 1 Grass to console themselves with the new throne they established at Tehuantepec.[65]

It appears that another political crisis was triggered by the death of Cosijopii's son, Cosijoeza in the early 1500s, when the lord of Xalapa rejected the king's deathbed selection of the prince Bichana Lachi as his successor and seized the opportunity to revolt. No mention of an insurrection is found in the account of a peaceful, uncontested inheritance of the Tehuantepec throne that Bichana Lachi/Don Juan Cortés and his widow presented in defense of the cacique's patrimonial claims. No mention of battles between the towns surfaced in Burgoa's recounting of Isthmian history.[66] However, chronic hostilities erupted easily into armed confrontation, if the early account given by Hernán Cortés's lieutenant Pedro de Alvarado is to be believed. Responding to one of thirty-six counts of criminal malfeasance that had been brought against him in 1529 before the Audiencia of New Spain, Alvarado denied the charge that he had been bribed to turn against the lord of Xalapa, when pursuing the lord's escaped slave in Tehuantepec. According to the accusation, this slave offered Alvarado whatever he wanted from a room full of gold, silver, pearls, jewelry, feathers, and precious stones in Tehuantepec, if he would bring him the lord of Xalapa. Alvarado complied and delivered the cacique in return for ten loads of the finest objects in the room and later led an army of 24,000 Indian warriors to a brutal siege of Xalapa, in which more than 20,000 were killed.[67]

Answering these charges, Alvarado countered that this supposed slave was none other than Xolo (presumably the same Xolotl referred to in other documents as Don Juan Cortés's *mayordomo* or advisor), who served as governor of the province of Tehuantepec on behalf of the deceased king's children:

> and to the rest, I say that this "slave" was the governor of Tehuantepec, that I never knew him as such slave but instead as a very important person who was in charge of that land and finding him in this position and a servant of Your Majesty, there was no reason to bring him to that other lord of Xalapa, who was only lord because of the commission of the sons of the lord of Tehuantepec, and he was governor of that land because after the death of the lord of that province, the lord of Xalapa rose up against them, among whom there were many great wars, and I pacified them and since then until now they have been and are in your royal service, and I never delivered to Xolo, governor of Tehuantepec, the lord of Xalapa.[68]

This rebel Xalapa lord must himself have been of high birth, for only a member of the royal clan or *tijacoqui* would have such an important governing role within Tehuantepec's domain. Political and economic opportunism doubtlessly fueled his rebellion, but the youth of the designated heir, who was only a young boy at the time of his father's death, was another weak thread that allowed the fabric of empire to be torn. Too young to display the qualities of kingship or to understand a king's ritual duties, the child Bichana Lachi would have ruled through his Mexica mother and the regent Xolotl, and these persons may have been perceived as inappropriate temporary guardians of the Zapotec royal ancestors. Paradoxically, the spiritual power of royal blood could be both the binding agent that allied commoners to their ruler and the root of political fragmentation within the nobility.

For the ancient Zapotecs, political authority did not exist apart from the spiritual authority invested in kings by virtue of their kinship with powerful deceased ancestors. When Spanish administrators later sought to separate royal blood and noble status from the pagan belief systems that had legitimized the polity's social divisions, they undermined the same native political institutions through which they hoped to direct the flow of goods and labor.

Markets, Trade, and Warfare

The Xalapa insurrection adds a discordant note to the assertions of Tehuantepec's ruling elite that its hold on the conquest state and neighboring polities went unchallenged by the province's lords. That there were external threats, however, was a fact fully acknowledged by colonial-period Zapotec sources, which expanded at length on the persistent menace of Aztec imperial designs. Before taking up this final topic of the nature of Tehuantepec's relationship with Tenochtitlan, I will first examine what evidence there is for more peaceful interchange with towns outside the polity's tributary boundaries.

Markets and trade

Local and long-distance exchange of economic goods is a subject of abiding interest among Mesoamerican prehistorians, who have benefited from the similarly keen interest in the production and distribution of goods held by early Spanish observers. Descriptions of the operation of the Aztec marketplace at Tlatelolco provided by the conquistadors have been the starting point for numerous studies of the rotating Nahua market known as the *tianguiz*.[69] Among Zapotec towns, Córdova recorded that the *quèya* or *quiya* was a similar periodic market. Cloth was one of the goods he noted being sold in this market, along with cacao, maize, and beans (among things which can be counted), but the range of goods is likely to have been much broader. Permanent shops or *tiendas* not associated with the marketplace existed as well for such artisan-specialists as barbers, weavers, potters, goldsmiths, herbalists, and makers of *lienzos* or cloth strips. Although there is no direct evidence to support this conjecture, it seems likely that most of the market activity in a town like Tehuantepec would be generated by the elite, who as proprietors of some of the region's most productive lands were more likely both to have surplus produce to sell and the money to buy goods produced by an artisan or sold by a merchant (*pénicònija*). A 1555 viceregal edict ordering non-Indian middlemen out of the Tehuantepec *tianquiz* because of complaints that they were driving up the price of food and other commodities suggests that, at least thirty years after the conquest, enough agricultural surplus was produced on such lands to provision Tehuantepec's market.[70]

One class of indigenous merchant, the wholesaler or *cónijaxéni,* dealt primarily in long-distance trade. Demand for Isthmian products was strong in the valley and southern highlands of Oaxaca, according to the accounts of several towns that responded to the Relación Geográfica.[71] From the eastern Oaxaca Valley, traders from Macuilxóchitl, Teotitlán del Valle, Teticpac, Taliztaca, and Tlacolula journeyed to Tehuantepec to obtain cotton grown on the coastal plain, which local weavers then spun and wove into cloth. Macuilxóchitl also bought salted shrimp and fish in

Tehuantepec, for which they traded home-grown corn, turkeys, beans, chiles, and squash. Closely tied economically though they were to Tehuantepec, none of these five communities needed Isthmus salt, for they had their own local sources from which dark-colored loaves of salt were made until the Spaniards discouraged its use.

Guaxilotitlán in the western or Etla arm of the valley procured salt as well as cotton, cacao, and fish from Tehuantepec. Salt was brought to Nexapa, Xuchítepec, Chichicapa, and Amatlán by traders who came from Tehuantepec, according to the Relaciones Geográficas of these towns. The Isthmus *salinas* were the property of the Tehuantepec ruler, whose *mayordomos* oversaw salt production and kept accounts of what was sold to the merchants who paid in copper axes, gold, precious stones, fine cloth, and jaguar skins. In 1554 the ninety-year-old Don Alonso of Xalapa testified that he had been taken to see the *salinas* several times by Don Juan Cortés's father Itzquiahuitl/Cosijoeza, whom he had known for thirty years:

> And he had his *mayordomos* who were in charge of guarding these salt beds and collecting salt from them and selling it. And several times this witness saw and was taken by Itzquiahuitl to see that these *mayordomos* brought him little axes and gold and stones and cotton cloth and tiger skins, which were the proceeds of the salt they sold and they answered to him in all matters as lord of these salt beds, which this witness saw him hold and possess until he died without any contradiction from anyone.[72]

Aztec encounters

With the province yielding such important trade goods as salt, cotton, and cacao, it is no surprise that other conquest states challenged the Zapotec ruler's control. For the Aztecs, the preeminent polity of the late precolumbian world, long-distance traders or *pochteca* often served as the front line for military conquest and political subjugation of such strategic resource zones. The first documented Aztec challenge, however, was less ambitious in its intent and came early in Yecaquiahuitl/Cosijopii's tenure over his newly conquered domain, if the proposed timing of the Zapotec *entrada* in the 1460s holds true. According to Fr. José de Acosta's Mexican sources, the appointed ruler of Tenochtitlan, Axayacatl, included Tehuantepec in his precoronation journey of conquest. Very quickly he passed to:

> the province of Tehuantepec, which is 200 leagues from Mexico, and in it he gave battle to a powerful and innumerable army, which had been joined to-

gether from that province and the surrounding territories. The first to leave his camp was the king himself, parading before his enemies, from whom he began to flee when they attacked in order to bring them to an ambush, where he had many soldiers covered with straw; [the soldiers] jumped out unexpectedly, and those who had been fleeing turned around in such a manner that they cut those of Tehuantepec down the middle, and they gave it to them, making a cruel slaughter and, continuing on, they destroyed their city and its temple, and to all the surrounding towns they gave severe punishment; and without stopping, they went on conquering until Guatulco.[73]

Axayacatl returned from this expedition with many riches and prisoners for sacrifice at his coronation in 1469, but the gains made did not include any permanent control over the province. Indeed there is no independent confirmation that the battle took place; it is unmentioned either by other primary Mexican sources or in Zapotec accounts.

During the reign of Ahuitzotl in Tenochtitlan (1486–1502), however, most non-Zapotec chroniclers of the early colonial period confirm that Tehuantepec was soundly defeated by the Aztec army and forced to pay tribute, if only for a period of time.[74] The Dominican cleric Fr. Diego Durán and the mestizo writer Hernando Alvarado Tezózomoc offered the most detailed descriptions of the events that led to war, and both these authors, reliant as they were on Tenochtitlan's historical accounts, agreed that the slaughter of Mexican traders was the precipitating event.[75] A large caravan of long-distance merchants from several towns in the Valley of Mexico had banded together to travel to the coastal towns of Tehuantepec, Xolotlan, Izhuatlan, Miahuatlan, and Amaxtlan (Tezózomoc includes Xuchtlan or Xochitlan in the list as well) in pursuit of luxury goods for the markets of Mexico, as was the practice of the *pochteca*. Their claim that they were only miserable merchants so angered the townspeople, according to Tezózomoc, that they killed the traders in their sleep, an explanation that is more persuasive when taken in light of the Aztec practice of using the *pochteca* as the first stage of territorial expansion. Durán elaborated further, saying that the coastal peoples attacked:

so that they would not come each year, as they had come, to skim and rob the riches which they took from those cities with the trifles and lowly goods that they brought, in order to return with gold and jewels and feathers and other rich things that they took away, with which they returned home laden; and there were so many that were accommodated that in all the year the roads were never empty of these merchants and dealers, because not only did the Mexicans themselves follow this route, but it was also followed by Texcocans,

> Tepanecas, Zuchimilcas, Chalcas, Tlahuicas, Tlaxcaltecas, and Chulultecas, finally those from all the provinces near and surrounding the volcano, and not just one or two from each city, but hundreds and hundreds, laden with lowly things.[76]

According to Durán these towns conspired to station watch guards along trade routes and kill all those who came to trade. By the time word got back to Tenochtitlan, the roads were full of corpses and the remains of bodies scavenged by wild animals. Lured by the promise of plunder from these rich cities, a huge army was recruited by the allied kings of Tenochtitlan, Texcoco, and Tlacopan, leaving the Aztec capital populated only by women, children, and the elderly. Tehuantepec was the last of the conspirators to meet the Aztec army in battle, but its soldiers were routed after many hours of pitched battle, and the Aztecs plundered the city before Ahuitzotl's captains could call off their greedy troops. The defeated lords of Tehuantepec then fell upon the mercy of Ahuitzotl, presenting him with rich gifts and agreeing to pay regular tribute to the Aztec king, whom they would thenceforth recognize as their lord.[77] When the coastal provinces of Xoconochco, Xolotla, and Maçateca soon after began attacking *pochteca* and other travelers and marauding the neighboring Isthmus villages, Ahuitzotl again amassed a huge army and joined with the lord of Tehuantepec to vanquish these rich and powerful provinces.

Ahuitzotl died shortly after his return to Tenochtitlan, and Tehuantepec proved to be less than a faithful subject, failing to send a delegation to the coronation ceremonies of his successor Motecuhzoma and offering belated congratulations only after seeing how many men were sacrificed and how harshly the new ruler dealt with recalcitrants. Motecuhzoma agreed to the requests of the Tehuantepec lords to provide a royal bride for the Zapotec king. According to Durán, the Mexican queen sabotaged her father's secret plan to destroy the city sometime after the birth of their son, informing her husband, who had 10,000 Aztec infiltrators killed that very night. Afterward Motecuhzoma treated the ruler of Tehuantepec with great respect.[78]

The Zapotec account of this encounter is, not surprisingly, dramatically different from that remembered by the Mexicans. In Burgoa's version, summarized in the previous chapter, the ruler of Tenochtitlan was provoked by the Zaachila lord's recent conquest of Tehuantepec and sent his most valiant captains in command of a huge force to take Cosijoeza prisoner and teach the other nations a lesson about greed. Outnumbered but not outsmarted, the Tehuantepec ruler first fortified the city's plazas then withdrew with his soldiers and enough supplies to last a year to the mountaintop retreat at Guiengola. Nighttime raids on the tired Mexican forces assembled below so weakened and demoralized the foreigners that the Aztec ruler was forced to sign a peace treaty after seven months of stalemate. The bold Cosijoeza then pushed on to wage battle with the province of Soconusco, which he conquered with the aid of the Chiapanecos. Thus frustrated in his access to this lucrative province, the Aztec ruler wisely chose to secure a stronger alliance with the wily Zapotec by promising him his daughter's hand in marriage. Here Burgoa inserted a romantic subplot worthy of the European chivalric tradition that must in part underlie its inclusion in this tale of war and politics. The maiden, who was known as Cotton Puff for her delicate beauty, enlisted the help of powerful sorcerers to make herself appear before the bathing Cosijoeza. The passion kindled between them hastened the once reluctant bridegroom to proceed with their wedding and sealed the loyalty of the bride, even in the face of her father's later treachery.[79]

There are enough correspondences between the Tenochca and Zapotec accounts to make it evident that they represent two quite different perspectives on the same historical encounter. Although Burgoa's recounting of Zapotec history is unequivocal in its assertion of Tehuantepec's undefeated status, some of the heroic "facts" are unlikely or likely to have been more complicated than presented. An unprovoked Zapotec conquest of the Soconusco area with only the assistance of the Chiapanecos is unlikely. Given that region's well-established importance to the Mexicans, its inclusion in the Codex Mendoza tribute pages, and archaeological support for strong Central Mexican ties at several sites in the area, the Aztec claim that the Zapotecs merely assisted in their conquest of these towns, which had been harassing Tehuantepec's subject villages, is more persuasive.[80] Even Durán's sources acknowledged the contribution made by the Zapotec forces, however. The chronicler related a speech purportedly given by Ahuitzotl to his tired troops before the final battle against Soconusco, in which he chastised them for their lack of fortitude, saying that if the Zapotecs had not been helping them, they would surely all have been killed because they had fought so poorly.[81]

The marriage of Cosijoeza and Pelaxilla was more complicated than Burgoa's romantic tale would suggest. Whether or not the couple shared a great love in the few years they had together before Cosijoeza's death, the context of this alliance argues strongly for its institutional role as a means of extending Aztec political control. Arranged marriages between the local lord and a daughter of the Tenochca royal family were a preferred alternative to the imposition of an Aztec governor in conquered towns. The succession of a son born of this alliance, regardless of the presence of older children from other marriages, was thought to secure the town's place in Tenochtitlan's sphere of influence.[82] Since Tehuantepec popular history remembered the existence of two older half-siblings of Don Juan Cortés who did not rule, even though the son of Pelaxilla was too young to govern after his father's death, this marriage looks very much like a political stratagem on the part of the Aztec ruler to place Mexican blood on the Tehuantepec throne.

Nonetheless, it does not seem to have been the case that Tehuantepec was simply an ordinary, tribute-paying subordinate of the Aztec empire. Although mentioned as conquests of Ahuitzotl, Tehuantepec and its dependencies are not given a page in the Codex Mendoza showing their tribute schedule to the Triple Alliance, unlike the Soconusco towns and many other Oaxaca communities. Tehuantepec and Xochitlan do appear on the Memorial de Tlacopan, however, and according to Pedro Carrasco, this is one of several discrepancies between the two tribute documents that may reflect the latter's inclusion of towns obliged to perform other services for the empire than payment in kind, such as provisions for war or military services.[83]

Don Fernando de Alva Ixtlilxóchitl related a somewhat different sequence of battles in Tehuantepec between the Zapotecs and the Mexica during the reigns of Ahuitzotl and Motecuhzoma in Tenochtitlan. Reflecting his postconquest Catholic sensibilities, the Texcocan chronicler wrote that in 1496 the Triple Alliance armies did battle against the province of Tehuantepec "in which they were crushed and lost much of their fame and reputation, and God showed his punishment and anger that he had against [the Mexica] for the many sacrifices that they had made, and he did not stop here but sent them other punishments, as will be seen shortly. In the following year of 1497, they subjugated another two provinces, those of Amaxtlan and Xochitlan."[84]

The disgrace of failure at Tehuantepec was finally mitigated in 1499 by Ixtlilxóchitl's account, when the Mexican armies gained the upper hand in battle at a town called Amextloapan, where several thousand *tehuantepecas* died and 17,400 others were taken prisoner. Though the town of Xaltepec was taken the following year, an insurrection of several Oaxaca towns including Tehuantepec against the Mexican garrison there had to be crushed soon after, during the reign of Motecuhzoma.[85]

That Tehuantepec itself may not have been vanquished by the Triple Alliance, though many of its soldiers died in battle and several of its dependencies were captured, is supported by the chronology of Aztec rulers given by Fr. Bernardino de Sahagún, who did not list the Zapotec city-state among the conquests of the last two Aztec rulers. The Franciscan friar attributed to Ahuitzotl the subjugation of "Tziuhcoac, and Molonco, Tlapan, Chiapan, Xaltepec, Izoatlan, Xochtlan, Amaxtlan, Mapachtepec, Xoconochco, Ayotlan, Maçatlan, and Coyoacan."[86] Despite Tehuantepec's omission from the Sahagún list, the three Isthmus towns cited by most other chroniclers are included: Izoatlan (Ixhuatlan), Xochtlan (Xochitlan, now Juchitán), and Amaxtlan (Amatitlan, since disappeared).

Why should the three coastal localities have attracted the persistent attention of the Aztecs? Mexican historical sources typically provide little motivation for a conquest other than the repeated assertion that the town in question was a populous and formidable enemy or could provide rich luxuries in tribute. But nothing known about these particular places from the sixteenth-century historical record indicates that any one of them was a major center in the late 1400s. Nor is the oft-cited strategic importance of the province as a gateway to the rich cacao orchards of Soconusco reflected in the location of any of the three easily bypassed communities of the coastal plain. What Ixhuatlan, Xochitlan, and Amatitlan do have in common, however, is their location near important salt pans. All three are specifically cited in the suit brought by the *fiscal* Dr. Cespedes de Cardenas against the heirs of Don Juan Cortés. Arguing that the cacique had improperly infringed on property rightfully belonging to the Crown, the *fiscal* claimed five specific *salinas* on behalf of the king of Spain: (1) those near Tehuantepec itself, (2) a place called "los Zapotecos," (3) Xochitlan, (4) Ixtaltepec next to Amatitlan, and (5) Iztatla of the pueblo of Ixhuatlan.[87] Besides provisioning the bishopric of Oaxaca in 1567, these *salinas* provided salt for Chiapas and Soconusco, and therein lies the probable economic value of the three conquered towns for the Triple Alliance.

Securing control over the major salt beds east of the Río de los Perros would have given the Aztec ruler and his allies an important and profitable trade resource with which to augment the obsidian and luxury goods already being exported long-distance to the cacao producers of Soconusco. It was yet another wedge used by the Mexicans to position themselves in the economic and political arena at the southeastern limits of Mesoamerica. According to this scenario, both the Tenochtitlan and the Tehuantepec rulers might legitimately claim victory out of the bloody encounters that took place between their armies in the final decade of the fifteenth century. Cosijoeza could rightly boast of a successful military ploy that frustrated the imperial objectives of battle-hardened Mexican commanders, while he must simultaneously have welcomed the ensuing truce that offered Zapotec soldiers participation in a decisive campaign in Soconusco and himself a prestigious marital alliance. Although Ahuitzotl was unable to penetrate the *coquitao*'s fortified retreat atop Guiengola, it appears that the Mexicans may have entered the plazas of Tehuantepec, where they extorted some of the prized finery described in detail by Aztec chroniclers from the town's *principales*. Were the eastern *salinas* part of the arrangement by which Tehuantepec's autonomy was bartered? Their repeated citation in all the Mexican histories argues forcibly for Aztec control, but it is not known on what terms. If lost for a time, surely they were among the first properties to be reclaimed by the Zapotec royal family when word of Cortés's victory over Tenochtitlan spread across the land. Whatever the Aztec ruler's unfulfilled intentions may have been in the marriage between his sister and Cosijoeza, their alliance quelled the substantial threat that such a formidable foe as the Tehuantepec king might have posed to the Mexicans' Soconusco expansion.

Summary

In just a few decades, the Zapotec invaders established themselves as the preeminent polity of the Isthmus. Their story is not an unfamiliar one in Late Postclassic Mesoamerica. Whether by more subtle ploys of marriage alliance or through bald-faced military conquest, it was a time when bold leaders sought to enhance their names, expunge memories of past defeats, and garner the wealth that underwrote the lavish lifestyles of the ruling class. The well-chronicled, rags-to-riches tale of the Aztecs was but one extreme variant of a story of political ambition replayed throughout Mesoamerica during a time of growing populations, expanding economic needs, and ensuing social upheaval. A domino-like impact of the Mixtec expansion into the Oaxaca Valley reverberated all along the Pacific coast, as less powerful Zoque, Huave, Chontal, and Nahua communities were displaced by or subjugated to one of two immigrant kingdoms—the Zapotecs of Tehuantepec or the Mixtecs of Tututepec.

For the Zapotecs, it appears that subduing the local population was the easiest part of this imperial dream. Building a new polity was a complicated matter, and Zapotec historical testimony from the sixteenth century, however idealized in its presentation of actual events, minimally tells us what were considered to be the key ingredients. Political legitimacy was invested in the royal conqueror himself, by virtue of his claim to descent from the kings of Zaachila. The functioning of the state, however, depended on the cooperation of lesser lords and nobles, who appear to have been instrumental both in mustering the needed force of soldier-settlers and in day-to-day matters of governance. Choice private lands in fertile zones of irrigated cacao orchards and cotton fields surely eased the transition to the hot coastal plain, even if the ruler did reserve the most productive lands for himself. Those who followed these military leaders to the Isthmus, the commoner-citizens whose labor as farmers, soldiers, and construction workers constituted the primary resource of the state, also found economic opportunities in a new environment. Here there was sufficient space to accommodate a population squeezed by new immigrants at home. Furthermore, the ability to carve out settlements and farmlands that preserved familiar ties of community and kinship helped anchor the *pèniqueche* to this unaccustomed landscape. Even temporary day laborers who came from mountain communities seeking work and the *terrazgueros* bound to private fields of the Tehuantepec nobility may have found their lot in life improved in a land rich in natural resources and prosperous from long-distance trade.

But that was the ideal picture. Forging a new polity in an alien environment was in fact a tenuous operation, particularly when the city-state that emerged held twice the population of its contemporaries at home and had claim to a territory several times that of the Oaxaca Valley. It was, in fact, a scale of political integration that had not been achieved by the Zapotecs since the eighth-century collapse of Monte Albán, and it is unlikely that this important Classic-period empire had been managed through the same political institutions that survived the Postclassic Balkanization of Oaxaca. The Tehuantepec polity that emerged so quickly in the fifteenth century was far more precarious than the assertions of kingly authority a century later would suggest. Menaced not just by outside military power, the Tehuantepec rulers had to contend with centripetal forces within Isthmus Zapotec society that threatened to fracture the religious and ritual bonds that promoted its integration. Illuminated next against the backdrop of the severest challenge met by the young Tehuantepec state, the Spanish conquest of Mesoamerica, these weaknesses and strengths will be seen to have presaged the kind of society the Isthmus Zapotec created under colonial rule.

CHAPTER THREE

The Social Fabric Is Torn

Political and Religious Change, 1521–1562

The preceding chapters have examined historical, archaeological, and linguistic evidence for Tehuantepec's foundation as a late Zapotec capital and the nature of the city-state's political organization, both horizontally, into its constituent barrios and subordinate communities, and vertically, in the division of its population into social classes with discrete rights, duties, and powers. These features of social and political organization were predicated on widespread Mesoamerican assumptions about the organization of the universe and the mutual obligations between human society and the supernatural forces governing its perpetuation. Sharing ideas and values among contemporary states left many opportunities for military and economic competition, nonetheless, as the ongoing struggle between Tehuantepec's kings and the powerful Mexica rulers makes clear. In the course of campaigns to exert hegemony over others and proclaim one's own polity the sacred center of humanity, it was common Mesoamerican practice for rival temples to be sacked and images of divine patrons to be taken hostage in reflection of the realigned political and supernatural forces.

The arrival of Hernán Cortés and his army of Spanish mercenaries on Mesoamerican shores must have been regarded by native observers from the perspective provided by their own long-standing institutions of political, economic, and spiritual control. Despite their pale complexions and stranger garb and manners, the Spaniards' military ambitions could be read initially in the familiar context of warfare and the expedient political alliances it engendered. Accordingly, different Mesoamerican peoples responded to these new arrivals based on their own varied perceptions of the strategic advantages and disadvantages they presented. At first contact, such responses ranged widely, from the Tlaxcaltecans making a notoriously decisive early alliance with the Spaniards, to the Mixtecs waging fierce if futile opposition to the Spaniards entering Oaxaca. No matter what their initial response, it would become all too clear to native peoples as the decades of Spanish rule wore on that this foreign polity operated under a model of conquest that reduced proud native kings to bureaucratic administrators and under a theology that demanded the elimination of familiar gods and rituals. For some groups, overt acts of defiance followed once the hand of colonial control was revealed. Matthew Restall has demonstrated that the granting of *encomiendas* was the initial trigger for resistance among the Yucatec Maya, a resistance that would be perpetuated by some Maya leaders, while others found new avenues for advancing their own political ambitions under the colonial state.[1]

It is in the context of disparate cultural assumptions dividing native and European perceptions of one another and the shifting strategic values their encounter presented that I consider the confrontation between the Tehuantepec polity and the Spanish conquest state. Partly because both sides claimed, each for its own reasons, that Tehuantepec had submitted peaceably to Cortés, the Spanish subjugation of the Isthmian province has never received more than passing mention in general histories of Mexico. Detailed scrutiny of the historical record for Tehuantepec, including my own earlier efforts, typically begins in the last half of the sixteenth century, when a substantial documentary base eases ethnohistorical reconstruction. To approach an understanding of the experiences of people who lived through the conquest and faced for the first time the startling dislocation of a familiar world, however, requires a closer inspection of the events and policies that shaped the first decades under Spanish rule.

Although the record is limited, the period between the conquest of Tenochtitlan in 1521 and the death of the last precolumbian ruler of Tehuantepec in 1562 brackets a critical era of transition. The year 1562 coincidently heralds the imposition of the mature colonial state, with the transfer of the province a year later from Hernán Cortés's seignorial domain to the full authority of the Spanish Crown and its delegated representatives in New Spain. While attempting to reconstruct the events surrounding the conquest of Tehuantepec with additional documentation, I will focus more broadly on the challenge posed to the polity's survival by the subordination of indigenous values to the ideology of the sixteenth-century Spanish empire.

Cortés and the Institutions of the Conquest State

Exactly when the Xalapa massacre that figures in Pedro de Alvarado's 1526 *residencia* took place is unstated, but the chronological nature of the list of charges and Alvarado's own testimony indicate that the incident occurred shortly after he succeeded in brutally quashing a rebellion in the coastal Mixtec kingdom of Tututepec in March 1522. As a reward for his services, Alvarado received both Tututepec with its dependencies and Xalapa as *encomiendas* (territorially based allotments of tribute-paying natives) from Hernán Cortés in August 24, 1522.[2] Although he did not mention Xalapa at the time, Cortés justified the severity of the Tututepec campaign in his third letter to Charles V by the actions of its people, who "had done much harm to those who had offered themselves as Your Majesty's vassals, and to the people of Tecoantepeque because they had permitted us to pass through their lands on our way to the Southern Sea."[3] That passage transpired on one of two small expeditions Cortés sent out immediately after the fall of Tenochtitlan in August 1521 in search of a port that would link his conquest strategically with the long-sought trade route with Asia. Tehuantepec's hospitality extended beyond safeguarding the foreigners' journey, however, for a short time later:

> the lord of the province of Tecoantepeque, which lies by the Southern Sea and through which the two Spaniards passed on their journey there, sent me certain of his chieftains, through whom he offered himself as Your Majesty's subject; he also made me a gift of gold ornaments, jewelry and articles of featherwork, all of which I handed over to Your Majesty's treasurer. I then thanked those messengers for what they had said to me on their lord's behalf, and gave them certain things with which they returned very happy.[4]

Thus allied from the outset with Cortés, the lord of Tehuantepec or his regent Xolotl found Alvarado to be a useful friend who demolished his nearest competitor, the lord of Tututepec, and who helped Tehuantepec's warriors put down the Xalapa lord's treacherous rebellion. When an opportunity came to assist the Spaniards at the beginning of 1524, the young king Bichana Lachi did so willingly, hosting the huge army of over four hundred Spanish soldiers and their Central Mexican allies, who rested in Tehuantepec before mounting a crushing attack on the southern Maya kingdoms of Chiapas and Guatemala.

Although their contribution was never acknowledged by Alvarado in his surviving reports on these battles, many Zapotec informants recounted on behalf of Don Juan Cortés's widow how the Tehuantepec cacique had not only fed this army, but sent a large force of his own men under the command of two of his best captains to participate in the Guatemala campaign. A typical account is that of seventy-year-old Alonso Días, *principal* of the Tehuantepec barrio of Totoncalco, whose own father had been conscripted: "Don Juan received them in peace and served them and favored him and those who came with him with food and supplies, and so he sent with him people from this town and the father of this witness went with them, serving them." Domingo Hernández, *principal* of the barrio of Tecpantilca, added the names of the Zapotec captains, Cotoguela and Alonso Peo, who he claimed were in command of four thousand men in the conquest of Guatemala, "and where the Spaniards died, they died as well." These events seem also to have been recorded in native-style *pinturas*, according to the Spaniard Juan Bautista de Avendaño, who viewed them in 1552 and later testified for Don Juan's widow that her husband had served the king and his captains and ministers well in the conquest and pacification of the provinces of Guatemala and Chiapas.[5]

It would appear then that the Tehuantepec ruler's well-known early submission to Cortés was no hollow pledge, but rather a serious bond of mutual obligation contracted by Bichana Lachi or his regent and sealed with the presents sent to the powerful Spaniard in Tenochtitlan. Whether or not the Tututepec venture was actually launched at the request of the Isthmus Zapotecs, the Xalapa campaign that followed at least demonstrates that Cortés's lieutenant could be enlisted (or bribed) to take up arms against the Tehuantepec king's enemies. And, as the native witnesses made clear in his widow's suit, the king reciprocated with no small expenditure of his own supplies and men to ensure Spanish victory in Alvarado's conquest of Guatemala.

A troubled alliance

Superficially, both the alliance and the mutual aid it entailed were familiar Mesoamerican practice; even the Chiapas-Guatemala expedition retraced part of a victorious campaign forged years before between Cosijoeza and Ahuitzotl against the Chiapanecs. On the Spanish side, it was precisely this kind of early submission and military support that was rewarded by allowing native lords to retain control over their kingdoms after the imposition of the colonial state. Not surprisingly, when the documentary record finally provides more abundant references to Tehuantepec's native population at mid-century, the baptized king, Don Juan Cortés, is seen sitting firmly in control of his domain.

Something in the alliance seems to have gone seriously wrong in the period between Alvarado's return to Mexico in 1526 and Cortés's appointment of Juan de Toledo as *alcalde mayor* for the province in 1538, something lost in the oral histories that Burgoa transcribed over a century later. Fortunately that disjuncture is alluded to more directly in the litigation records involving Don Juan and later his widow, as they took recourse in the Spanish courts to reestablish patrimonial rights. Testimony provided by both Tehuantepec's native population and its Spanish *vecinos* shows the extent to which local autonomy had been lost in those early years, although reasons for its withdrawal can only be inferred from sparse clues.

The natives who testified on behalf of Doña Magdalena in 1570–71 emphasized Don Juan's peaceful receipt of Cortés and his generous military support of Alvarado's campaign, but that is not the case for those called by Don Juan himself to establish his claim to the restitution of the Isthmian salt beds. Several 1554 witnesses volunteered the same information given by the ninety-year-old Don Juan of Nanacatepec (Santiago Guevea), that some thirty years earlier the Spaniards had won control of the province from Don Juan in war, leaving him with just his patrimonial *estancias* and *salinas* to support himself. Alonso de Chila, *principal* of Amatitlan, testified that "they gained the province by force and war ('por fuerça y guerra') from Don Juan, and they took away his lordship over all the province." Luís Netela, a *principal* of the villa of Tehuantepec, claimed that "the Spaniards came and entered the province by war ('por guerra') and they vanquished Don Juan Cortés and they took away the lordship which he had before."[6]

Can it be that the conquest of Tehuantepec was achieved by force and not by the voluntary submission recounted in Cortés's letter, or might this not be a case of *post facto* rationalization by Tehuantepec's native nobility, for whom such loss of political autonomy was conceivable only in the context of crushing military defeat? That the inhabitants of the province were in a state of revolt not long after Alvarado's Guatemala campaign is attested to by Francisco Maldonado, who came to Tehuantepec in 1526 under the commission of Cortés's appointed governor of New Spain, Marcos de Aguilar. Maldonado's activities during his few years in the province were challenged in a July 1529 *residencia* taken by Martín López, whom Cortés's enemies in the first Audiencia managed to install briefly as *alcalde mayor* during the conqueror's absence in Spain. Although Maldonado's primary mission in Tehuantepec was that of constructing ships for expeditions to the Spice Islands, he found it necessary to first arm the shipwrights he had brought with him from Spain to conquer and pacify the province:.

> This Marcos de Aguilar, as *justicia mayor* for him [Cortés], gave me sufficient powers, ordering me to build certain ships in fulfillment of the mandate of His Majesty, by the provisions of which I was commanded to take people from wherever I could find them. And I, on the basis of that order, went to the towns of Medellín and Villa Rica and took people and shipwrights, on whom I spent much money, and I came to this village of Tehuantepec with all of them. Upon arrival I found that all the neighboring villages were at war, for which reason I had to attempt to conquer and pacify them, which I did with the help of God and with myself and the help of those who came with me, for which I spent a large sum of gold pesos and later I commenced work on making ships, which was my command for the service of his Majesty.[7]

Maldonado maintained that he had not conquered the province in order to exploit the riches of the land, which were few in his estimation—"como es la tierra estéril e de ningún provecho"—but in order to pacify it so that he might fulfill his charge to serve the king of Spain. That lengthy process cost him plenty of his own money, he claimed, since he had to pay his companions at least 10 pesos a month, not to mention the loss of horses and arms.

Don Juan's role in this uprising is not clear, since Maldonado does not mention him and refers only vaguely to his own subsequent interaction with the native lords of the town. Maldonado's challenger, Martín López, however, reported that the province was so severely underpopulated in 1529 that the success of the shipbuilding operation there was seriously compromised. He attributed the lack of local manpower to the fact that so many men had left the province with its native lord: "because all the rest of the people who would help to build these ships went to Chiapas with Don Juan and many others to Guatemala, and of all of them no more than two *maestros* and one blacksmith and one carpenter remained in this village."[8] Conceivably, their absence might have stemmed from the Spanish campaign in Chiapas and Guatemala, but Alvarado himself had returned to Mexico in 1526, leaving the conquered Maya provinces in a state of unrest. Another, perhaps more likely reason for the withdrawal of the cacique and so many of his followers was Maldonado's own brutal "pacification" efforts.

That Don Juan, despite his services to Alvarado, may have been punished by Cortés shortly after the Guatemala campaign is suggested by two sets of facts well supported by testimony in Doña Magdalena's 1570 suit. First, a large group of about one hundred Nahuatl-speaking men (referred to as "mexicanos," a designation that suggests an ethnic affiliation with one or more Valley of Mexico towns) and their families were settled in the province after the close of Alvarado's Chiapas-Guatemala expedition. Once Tehuantepec was formally incorporated in 1529 into Cortés's vast seignorial domain, the Marquesado del Valle, it was from their ranks and not that of the hereditary Zapotec nobility that Cortés's provincial administrators appointed *principales* and *calpixques* in each of the villages and *estancias* subject to the town of Tehuantepec.[9] When Juan de Toledo arrived in Tehuantepec in 1538 to serve as *alcalde mayor* for the Marqués, he found that the Mexicans Luís and Diego were serving as *principales* and *tlacatecuhtli* or ruler. Toledo, with the Marqués's approval, restored Don Juan to power in order to make the collection of tributes and requisition of supplies and laborers more efficient, as he recalled in testimony for the *fiscal*.

> When the Marqués departed from the town, he left as its *principales* and *tlacateotl* [sic] a certain Luís Mexicano and the aforementioned Diego and Don Juan remained without office as lord or governor. And this witness, having the responsibility after the Marqués left of maintaining and provisioning twelve or thirteen groups of slaves with their miners and Spanish *mayordomos* and the *alcalde* of the mines and the shipyard of his boats with the shipwright Fernando Cortés and many other Spaniards and people to support and many other things to provide, came to realize that this Don Juan Cortés was the natural lord of this town and province. And he named him such and charged him with its government and with the care of the collection of tribute and people of service for these mines and supplies for them and the shipyard. And he removed Luís Mexicano, whom the Marqués had placed earlier [in this role] and this witness, communicating all this with the Marqués by letter, saw that it worked well and so he remained since that time forward as lord.[10]

If the stripping of all Bichana Lachi/Don Juan's traditional governing roles had been an intentional act, one authorized by Cortés himself, the rebellion that may have provoked it would not be inconsistent with the long history of temporary alliances between past Zapotec kings and the Aztec rulers whom Cortés replaced. Such alliances were strictly utilitarian responses to the perception of how powerful one's enemy was and how helpful joint military ventures might be to the expansion of one's own territorial ambitions. With precolumbian city-state alliances traditionally based on such fragile bonds, it should not have been long before the Zapotec king attempted to test the limits of Spanish domination. Alternatively, the rewarding of the conquistador's Nahua allies with choice new lands to settle and positions of authority over regional native affairs may simply have been a more pressing priority than paying attention to traditional government in this remote province, which held such high strategic value in Cortés's political and entrepreneurial imagination.

The imposition of Nahua receivership, or perhaps the disputes which brought it about, wrecked havoc in the lives of the Tehuantepec king's subjects, whose long history of poor relationships with the Mexica added further insult to their subordination. Those who were sympathetic to his widow remembered before the court in 1570 and 1571 that the "mexicanos" were the instrument of these problems, causing the native inhabitants much injury through their mistreatment. As a consequence many people abandoned their homes, leaving the town's barrios and villages deserted. Perhaps it was following the *alcalde mayor* Juan de Toledo's reinstatement of the cacique as lord and governor that Don Juan himself went to the neighboring villages and persuaded his subjects to return to their homes. The testimony of Diego Ruíz is typical of these accounts:

> at the time that the province was conquered and pacified by order of Don Hernando Cortés, the natives of these *estancias*, like others of the head town itself and other parts of the province, ran away and many of them left out of fear of the Spaniards, and they stayed in the surrounding villages, where they could live more securely. And after the pacification of the province was finished, Don Juan Cortés looked for them and went to bring those who were of his patrimony back to the proper *estancias* where they should live as his patrimonial Indians.[11]

At issue in this particular case, of course, was whether the inhabitants of those *estancias* Don Juan had claimed to be his patrimonial estates were free citizens, forcibly moved from their proper communities, or *indios terrazgueros*, who had fled during this period of instability from the lands to which they were bound. Juan de Toledo maintained that all *estancias* paid tribute to the Marqués, but various *visitadores* sent by the Audiencia apparently were persuaded of the patrimonial status of the Indians from the disputed *estancias*, for they were excluded from the Marqués's tribute lists and, despite frequent challenges from the Marquesado administrators, remained so until the Crown regained control of the province in 1563.

The cacique's role under Marquesado administrators

After ten or twelve years of hated subjugation to both the Spaniards and their Nahua surrogates, Don Juan Cortés was at last reinstated as native lord and governor of the Tehuantepec province. Much had been lost in the intervening decade and the ruler, now in his mid-thirties, had ample time to reflect upon the changed political landscape. Overt resistance to the Spanish overlords was fruitless, but the terms by which his new political status was sustained were harsher than any imposed by the Aztecs on his father and grandfather. As governor, he was responsible for delivering to the Marqués's *alcalde mayor* all the tribute in gold, specie, and labor mandated by his administrator and approved by the Audiencia. Much of that tribute was dedicated to servicing the demanding shipbuilding and mining enterprises that the Marquesado maintained in the Isthmus, and Juan de Toledo's interest in reinstating the cacique was a purely pragmatic means to filling these needs.

In 1542 the *oidor* Lic. Alonso Maldonado brought Don Juan and some of the other *principales* before him in Tehuantepec to confirm a previously mandated tribute schedule that had not been properly documented. He authorized Juan de Toledo to collect a sum of 1,650 pesos worth of gold from the province, delivered in four parts annually, as well as a long list of goods and services, many specific to individual communities, much of it destined for the Marquesado mining and shipbuilding activities. Support for the *alcalde mayor*'s household and administrative needs was varied—making and repairing the Marqués's houses in which the *alcalde mayor* resided, transporting letters and messages for his estate, planting corn, beans, and chiles, providing dishes and cooking pots, household labor, and a daily supply of twenty eggs, four turkeys, two chickens, and whatever fish, firewood, fruit, and herbs might be necessary. In addition, Tehuantepec had to supply 80 lengths of cloth suitable for the mine's slaves each quarter as well as deliver two hundred chickens and two hundred hens to feed them and whatever other supplies were needed from time to time. When the mines moved, Tehuantepec natives were obliged to construct new houses and shelters.

The coastal Huave villages also had specific obligations toward the mining operations: Tepeguazontlan had to bring eighty loads of lime every fifty days, while Itzactepec del Mar brought eighty loads of shrimp and Guazontlan eighty loads of fish to the mines. The complex shipbuilding effort was sustained by local community support at several points. The mountain sawmill where the ships' timbers were cut required food for the Spaniards and slaves working there, as well as the labor services of ten Indians from the village of Macuiltepec; the Zoque-speaking communities of Chimalapa, Nectepec, Ocotepec, and Acasebastepec were to make pitch and otherwise help Macuiltepec in these tasks. Transport-

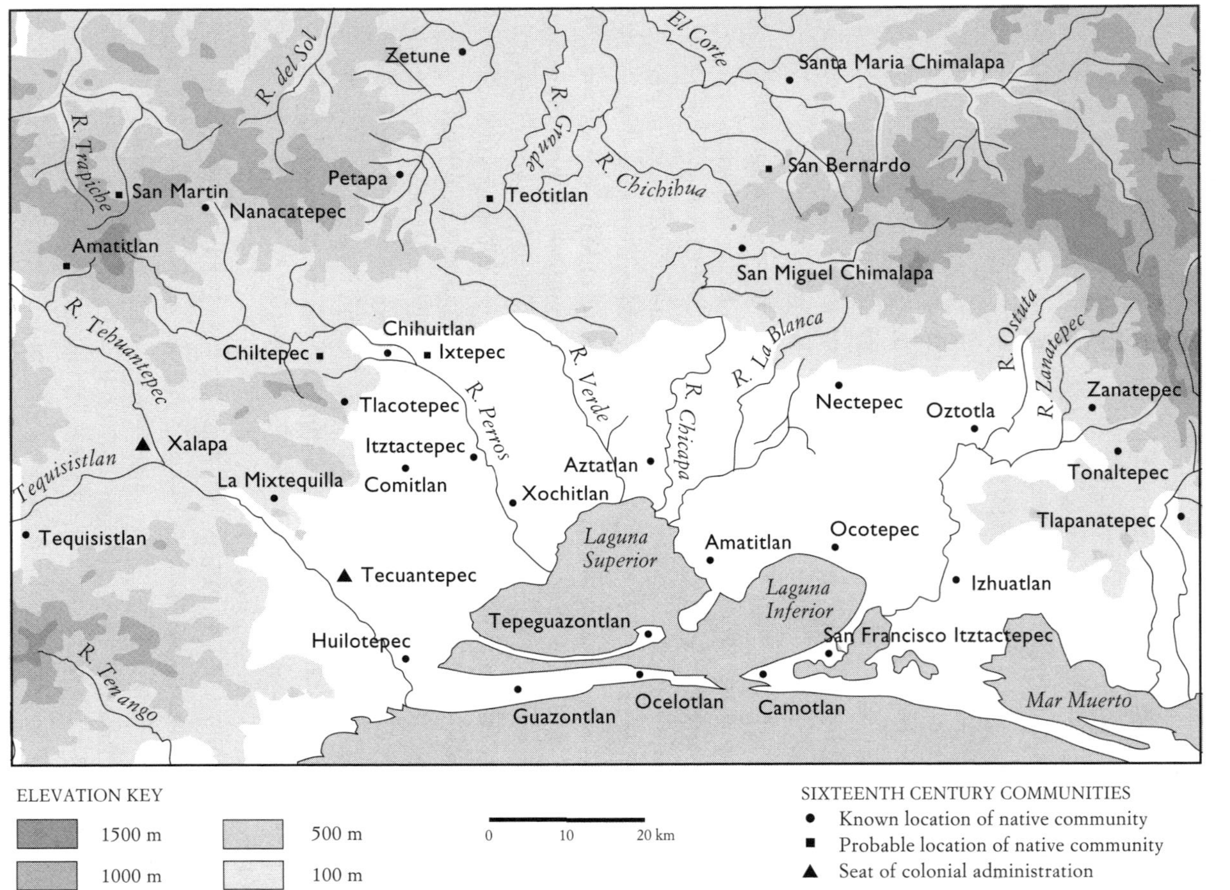

MAP 3.1. The Tehuantepec province in the sixteenth century.

ing the planks and masts and rigging down river to the coastal shipyard fell to the Zapotec towns of Itztactepec, Chiltepec, Teotitlan, and Comitlan, while the barrio of Cuilapan was required to provide whatever services were necessary for the ships under construction. The barrio of Cia made and supplied charcoal and nothing else.[12]

Three years later these requirements were simplified in compliance with the New Laws, which were intended to curb some of the excessive tribute demands made by the colony's *encomenderos*. All labor services were banned in Tehuantepec, as they were to be in privately held *encomiendas* throughout New Spain. Tribute in food was limited to specific amounts of corn (4,020 *fanegas*), beans (160 loads) and chiles (130 loads), to be partitioned between the mines and the shipyard as needed, while every ninety days an additional two hundred hens, forty loads of fish, and eighty loads of shrimp were to be taken to the mines to feed the slaves working there, along with forty loads of salt for processing the ore. Household supplies for the Marqués's administrator and staff in Tehuantepec itself were limited to the daily delivery of two hens, two turkeys, four loads of firewood, ten loads of herbs, twenty eggs, six melons, six tomatoes, and six Indians to bring water and serve in the house and five others to prepare food; on Fridays and Saturdays, twenty fish, a gourd of shrimp, and an additional twenty eggs substituted for the poultry. In response to a formal complaint by the Tehuantepec natives that they were unable to meet this tribute schedule, the requirements were moderated and simplified further in 1553 to 1,470 pesos of common gold and 2,940 *fanegas* of corn and nothing more.[13]

However much the exquisitely precise plan of 1545 appears to have been less open-ended and burdensome than the previous authorization, it is certain that labor service did not stop, but merely changed its appearance. Requisitions of laborers now had to be paid, and the Marquesado administrators kept careful records of the numbers of natives working on specific *repartimiento* details and of the wages paid to their indigenous overseers or *tequitlatos*. In 1556, for example, more than 1,100 men were drafted from Isthmus communities for periods ranging from one week to one month to perform various auxiliary tasks associated with the construction of the galleon *Sancti Spiritus*, the last of the ships to be built in Tehuantepec. Their jobs included such varied activities as transporting timbers from the mountain sawmill or European cable from the Coatzalcoalcos River port of Utlatepec to the shipyard and making charcoal for the ironworks or tar for the ship's planking. Shortly before Christmas, three hundred natives from Xalapa were paid for six days work helping with the launching of the ship. Nearly two-thirds of all laborers were drawn from Zapotec-speaking communities, but Huave and Zoque villages contributed transport and labor service as well, a burden borne in addition to the Huaves' paid procurement of fish for the Marquesado.[14]

Many of the jobs were more dangerous than the account records alone would suggest. Martín López complained to the king in 1529 at the outset of this venture that building and launching ships in this dangerous port should be stopped because of the hazards it was causing the native inhabitants: "to avoid the great dangers and deaths that increase daily among the natives of this province because of these ships, from hauling wood from the mountains and many other labors and aggravations, I say have mercy that those ships that now are in the shipyard are enough."[15] Despite the toll on human life and the loss of numerous ships that were to run aground at the narrow entrance to the open sea, the shipyard remained active until the province and port were finally removed from the Marquesado. Memories of these hardships remained strong over a century later, when Burgoa recorded Huave accounts of the many men who had died in ill-fated efforts to launch ships from the poorly placed Tehuantepec facility.[16]

What specific role Don Juan Cortés played in the *repartimientos* that serviced Marquesado enterprises is difficult to determine from the documentary data at hand, but he would ultimately have been responsible for partitioning labor requisitions among the *tequitlatos* of his subject barrios and *estancias*, although the choice of which individuals served when would have been a decision made by the native barrio officials. This was, after all, the mechanism by which labor service was allocated for traditional public works projects. As Spanish-sanctioned governor of the province, he was already responsible for delivering all other tribute to the *alcalde mayor.*

Under Spanish rule, however, there was another level of accountability, and the cacique himself might be punished if things did not go well. That was clear at the outset of Juan de Toledo's tenure, if we are to believe the many Zapotec witnesses who claimed to have seen Don Juan's mistreatment at the *alcalde mayor*'s hands. The very fact that Toledo was the first to place the responsibility for complying with the Marqués's labor and tribute demands directly in the hands of the Zapotec cacique may have made their relationship particularly strained. Juan Pérez was called in 1572 to refute some aspects of the former administrator's testimony regarding the patrimonial *estancias* and said he had seen Juan de Toledo beat the cacique with sticks. Diego López confirmed the beatings, and Gaspar de la Cueva added that Toledo had thrown Don Juan in jail for many days. Reasons given for this ill treatment varied—one witness attributed their enmity to the two men's different natures. Juan Díaz, who served as *nahuatlato* or interpreter for the *alcalde mayor*, suggested that Don Juan's failure to bring Toledo presents when he was in office reflected their mutual hostility. Don Juan clearly found this subordination difficult to bear.[17]

Toledo himself seems to have had little sympathy for local cultural traditions except as they facilitated or hindered his managerial role, nor was the Marquesado administration particularly interested in his handling of native affairs. When his term of office as *alcalde mayor* ended in 1543, Toledo was held accountable for every tool made or delivered to the mines and shipyards, but no questions were asked in the formal *residencia* concerning his treatment of the native population.[18]

The heavy hand of colonial rule did not lessen under Toledo's replacement in the mid–1540s, Pedro de Alcala. By his own testimony, Alcala recalled in 1571 that he had confronted Don Juan after hearing that the cacique had illegally appropriated the tribute owed the Marqués by several *estancias*, but the Audiencia's *visitadores* upheld the cacique's patrimonial claims:

> During the time that he was *alcalde mayor* of this town, he heard that Don Juan had usurped and concealed certain *estancias* subject to the town of Tehuantepec, those that he had concealed are Atotonilco, Tlacotepec, Amatitlan, and that as soon as he heard of this he called for Don Juan and he came and admitted that he had concealed these *estancias*, which were mandated to serve and contribute according to their potential to the tribute which they were obliged to give to the Marqués. And Don Juan apologized, saying that they were his and from his patrimony and of little consequence. . . . And so he brought several times cloth and other things of little value to this witness, saying that this was what the *estancias* gave for tribute and that a little earlier Diego Ramírez had come as *visitador* to make a census of the province by order of the viceroy Don Antonio de Mendoza, and that this *visitador* returned the *estancias* to Don Juan and this witness does not know why he returned them and he gave notice to Lic. Altamirano, who was governor of the [Marquesado] so that he could find a remedy.[19]

But Alcala's efforts to thwart Don Juan's patrimonial claims did not stop here. In 1546 the *alcalde mayor* renounced the cacique's exclusive rights to the salt beds inherited from Itzquiahuitl/Cosijopii and told the barrio leaders of Tecolapa (Santa Cruz Tagolaba) to harvest salt for themselves from the salt beds that lay adjacent to their own community lands. As Marcos Lecal of Xalapa told the story in 1554:

> It could be eight years, more or less, that Pedro de Alcala, being at the time *alcalde mayor* in this province for the Marqués del Valle, ordered Juan Tecolapa and Gaspar Layche and the Indians of the barrio of this town known as Tecolapateca, and made them understand that, since the salt beds which he had possessed were not his and were communal property belonging to everyone, and that since they possessed lands up to these salt beds, that they could take the salt in them against the wishes of Don Juan, all of which Pedro de Alcala said to these Indians of the aforementioned Tecolapateca. And this witness heard that these Indians, having seen that which Pedro de Alcala had said to them as *alcalde mayor*, in his name went to the *salinas* against the wishes of Don Juan and they took a great quantity of salt against his will and this is what this witness knows and saw and heard about.[20]

Don Juan himself claimed in the interrogatory he filed in September before the judge Alonso de Buyca, who had been commissioned to investigate the province, that Pedro de Alcala had done this deed out of hatred and enmity ("por odio y enemistad") and never repaid him for the 40 *jacales* of salt that had been improperly taken from the *salinas* against his will.

The relationship between cacique and *alcalde mayor* did not improve under the administration of Pedro Pacheco in the early 1550s. It was Pacheco who ordered that the Zapotec governor be subjected to a *residencia secreta* the year before the visit of Buyca's special commission. This formal investigation into the conduct of an official was typically instigated at the end of an officeholder's term. For Spanish administrators, the *residencias* of outgoing *alcaldes mayores* were normally conducted by their replacements; Lillian Thomas and I have suggested elsewhere that this investigation of Don Juan may have marked the end of his first two-year stint as *gobernador* in a newly inaugurated, formal *cabildo*-style native government in Tehuantepec. Whatever its impetus, Don Juan's *residencia* resulted in the cacique being formally tried on two counts of criminal behavior before the same Pedro Pacheco. In this case the charges were brought by his own native subjects.[21]

One set of complainants consisted of three Nahuatl-speaking residents of the town, who protested that they had been severely beaten in the cacique's presence and that one of their number had been left for dead in

FIG. 3.1. Drawing of abuses suffered by Mexican Indian residents of Tehuantepec accompanying their 1553 criminal complaint against Don Juan Cortés, governor of Tehuantepec. The original drawing, made on European paper with European ink, was published as Códice Num. 29 in *Códices indígenas de algunos pueblos del Marquesado del Valle de Oaxaca* (1933) by the Archivo General de la Nación. Reproduced by permission of the Archivo General de la Nación.

an irrigation ditch during a community work project. Taken in the context of long-standing hostilities between the Zapotec ruler and the "mexicanos" installed in the province by the Marqués, we might find plausible the allegation by the complainants that Don Juan had done this because of his hatred and enmity ("odio y enemistad") for the Mexicans. However, Don Juan recanted his confession to a role in these beatings after formal charges were made, saying that it had been taken while being held in jail and in fear of being whipped. He confirmed his presence at the irrigation works, but maintained that the punishment of these uncooperative workers was ordered by his *tequitlato* overseer, a claim that received mixed support from other native witnesses during the governor's *residencia.* Although the cacique had managed to reclaim both the offices and the prime agricultural lands briefly usurped by Cortés's Nahua allies, making these recalcitrant Mexican foreigners accede to the duties and obligations expected of commoner citizens was an ongoing struggle.

FIG. 3.2. Depiction of abuses suffered by Zapotec complainants under Don Juan Cortés, governor of Tehuantepec. The indigenous-style drawing was executed on maguey paper with *huizache* ink; Archivo General de la Nación, Hospital de Jesús, leg. 450, papeles sueltos, exp. 1, catalog no. 3125. Reproduced by permission of the Archivo General de la Nación.

The other complaint was made by Zapotec commoners, all residents of the Tehuantepec barrio overseen by the *tequitlato* Domingo Goma, and it signaled a more significant erosion of the Zapotec king's traditional authority. As described more fully in the previous chapter, the four commoners accused the tribute collector and Don Juan of exacting excessive tribute payments in cacao, *mantas*, and coins. They complained that they were worn out from tribute demands so high that they were destroying all the commoners of the town, tribute which they suggested was going to finance Don Juan's personal expenses. Domingo Goma countered with a complicated accounting of what had been taken and for what purposes, but the very notion that the ruler and his administrators might be held accountable to some outside judge for their actions was a pernicious wedge in the structure that bound the social and political divisions of the Zapotec city-state.

The commoners' accusation was a logical consequence, as Thomas and I have argued, of the introduced Spanish form of civil government with its idealized concept of justice. Based on humanistic understandings of natural law, which saw the proper role of government to lie in the safeguarding of the interests of every sector of society as codified in law, Spanish justice held all officials, even in principle the king, accountable for their actions through judicial review. For the ancient Zapotecs, the king was accountable ultimately only to the divine ancestors who watched over the affairs of mortals, however much his practical ability to enforce his will may have depended upon the cooperation of the nobility and upon the political authority he held over his commoner subjects.[22]

In the case of the 1553 complaints, the assertion of this authority behind the scenes, doubtlessly reinforced by physical threat, undermined the newly imposed colonial judicial system. Both the Zapotec and Mexican complainants abruptly withdrew their charges in the interest of peace and harmony ("por bien de paz y concordia") and not out of fear that justice would not be done ("no por temor de falta de justicia"). Still the stage had been set for a different kind of relationship between the cacique and his subjects under Spanish colonial rule.

A year and a half later, Viceroy Luís de Velasco issued a series of edicts concerning the province and especially its hereditary lord, which spelled out more specifically the kind of contractual obligations between the Zapotec governor and the Spanish Crown on the one hand and between the governor and his people on the other that was authorized by the colonial government. Because he was informed that Don Juan was cacique by birthright and custom ("de casta y derecha de convención de los caciques y señores de esta villa") and because of his services to the king in the pacification of the provinces of Guatemala and other parts, the viceroy ordered that the natives of the town and its subject villages obey him as their natural lord, without rebellion, under penalty of exile or prosecution. Possession of his patrimonial lands, villages, commoners, and other properties was to be restored to him, and anyone who infringed on that possession was subject to penalties and fines. Specific orders were given to the officials of the Marquesado that Don Juan be left to enjoy his properties and his office, the conduct of which was spelled out in more detail:

> and he was allowed to use his office freely and to meet with the rest of the *principales* and officials of the Republic of the Indians in his public house and to order and to arrange that which among them they see fit for the service of Our Lord and the well-being of the natives, and the execution of justice and punishment of public sins, and his own properties and accounts of his council, without anyone interfering in them, not even in any part of them, in the manner that it was done in the past and as in the rest of the villages of this New Spain of the Royal Crown of His Majesty, and they are permitted to name of-

> ficials and persons of their choosing for the good of the Republic of the Indians and the execution of the ordinances of the Royal Audiencia and all else that remains in his power.[23]

In return for these privileges, Don Juan also incurred obligations. He was to respect the Marqués and his officials, treat the Spanish residents and visitors to the town well, and administer to his own subjects with love and kindness, watching over their well-being, not taking their lands and enterprises, and not charging them more tribute than that for which they were obligated. In words that were to cast a foreboding shadow over the last decade of Don Juan's life, the cacique was instructed as well to see to his subjects' instruction in Catholic doctrine and conversion to Christianity ("tenga cuidado de su doctrina y conversión").[24]

The Imposition of Christianity in Tehuantepec

Making good Christians out of the indigenous population of New Spain was, of course, a fundamental and abiding goal of the colonial state, however much the papal charge underwriting Spain's political and economic subjugation of native peoples had become a contested issue for humanist theologians by 1550. Far from the Valladolid epicenter of this debate, the Dominicans of Oaxaca launched an active campaign to establish permanent missions throughout the geographically and linguistically diverse region. At mid-century the growing number of stone and brick churches built to serve distant towns in the diocese gave physical support to the doctrinal efforts of an expanding cohort of preachers adept in the languages of their native charges. While the missionaries' intent was to save each and every soul through the spread of Catholic faith, caciques and other native elite were especially targeted as leaders and role models for their communities. As such their successes as Christian converts as well as their failures received particular notice whenever the Dominican order's chroniclers or critics assessed the Oaxaca chapter's effectiveness.

The early mission in Tehuantepec

At the time of Dr. Quesada's *visita* to the province in 1554, Don Juan Cortés seemed to embody all that might be desired of an important convert to Catholicism for the colonial authorities. At the cacique's direction, a sumptuous two-story convent to house the Dominican mission in Tehuantepec was under construction, finally receiving its charter of admission in 1555. Don Juan ensured that the eight friars and the servants who were to reside there would have a daily supply of fresh fish to replace the meat they forswore by ordering its provision from the two hundred households of San Blas barrio.[25] The edifice seemed to give testimony in brick and mortar to the strength of Don Juan's support for the church and its ministers.

When the cacique's own conversion to Christianity took place is not well established. Burgoa stated that Hernán Cortés himself was responsible for baptizing the Tehuantepec king, which Bichana Lachi submitted to willingly, assuming his better-known Christian name of Don Juan Cortés. Perhaps as impressive as the conquistador's theology was the round of artillery fire with which the conversion was celebrated, which according to Burgoa, seemed to the assembled Zapotecs to be thunder and lightning given to the Spaniards by the gods themselves: "he had the artillery fire a round, which appeared to them to be something beyond their understanding of nature, and that it was thunder and lightning that the gods had given the Spaniards, and they were even more afraid of this conviction when they saw the fire and the unseen bullet flying through the air that wounded at great distance."[26] That Cortés personally played a role in Don Juan's baptism may be as doubtful as Burgoa's claim that the celebratory gunfire frightened the assembled Indians, if we remember that Pedro de Alvarado had already provided the Zapotecs considerable firsthand experience with Spanish gun powder. Moreover, although the founder of the Dominican chapter in New Spain, Fr. Domingo de Betanzos, persuaded Cortés to support the order's missionary efforts in Oaxaca as early as 1527, there is little evidence that Cortés himself came to Tehuantepec until he returned from Spain with the title of Marqués del Valle.

The early Dominican mission, however, did make it as far as the Isthmus. Betanzos sent two religious brethren to Oaxaca: Fr. Gonzalo Lucero, who went to work in the Mixteca, and Fr. Bernardino de Minaya, who had not yet been ordained as a preacher, but whose restless energy touched many Zapotec-speaking communities. Fr. Bernardino was present in Tehuantepec when Martín López arrived in 1529 to assert the authority of the first Audiencia over Cortés's enterprises. Known in Oaxaca for his Nahuatl skills and proselytization of the more acculturated Indians or *ladinos*, Fr. Bernardino may have had more impact on the Nahua allies of Cortés than on the subordinate Zapotec-speaking population. Other Dominicans who spent brief periods in Tehuantepec during the first decades following the conquest included Fr. Pedro de Santa María, Fr. Luís Cancer, and even the redoubtable Fr. Bartolomé de las Casas, who stopped there for a time on his way to Chiapas.[27]

As verified by several letters written from Tehuantepec, Hernán Cortés himself came to Tehuantepec in late 1532, when he made the long journey to hasten the construction of several vessels then at the shipyard, a haste intensified according to his secretary by the beleaguered conqueror's desire to outflank his enemies in the exploration of the Pacific Coast and to avenge the deaths of an earlier exploratory mission.[28] The Franciscan chronicler Motolinía suggested that the ships were originally commissioned for his fellow communicant Fr. Martín de Valencia, religious leader of the first twelve missionaries who arrived in New Spain in 1524. After eight years' teaching in Mexico City, Valencia was eager to missionize new lands and he went to Tehuantepec in 1532 to await the construction of ships promised him by Cortés. When, despite the Marqués's personal intervention, they could not be finished after seven months' wait, Valencia returned to Mexico. During the interim, however, the Franciscans learned Zapotec and spent their time teaching Catholic doctrine to the natives of the area in their own tongue. Valencia left his three religious brethren in Tehuantepec to await the ships' construction, but they did not finally set sail until 1538 on an unsuccessful expedition, one spoiled by dissension in the ranks of Cortés's men.[29]

By this time the diocese had acquired the steady hand of Juan López de Zárate, who in 1535 was the first bishop appointed for Oaxaca and who for the next twenty years oversaw its Catholic mission. Still, missionary efforts in this vast territory continued to be hampered by the small but expanding number of friars. It may not have been until the 1540s that a permanent religious "house" was finally established in Tehuantepec with Fr. Gregorio de Beteta, former bishop of Cartagena, serving as the parish's first vicar. The penitent Beteta's missionary zeal remained unsatisfied, however, until he finally realized his ambition to go to La Florida, where there were said to be large populations of natives needing conversion. His successor in Tehuantepec, Fr. Bernardo de Albuquerque, was more deeply committed to the Zapotecs, among whose towns and villages he had devoted his missionary efforts since arriving in New Spain, and to the Oaxaca diocese, over which he was appointed bishop in 1555 upon the recommendation of Las Casas.[30]

A 1548 royal decree mandated the establishment of monasteries in native villages to aid their religious instruction, and planning for the con-

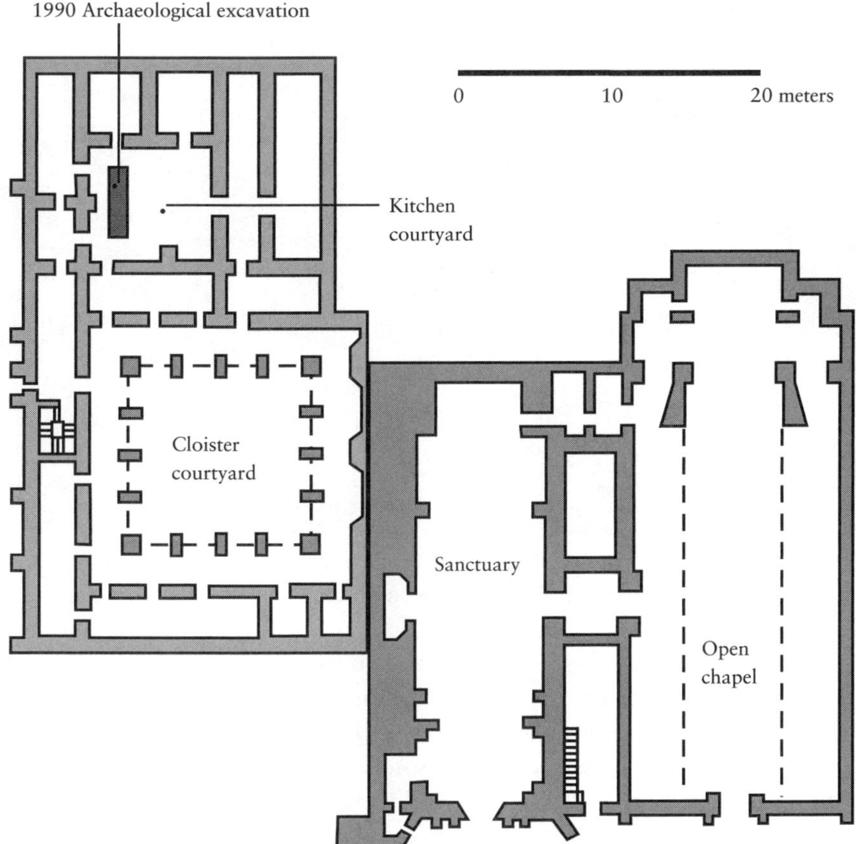

MAP 3.2. Ground plan of the Tehuantepec church and convent complex. Based on Martha Lis Garrido Cardona, *Monumentos coloniales religiosos del istmo de Tehuantepec*, fig. 13 (Mexico: Instituto Nacional de Antropología e Historia, 1995).

struction of Tehuantepec's convent must have followed soon thereafter. Fr. Alonso de Espinosa served as the convent's first prior, with Fr. Diego de Azevedo serving as preacher. The plan of the open-air chapel, completed sometime after the convent itself was formally accepted in 1555, is strikingly similar to that of the open chapel at Teposcolula, the inventive design of which has been attributed to the hand of the Dominicans' master architect, Fr. Francisco de Marín. Albuquerque, who was prior of the Oaxaca convent in 1547, when Fr. Marín was assigned there, may have been responsible for the Tehuantepec project's conception.[31] Both the am-

FIG. 3.3. The Tehuantepec church. The convent wall can be seen behind the bell tower on the left; the facade of the open-air chapel is seen on the right.

bitiousness of the open-air chapel plan and the sheer size of the adjacent convent, which has one of the largest cloister courtyards in Oaxaca, attest to Tehuantepec's importance to the Dominican evangelization program and the wealth and power of its native lord, who enlisted hundreds of his subjects to make bricks and build walls for the friars. That importance persisted even after the ravages of introduced epidemic diseases depleted the province's population, leaving under 12,000 Indians in the town of Tehuantepec and less than 5,000 in its twenty-seven subject villages at mid-century, about one-half of the estimated prehispanic total.[32]

Evangelical themes

As to the message imparted by these early Tehuantepec missionaries and the means by which it was communicated to the Zapotecs, there is little direct information from the Isthmus, and practices reported elsewhere must serve as guides to the conversion strategies.[33] By the time the first Dominicans established themselves in Oaxaca, the transitory result of mass conversions was widely lamented, and the early Dominican preachers were known for their inventive evangelization methods. The first to make contact with many mountainous villages, Fr. Gonzalo Lucero developed what was considered to be a particularly effective approach in his work among the Mixtecs. He concluded from his experiences that the slow teaching of small parts of the Christian dogma was the only way to convert his charges from their pagan ways: "The Indians are a phlegmatic people, and with prolonged effort they obtain many estimable works. If they are made to hurry and taken beyond their speed, without covering what they are given, they lose what they had and make nothing of importance."[34] Lucero used a variety of visual aids to impress his charges with the falsity of their pagan beliefs and the fundamental precepts of Catholic doctrine. He brought a sphere with him to demonstrate the prevailing Ptolemaic view of the heavens in which the celestial bodies moved around the earth according to the will of God rather than their own, so as to discredit indigenous deification of the sun, moon, and stars. Several large cloth paintings were brought out in each village he reached in his preaching circuit. One illustrated the rewards of heaven and punishments of hell awaiting individuals after death. Another depicted two giant canoes filled with natives, one bearing a group of praying, rosary-bearing men and women accompanied by angels, the other filled with drunken and debauched individuals who ignored the pleas of the angels flying overhead, while demons alongside diverted the canoe to the gates of hell.[35]

Pictorial aids such as this continued to be used throughout the sixteenth century, and they even appear in Burgoa's account of the 1609 Pinopiaa idolatry in Xalapa discussed earlier. But as permanent monasteries became widely established, officially promulgated catechisms delivered in the native language of the town became the primary vehicle for indoctrination. The first Zapotec *doctrina* to be published was Fr. Pedro de Feria's *Doctrina christiana en lengua castellana y çapoteca* (1567). Much renowned for his eloquence, Feria doubtlessly built upon arguments and analogies already in use among his Oaxaca brethren when he composed his bilingual treatise. It should not be too great a leap to view this widely used work as the culmination of conversion strategies that were employed in Tehuantepec and other Zapotec-speaking towns in the 1550s and 1560s.

Feria, like Lucero before him, attacked the substance of pagan belief and ritual, but his approach was more subtle. While presenting in Zapotec the major teachings of Catholic doctrine concerning belief, prayer, law, sin, and redemption, Feria simultaneously demolished what he considered to be the essence of Zapotec religion in a three-pronged attack on native ideology, the falsity of its gods, and the mortal danger which continued idolatry presented to the newly baptized. True belief, he asserted, focused on the immortality of the soul, a concept which Feria refused to translate into Zapotec, using the Spanish "*ánima*" in both languages, rather than the material needs of the body. But the propitiation of false gods, in his view, was devoted to ensuring the fulfillment of temporal desires:

> Now you will understand how vain and how without basis your ancient religion was, for you only sought in it corporal and temporal things. You tell me, my children, how you cut your tongues and ears, when the priests sacrificed men in the temples of the demons, when you did whatever other thing that your old religion commanded of you, that you sought to do it and that you prayed to these false gods. You only prayed to be free of illness: to live a long time in this world: to have good storms, to have children, to enjoy this world: you were only concerned with these things of the body, and only these things did you remember: and only for these did you pray to your false gods.[36]

Rather than worship the one true God who had created the universe, a god whose existence is as apparent as the watchmaker's existence is manifest in the watch he created, the devil had made them worship innumerable deities. These deities were no more than illusions; like the illusions of men walking that the darkness makes of leaves and trees, the darkness that covered their hearts had created illusions of gods. For if these pagan gods had been all powerful, where had they disappeared to after the arrival of the Christians?[37]

The humanist Feria offered a quasirational derivation for the practice of worshiping idols made of stone or wood. Such an image, he suggested, might be made by a parent after the death of a child in order to comfort himself. Generations later, when their descendants had forgotten the original intention of these statues, the devil was able to persuade people to make temples for them and place singers and dancers there. In some cases, it was tyrannical kings who had ordered the villages to make images of them and treat them with reverence, and after time people came to worship these images as if they were gods, having been convinced of that by the devil, who entered these statues and spoke things to persuade them of their divinity. "And in this manner it was converted into idolatry, by chance, that those figures of stone, which had been made by hand from human artifices, later men came to adore as their gods through the trickery of the devil; and they celebrated grand holidays for them and they made sacrifices and they tore their flesh, cutting their tongues and their ears and other parts of their bodies, and they sacrificed men before them to placate them: and all of it was in order to have them agree to their petitions."[38]

But idolatry was an abomination to the true God, and its practitioners, particularly those who had received the rites of baptism, were accorded the severest of punishments in this life and in hell. As evidence of this fact, Feria pointed to the terrible mortality which the Indians continued to experience, which he suspected was due to their continued veneration of pagan idols. For, while the Spaniards also committed sins, theirs were not the unforgivable sin of idolatry. God punishes them, but He does not exterminate them.

> I do not know what would be the cause of this: only God knows the answer. But I have a suspicion, that the sin of idolatry is the cause, because God is punishing you. In ancient times you were like the grasses of the field and like the sands of the sea, with always an infinite number of people dying from the incessant wars and from the great tributes of those days. Now all of you are at peace and no one makes war against another, and with all this you are dwindling.[39]

Feria gave special instruction to the Indian officials. He warned them not to mistreat their subjects by abusing their labor or taking goods or money from them or by failing to listen to their grievances, actions which he said were violations of the seventh commandment to do no injury. But at the same time he charged these community leaders ("como son governador, alcaldes, fiscal, alguaziles, tequitlatos, y los demás principales") to safeguard the proper respect for the Cross and to see that those who failed to honor it were severely reprimanded.[40]

The apostasy of Don Juan

At mid-century such admonitions appear to have been heeded at least outwardly by Don Juan Cortés, governor of Tehuantepec. According to the terms of Don Luís de Velasco's 1555 decrees, the accommodation to Spanish rule that the cacique finally achieved severely limited his opportunities to benefit materially from his subjects. While other officials and *principales* of the town received an annual tribute of 20 *fanegas* of corn grown on a communal plot of land, Don Juan's remuneration for his official duties was set at 100 pesos paid annually by the townspeople. Most of his income derived from the tribute obligations of his patrimonial Indians, with each married couple paying 1 *fanega* of corn and 4 *tomines* of gold each year, the same rate at which most natives paid tribute to the Marqués del Valle. Any other service which was asked of them had to be paid and paid in the presence of the vicar of the monastery, with the ultimate penalty for noncompliance being the loss of any rights to these tributaries which Don Juan or his heirs might claim.[41]

As one of those officials Feria would charge with the responsibility of seeing that the church and its symbols were properly honored, the cacique's record of public support for the Dominicans' evangelization efforts was generous and enthusiastic. The Marqués was obliged to maintain the mission from the province's tributary income, but it was Don Juan who made possible such an ambitious project as the construction of the convent and chapel. Although the details of this incident are murky, it even appears that Don Juan had a hand in the discovery of idolaters in the province. Two Indians from the village of Chihuitán, Don Hernando Cortés and Domingo Hernández, testified in 1571 against his widow's claims to patrimonial *estancias* inherited by Don Juan's children. Five witnesses called by Doña Magdalena in rebuttal testified that these men were notorious enemies of the cacique and his wife because they made public their witchcraft and idolatry. For punishment they were first jailed and then made to sit in front of the church door wearing the cone-shaped idolater's hat (*coroza*) inscribed with their crimes.[42]

Rather than an incident of deeply felt moral outrage on the part of Don Juan, however, the idolatry accusation seems rather to have been a socially acceptable means of subduing men whom all the witnesses agreed were notoriously vile and lowly persons and, according to one testimony, foreigners (" *extranjeros*"). That this accusation was made during Albuquerque's tenure as Bishop of Oaxaca may add a further political note to its timing. David Tavárez points out in a detailed analysis of colonial anti-idolatry campaigns in the dioceses of Mexico and Oaxaca that Albuquerque was an ardent crusader, who initiated a far-reaching program to rid native communities of clandestine pagan practices during his long tenure as bishop. Although the campaign is known directly from just a few prominent cases, natives complained so ardently about the excessive punishments inflicted by Dominican vicars whom the bishop appointed as extirpators that the Audiencia finally compelled Albuquerque to put an end to these commissions in 1571.[43] The Tehuantepec vicar, Fr. Bernardo de Santa María, who had been in Tehuantepec since the construction of the convent in 1554, was an active participant in Albuquerque's extirpation campaign, having located the cave known as Corazon del Reino in his search for signs of continued idolatrous activity in the province. In this context, Don Juan's accusations against the Chihuitán "foreigners" might be seen as an effort to deflect the vicar's attention from activities that were more central to Zapotec religiosity. Despite his baptism and his unflagging support for the Dominicans, the exclusive tenets of Catholic doctrine had not been accepted by Don Juan, who was himself caught in idolatrous acts in 1562.

According to Fr. Francisco Burgoa, whose *Geográfica descripción* provided a detailed account of Don Juan's apostasy, the cacique had resumed his ancient role as supreme priest. Each night he received large numbers of people from many villages bearing animals and other gifts in his palace. A Spaniard residing in the town who thought he might benefit from the cacique's well-known largesse disguised himself in native dress and entered the palace carrying a load of firewood, where he spied an inner room in which a stone figure rested on an altar surrounded by candles and smoking incense burners. When Fr. Santa María was told of this, he summoned Don Juan and questioned him closely about his actions. The cacique assured him of the sincerity of his Catholic beliefs and claimed that the suspicious strangers from Mitla who accompanied him everywhere were nothing more than trusted counselors who had advised his father. But Fr. Santa María's doubts were not satisfied and he entrusted a native convert who served as church treasurer to keep his eyes open for suspicious activities. When the convert reported that the Mitla elders seemed to be making preparations for another ceremony, the vicar enlisted the help of the *alcalde mayor* to make a secret raid on the palace at midnight. Don Juan was caught *en flagrante,* attired in the white robes and feathered headdress of the highest priest. He was attended by the six elderly *mitleños*, all of whose hands were bloody from the sacrifices of birds and animals.[44]

The Mitla priests were immediately thrown in jail, but Fr. Santa María, out of respect for the cacique's many kindnesses to the Dominicans, brought Don Juan to the convent while the proper course of action was charted. Bishop Albuquerque dispatched two learned Dominicans, Fr. Juan de Mata and the eminent linguist Fr. Juan de Córdova, to Tehuantepec to sit in ecclesiastical court over the matter. Don Juan insisted that his case touched on matters that concerned the king of Spain and that he should therefore be judged not by the friars but by the viceroy and Audiencia. In Mexico the case dragged on at great expense for an entire year, ending with Don Juan finally admitting guilt and being stripped of his villages, his office, and his rents in punishment. Allowed to return home to Tehuantepec, the cacique made it no farther than

Nexapa, where he was struck down by a severe stroke or heart attack and died before receiving the final sacraments of his baptism.[45]

Confirmation of the facts elaborated upon in such great detail by Burgoa is strangely lacking from earlier Dominican chronicles, even though the most comprehensive of these works, Dávila Padilla's *Historia de la fundación y discurso de la provincia de Santiago de México* (1596), like Burgoa's own *Palestra historial*, is replete with accounts of idolatry on the part of other Zapotec caciques during this same period. It would be tempting to regard this story as apocryphal, were it not for the fact that the Crown *fiscal*, Dr. Cespedes de Cárdenas, claimed not long after these events in 1567 that the deceased Don Juan, whom he accused of stealing the Tehuantepec salt beds, was an idolator and sacrificer:

> and a certain Don Juan, cacique of the town of Tehuantepec, without doubt entered these *salinas*, he, who for idolatry and for being a sacrificer was punished and castigated and removed from office in the sentence for his crime, died and Doña Magdalena, who is said to be his wife, conspired with the *principales* and natives of the town and divided up among them these salt beds, and they have them and detain them, harvesting and taking advantage of these things that are not theirs nor do they belong to them.[46]

The issue of Don Juan's apostasy was not raised again in the protracted suit between the fiscal and his widow, and the very person who might have been most disappointed personally by the cacique's idolatry, Fr. Bernardo de Santa María, now vicar of Xalapa, appeared as a witness on Doña Magdalena's behalf in 1571. So close were the bonds of gratitude and affection between the missionaries and Don Juan and his family that the Dominicans found no easy moral lessons to promote from the sorry failure of their convert. Never at a loss for words, Burgoa took the incident and turned it into an indictment against the greed of the Spanish settlers who spoke only of gold and nothing of God, saying that Don Juan had been convinced that by giving the gold that had been required of his people, they would be left to live by their own law.[47]

But the greater theological problem may have been the failure of the missionaries to comprehend the true nature of Zapotec religion. Even the eloquent and learned Fr. Pedro de Feria had it wrong when he asserted that the object of ancient religious practice was the gratification of individual material needs, while Christianity rested on transcendent principles. What he failed to see was that the performance of ritual was itself a transcendent practice, a fulfillment of the human community's commitment to sacrifice its own blood, its own life substance to ensure that the cosmos would maintain its momentum. Don Juan Cortés, as the supreme spiritual leader of his community, could no more abandon his obligations to fulfill that commitment at sanctioned occasions than he could abandon the political authority inherited from his ancestors. What the friars considered to be the moral course for individuals was incompatible with the spiritual needs of the political community. As long as the Tehuantepec cacique lived, he would be bound by the demands of the gods. Only after Don Juan's death might there be room for forging a new spiritual contract.

Assessing the spiritual conquest's wider impact in Tehuantepec

As Tavárez cautions, focusing on those continued prehispanic ritual practices that colonial anti-idolatry campaigns revealed can produce a distorted view of the nature of native religious beliefs and the perceptions individuals held about the Catholic teachings to which they were subject. Not only must the practices be viewed through the lens of Spanish cultural biases, but their clandestine nature makes it difficult to detect how central a role they played in a transformed religiosity among the native population as a whole.[48]

For Tehuantepec, unfortunately, the only direct information concerning native responses during these early decades to the introduced theology and rituals of Christianity centers on the person of the traditional ruler, Don Juan Cortés. Burgoa's account of his idolatry exposé provides glimpses of what must have been a broader division within the Zapotec population as a whole regarding the role Catholicism would play in their lives. It was a division that posed the larger majority unconvinced by Catholicism's claims to exclusivity, as indicated by the crowds attending Don Juan's ritual performances, against a smaller number of individuals who, like the native treasurer of the church willing to spy on suspicious activity for the vicar, appear to have committed themselves wholeheartedly to the evangelization project. Nothing in Burgoa's account informs us of the social groups to which these divisions pertained, but it would be unusual for a society as large and diverse as that of the Isthmus Zapotecs if there were not political, economic, and personal agendas that propelled individuals to place themselves on one side or the other of this divide, no matter what their religious understandings may have been.

It would be wrong, however, to suppose that Christianity's hold on the native population depended solely on the opportunities for social advancement it offered some or the reality of coercive sanctions it used against the unwilling. Once the temples to familiar gods had been destroyed, the Dominicans did not waste much time before erecting impressive edifices often literally in their place. The open-air form of chapels like that built in Tehuantepec was an intentional adaptation of the European model in order to situate Christian worship in a familiar and appealing outdoor context for religious performance.

There are few glimpses of the performances themselves, other than surviving texts of Zapotec sermons like Feria's, but the Dominicans were known to use dramatic pageantry to impress native audiences, and music was an attractive part of the ritual tableau. Dávila Padilla commented on the enthusiasm for religious music among new communicants, which native cantors, adept at singing and playing many instruments, quickly taught to others. Traces of these early Christian songs in Sierra Zapotec were still part of local ritual knowledge uncovered in a much later anti-idolatry campaign, according to Tavárez's close textual analysis. In sixteenth-century Tehuantepec, inviting songs and pageants would have been an important component of doctrinal pedagogy as well. A hundred years after Don Juan's idolatry, these early evangelical roots still bore fruit in the ardent participation of Tehuantepec's barrio parishes in choral processions to the main church, as witnessed by Burgoa.[49]

That most native people participated willingly in these mandatory religious spectacles is to be expected, and some may have embraced fully the message of faith and salvation the missionaries offered, along with the colorful foreign ritual dramas in which it was cast. For the majority, reception of these new ideas was selective and contextual, competing on a deep psychological level with traditional beliefs and practices inexorably linked to the local landscape and the passage of time. The dynamic interchange between the two opposing systems of thought and practice would play out over the years ahead in both the collective and the elective spheres of social life, to employ Tavárez's subtle distinction concerning public and individual ritual performances.[50] Although the current archaeological and historical records for Tehuantepec do not illuminate more than the occasional flicker of evidence pertinent to Zapotec religiosity over the colonial period as a whole, what is known from other regions of New Spain makes it clear that the terms of this interchange remained a subject of ongoing negotiation in daily life.

CHAPTER FOUR

The Colonial Political Economy Takes Root

Archaeological and Documentary Evidence, 1563–1660

For the Dominican friars, ministering to their native charges involved more than matters of theology. Once the initial evangelization efforts had settled into a long-term program of indoctrination and observance, economic and political considerations intermingled with the spiritual on an ever-increasing scale. To the extent that such considerations reflect the complex human and ecological transformations taking place as Tehuantepec was incorporated more fully into the colonial political economy, the convent's record during its first century mirrors broader developments in the province and serves as a useful introduction to a critical period of cultural adaptation for the indigenous population. It is a period that begins locally with the transfer of the province from the Marquesado to Crown control and ends with the political crisis engendered by the well-known Tehuantepec revolt of 1660.

When comparing the province's early colonial history with developments in New Spain as a whole, it is clear that this period corresponds both to the rough chronological frame and to the kinds of cultural change typical of what James Lockhart has referred to as Stage 2 in the accommodation of Central Mexican native society to Spanish colonialism. Spanning the one hundred years between 1540–50 and 1640–50, Stage 2 (also termed the "middle years") is distinguished linguistically by an active absorption of Spanish loan words into Nahuatl vocabulary as the native population became more familiar with the material culture and institutions of the colonial state. Because of the widespread adoption of alphabetic writing among the Nahua during this period, Nahuatl-language wills and other documents give ample testimony to the scale at which Spanish introductions influenced native society, from imposed local government structures to accumulated household goods. At the same time these texts underscore the resiliency of indigenous patterns of thought and principles of organization.[1]

Unfortunately, no similarly rich corpus of early colonial Zapotec texts from Tehuantepec has yet been uncovered that might provide the heterogeneous internal perspective on Isthmus community life advanced by Lockhart and other "New Philologists" for many regions of New Spain.[2] Much of what can be said presently about the "middle years" in Tehuantepec depends on more conventional Spanish-language sources, some of them written on behalf of native petitioners, but all of them intended for review by outside authorities. To counterbalance the often biased and selective vision of Spanish administrators and clerics, this discussion draws as well from a sample of early colonial archaeological materials. Architecture, settlement patterns, and faunal remains, along with pottery, stone, and metal artifacts provide another type of silent "text" with which to interpret adaptive changes taking place within the native community.

It was not merely the native community that underwent change during these "middle years," a period in which bureaucratic processes became normalized and Spanish settlers found alternatives to the diminishing resources of native labor and precious metals that seemed so limitless in 1521. For both colonist and native alike, a variety of cultural predispositions, personal proclivities, and political considerations might mediate the impact of colonial economic institutions and opportunities on individual lives. The discussion that follows attempts to draw out some of the variability of economic activity among the Tehuantepec province's increasingly diverse inhabitants, after first framing its local setting in native population decline and settlement pattern change. To this end, the economic history of the province's Dominican mission serves as a lens with which to preview Tehuantepec during the middle years of Spanish colonialism.

The Growth of the Dominican Enterprise in Tehuantepec

Just maintaining the Tehuantepec church, its convent, the four to eight resident friars and their attendants, not to mention the one hundred or more people who regularly sought its shelter, was a costly endeavor. During Don Juan's lifetime, the cacique himself guaranteed some portion of the convent's necessary requirements with provisions of fish and local produce for the friars as well as materials needed for the sacraments.[3] Most of the convent's financial support in these early years came from the Marqués del Valle, who by viceregal decree was obliged to provide for both the Tehuantepec and Xalapa monasteries beyond the yearly salary of 200 pesos paid to the Spanish master builder who oversaw their construction. The Marqués had to deliver to the Tehuantepec convent regular supplies that included 100 *fanegas* of maize, 40 *fanegas* of wheat (produced in his Oaxaca Valley jurisdiction), 6 *arrobas* of wine, 6 *arrobas* of oil, 12 pounds of wax candles, 6 pigs, 25 *arrobas* of wool, and 8 *arrobas* of tallow from the tributes, rents, and other enterprises which he maintained in the province.[4]

Although the Dominicans were compelled to seek formal stipulation of these payments in 1554 because of some irregularity in past support, the Marqués, like all the colony's entrepreneurs, was subject to ecclesiastical tithes that constituted an additional contribution to church revenues. His *alcalde mayor* testified over a decade earlier, long before construction on the convents began, that Hernán Cortés regularly tithed to the church out of Christian duty a portion of his income from the maize he received in tribute from the province's inhabitants and from the livestock increase on the Haciendas Marquesanas. For the three years before Hernán Cortés's death in 1543, the sale of 4 horses, 83 cattle, and 860 sheep belonging to the Marqués and his administrator and partner, Juan de Toledo, on their newly established ranches had helped fill church coffers.[5]

In 1563, a few short months after the death of the cacique Don Juan, the Tehuantepec province minus Xalapa was taken out of the Marquesado and returned to Crown control. Ensuing administrative changes greatly curbed the cacique family's traditional prerogatives, most notably the loss of entire communities of patrimonial Indians or *terrazgueros*, one of the principal issues in Doña Magdalena de Zúñiga's 1572 suit against the royal *fiscal*. Without *terrazguero* labor services, upon which Don Juan's royal household relied for much of its maintenance, his widow may have been hard pressed to continue the cacique's long-standing daily support for the convent. That she found other ways to express her gratitude to the friars to whom she often turned for advice and consolation was acknowledged a century later by Fr. Francisco de Burgoa, who recalled Magdalena's generous gift to the Tehuantepec convent of several important properties. These included irrigated orchards and cool bathing springs near Laollaga, several salt beds on the coastal lagoon, as well as the endowment of a rich chapel (*capellanía*). Fifty pesos of the endowment's income were to be given in charity to each of the order's *provinciales* who visited Tehuantepec, that they might ensure the performance of masses requested in her will.[6]

Other gifts of property and money from wealthy natives and the province's small but growing Spanish population enabled the convent to secure a healthy income, and the Dominicans were prospering by the mid-seventeenth century. According to a 1643 petition from Tehuantepec landowners responding to a mandated retitling or *composición* of their properties, the town's convent had become a significant investor in the provincial ranching industry. Besides owning three large *estancias* on which mules and burros were raised, the convent and its lay supporting institutions, which included the Cofradía de la Santa Vera Cruz and an unidentified church *capellanía* (possibly the one funded by Doña Magdalena), held mortgages totaling 10,600 pesos on nine Spanish estates.[7] A comparison with the late sixteenth-century report on Oaxaca ecclesiastical properties cited by William Taylor shows that the Tehuantepec convent's finances matched or exceeded those of most other Dominican institutions; the well-endowed Cuilapan monastery, for example, had six sheep ranches, a small agricultural farm, and some 8–13,000 pesos worth of liens on properties in the capital of Antiquera.[8]

As it was securing its financial base of operations, the Tehuantepec convent also expanded its physical presence in the province, especially among the Zapotec-speaking communities of the western coastal plain. Burgoa might lament the poverty of the Zoque *cabecera* of Zanatepec, with its tiny church made of thatch and its rude quarters for the two resident friars that resembled a dilapidated ranch more than a house of worship, but no such complaints would be voiced about churches constructed among pueblos within Tehuantepec's *visita*.[9] Today, towns and villages all across the western coastal plain attest to the late sixteenth- to early seventeenth-century architectural underpinnings of their earliest churches, even when the original, buttressed stone and brick walls and vaulted chapel ceilings have been replastered and remodeled to suit a different era's aesthetic.

Among these rural communities, the size of the early church is a rough indicator of the community's early colonial population and wealth. The

FIG. 4.1. The Chihuitán church.

upper Río de los Perros village of Chihuitán, for example, boasts a handsome church dedicated to San Pedro with an enormous walled atrium appropriate to a much bigger town than today's sleepy community. One of its neighbors in the Isthmus foothills, Santa María Magdalena Tlacotepec, on the other hand, has replaced its small early colonial chapel with two more modern buildings that now dwarf the partially collapsed edifice. The domed vault of the tiny *capilla mayor* still stands at the head of the ruined single-nave church, with remnants of bright blue paint decorating the white-washed walls.

In Tehuantepec itself, circa-1600 parish churches dominate most of the city's barrios, and their location, with respect to archaeological traces of the barrios' precolumbian predecessors, confirms the dislocation suffered by commoner communities from high mortality rates in the early colonial period and civil and ecclesiastical *congregaciones*. As a case in point, the barrio of Santa Cruz Tagolaba, which may have held a population of 1,000 to 1,200 people on the eve of the conquest in the dispersed habitation zone surrounding the Panteón Antiguo site, was relocated nearly 1

FIG. 4.2. Ruins of the Tlacotepec church.

km closer to the town center. There new adobe homes were built Spanish-style on brick and rock foundations, with contiguous walls facing the regularly aligned streets that radiated out from the parish church (see Map 1.3).

Depopulation and Congregación in Town and Pueblo

Tagolaba's reduction to one-fifth its precolumbian physical size reflects in part the more tightly aggregated plan of the new settlement. The major factor influencing the size of this and other early seventeenth-century communities, however, was the dramatic native depopulation experienced in Tehuantepec, like other parts of New Spain, as Old World diseases from smallpox to influenza raged among previously unexposed populations. The comprehensive census conducted by Baltasar de San Miguel in 1550 tallied 16,726 people in the province, a number which might be raised as much as 20 percent to include members of the nobility or their slaves and serfs, whom Borah and Cook found to be regularly excluded from the larger census of which San Miguel's survey was a part.[10] San Miguel reported a total of 11,845 men, women, and children living in Tehuantepec proper and its forty-nine barrios, which was about 71 percent of the province's total population. Even raising the urban population to 14,214 to include any uncounted *principales* and their retainers indicates a population loss of over 40 percent from the archaeological estimate of 25,000 people living in Tehuantepec on the eve of the conquest.

This reduction represented only the first wave of the rising tide of disease and death that swept across the Isthmian coastal plain. More impressionistic figures given later in the century range between three thousand tribute-paying households estimated for the province by Bishop Albuquerque in the mid–1560s and 3,200 *vecinos* or adult males cited by the Tehuantepec *alcalde mayor* in his 1580 Relación Geográfica. These numbers can be contrasted with the 5,259 full-tributary equivalents for the province as a whole and 3,705 urban tributaries represented in San Miguel's earlier count. By 1580, when the *alcalde mayor* estimated 1,200 tributaries residing in the *cabecera,* the urban population was one-third what it had been thirty years earlier or about 20 percent of its precolumbian base.[11]

The enormity of indigenous mortality here as elsewhere in Spain's American colonies did not escape contemporary observers. Among them, the late sixteenth-century Dominican chronicler Fr. Augustín Dávila Padilla noted several major pandemics that had afflicted New Spain in 1543 and again in 1566–67, when the viceroy ordered a census that revealed more than two million native deaths. At the time of his writing in 1592, the Mixteca region of Oaxaca was still in the midst of a major measles epidemic that began the year before, devastating the countryside and carrying with it a huge childhood mortality. In his own village, ten to sixteen children died each day, according to the Dominican, and it was typical for the surrounding towns that 1–2,000 children died for every 2,000 surviving adult males. The chronicler fretted that it would not be long before the prophecy of the Mexican chapter's founder, Fr. Domingo de Betanzos, would prove true, and that the natives would be extinguished, as had been the case in Hispaniola, leaving people in future generations to ask what color the indigenous people had been.[12]

Fortunately, his fears would not be borne out, and most regions of New Spain witnessed a slow population recovery beginning in the 1600s. Tributary records for Tehuantepec document further population decline at the turn of the century, but by 1623 a figure of 2,437 tributaries may represent something close to the provincial nadir. Epidemic disease continued to impact the native population, precipitating a request for a new count just thirty years later, when the Tehuantepec town council or *ca-*

bildo was left unable to raise its tribute assessment following one particularly severe siege. Despite such temporary setbacks, the course of demographic recovery had been set; even a modest population increase in the province is indicated by a 1687 report of 2,788 tributaries.[13] Here, as elsewhere in New Spain, the native population had by mid-century at last accumulated sufficient immunity to the introduced European diseases that the majority of adults might survive the impact of new epidemics, allowing natural fertility rates to compensate quickly for most short-term population losses.[14]

The horrendous population losses experienced throughout the first century of Spanish rule were used to justify the implementation of long-standing civil and ecclesiastical policies of *congregación*. Aggregating dispersed populations into nucleated communities had been a high priority for the missionary orders in New Spain since 1537, when the Audiencia's bishops appealed to the king for permission to resettle natives into villages and to burn their temples and idols so as to more efficiently bring them into the Christian fold. This position was reiterated in each of the three Provincial Councils that met in the sixteenth century to formulate consistent policies that would address and improve the Indian's legal and spiritual status. Living in settled villages with proper government would help the natives behave like civilized beings, asserted Fr. Juan de la Plaza, S.J., in his summation of written *memoriales* presented to the assembled clergy at the 1585 Provincial Council. In one of these *memoriales*, Fr. Pedro de Feria, the erudite compiler of the Zapotec-language catechism who now served as bishop of Chiapas, expressed his vexation with the poor progress he had seen in thirty years of missionary experience and affirmed the centrality of *congregación* in the struggle to keep the indigenous population on the correct spiritual path. Feria attributed the natives' continual backsliding into idolatry to their weak character and intellectual inferiority; "the Indians, because they are of a low and imperfect nature, have to be ruled and governed more through fear than through love."[15]

As the Dominicans expanded their reach throughout Oaxaca, *congregación* was a fundamental tool for religious instruction, particularly in mountainous areas where the native population was widely dispersed. Such practices extended as far as the Isthmus, to judge from a 1563 petition from the nearby Chontal community of Tequisistlán requesting the selection of a different site for their recently congregated village and the forcible return of those who fled at the prospect of the first relocation.

Even the Tehuantepec polity, with its urban *cabecera* and network of subject pueblos, underwent some population restructuring in the first decades of colonial rule, according to the response of native informants to one of the 1580 Relación Geográfica questions. Discussing the various factors thought to be responsible for the decline in longevity, they cited certain lifestyle changes like drinking chocolate and Spanish wine, eating too much, and, surprisingly, working less hard than they did under native rule, but gave the principal cause as having been "gathered together in this *cabecera* and its other subject villages," when formerly they lived dispersed among the valleys and countryside.[16]

Archaeological indicators of this precolumbian settlement dispersal abound along the Río de los Perros floodplain, where my earlier surface survey found the Late Postclassic period of Zapotec domination to be characterized by the proliferation of many small sites under 1 ha in area extent. The twenty-four sites of this type presumably were the homesteads of single or joint families, socially and politically affiliated to the four or five named villages in the 100 km^2 area.[17] Outside the pueblo of Chihuitán, where several widely scattered sites were identified in 1972, my more recent field studies located an additional late precolumbian rural hamlet that illustrates the early colonial aggregation process. Situated on a far slope of the Cerro Tablón, this Late Postclassic settlement on the grounds of Rancho Santa Cruz was abandoned shortly after the conquest and its population joined together with neighboring household groups to form a slightly larger settlement of 2 to 3 ha, where pottery styles indicate occupation continued into the seventeenth century.[18]

Not all settlements were subject to early relocation, however, and Tehuantepec's larger barrios may have held on to their original neighborhoods longer than others. At the Panteón Antiguo site, signs of repair at the deteriorated administrative building or "*palacio*" and the occasional occurrence of European-style pottery confirm that some group of people continued to live there for a period of time. By the second half of the sixteenth century, however, consolidating the dispersed urban barrio populations became an ecclesiastical priority.

Baltasar de San Miguel counted forty-nine barrios of Tehuantepec and twenty-seven subject villages in 1550. Thirty years later, the indigenous-style map accompanying the province's 1580 Relación Geográfica continued to portray urban Tehuantepec as an aggregate of spatially separate barrios, but now only thirty-one such entities were depicted (see Fig. 2.1. Relación Geográfica map). Dramatic population losses in the intervening

FIG. 4.3. Excavations at Rancho Santa Cruz. Cerro Tablón is in the background.

period, acknowledged in the Relación, seem to have had a disproportionate impact on the urban center. If the 1580 count of 1,200 urban *vecinos* is reliable, some 60 percent of the town's inhabitants had died or relocated since 1550, compared to a loss perhaps as little as 23 percent in the countryside (based on two thousand tributaries). Such a decline would have decimated any small barrios, which disappeared as their dwindling populations were relocated into the remaining thirty-one barrios.

By the seventeenth century, however, settlement relocation had become more intrusive and far-reaching for a number of the Isthmus's pueblos and *estancias*, as a late sixteenth-century royal order to congregate dispersed groups of Indians into sizable communities was implemented in targeted areas throughout New Spain.[19] In the Tehuantepec province, this program primarily involved the transplanting of rural hamlets and villages to new, more accessible sites, although the disappearance of seven smaller pueblos located on the 1580 Relación Geográfica map may date to this period as well (see Map 3.1). Two Huave communities, San Dionisio del Mar (Tepeguazontlan) and San Francisco del Mar (Ixtaltepec del Mar), were moved from sites on remote barrier beaches to places more easily reached by horseback, and the Zapotec community of Ixtepec was relocated from its mountainous setting to the floodplain of the Rió de los Perros. The Zoque community of Tlapanatepec appears to have experienced a similar relocation even before this period, for in their 1583 attempt to block a requested land grant, Tlapanatepec community leaders threatened to move back to the former site.[20]

Responding to continued population losses, such practices paradoxically instituted unhealthy living conditions that further hastened morbidity. In more mountainous parts of Oaxaca, the *congregaciónes* created widespread social dislocation and misery, compelling the Dominican provincial Fr. Antonio de la Serna to write the Viceroy in 1601 complaining that the whole ecclesiastical province was threatened with ruination because of these resettlement policies and the suffering that ensued. Fr. Antonio's outrage was sympathetically reported in Burgoa's 1670 biographical chronicle of the order, *Palestra historial*, in which he lambasted the Spanish *hacendados* and the secular clergy who served their interests, treating the Indians "like chess pieces."[21]

The Battle for Indigenous Souls and Services

The Dominican complaint against the implementation of a policy the Order had long supported must be viewed within the context of a simmering political conflict between the religious orders of New Spain and the colony's diocesan administrative structure. With the bishops appealing to the king for proclamations affirming their authority over the monasteries and the friars appealing to the pope for privileges of autonomy, this conflict rekindled itself repeatedly in the closing decades of the sixteenth century. Held against the Dominicans and other religious orders was the rapidity with which they had accumulated vast revenue-producing holdings, the income of which should have been subject to the same tithes that the agents of the Crown were charged with collecting. Civil initiatives of the 1570s attempted to curb the religious orders' accumulation of wealth and property, but the faithful continued to cede lucrative holdings to the friars without reserving the mandated tithes, two-ninths of which were earmarked for secular purposes.

In the 1640s the reformist Juan de Palafox y Mendoza launched a concentrated campaign during his brief tenure as archbishop of New Spain to control the lavish excesses of public ritual and limit the properties held by religious orders, the support of which Palafox found exacted too great a burden on the long-suffering natives.[22] The campaign was met with resistance and noncompliance, as were his earlier attempts as Tlaxcala's bishop to transfer most of that province's indigenous communities from the control of the religious orders or "regular" clergy to that of "secular" or parish priests. The religious orders felt themselves to be under siege, and they responded aggressively to all encroachments on their authority and autonomy. In an impassioned defense of their disobedience, Lic. Luís de la Palma y Freites wrote on behalf of the Dominicans, Franciscans, and Augustinians that the removal of these *doctrinas* had caused the native communities tremendous hardships. The secular clerics were ignorant of native languages, refused to travel outside the parish center to visit the sick and administer sacraments, charged excessive fees for burials, marriages, and baptisms, and forbade the celebration of popular fiestas to the communities' patron saints. Worse still, the priests squandered community resources to build parish churches, and then handed over native laborers to the *estancieros* for twelve to fifteen days of work against their will.[23]

In Oaxaca the policies of unsympathetic bishops had affected the Dominicans in many aspects of religious life, from the examination of candidates for ministerial vacancies to the wholesale transfer of native parishes to the administration of secular clergy. As the province's *juez conservador*, Fr. Diego Ybañes eloquently argued in a pamphlet published around1631 favoring the retention of Oaxaca's native parishes by the Dominicans, what value would it be to convert the Indians without conserving their faith through the maintenance of preaching, confession, and the administration of the sacraments?[24] By implication, only the friars, with their proficiency in Zapotec and other indigenous languages and their willingness to serve in the poorest and most remote pueblos, where they had gained the loyalty and trust of the natives, were qualified for the task.

It was a claim that may not have had perfect resonance among native communities, which in the Tehuantepec province, as elsewhere within the diocese, had reason to fault the actual practices of the Dominican friars in their midst. Two Tehuantepec complaints that reached as far as the General Indian Court in Mexico City illustrate how thoroughly that trust between the friars and the indigenous population might be breached. The community of Ixtaltepec successfully petitioned the viceroy in 1590 to order the *religiosos* not to make a yearly accounting of the properties and income which belonged to its *hospital* or community fund, a duty which was the formal responsibility of the civil authorities and the practice of which by the friars they considered to be extremely meddlesome. To guard against the implied danger to the fund's 115 pesos, Viceroy Velasco ordered that a box with three keys, one each for the *alcalde mayor*, the convent, and the fund's *mayordomo*, be established, and that the use of the income be restricted to the fund's chartered care of the poor.[25]

More direct and personal charges of abuse of authority were levied against Fr. Francisco Estevan, vicar of the pueblo of Zanatepec, the largest Zoque-speaking community in the province. In 1635 the viceroy ordered that the Dominican provincial of Oaxaca take remedial action against this friar, who had been accused by the local cacique, Don Pablo de Mendoza, of stealing the property he was to inherit from his deceased father and charging excessive fees for performing the sacraments and other religious services. A price list for the vicar's services was supplied in the complaint. For the festival of La Purificación de Nuestra Señora, he charged the community 1½ *pesos* and 2 *mantas* plus a standard 2 *reales* from each of its eighty-five tributaries. To hear confessions during Lent, the fee was 3 *pesos*, 2 *reales*, and 4 *mantas*, with 2 *reales* charged per tributary; an additional 2 *reales* was assessed per tributary for Thursday, Friday, and Sunday services during Holy Week beyond the fee of 2 *pesos*, 6 *reales*, and 4 *mantas*.

Similar fees paid from community funds rounded out the rest of the religious calendar, giving the vicar a cash income of over 236 *pesos*, nearly three times the tribute paid by the community to the Crown. If, as seems likely, Fr. Francisco charged additional fees for administering the sacraments at baptisms, marriages, and death beds, that income was even higher. Meanwhile he demanded weekly provisions of corn (20 *fanegas*), fruit and butter (60 *pesos* worth), turkeys (three), and Spanish hens (ten), in addition to substantial personal services. All the boys and girls of the village were occupied either tending the more than five hundred poultry belonging to the vicar or in collecting honey and performing other tasks in his service without pay, so that they had no time to help their parents.[26] That this level of extortion could occur at the hands of a member of a religious order well known for its extreme practices of penitence and poverty only one hundred years earlier is symptomatic of an era in which moral principle was severely compromised by personal greed. That the Dominican provincial had previously been so ineffective in responding to native complaints and controlling the excesses of this one individual suggests how well founded Palafox's impetus to ecclesiastical reform may have been.

Profiteering at the expense of native people had become a widespread reality in the maturing colony. Its lure reached into all sectors of Spanish religious and civil authority, but the opportunities for coercive entrepreneurial activities were broadest among the Crown-appointed administrators, the *corregidores* and *alcaldes mayores*. In 1637 Fr. Geronymo Moreno, who had served as provincial of the Oaxaca Dominicans and was himself gifted in Zapotec, published a treatise titled *Reglas ciertas y precisamente necessarias para juezes, y ministros de justicia de las Indias, y para sus Confessores*, a book quickly rushed to print by the Holy Office because of what the censors perceived to be the urgent need for such a work in the prevailing climate of greed and injustice toward the Indians.[27] In his book Moreno spelled out twenty-eight rules of proper comportment for Spanish officials and their confessors, so that the officials would no longer be able to plead ignorance as a justification for their misdeeds, nor their priests fail to question them about such actions and require appropriate repentance and restitution.

Moreno distinguished a multitude of unjust practices commonplace among Spanish officials in their dealings with natives, a list that can be distilled into several larger issues: abuses committed in the exercise of official duties, the purchase of lands and ranches in their jurisdictions, and the abuse of *repartimiento* privileges that had been reassigned to the *corregidores* and *alcaldes mayores* by viceregal decree in 1624. Many of the specific practices had been outlawed by the king or his viceroy and already carried the weight of criminal penalty. Moreno followed a Thomist argument in asserting that just laws enacted by secular kings carried a further moral obligation of conscience, and that the infraction of such laws concerning serious issues of human justice was properly to be considered a mortal sin.

> To the extent that there are human laws, imposed by secular authorities, that compel the conscience: and leaving aside those opinions surrounding the determination of how human law acquires the force to make mortal blame, and referring the reader to St. Thomas (I, 2, q. 96) and his interpreters, I say that the force of the law to [lay] mortal blame arises not from the words of the mandate or prohibition, but rather from the gravity of the matter that is mandated or prohibited in the law.[28]

Not only were these infractions sins on the part of the officials who perpetrated them, but all those who aided and abetted their practice were complicit as well, from those who actively encouraged and assisted officials in unjust activities to those who, including native *principales*, failed to speak against these wrongdoings. The strongest admonitions were directed toward ecclesiastics who permitted these practices by failing to seek out the truth and by absolving their powerful penitents in the confession booth. According to Moreno, the confessor likewise committed a mortal sin by this failure and, should he further fail to make the penitent restore damages to the victims of his abuse, he must himself make restitution.[29]

The widespread misdeeds Moreno condemned have been amply documented in the history of Spain's flawed struggle to extend administrative control and dispense justice over its broad and ethnically diverse American domain. A frequent complaint in New Spain was that officials abused their native charges by demanding unpaid personal services or extorted excessive gifts and fines during too-frequent *visitas* among the communities of their jurisdictions. With witnesses easily bribed to ensure a favorable *residencia* for the corrupt official, there were few effective sanctions in place to control the misconduct of a distant bureaucrat or the blind eye he turned to gambling and more serious criminal infractions. Nearly half of Moreno's list of sinful acts is a litany of abuses resulting from the practice of permitting *corregidores* to engage in the *repartimiento de efectos,* or the required production of goods for sale and its inverse, the obligatory purchase of manufactured commodities. Rationalized as a vehicle for integrating reluctant native producers and consumers into the colonial market economy, the *repartimiento* system quickly became a cash cow for administrators. Ultimately, lucrative *repartimientos* became both the sole objective for would-be officeholders, who counted on reaping quick profits for themselves and their financial backers, and an outrageous, indirect source of income for the cash-strapped royal treasury, which tacitly acknowledged the profiteering opportunities inherent in the provincial offices it sold to these entrepreneurs.[30]

Even at this early stage of *corregidor* involvement, Moreno's rules of conduct reveal the outline of a system designed solely to squeeze more goods and labor out of hard-pressed Indian tributaries. Money was advanced to communities for the production of agricultural commodities that could not be grown on their lands or which no longer were being grown in the quantities anticipated by the loans, forcing natives to travel to producing pueblos to buy the same, usually at a higher price than the *corregidor* contracted to pay for the crop at harvest. Sometimes these goods were procured from the *corregidor*'s own agents or *criados* at inflated prices. The Dominican underscored the particular hardships these practices inflicted on native women, whom he acknowledged as holding an independent economic role in their families. Households were forced to produce cotton thread, but paid only for the value of the raw cotton and not the time women spent spinning it. Women were obliged to weave as many as three lengths of cloth per year, often of larger than normal size and for a price less than market rates, in order to meet household *repartimiento* demands. This obligation, Moreno claimed, interfered with their ability to clothe their own children and to produce some additional *mantas* that might be sold to meet household expenses.

While other abuses of the *repartimiento* system may have been cruel and exploitative, the forced sale of merchandise by the *corregidor* or his agents could have a ludicrous side, as Moreno pointed out in a telling anecdote. In 1612 on a visit to one community in the Oaxaca diocese, the friar noticed that the natives were all wearing short cloaks of different colors. The cloaks, he was told, were fashioned from *repartimientos* of half-yard lengths of thin cloth which each household was forced to buy from their *justicia mayor*, and they could not think of any other use for it. If it were not bad enough that natives were forced to buy goods from these officials at excessively high prices, it was all the worse that the goods in question so frequently were unwanted, like the required purchase of spurs by one who has no horse.[31]

Moreno dismissed any arguments that such sales were a good means of drawing natives into an expanding colonial market economy, since the monopolistic practices of the officials actually interfered with free trade. Moreover, the contracts with native *principales* upon which such interchanges rested were themselves invalid. Because of the tremendous fear in which natives regarded these officials, fear of being jailed or whipped or fined impossible amounts, the contracts were not freely entered into and therefore not legal. The only way in which a Spanish official might legitimately engage in commerce with the natives of his jurisdiction, according to Moreno, was to permit the free movement of other merchants within his jurisdiction and open a shop in his home to which those who wished to buy or sell could come of their own volition. Just how little impact Moreno's appeal to moral and juridical principles had on these merchandising monopolies can be seen almost twenty years later, when the survivors of Tehuantepec's mid-century epidemic complained to the viceroy that their *alcalde mayor* insisted on collecting *repartimiento* debts due from those who had died on the machetes, candle wax, cloth, manufactured items, and other goods which he had distributed among the province's population.[32]

Excessive production quotas in the *repartimiento* system had, Moreno observed, turned the land sterile and unproductive, as Indians resorted to destroying the crops which were the object of official greed. Moreno pointed to Tehuantepec in particular, where he knew of several pueblos in which large harvests of 400 *cargas* of cacao had once been the norm, but there was no longer even a sign of the once extensive cacao groves, the trees all having been cut by the Indians to avoid meeting the excessive demands of the *alcalde mayor.* Similar destructive protests had befallen other of Oaxaca's more visible and profitable commodities, among them silk production in the Mixteca from introduced mulberry trees and the highly profitable silkworms that fed upon them or the dye industry based on the native cochineal insect that grew on the cultivated nopal cactus.[33]

Much as the publication of Moreno's *Reglas ciertas* was applauded by the highest religious and civil authorities in New Spain, there is little to suggest that the moral arguments and sanctions he espoused had a significant impact on official conduct, which in fact grew more egregious in Tehuantepec during the latter half of the seventeenth century. Although it is unclear how widely his book was disseminated, at least the copy presently in the collection of the John Carter Brown Library shows evidence of serious study. Besides the eighteenth-century signature of one owner and embossed stamp of another, the book has several marginal annotations referring to laws and decrees relevant to Moreno's arguments that were promulgated in 1694.

The Growth of the Spanish Ranching Economy

However distasteful the reality of these commercial monopolies may have been, the Crown had few qualms about promoting another form of Spanish economic activity, the raising of European livestock. Old World animals were first introduced to the Isthmus by Hernán Cortés, who began his Isthmus ranching with a large pig-raising venture in Xalapa within a few years of the fall of Tenochtitlan.[34] During the five-year period that he served as *alcalde mayor* for Cortés and *mayordomo* of the Tehuantepec estates, Juan de Toledo greatly expanded the livestock enterprise, which he managed in equal partnership with the Marqués, buying breeding stock and establishing *estancias* as needed throughout the province. At his 1543 end-of-term *residencia*, Toledo cited the following inventory made just two months earlier: 13,007 sheep, 700 cattle, and 185 horses remained on the ranches; 4,272 burros had been sold in Guatemala or other parts and another 700 sent to the Chicapa mines; an additional 131 young bulls, 14 horses, and 12 mares had been traded in Guatemala from the livestock increase, not counting the quantity mentioned earlier that the haciendas sold in tithe for the church.[35]

Twenty-five years later, when Hernán Cortés's son and heir Martín was accused of participating in a seditious conspiracy and the Marquesado properties were temporarily sequestered by the Crown, the Tehuantepec ranches had been consolidated into seven major estates. According to the government inventory of 1570, three of these *estancias*, Guazontlán, Huilotepec, and Las Salinas, which were located between Tehuantepec and the barrier beach forming the Laguna Superior, were primarily dedicated to raising some eight thousand sheep and goats (*ganado menor*) during the previous two years. The remaining four, La Ventosa, Tarifa, Las Cruces, and Almoloya, were extensive *ganado mayor* or large livestock ranches situated in more sparsely occupied areas of the eastern coastal plain and nearby foothills. La Ventosa was by far the largest, with 20,000 head of cattle destined for the Oaxaca market and a small horse and donkey breeding enterprise as well. The smallest ranch, Almoloya, held 1,300 young bulls and 250 colts. Altogether 30,591 large animals were raised on the Tehuantepec Haciendas Marquesanas, 96 percent of which were cattle.[36]

Just four years later, when the Marquesado properties had been returned to Cortés, the hacienda account records suggest some losses in the Tehuantepec ranches. Two sheep *estancias* were vacant, and the total number of *ganado menor* was under five thousand head. Horses, mules, and donkeys had increased slightly by a couple of hundred animals, but no accounting of the number of cattle could be given by Juan Ximénez, the haciendas' *mayordomo*, who may not have been able to hold a roundup during the sequestration of the vast herds that ranged freely on the estancia lands.[37] In the 1580s the second Marqués del Valle began an attempt to expand and invigorate the ranches, petitioning the Crown for fourteen additional *estancia* grants in the Isthmus between 1582 and 1597 and purchasing or receiving as a gift two other *ganado mayor* ranches. Just how entrepreneurial this expansion was is indicated by the *Instrucción* issued in 1588 to the newly appointed Tehuantepec *mayordomo*, Juan Pérez de Ocariz, by the Marquesado's governor, Francisco de

Quintana Dueñas. Lamenting the disrepair into which the haciendas had fallen, Quintana set explicit instructions for their restoration and for their profitable incorporation into the efficiently integrated Marquesado enterprises.[38]

This renewed attention from the estate governor may have been prompted in part by competition the Marqués faced in a rapidly developing Isthmus ranching boom. A scattering of petitions for *estancia* grants in the province had reached the Audiencia in Mexico City each decade since the removal of Tehuantepec from the Marquesado in 1563. The rate at which such *mercedes* were requested accelerated dramatically in the early 1580s and did not decline again until the turn of the century, when a shortage of remaining vacant land helped bring the ranching expansion to a close. Over two hundred grants were made to Spaniards for diverse agricultural purposes, including both *caballerías* for growing maize and *estancias de ganado menor* on which sheep and goats could be raised. The majority of these petitions were to establish ranches for larger livestock, sometimes horses, mules, and asses, but principally cattle. By 1609 a formal stockmen's association or *mesta* had formed and the province became one of the major *mesta* centers of New Spain.[39]

Cattle breeding was particularly well suited to the arid climate and expansive terrain of the southern Isthmus. The distinctiveness of the region's economic focus is highlighted by comparing the pattern of Tehuantepec's land grants with that of two other regions closely linked to the Marquesado del Valle. In Morelos Cheryl English Martin's review of viceregal *mercedes* during the peak years of Tehuantepec's ranching boom shows only three *sitios de ganado mayor*, while fourteen sheep ranches were granted. Livestock ranching generally was a less significant economic activity for Spanish settlers in this region, where the warm climate and irrigable lands made sugarcane production a primary focus and eighty-four and a half agricultural *caballerías* were ceded. In the Oaxaca Valley, only twenty-five *mercedes* in total were granted to Spaniards in the sixteenth and early seventeenth centuries, thirteen of these transpiring between 1580 and 1620. The nine *estancia* grants made on valley lands during these forty years were about evenly divided between large and small animal requests, according to data presented by Taylor, who found that the primary growth of successful Spanish estates in the valley occurred later in the seventeenth century. The mixed agricultural base of these later estates required fertile, well-watered soils, typically obtained on lands purchased from the native nobility.[40] Spanish *vecinos* of Ante-

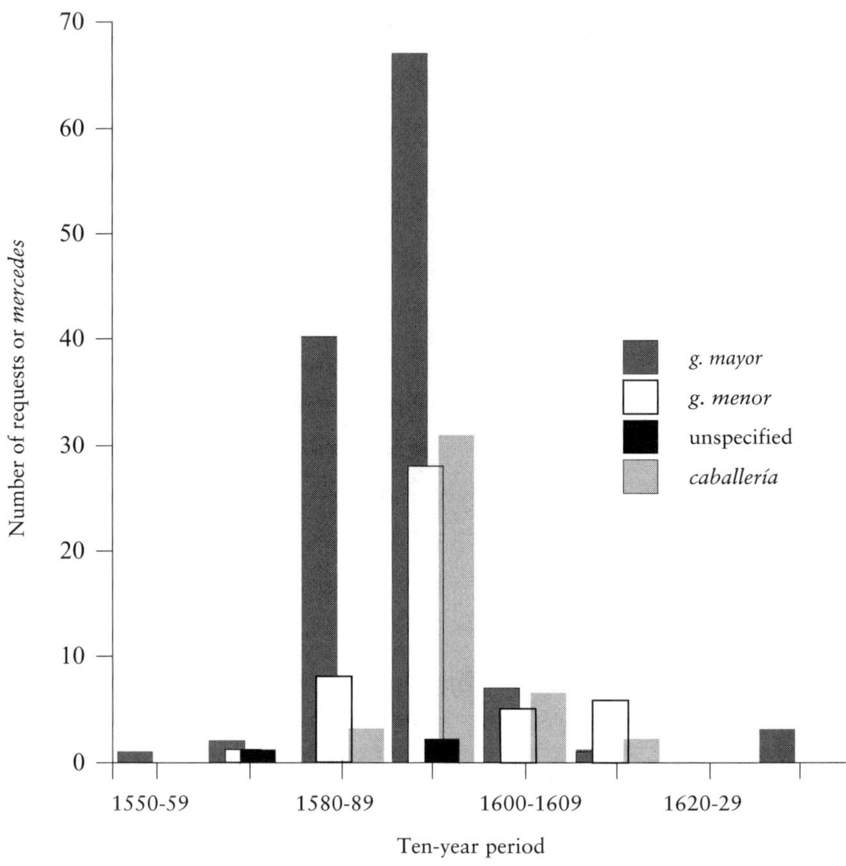

FIG. 4.4. Land requests and grants awarded to nonnatives during the Tehuantepec ranching boom. Source: Archivo General de la Nación Mercedes, various.

quera, the valley's principal town, are occasionally named among the recipients of *ganado mayor* grants in nearby Tehuantepec, however, where broad expanses of untilled land in sparsely populated areas of the coastal plain were more promising for raising livestock.

Cattle ranching held many attractions for the growing number of Spaniards trying to make a living in the maturing colonial economy. There were multiple and complimentary economic uses for the animals, whose meat fed nearby markets and whose tanned hides and tallow might be shipped great distances. Being a rancher was a socially acceptable occupation in a culture that disdained the manual labor of agriculture. More important, ranching was not dependent upon a large labor force, an especially significant factor toward the end of the sixteenth century, when native populations throughout New Spain had declined drastically. As Lesley Bird Simpson pointed out many years ago, the rise of ranching and the demise of the native population were closely correlated phenomena. Civil and ecclesiastical *congregaciones* drew the once scattered native communities into aggregated towns and villages, where their reduced numbers might more easily be administered, leaving large rural areas vacant (*tierras baldías* or *despobladas*) and, according to colonial law, free for the Crown to transfer to new landowners.[41]

Their numbers initially unchecked by accustomed parasites and predators, the Old World animals flourished at first in their New World setting and multiplied at phenomenal rates during the ranching boom. Passing through the Tehuantepec province in 1629, the Jesuit priest Bernabé Cobo estimated that sheep herds alone on the outskirts of the *cabecera* numbered over 50,000 animals.[42] Cattle thrived particularly well on the eastern coastal plain's mix of thorn forest and palm-studded grasslands, where four extensive ranches belonging to the Dominican convent in Oaxaca were said to have a value of 33,000 pesos in 1597.[43] Even in relatively low population areas, such vast estates could have too much success, as free-ranging cattle strayed well beyond the ranch boundaries and onto native farms between what should have been yearly round-ups or *sacas*, when herds were counted, branded, and excess individuals culled. In 1592 the Audiencia responded to a request by the convent to slaughter an unusually large number of stray cattle from its Chicapa and La Isla *estancias*, which had been the source of great aggravation to the communities of Amatitlán, Ixhuatlán, Ostutla, Niltepec, and Zanatepec. Testifying as one who had been in the cattle business all his life, the creole witness Cristóbal Ruíz de Andrada concurred that indeed the Dominicans had too many cattle on these ranches. Rather than get rid of the animals altogether, he maintained that they should be branded and three to four thousand head slaughtered to reduce the damage to native fields.[44]

Ruíz de Andrada indeed did have considerable ranching experience, coming from one of the longest-settled Spanish families in Tehuantepec. His father, Diego Ruíz de Andrada, had served twice as *mayordomo* of the Marquesado's Tehuantepec haciendas, once in the early 1550s, when the primary labor force for the *estancias* was a small number of indigenous slaves and day laborers, and again in the1580s, when the task of resurrecting the deteriorated ranches seems to have been beyond his abilities. A well-established and well-regarded *vecino* of Tehuantepec, Diego Ruíz de Andrada was one of three informants called upon by the *alcalde mayor* from the town's twenty-five resident Spaniards to provide information for the 1580 Relación Geográfica.[45]

Diego himself received two *ganado mayor* grants from the Crown, according to available documentation. An early *merced* gave him title in 1567 to some lands near the community of Ixtaltepec along the present-day Río de los Perros, then known as the Zopiloapa River. Not more than a few years before his death, Diego made a second formal petition in 1595 for some property near the pueblo of Ixtepec. The most substantial of his properties may have been an *estancia* apparently given him by the Marqués prior to the province's return to Crown authority.[46] The ranch known as Buenavista was sold back to the Marqués in 1587, along with its houses, corrals, other buildings, and more than sixty cattle, for a grand sum of 600 pesos. It was a transfer made under some duress, for the Marquesado's governor, Francisco Quintana Dueñas, accepted the property in settlement of debts or obligations Ruíz de Andrada had incurred as *mayordomo* during this period.[47] Although it took some legal maneuvering to force the Ruíz de Andrada family to actually relinquish control of the transferred Buenavista animals and pasturage, the Marquesado maintained friendly ties over the years, hiring Cristóbal as a part-time overseer on occasion, selling livestock to family members in other years.[48]

Besides Cristóbal, who received grants for two *estancias de ganado mayor*, both his brother Antonio and his own son Melchor received grants in the 1590s; Antonio also requested a *caballería* for planting, as did their sister, Inés Alonso Rondon. Their combined holdings made the Ruíz de Andrada family one of the largest Spanish landowners in the province outside of the Marquesado and the Dominican convent of Oaxaca. A closer look at the history of one of these holdings, the Ixtaltepec ranch that came to be known as Zopiloapa, shows how difficult it was, even for well-entrenched families like this one, to hold on to such properties and squeeze a profit from them. Despite the apparent attractiveness of the coastal plain habitat for introduced livestock, Isthmian ranchers would find their dreams of easy wealth broken by the reality of periodic drought and disease, native resistance, and intermittent financial crisis as the seventeenth century unfolded.

In the early 1600s, when the ranch was populated by houses and corrals with 400 breed mares, Antonio was ceded all rights to the Zopiloapa property by his two surviving siblings and nephew. Antonio's daughter,

Ana Ruíz de Andrada, later brought this ranch as dowry into her marriage with Juan de Zepeda, another *vecino* of Tehuantepec. Moving to Antequera after her husband's death, Ana sold the Zopiloapa property in 1636 for the sum of 2,300 pesos to Gerónimo de Espinosa, who had been the Marquesado-appointed *alcalde mayor* of Xalapa. By this time the property included title to another Ixtaltepec ranch, an *estancia de ganado menor*, originally given in *merced* to the native community in 1585, but subsequently transferred to Spanish hands before it was purchased for 200 pesos by Ana's husband. By 1643 Espinosa was using both ranches to raise *ganado mayor*, and nearly half its value (1,000 pesos) was held in mortgage by the Cofradía de Santa Vera Cruz. The only identifiable member of the Ruíz de Andrada family still possessing land in the province according to the 1643 *composición de tierras* petition was the widow María Ruíz de Andrada, who held a single *caballería* of land on which she raised corn.[49]

As summarized by Lolita Gutiérrez Brockington in her study of the Tehuantepec Haciendas Marquesanas, Gerónimo de Espinosa's saga provides a close view of how difficult livestock management might be in the waning years of the province's ranching boom. After serving as second-in-charge on the Cuernavaca sugar plantations for a few years, Espinosa was sent to Tehuantepec to run the Marquesado's haciendas as *mayordomo* in 1604. He kept this title until the estate shifted to a system of leasing out the ranches in 1620, at which time Espinosa became the first lessee and retained his position as Marqués-appointed *alcalde mayor* of Xalapa, holding both roles until a few years prior to his purchase of the Zopiloapa hacienda. Testimony presented during his 1621 *visita* recounted many of the obstacles Tehuantepec ranchers faced. Periodic droughts inflicted the heaviest toll on livestock in this hot, semiarid climate; one witness estimated that four hundred Marquesado mares had died during a recent drought, and he personally had counted twenty-seven dead mares along the road on one day. Livestock diseases that eventually found their way to the New World added to the mortality, as did commonplace complications from the primitive castration process that could itself result in losses as great as 70 percent of gelded mules. Adding to these hazards of serious drought and disease, all the Spanish ranchers complained of persistent problems from native raiders, who would even slaughter calves in their corrals.[50]

With so many perils affecting its success, it is no wonder that the longevity of a ranching enterprise was strongly associated with its herd size and degree of capitalization. A large herd might more easily sustain a sudden increase in mortality if its core breeding stock survived to multiply in more propitious years. While most individual landowners were dependent upon income from their livestock to support themselves and to pay mortgage interest, ranch owners with significant financial backing could endure a stretch of bad weather or epidemic disease and even replenish depleted stock and finance needed repairs to corrals and other ranch structures. Indeed Brockington's calculations for annual income from livestock and animal byproduct sales minus operating expenses on the Tehuantepec Haciendas Marquesanas show the Isthmus ranching venture running a slight deficit for five of the eight years between 1589 and 1619 for which she has comparative data. These figures do not, however, include the principal function of the Tehuantepec haciendas, the export of animals and hides to other parts of the estate, where they made a steady contribution to the Marquesado's overall profitability.[51]

It is no surprise then that the number of private landowners that survived the boom years was quite small by 1643, if the *memoria* recorded by the *alcalde mayor* at the time is an accurate reflection of "the ranches and livestock and lands for cultivating maize that exist in the province of Tehuantepec and the manner in which their owners presently possess them."[52] Only seventeen individuals were identified by name in the original document which was included in a later petition to reduce the fee demanded by the Crown for formal land titles. Not all these private landowners were Spaniards, for one of the original parties included the indigenous heirs of a cacique. The following year an eighteenth landowner, a Chihuitán noblewoman and her mulatto slave husband, petitioned to have their names added to the *composición.* Most individuals claimed to hold either one or two properties, more rarely three. Many of the *estancias* were unpopulated, but those that were active usually supported only two to four hundred head of cattle, horses or mules; a couple were used to raise goats and sheep. Just four of the active livestock ranches were free of any mortgage encumbrance, and mortgages to the convent, its *cofradía* or *capellanía* ranged in size from 200 to 5,000 pesos. Gerónimo de Espinosa, with his two *estancias* mortgaged for 1,000 pesos and populated by one thousand head of mares, burros, and cattle, was one of the more successful private ranchers.

The *alcalde mayor* acknowledged that the properties "most numerous and of greatest worth" were those held in the province by the Marqués del Valle, the Convento de Santo Domingo de Oaxaca, and the three mule-breeding ranches owned by the Tehuantepec convent.

The once profitable Haciendas Marquesanas, however, had already begun to slide into serious decline under the tenants who replaced the pre-1621 *mayordomo* managers. Without the steady influx of outside capital, even the capable Espinosa had trouble making timely rent payments, though his problems were apparently not so severe as to preclude his leasing the ranches yet again in the late 1640s. Lessees who followed Espinosa mismanaged the estates to the point of near ruin, leaving neglected animals to die or slaughtering them indiscriminately for local meat markets.[53] Fr. Francisco de Burgoa, observing the Marquesado haciendas at mid-century, lamented their deteriorated state, which he attributed to bad administration and inattention on the part of these Xalapa officials who, having purchased their titles, could not be bothered with overseeing the estate properties.

The friar avoided turning a critical eye to the management of the Santo Domingo convent's *estancias*. Instead he praised the expansiveness of the holdings, which stretched for 22 leagues to the Guatemala border, hosting a large mule-breeding ranch and several cattle ranches. The principal cattle ranch was known as "La Mezquitana," after its founder Don Matías de la Mezquita, a prominent Spanish *vecino* of Tehuantepec, who had left the ranch with its slaves and furnishings to the convent in support of a *capellanía*.[54] Pious testamentary acts such as de la Mezquita's donation may have been the final disposition of many of Tehuantepec's private land grants, once the grand ambitions of the province's short-lived ranching boom gave way to the practical concerns of surviving financially in an arid and unpredictable climate.

What had endured by the mid-seventeenth century were several corporately owned estates controlling a considerable amount of land, particularly in the eastern half of the coastal plain, and a small number of privately owned ranches, endowed with sufficient pasturage and year-round water to ensure the viability of the enterprise, even if actual ranch ownership might change hands from time to time. Problems of management and problems of drought and disease continued to affect the short-term profitability of Isthmus ranching throughout the colonial period and beyond. But the long-term impact of the ranching boom on the province's native population was profound, transforming the regional ecology and economy and spawning community dislocations and territorial conflicts that permanently realigned social relationships. Fully understanding the nature of these changes requires a closer look at the indigenous economy during this period.

Native Communities and the Colonial Economy

Fr. Burgoa held the Zapotecs of Tehuantepec in high regard, referring to the 1,500 families living in the town in the second half of the seventeenth century as "a highly capable, Hispanicized, politically organized, liberal, hard-working people" ("toda gente hábil, ladinos, políticos, liberales, trabajadores").[55] Their traditional long-distance commercial ventures had expanded through the addition of Old World pack animals. Some natives from the town operated teams of forty to fifty mules, traveling as far as Mexico City, Veracruz, Chiapas, and Guatemala to trade in cacao, assorted textiles, soap, machetes, axes, tackle for horses and mules, and plows and plow blades. According to the admiring cleric, they looked for all the world like Spaniards when met on the road, dressed from head to toe in Western clothes and seated on fine saddles on good mules. Although Burgoa failed to mention these items when listing the manufactured items sought by Zapotec traders, such distinctive coastal products as fish, shrimp, and salt must have been among the goods carried from Tehuantepec to distant locales, as they had been since precolumbian times.

The town itself was split into two sectors occupying either side of the river, with the larger eastern side divided into eighteen barrios, each with its own chapel and choir. Irrigated fields in the eastern sector supported extensive fruit orchards, the produce of which included melons, watermelons, papayas, and sugarcane, all introduced Old World domesticates, among other notable delicacies. Supporting his characterization of Tehuantepec's "opulence," the cleric found the daily repast with its two-hour break from the tropical sun equal to holiday fare because of the diverse offerings of salted meat, fresh fish, birds, turtle and iguana eggs, fruits, shrimp, and other foods that graced the local table.

Not much had changed in the local economy since it was last chronicled in some detail nearly a hundred years before for the 1580 Relación Geográfica by the *alcalde mayor*, Juan de Torres.[56] Aridity and poor soils limited agricultural production on most of the coastal plain, but irrigation from the Tehuantepec River was used to support crops then as later. In addition to major plantings of maize, beans, chiles, and cotton, most pueblos also grew a mixture of native and introduced plants. Torres's informants gave the *alcalde mayor* a list of crops that included avocados, sweet potatoes, *chico zapote*, native plums, Spanish melons, native and Spanish squashes, introduced bananas, oranges, lemons, and limes, and the South American domesticate, pineapple. Three or four of the villages were able to grow cacao. As was noted earlier, drinking chocolate on a regular basis and imbibing Spanish wine were, in the opinion of the *relación* informants, major contributors to the poor health and shortened life expectancy of the native population, along with a diet that now included beef and mutton.

Taking a more moderate view of the industriousness of the indigenous population than did the effusive Burgoa, Torres considered the Zapotecs to be of average intelligence, with some hard workers and some idlers among them. Most made their living as farmers, but some individuals specialized in hunting or fishing and still others were merchants. Much buying and selling went on in the town and provincial markets, where Zapotec women sold cotton clothing and the men traded cacao, fish, shrimp, salt, cotton, and cloth. Some journeyed as far as Soconusco to trade these local products, a business which supported most of the twenty-five Spanish *vecinos* living in the town in 1580 as well. Much of the fish and shrimp came from the Huave communities, for whom these lagoon resources were their primary sustenance. Salt production, however, was still a patrimonial privilege for Don Juan Cortés's heir, Don Felipe, whose rightful possession of two lagoons producing exceptionally fine quality salt had been confirmed by royal decree, as the *alcalde mayor* acknowledged: "These two lagoons belong to Don Felipe Cortés, native cacique of this province and legitimate son of Don Juan Cortés, who was its lord in ancient times and possessed them as his own and had a royal decree [for their ownership]."[57]

The growth of ranching among the Zapotec elite

Although Don Juan's children had finally managed to secure their claim to the Tehuantepec *salinas* after the long battles their mother, Doña Magdalena de Zúñiga, had waged so determinedly on their behalf ten years before, even she appears not to have been able to resurrect the patrimonial privilege of *terrazguero* labor, upon which the productivity of privately held lands had traditionally rested. In an ironic turn of events, it may have been the widow's own readiness to appeal to Spanish authority that contributed to the loss of this important patrimonial privilege. Soon after the province was restored to royal authority in 1563, Viceroy Don Luís de Velasco ordered Juan de Salinas, the first Crown-appointed *alcalde mayor,* to investigate the status of these serfs upon the complaint from the deceased cacique's minor children that they and other workers were failing to perform their customary labor services. The resulting investigation led Salinas to dismiss all *terrazguero* exemptions from Tehuantepec's tribute lists, not just those claimed by the cacique's heirs but those claimed by other *principales* as well.[58] Faced with the forfeiture of compulsory labor to farm patrimonial fields and service their household, the widow complained bitterly to her sympathetic friends among the Dominican friars that her children were destroyed and without any remedy.[59] However heartfelt her concern about their financial setback, as adults Doña Magdalena's children were able to find other means of support in the new economy, as did other members of Tehuantepec's hereditary elite.

There is no further reference to *terrazgueros* in the Isthmus documentary record, although Taylor reports that entire barrios of *terrazguero* laborers were retained by certain Oaxaca Valley caciques until the eighteenth century.[60] That the particular *cacicazgos* involved—Cuilapan, Etla, and Oaxaca—were all part of the Marqués del Valle's Cuatro Villas jurisdiction and thus paid tribute to the Marqués and not to the Crown may help explain the surprisingly late survival of this indigenous social category. As Gibson pointed out many years ago, the exemption of large numbers of people from tribute obligations to either Spanish *encomenderos* or the royal treasury was a luxury that the colonial state could afford only as long as large numbers of tribute-paying Indians survived. As the Indian population declined precipitously in the Valley of Mexico, all indigenous social groups below the status of *macehual* or commoner were absorbed into the category of tribute payers by the end of the sixteenth century.[61] Very likely the Tehuantepec province's transfer from Marquesado to Crown authority in 1563 only hastened the inevitable loss of this source of labor service for the Zapotec elite.

Not surprisingly then, ranching emerged toward the end of the sixteenth-century demographic collapse as a viable economic activity for those members of the indigenous nobility who could neither pay nor coerce the laboring force needed to farm private lands. This activity seems to be different both in scale and in kind from the more limited but eager interest in raising horses and mules that Tehuantepec elites had expressed in the early half of the sixteenth century. In the decades shortly after the Spanish conquest, riding on horseback, like other forms of emulating the attire and material possessions of the conquerors, conferred a degree of added prestige to the Tehuantepec cacique and *principales*. Even in the 1550s, there were clear economic benefits to be realized from native livestock ownership; on one profitable occasion, the cacique Don Juan was paid 45½ pesos by the *alcalde mayor* Juan Ximénez for thirteen horses he needed at Utlatepec on the headwaters of the Coatzalcoalcos River, where they were used to transport cable and other materials to the Marquesado's Isthmus shipyard.[62]

No personal motivations are disclosed in the formal language of later ranching *mercedes*, but the number and identity of individual Zapotecs who sought and procured rights to keep livestock during the Spanish ranching boom suggest the powerful economic appeal these ranches held for the indigenous nobility.[63] References to existing *estancias* as well as actual petitions or viceregal grants for livestock raising name thirty-four individual native ranchers in the province, with an additional petitioner each in Xalapa and the Chontal community of Tequisistlán. Though a handful of petitions were registered in 1555 (associated with the *visita* of Dr. Quesada) or scattered across the intervening decades, the majority of private native *estancias* (forty-eight) were requested during the Spanish ranching boom years (1580–1620). By contrast, the much larger population of nobles living in the Oaxaca Valley requested only twenty-seven livestock *estancia* permits during the entire early colonial period.[64]

Native petitions peaked during the ranching boom, like those of their Spanish neighbors, but the kind of land use favored by the indigenous elite differed sharply. Only one native request was for agricultural lands or *caballerías*. Five individuals are known to have been engaged in large-animal raising, but the majority of these ranches were established well be-

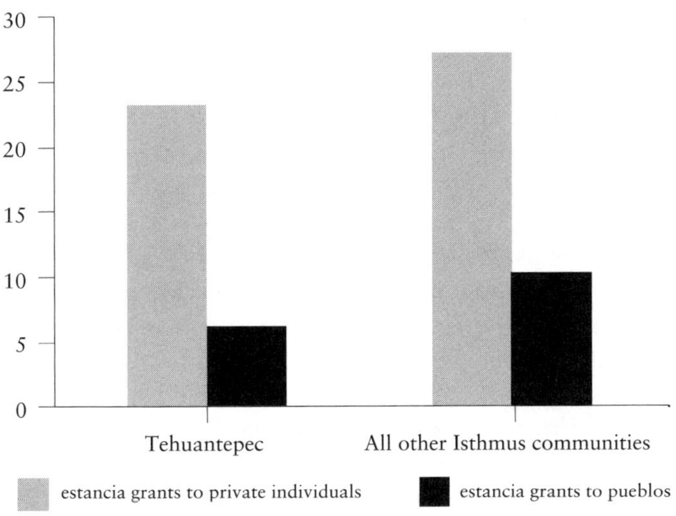

FIG. 4.5. Land requests and grants awarded to natives during the Tehuantepec ranching boom years, 1580–1620. Source: Archivo General de la Nación Mercedes, various.

fore the ranching boom, since their only documentation in the *mercedes* records is as neighboring *estancias* to other requested land grants. The vast majority of private individuals specifically asked for permits to raise sheep or goats, and forty-four such requests are documented. Viceregal policies discouraged native involvement in large-animal husbandry at this time, but sheep and goats may also have been more compatible with traditional social and economic activities, being easily tended by juvenile members of an extended family household and easily marketed for local consumption.[65] For the many individual petitioners who requested livestock permits on lands which already belonged to them, a preference for smaller animals with less destructive impact on neighboring *milpas* would have been the more sensitive land use choice. Not everyone was so responsive. Mateo López, the cacique of the Huave community of Ocelotlán, finally provoked the communities of Ocelotlán and Guazontlán to bring suit against him before the Audiencia on account of his long-standing disregard for the damage caused by his small mule-breeding ranch, where he kept too many animals (more than one hundred mares and burros) on too small a parcel of land.[66] His example and Burgoa's reference to Tehuantepec's expensively attired Zapotec muleteers are reminders that an important segment of the native livestock industry was invested in *ganado mayor* production as well, an importance unacknowledged in land grant records.

With one or two ambiguous exceptions, all the would-be ranchers identified themselves as members of the nobility in their communities (*principal* or cacique); most assumed the honorific title of *don* or *doña*, which remained restricted to the highest nobility at the time of the ranching boom. Nobles from almost half (fourteen) of the thirty-one communities listed in 1580 as subject to the *villa* of Tehuantepec are included in the sample, but only six pueblos had more than one petitioner. As might be expected from its position as the seat of Zapotec political power and as the largest community in the province, Tehuantepec itself had many more elite ranchers (twelve) during this boom than the largest number (three) recorded among the five other communities with more than one petitioner. Tehuantepec's native grantees included two women who petitioned jointly with a spouse or male kinsman.

Little descriptive social information accompanies the formal language of the land grants or their petitions in most cases. In the absence of specific data, the erratic Spanish naming practices used by the sixteenth-century Isthmus Zapotec make shared surnames unreliable clues to kinship relationships. For the Tehuantepec elite, fortunately, information from other sources can sometimes help identify the social position of the petitioner. During the ranching boom years, several individuals close to the royal family requested *estancia* permits. These affiliations ranged from that of Don Juan Cortés's last *mayordomo* and onetime governor of the town, Don Francisco Vásquez, who petitioned twice for his own *sitios de ganado menor*, to the cacique's son, Don Juan Bautista de Avendaño, who received a single 1589 permit for a small animal *estancia* in the vicinity of the piedmont town of Chiltepec.[67] There are no documented land grant petitions from the two other legitimate heirs, Don Juan Bautista's older brother, Don Felipe Cortés, and his sister, Doña Juana de Zúñiga, but this omission does not preclude their participation in the booming livestock industry through properties inherited earlier from their father.

These three children, by virtue of their birth in a church-consecrated marriage between a middle-aged Don Juan Cortés and his young bride, Doña Magdalena de Zúñiga, were recognized as the legitimate heirs under Spanish law. The cacique had other children by previous marriages or liaisons, but early death or documentary omission has left only one of these offspring more fully identified in sixteenth-century records. Don Francisco de Figueroa was described by the former vicar of Tehuantepec, Fr. Bernardo de Santa María, as the illegitimate son of Don Juan, who journeyed to Mexico City in the 1560s on behalf of Doña Magdalena in her suit to reclaim the patrimonial properties inherited by her children. In 1598 Figueroa sought formal rights to a sheep *estancia* on some vacant lands two leagues from the pueblo of Chihuitán and one league from neighboring Ixtepec. Community leaders voiced no objection to either the ranch's location or its petitioner, who was described as a Chihuitán native, when the *alcalde mayor* presented Figueroa's request before the assembled congregants on a feast day, Sunday, July 9. In support of his petition, Figueroa brought four Spanish witnesses, all *vecinos* of Tehuantepec, as well as six native men, three from Chihuitán and three from neighboring Ixtepec. The well-orchestrated proceedings concluded without incident, and Figueroa joined the growing ranks of Zapotec pastoralists.[68]

Chihuitán's close ties with the Tehuantepec royal family are demonstrated through other elite participants in the ranching boom. Fabian de Zárate, who identified himself as a nephew of Don Felipe Cortés and *principal* of the villa of Tehuantepec, began acquiring livestock *estancia* permits in 1601 and by 1614 had requested seven *sitios* in the vicinity of Chihuitán on which he could raise sheep or goats. Two of these were specified as being on his own land and a third was located on lands that had belonged to his uncle. Apparently Zárate inherited more than some vacant land from his uncle, for in 1613, five years after his request for an *estancia* on Don Felipe Cortés's former property, Zárate referred to himself as cacique of the villa of Tehuantepec. One year later his final *estancia* petition claimed that he was cacique of the community of Chihuitán.[69]

Assuming that Zárate's claim to the Tehuantepec *cacicazgo* was legitimate, an issue to be pursued later, his example underscores the value of livestock breeding to the Isthmus's indigenous elite. Struggling to maintain a superior social and economic status after the withdrawal of *terrazguero* labor and the closure of traditional income revenues from native offices, Tehuantepec's noble households seized on the ranching venture for their economic support with surprising alacrity. By the time the indigenous *pintura* known as the Mapa de Huilotepec was drawn—probably no later than the 1580s, during the later years of Don Felipe's tenure as cacique—the establishment of sheepfolds and other forms of livestock breeding on private lands had begun (see Fig. 2.3).

With horizontal lines dividing the area between the town of Tehuantepec and the sea into parcels of variable width, the long strip of painted cloth appears to have served as a kind of royal deed map. Its genealogical portrayal of the four Tehuantepec kings and their principal advisors in the map's upper section implicitly sanctions the territorial division pictured below. Crudely drawn codex-style figures representing individual native owners are seated on the parcels, each with his Zapotec name written in Latin letters following the noble title *xoana* (*joana*). Nearer to the sea, U-shaped corral representations make their appearance on some of these same private lands, with the name and sometimes the image of the owner depicted as well. A unique document for the Tehuantepec province, the Mapa de Huilotepec is an important native record of late sixteenth-century private land titles that, much like the slightly earlier Lienzo de Guevea discussed in Chapter 1, legitimized its territorial claims by reference to the authority of the Tehuantepec royal family. In the case of the Guevea map, however, the territorial claim is one made by the community as a whole, not one based on individual privilege.

The impact of the colonial political economy on community life

The deference of subordinate communities to the political authority of conquest kings and their descendants that both these sixteenth-century Isthmus cadastral maps symbolize would eventually become another casualty of Spanish colonial rule. Throughout New Spain the often convoluted relationships between autonomous polities and their outlying dependencies were pushed aside in the sixteenth century by Spanish bureaucrats who could neither comprehend their underlying cultural premises nor condone their interference with the efficient delivery of tribute to Crown coffers.[70] That Tehuantepec had retained and perhaps even enhanced the traditional dependency of its subject villages and hamlets on the town where Don Juan Cortés resided may have had as much to do with the force of this ruler's persona as it did with the special political arrangements forged under the Marquesado. When Don Juan died and the province reverted to Crown control in 1563, Tehuantepec's territorial structures succumbed to the centripetal pressures at work elsewhere.

Where once-subject rural communities, like the urban barrios, were administered by a community headman and tribute collector, newly autonomous Zapotec villages now sought to install their own elected Spanish-style *cabildos* or town councils, as did the pueblo of Ixtaltepec as early as 1568.[71] Cacique status, once reserved for traditionally invested lords of independent towns, now was widely claimed by former *principales* among Tehuantepec's villages and hamlets by the end of the sixteenth century. Ixtaltepec again provides a prototype for what the *estancia* request records suggest was a common pattern. In 1590 Don Martín López claimed to be cacique of the village in his successful request for a sheep or goat *estancia*, and the following year petitioned to have a man and woman assigned to him for personal service as befitted his elevated status.[72]

With independence came not only freedom from labor obligations to the former *cabecera* but a newfound juridical right to take actions and inaugurate institutions of benefit to the community as a whole.[73] In Ixtaltepec, as was seen earlier in the community's 1590 complaint about meddlesome clerics, the pueblo took advantage of introduced Spanish institutions to create a village fund, out of which the poor could be cared for and other community needs addressed. One of the more widely documented new forms of collective action was the establishment of community livestock *estancias*. Here Ixtaltepec appears to have been especially diligent in its search for new means of providing community funds, seeking or receiving grants for three separate sites for raising small animals "for the benefit of its community" between 1584 and 1590.[74] Unlike private owners whose income may have been dependent upon the sale of excess animals each year, community-held *estancias* must have functioned more as a living bank, perhaps providing animals for special community feasts but otherwise maintaining assets in reserve until specific needs, from covering tribute shortfalls to supporting religious festivals, dictated their sale.[75]

Other Isthmian communities known to have founded collective *estancias* during the ranching boom years include Zanatepec and Ostutla in the Zoque-speaking area, and Tehuantepec, Chihuitán, Teotitlán, Tlacotepec, and Comitán in the Zapotec-speaking western sector of the coastal plain. As was the case with private Indian *estancias*, the town of Tehuantepec also had the largest number of community ranches, recording six out of the sixteen *ganado menor* grants. In light of the frequency and broad distribution of private native ranches among communities and ethnic groups in the province, the relatively small number of community *estancias* is somewhat puzzling. By comparison, in the Oaxaca Valley, where elite requests for ranching permits lagged considerably behind those registered in the Tehuantepec province, some twenty-two sheep *estancias* were granted to native communities in this same period, out of the thirty-three Oaxaca community ranches granted during the early colonial period as a whole.[76]

Perhaps a substantial number of Isthmus communities simply failed to seek formal permission for livestock *sitios* they had already established within their community boundaries, or perhaps the economic and social utility attributed to them was illusory. After all, not every *estancia* granted to a native community maintained its original purpose or even its community ownership. One of the Ixtaltepec sheep ranches was alleged to have been sold to a Spaniard not long after it was granted. Moreover, the sale of an *estancia* seems to have facilitated its conversion to uses other than those stipulated in the original grant, though such a practice could lead to the rescinding of the grant. This was the allegation made by a Spanish resident of Tehuantepec in a rare complaint against native landowners brought before the Audiencia in 1636. Juan del Moral, who was himself the owner of several large animal *estancias* in the province, argued that the indigenous proprietors of a neighboring *sitio de ganado menor* were keeping a large number of cattle on the land, which was too small to support them. Its original purpose as a goat pasture would have been fine, he asserted in his petition, but the community of Tehuantepec, which received the original grant, sold the *estancia* to some other, unnamed native owners, and neither party would respond to his complaints about the damages these cattle inflicted on his lands.[77]

After the ranching boom passed, religious sodalities provided another means of collective ownership of herds for at least some groups. In the course of its early eighteenth-century boundary dispute with a neighboring Dominican hacienda, the Huave community of San Francisco del Mar presented a 1655 viceregal decree authorizing the possession of certain lands for raising cattle and mules in the name of its Cofradía de Nuestra Señora del Rosario.[78] Conversely, in 1736 the Zapotec pueblo of Juchitán (Xochitlan) sought to have community lands restored to it that the vicar of Tehuantepec had falsely appropriated for small livestock *cofradías* some twenty years before. Maintaining that these community lands had been the sole basis for cultivating cacao and other fruit that was used to support the church and to pay tribute shortfalls and other expenses, the community leaders denied that the pueblo had ever had such religious confraternities.[79] Whether or not this particular mechanism of establishing community holdings was widely used in the province, the San Francisco del Mar case signals the multiple avenues by which native communities might enter into ranching.

It was suggested earlier that maintaining small herds of sheep and goats may have functioned as a reserve bank for communities, allowing them to sell or use animals as needed for collective purposes. Unfortunately the documentary sources give little insight into the actual disposition of such livestock by native pueblos. Even turning to the much more extensively documented hacienda records of the Marquesado for clues as to regional marketing patterns for *ganado menor* does not make the picture much clearer. The Marquesado ranches raised almost six thousand head of sheep and goats during the early seventeenth century, but wool production from the much more numerous sheep was the major income the estate derived from these animals in 1609 and 1610. Fetching less than a peso each, the live animals were sold only in small numbers to different private parties. Indeed, the *mayordomo* Gerónimo de Espinosa complained that the climate was too hot for sheep and not worth the bother. As a consequence, most of the herds were leased out to other individuals by 1612.[80]

Only beef cattle were sold from Marquesado stocks to the Tehuantepec butcher shop during the ranching boom, and it is unlikely that any native-owned goats or sheep were marketed in such a formal setting, though animals may have been sold "on the hoof" in the native market or *tianguiz*, as it was known commonly by its Nahuatl name. Very likely the meat was consumed throughout the colonial period, as it is today on the Isthmus, at special occasions that required a feast in which many people would be served from a dish prepared from the entire animal. While it is not yet possible to say with certainty what mechanisms were used to buy and sell from native producers, be they private individuals or corporate entities, there is archaeological confirmation for the consumption of small livestock within at least one colonial Zapotec community, the Rancho Santa Cruz site situated at the foot of Cerro Tablón on the upper floodplain of the Río Perros.

The impact of *congregación* on the province's dispersed Late Postclassic settlement patterns was discussed briefly at the beginning of this chapter, when the Rancho Santa Cruz site was introduced as an example of the early colonial aggregation of small hamlets surrounding the community of Chihuitán. Responding to civil or ecclesiastical pressures, the small protohistoric settlement was relocated to a more easily accessed side of the mountain. No standing structures remain at the site; the perishable materials out of which house walls were formed have long disappeared, and indeed the community itself had vanished well before the 1801 *merced* that permitted construction of a sugar refinery at the ranch. Agricultural plowing has disturbed most of the subsurface deposits, but the remains of pottery and other artifacts are widely scattered across the surface of the site, which must at one time have been home to a few hundred people.

European-style trade wares represented in this artifact collection are known to have been manufactured between the late sixteenth and mid-eighteenth centuries, but changes in local pottery styles suggest the site was abandoned by the end of the seventeenth century. Our 1990 test excavations located one area with better preservation of household debris, and there the identification of two distinct stratigraphic levels and postholes associated with former building locations provided a better context for the material remains we recovered.[81]

What is preserved in the archaeological record under normal conditions is, of course, only a small, more durable fraction of the material goods that circulated originally in the community. Seldom are these remains found in the places where they actually were used; rather the archaeological record is in large part formed by refuse contexts where, having been eaten or broken or worn out, the material goods were finally discarded. Even this incomplete inventory of what was in use has advantages over the highly formalized documentary record of the time, with its emphasis on nonnative and elite affairs. Archaeological garbage is much more democratic and potentially more representative, accruing from all social sectors and providing direct testimony as to what did happen, rather than what powerful individuals would like to represent as happening.

In this context, the excavated sample of animal bones discarded at Rancho Santa Cruz supports what the record of *estancia* grants and permits only suggests. As expected, the native residents of this hamlet continued to hunt and trap the same animals that had traditionally been utilized by Tehuantepec's inhabitants for thousands of years before the Spaniards' arrival—deer, rabbit, armadillo, and iguana dominate the terrestrial game animals found in excavation. Indeed, oral testimony from local witnesses called to assess the impact of Don Francisco de Figueroa's requested Chihuitán sheep ranch indicates that hunting was a regular activity (the witnesses testified that they were familiar with Figueroa's property because they frequently passed by it when out hunting).

Added to this archaeological evidence for the consumption of a diverse array of wild game is a small faunal sample from introduced domesticated animals. A single cattle rib, one calcaneous from a sheep or goat, and several bone fragments attributed to some unidentifiable species of *ganado mayor* together comprise just 4 percent of the excavated faunal collection. Although these data confirm that introduced domesticates were eaten by natives, their low numbers and incomplete representation of an individual carcass are not consistent with the regular consumption of livestock by a small household or extended family unit. The model proposed above in which festive, perhaps community-wide, occasions prompted the butchering of one or more animals and the communal sharing of the prepared meat is a more reasonable interpretation of the archaeological record.[82]

Other classes of artifacts recovered at Rancho Santa Cruz illuminate just how widespread was the community's acceptance of introduced European-style goods. House construction patterns underwent some significant changes, with the adoption of fired clay bricks and roof tiles indicated by scattered finds at the site, albeit in such low numbers as to suggest either their limited construction use or their reuse at another site

FIG. 4.6. Iron nails from Rancho Santa Cruz excavations.

after the settlement was abandoned. A handful of forged iron artifacts was found in excavation, mostly nails and cotter pins used to frame and hinge wooden house doors, but a single iron fishhook suggests that the community sought other practical applications of the new metal technology.[83] The absence of knives or brush-cutting implements from this archaeological collection may be due just to its small size. Regional elites had acquired the right to carry swords along with the other trappings of Spanish dress as early as the mid-sixteenth century, and the more practical and presently indispensable machete was one of the items distributed through *repartimiento* monopolies by the Tehuantepec *alcaldes mayores*. On the other hand, stone tools made from locally available chert and quartzite are abundant in the sample and continued to be used by the site's occupants even after obsidian blades, long an item of long-distance trade in prehistoric Mesoamerica and present in the lower stratigraphic level, became harder to obtain in the colonial economy. The site's occupants may simply have found that familiar materials, easily obtained and quickly modified to produce a sharp working edge, were good enough for most utilitarian purposes.

Such practical considerations cannot be enlisted to account for the presence of one class of imported goods found at Rancho Santa Cruz, that of wheel-made, glazed European-style pottery. The sample of these broken trade vessels (just under two hundred potsherds) is a small percentage of the entire body of pottery collected, but its broad distribution across the site indicates that most households acquired at least one or two tin-glazed vessels. About 80 percent of the Chihuitán sample matches what colonial ceramic specialists Florence and Robert Lister identify as common-grade majolica wares. These are Spanish-tradition wares produced cheaply in or near Mexico City. Although they imitated more costly Puebla majolica styles, their potters economized by using low tin-content glazes and less expensive paint mixtures, which were applied in careless designs. Apparently manufactured just for local markets, the commonwares were never intended to travel long distances, and most historical archaeologists have assumed that their primary consumers were Spaniards and some high-status natives from towns around the Valley of Mexico.[84]

Thus the presence of commonware majolica pottery at Rancho Santa Cruz defies conventional wisdom. We should not find this pottery so far from Mexico City, yet similar goods have been recovered in archaeological excavations in the Mixteca Alta and the Soconusco, although sometimes in contexts that might more likely be associated with high social or

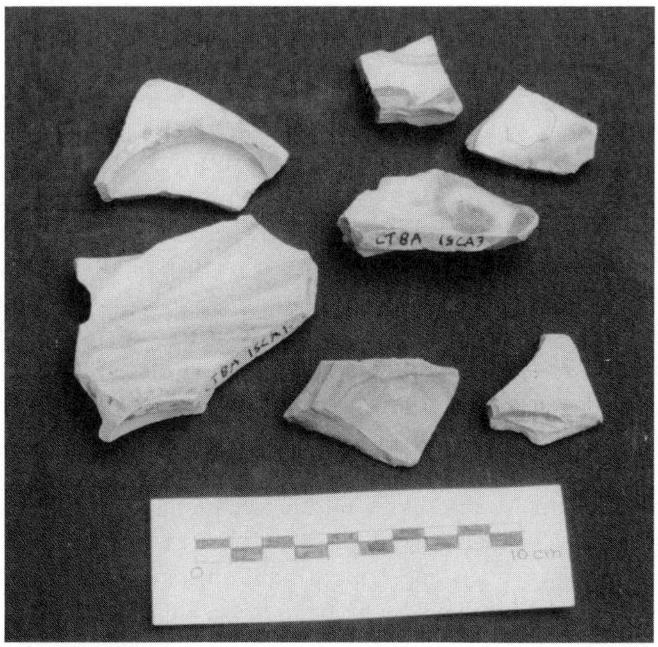

FIG. 4.7. Majolica pottery sherds from Rancho Santa Cruz excavations.

economic status among these sites' indigenous occupants.[85] Certainly it should not be associated with what otherwise would seem to be a native hamlet of mixed agriculturalists. Was there perhaps something special about the Rancho Santa Cruz community? Without comparative archaeological materials from other rural sites in the province, the degree to which this site is representative of moderate-status, early colonial Zapotec communities is difficult to assess. Although documentary sources make it clear that members of the Zapotec nobility were strongly connected to Chihuitán during this period, there is nothing that would suggest that the few hundred individuals inhabiting the Rancho Santa Cruz site were all accorded high status. Indeed, the kind and quality of non-European dietary and artifactual materials found at the site parallel the typical archaeological remains associated with moderate-status households in earlier Isthmian prehistory. What would be missing from such households in Late Postclassic times is the kind of fancy trade wares represented by the Spanish-style majolica. Their precolumbian equivalent, a type of polychrome-painted pottery, is not normally found outside of elite domestic and mortuary contexts in the Isthmus.

What the archaeology of the Rancho Santa Cruz community does affirm is that some rural villagers did reasonably well economically during the late sixteenth and seventeenth centuries. Subsistence practices appear not to have been much threatened by Spanish land acquisition, since the relocated community maintained a strategic location with respect to irrigable lands still watered today by canals fed from the river and nearby springs. Game resources remained diverse and newly available cattle, goats, and sheep added another protein source to the diet. Residents of the pueblo produced enough surplus of some as-yet-unknown commodity beyond that which was needed to meet their tribute obligations in order to procure both some utilitarian metal tools and imported pottery, with the latter valued more for its prestige than for its intrinsic usefulness.

Because Spanish traders in Oaxaca rarely included such fragile and heavy commodities as pottery among the goods they transported from village to village, it is more likely that native merchants, like those Burgoa describes plying their wares between Tehuantepec and distant markets, were the purveyors of these exotic items, just as their Mesoamerican forebears had traded prestigious pottery from one precolumbian city to another. Ronald Spores found documentary support for the inclusion of pottery among the commodities that colonial-period Mixtec traders transported to distant localities by pack train.[86] Though Burgoa does not list pottery along with cloth, soap, and assorted iron implements customarily traded by the Zapotec merchants, it would not be an unreasonable conjecture to add it to their inventory. Such a native-based distribution system, operating largely outside the formal purview of Spanish bureaucrats and tax collectors, clearly was responsible for trade in another type of colonial pottery identified in these collections. Ubiquitous at Rancho Santa Cruz, the finely made local pottery I have designated Tablón Orange was traded at least as far as the Soconusco region of the Chiapas coast. There Janine Gasco has found sherds of this type in archaeological collections from the early colonial site of Ocelocalco.[87]

The Isthmus potters modeled the reddish yellow-firing local clay used for Tablón Orange by hand into traditional shapes to form bowls, tortilla griddles, jars, and strainers before applying a thin clay slip or wash and painted decoration to the most visible surface of the more durable forms. The painted designs follow typical precolumbian decorative canons that, seen outside of its excavated colonial-period context, might easily assign this pottery a prehistoric manufacturing date, were it not such an abrupt departure from the region's Postclassic conventions. Compared to the Oaxaca Valley–related pottery that dominated most protohistoric kitchens in Tehuantepec, Tablón Orange would have been an exuberant stylistic change from the plain gray ware bowls and jars of the past, which were unadorned apart from the slender mold-made tripod feet that supported them. Although the gray ware continued in use, albeit without the serpent-head support decorations thought by the missionaries to harbor pagan ideas, the new painted pottery was widely popular. Straight or wavy lines were typically used to draw horizontal bands of red and white and sometimes black paint around the lip or corner of the bowls, forming larger panels often filled with the commonplace Mesoamerican "stepped-fret" design. Over time the width of the painted line became thinner and, by the second phase of colonial occupation at Rancho Santa Cruz, was applied more fluidly in circles, zigzags, and other geometric motifs, no longer confined to bounded fields of decoration. The longevity and resiliency of Tablón Orange on the Isthmus are evidenced by further modifications to the ware found in late eighteenth- or nineteenth-century contexts in Tehuantepec, long after the Rancho Santa Cruz site was abandoned, when the design elements were further simplified and the controlled use of the potter's wheel became the norm.

FIG. 4.8. Colonial-period Tablón Orange pottery; potsherds from a dish with modified stepped-fret design, collected in excavations at Rancho Santa Cruz.

It would be disingenuous to assume that the apparent prosperity of Rancho Santa Cruz was universally shared among the province's indigenous communities, or that the century and a half or so represented by the site's archaeological record was without economic hardship or social conflict for its inhabitants. While the eruption of long-simmering political and cultural tensions in the second half of the seventeenth century is the main focus of the chapter that follows, it is appropriate here to briefly outline some of the sources of tension that colonial economic pressures engendered for the Isthmus's native population.

As suggested previously, problems of livestock multiplying beyond the capacity of *estancia* boundaries to contain them were present almost from the beginning of the Marquesado's ranching ventures, leading to several viceregal edicts in 1554 and 1555 that removed troublesome cattle from community lands or gave license to native communities to shoot stray animals with bows and arrows.[88] During the ranching boom years, community complaints multiplied along with the livestock *mercedes*. The nine disputes from this period registered before the Audiencia very likely represent only the most flagrant and difficult cases, as communities may have been disposed to take matters into their own hands before resorting to the expensive and formidable process of appealing to the General Indian Court for relief. Such efforts are at the heart of Spanish complaints like the one voiced by witnesses called in the *residencia* of Gerónimo de

Espinoso, *mayordomo* of the Haciendas Marquesanas, who claimed that natives went so far as to slaughter animals in their corrals.

There are differences in the impact of introduced European livestock on the region's three major indigenous ethnic groups, differences resulting from a mix of microenvironmental, demographic, and underlying sociocultural variables. Fr. Burgoa was impressed by the ingenuity and cowpunching skills shown by the Zoque-speaking communities of the eastern side of the coastal plain. In a region where the overabundance of feral cattle and horses made it nearly impossible to grow corn, the Zoque economy had reoriented itself to take advantage of these four-legged pests. Even the Zoque woman, Burgoa recounted, was accustomed to saddling up her mare and roaming the bush in search of a wild cow, which, having roped it by the tail, she dragged back to her homestead and slaughtered to feed her family. The Zoque man, he continued, was such an experienced *vaquero* that he could domesticate feral cattle. Squadrons of men on horseback went out at night in search of the animals, which they would rope and corral for three or four months until even the fiercest of bulls had been tamed.[89]

Such an accommodation had come with a heavy price for the Zoque. The more humid vegetation of the eastern coastal plain and piedmont zone was a favored location for the establishment of Spanish ranches. Here the largest cattle and mule-breeding ranches of the Marquesado—La Ventosa, Buenavista, Chivela, Almoloya, and Las Cruces—were founded and the Dominican convent of Oaxaca had its immense *estancia* holdings. Over fifty additional grants were made to nonnatives in the Zoque towns of Tlapanatepec, Zanatepec, Ostutla, Niltepec (formerly Nectepec), Chimalapa, Ixhuatán (Ixhuatlán), and Aztatlán. Never very populous, these communities experienced the combined impact of high mortality from epidemic disease and competition for agricultural space with often disastrous results. Three of these Zoque villages (Ostutla, Ixhuatán, and Aztatlán) and an additional hamlet without known *estancia* grants (Tonaltepec) were abandoned during the seventeenth century, with their residents compelled to leave either because of a mandatory civil *congregación* or because life in that locality had become unendurable.

It is not the case that the rush to acquire ranch lands proceeded unobstructed in this prime sector. For nearly four years at the beginning of the ranching boom (1583–86), the community of Tlapanatepec successfully challenged efforts by one Spaniard, Juan Díaz Roldan, a resident of Antequera with important Tehuantepec friends, to receive viceregal permission to establish two *sitios de ganado mayor*, even though the sites were over two leagues distance from the Zoque village and far from any *milpas* farmed by its inhabitants. The community was resolute in its insistence that the only kind of ranching that Díaz might engage in without harm to their interests was raising goats or sheep or breeding mules. So opposed were they to the installation of cattle anywhere near their village, as the petitioner in fact desired, that the governor and *principales* of the village threatened to uproot themselves and return to the former site of their community, from which it appears they had been removed in some early *congregación*. The Spanish witnesses who testified in this case grumbled that the Zoque *principales* merely wanted to reserve this choice site for their own ranches. When the community leader Don Estevan Cortés did receive a ranch permit a few years later, however, it was in a different location and only for goats and sheep, which the community would have conceded to the Spanish petitioner as well.[90]

Such protests were not always effectual as the ranching boom rushed on. Repeated complaints by the natives of Zanatepec, Niltepec, and Ostutla about the number of cattle, mules, and horses kept by Alonso López finally led to an order from the viceroy that the Spaniard be deprived of his title as *teniente* to the *alcalde mayor* of Tehuantepec in 1619. The Zoque communities complained that for years they had not been able to plant corn or chiles or other crops because these animals destroyed their plantings, and López intimidated them with the threat of punishing them whenever they raised objections. This intimidation had even caused one of their communities, Ixhuatán, to be abandoned. All its inhabitants moved to Juquipilas in Chiapas and the remaining communities vowed that they would do the same if this problem were not corrected. Evidently the punishment was ineffectual, for another complaint was lodged against López for the excessive number of cattle he kept on his *estancia* in 1626, this time by the Dominican convent of Oaxaca, which owned a neighboring ranch.[91] Unable to provide enough people to repopulate Ixhuatán, the native officials of its *cabecera* Zanatepec transferred their rights to the Huave community of San Francisco del Mar in 1650.[92] Thus while some Zoque communities appeared to maintain themselves through the colonial period, in fact a significant population loss and even some shift of community ethnicity underlies the toponym continuity.

The lack of sufficient secure agricultural land, adjustment to the *vaquero* lifestyle, and social dislocations within the small Zoque communities may have pushed a number of these people to seek employment as day laborers on the province's haciendas. Unfortunately, detailed wage records are available just for the Marquesado *estancias*, and, as Brockington points out in her study of Marquesado labor practices, the manner in which native labor was enlisted and employed varied considerably during the long life of the haciendas. Least disruptive to indigenous social structure, though extremely exploitative, were the *repartimiento* labor drafts by which powerful ranchers could turn to the local *alcalde mayor* for requisitions of unskilled laborers to fulfill specific tasks. Payment for this labor went to the community officials—*alguaciles* or *calpixques*—who organized the workforce. By the time of the ranching boom, the Marquesado *estancias* primarily had need for short-term (*extraordinario*) allotments of draft labor in constructing temporary corrals and gateways used in the roundup of livestock for the *saca*, and these individuals presumably were drawn from Tehuantepec communities unidentified in the accounting records. The payment of 46 pesos, 5 *tomines* for such services in 1609 represents a sizable labor force assembled for the short duration of the *saca*; typical wages for native *vaqueros* that same year were 2 pesos per month. Draft allotments of native shepherds operated year-round (*ordinario*) and involved only men from Xalapa, which was still administered by the Marquesado.[93]

A much smaller number of natives worked as paid day laborers for the Marquesado, and their names were all recorded individually in hacienda account records. In 1609 there were nine full-time and twelve part-time native adults and boys who worked as *vaqueros* or shepherds according to Espinosa's records, a number and proportion that varied slightly from year to year during his administration. Seven of the part-time workers ought to be considered seasonal workers, since they were employed for six months or less. Despite some attrition, most of these seasonal and year-round workers were reemployed from year to year. Unfortunately the ledger summaries do not often give the community affiliation of native employees. An occasional surname like that of Miguel Mixe is suggestive of ethnic affiliation (Mixe and Zoque were interchangeable labels in the seventeenth century), but just the proximity of most of the Marquesado *estancias* to Zoque territory makes it likely that the majority of these day laborers, especially those who worked only seasonally, came from surrounding Zoque communities. Indeed the singling out of one seasonal employee, the *vaquero* Juan Pérez, who was identified as coming from the Zapotec town of Suchitlán (Xochitlan or Juchitán), indicates that this particular community affiliation was unusual.[94]

The small number of indigenous employees on the relatively well-managed Marquesado *estancias* makes it clear that wage labor for Spanish enterprises could not have been a substantial drain on the labor force of any Zapotec-speaking community. Nonetheless, ranch-hand jobs did provide an escape valve for those who could not support themselves in traditional agricultural and artisanal pursuits, as well as for those who may have chafed under the constraints of mutual obligation that structured Zapotec community life. The very existence of this outside pull may have encouraged communities to draw the boundaries more sharply between themselves and the external world.

Concluding Observations

Studies of the indigenous peoples of colonial-period Spanish America have shifted direction over the last few decades from a focus on their victimization at the hands of colonial institutions and individuals to a perspective that emphasizes native cultural resiliency in the face of profound social, demographic, and economic change. That historiographic trend is particularly apparent in regions of Mesoamerica like the Oaxaca Valley, the Mixteca Alta, and the northern Yucatán Peninsula, where complex precolumbian polities enjoyed relatively high population densities prior to European contact and where the Spanish presence was less intense numerically and economically than it was closer to the capital.[95] Certainly Tehuantepec, or at least its Zapotec-speaking western half, conforms to this pattern. Despite profound population losses and disruptive settlement changes, most Isthmus communities approached the midpoint of the colonial period physically intact and economically adjusted to their transformed landscape. Armed with a new set of legal and social institutions to compensate in part for the suppression of indigenous politico-religious hierarchies, Zapotec society seems to have met the challenges posed by a maturing colonial state.

To a mid-seventeenth-century observer traveling across the coastal plain, the Isthmus Zapotec community would have appeared relatively acculturated for a people whose homeland was so distant from the seat of Spanish colonial power in Mexico City. Ox-drawn plows were used to till at least some fields by mid-century, as they were in the Mixteca and Oaxaca Valley, for such tools were included among the trade goods imported by Tehuantepec's native merchants. With small herds of sheep or goats grazing the outskirts of most villages and an occasional horse or mule ambling through the village streets, scenes of rural life probably differed little from those sketched by late nineteenth- and early twentieth-century artists. The parish church was the focal point of each Zapotec village, with its vaulted sanctuary and imposing bell tower looming over the small adobe-walled and tile-roofed houses that congregated around it.

By virtue of its monumental architecture and central placement, the church reiterated a spiritual hegemony no longer dependent upon the temple-burning and idol-smashing displays of the first generation of evangelists. Anti-idolatry campaigns continued to root out clandestine ceremonial activities in more difficult to monitor mountain regions of Oaxaca into the eighteenth century, but there are few such reports from the Isthmus after Don Juan Cortés's death. And while the great majority of congregants who practiced the prescribed rituals and gathered within the church's walls each feast day could have understood the priest's admonitions only when delivered in Zapotec, an increasing number of elite men had mastered the art of signing their names with a confident script in formal testimony. Some, particularly among those residing in the *cabecera*, were sufficiently fluent in the Spanish language as well as costume and manners to be considered "muy ladino" (very Hispanicized).

To point to these outward manifestations of behavioral and material culture change as evidence of the acculturation or Hispanicization of the colonial Isthmus Zapotec would be to miss their true significance. As Douglas and Isherwood have reminded us, goods do more than serve bodily needs; they are the material vehicles by which individuals invest meaning in the world around them.[96] Exactly what those meanings may be when material goods cross cultural boundaries will depend on what uses and values the receiving culture attributes to them, rather than the role they played in their originating culture. Perhaps nowhere in modern Mexico is this distinction more apparent than among the contemporary Isthmus Zapotec, whose distinctive elements of traditional dress and artistic performance are based in large part on an eclectic blending of imported goods and technologies, all of which serve to reinforce cultural boundaries and consolidate internal social bonds. Such practices today alert us to the fact that the meanings and social uses the colonial period indigenous population applied to goods and customs of European origin clearly were not the same as those attributed to them by sixteenth- and seventeenth-century Spaniards, let alone their value for us commodity-driven moderns.

Since the Spaniards who monopolized the written record were neither interested in nor appreciative of the fact that familiar goods might have different meanings to the Zapotecs, available historical sources offer little direct help in deciphering this code. Two primary avenues remain open to the challenge. One is to adopt the perspective of "postprocessual archaeology," which is expressly concerned with determining the meaning behind material culture, and scrutinize the archaeological record for patterns in the manufacture, use, and disposal of goods that might reveal their specific cultural significance. To the extent possible, given the limited set of historic period data presently available for the Isthmus or other regions of New Spain, I have inferred some of the distinctive values that the early colonial Zapotecs may have attributed to new sets of material goods: the production and consumption of European livestock in contexts which suggest their significance in reinforcing community bonds rather than in maximizing profit; an incipient democratization of native society as luxury goods like imported pottery lost the sumptuary restrictions they held in precolumbian times; and an affirmation of interregional communication through Tehuantepec's active involvement in exchange relationships with distant native groups.

Like the unrealized promise of much postprocessualism, such inferences seem tentative and conjectural without abundant comparative archaeological data. In the chapter that follows I try another path in the attempt to tease distinctive cultural understandings out of the historical record. The latter half of the seventeenth and the early eighteenth centuries were marked by a series of intense and often violent political protests on the part of the Isthmus Zapotecs. Historians often point to similar acts of resistance and rebellion as indicators of the extent to which the subjugated indigenous population has been oppressed economically by the colonizers. Certainly the early colonial record described thus far is replete with enough incidents of abuse and injury to Tehuantepec's native inhabitants to warrant that approach to understanding the chaotic events of the next few decades.

Yet the very longevity of this record of oppression and the fact that violent resistance was not triggered earlier by such dramatic events as the heresy of Don Juan or the large-scale intrusion of voracious cattle onto the landscape call into question the sufficiency of an economic reductionist approach. Why did the Isthmus Zapotec, who had been so successful in retaining community lands and acquiring some measure of economic prosperity, mount this resistance? Why did it take place at this particular point in time, when indigenous adjustments to colonial rule had matured and the native population was beginning to regain its strength? As Jean and John Comaroff have pointed out in their history of the English missionary movement in South Africa, *Of Revelation and Revolution*:

> Colonizers everywhere try to gain control over the practices through which would-be subjects produce and reproduce the bases of their existence. No habit is too humble, no sign too insignificant to be implicated. And colonization always provokes struggles—albeit often tragically uneven ones—over power and meaning on the frontiers of empire. It is a process of "challenge and riposte" . . . often much too complex to be captured in simple equations of domination and resistance; or, for that matter, by grand models of the politics of imperialism or the economics of the modern world system.[97]

Rather than attempt to capture the complexity of these events in their entirety, here my primary focus on Isthmus Zapotec resistance will be the contested meanings underscored by indigenous protests and their forceful suppression by the colonial state. When political tensions and contradictory understandings between a powerful elite and a subordinate people boil over into public view, we have a rare opportunity to see from the historical distance just what were the limits to the colonial state's ability to control native peoples through the hegemony of acculturated ideas.

CHAPTER FIVE

Confronting Colonial Authority in 1660

Conflict gnawed at relationships between the Isthmus Zapotecs and the Spaniards who lived among them throughout much of the later seventeenth and early eighteenth centuries. Disputes over land ownership between the native community and creole ranchers could snarl proceedings in the General Indian Court for decades or erupt into violence provoked by the simple act of measuring land boundaries. However much the very nature of the archival record, which in large part reflects the efforts of colonial administrators to mediate conflict, may underrepresent the more peaceable interactions of daily life, it is the case that the province had acquired a widely acknowledged reputation for belligerence by the late seventeenth century. As the most vocal Spanish defender of the Tehuantepec natives, Fr. Alonso de Cuevas Dávalos, bishop of Oaxaca, characterized the province in an April 1660 letter written to the viceroy from Tehuantepec, it was

> among the largest provinces of the realm, with a warlike people, of courageous nature and disposition, artful in the Spanish language, many of them experienced with firearms for being given to hunting and especially devoted to the trade in hides; on that basis it can be calculated that, with little effort, more than 10,000 men would be ready to come to this parish from the surrounding mountains, bold like the climate of the land, as is witnessed by the atrocious happenings that have taken place, more in this one province than in all the others of this realm; and so wary are these men that I have heard and know things about them in this business that cannot be said of very experienced captains.[1]

The 1660 Rebellion in Tehuantepec

The cause of the bishop's trip to this most distant region of his ecclesiastical domain, where the arduous journey and oppressive late dry season heat threatened his delicate health, was the request made of him by the Duke of Alburquerque, viceroy of New Spain, to mediate a native revolt which had taken place just a few weeks earlier. On the Monday of Holy Week, March 22, 1660, a large crowd of 6,000 people had gathered in the central plaza of Tehuantepec in the late morning, angry at the harsh *repartimiento* demands for cotton cloth set by the *alcalde mayor* Don Juan de Avellán. Anticipating in a few days yet another round of merciless punishments that would meet that month's failed quota, the stick-and-stone wielding crowd vented its rage at the town's Casas Reales, where Avellán remained entrenched. When a torch succeeded in setting the royal stables on fire, the *alcalde mayor* ran out and was mortally wounded by a blow to the head in the barrage of stones that met him before he could reach the safety of the church's sanctuary. Three others were killed in the melee: an unnamed black slave; Don Gerónimo de Celi, Zapotec cacique of the town of Quiechapa in the district of Nexapa, who died accompanying Avellán and the slave; and Avellán's servant, a Spaniard named Miguel de Buenos Créditos, who was discovered hiding in some wool and dragged out into the square by the rebels, where he was executed with a single machete blow. Only Avellán's wife and children were spared, when an unnamed Zapotec woman reproached those who would have pummeled the family with stones as they fled the Casas Reales and brought them to the house of a Spanish *vecina*; there they remained hidden for several days until managing to slip out of town during the celebrations of Holy Friday. Although no other Spanish residents of the town were attacked, members of the sitting *cabildo* of Tehuantepec were forced to seek the shelter of the convent walls, and a new set of native government officials was promptly elected by the town's *principales*.[2]

Spontaneous acts of violent protest such as this were not uncommon in New Spain. Using late colonial judicial investigation records, William Taylor was able to document 142 indigenous uprisings from Central Mexico, the Mixteca Alta, and the Valley of Oaxaca in his comparative study of the structure and cause of peasant revolts during the period between 1680 and 1811.[3] Among Taylor's sample cases, targets of violence were typically Spanish administrators or clerics, few evidenced any planned leadership, and most burned themselves out a day or two after the immediate objectives of the uprising were reached. In the context of this climate of violent protest, even the murder of Avellán does not stand out as an isolated, extreme measure. Killings of targeted outsiders were documented in at least eighteen of the cases studied by Taylor, and the incidence might have been greater had not many hated officials been able to flee and save themselves from the crowd's wrath. Likewise in Tehuantepec, which was not included in Taylor's comparative study, active resistance to Spanish authority surfaced repeatedly in the seventeenth and eighteenth centuries. At the time of the 1660 rebellion, it was common knowledge among the members of the Audiencia that the natives of Tehuantepec had rebelled twice previously against their *alcaldes mayores,* once during the tenure of the previous viceroy, the Conde de Alva (1650–53), when Don Diego Fajardo was murdered, and once nearly twenty years earlier, when Don Pedro Portocanero was attacked and beaten and forced to flee town.[4]

If the basic facts of the 1660 rebellion in Tehuantepec are not exceptional, its historical legacy is nonetheless unique, for the modern Isthmus Zapotecs continue to cite this colonial period uprising as a pivotal event in their long-standing tradition of political independence and cultural resistance.[5] Scholarly studies of the Tehuantepec rebellion have multiplied in recent years as well, inspired at least in part by that Isthmian legacy, which makes the Tehuantepec region such an intriguing focus of research.[6] An important consideration adding to the rebellion's prominence has surely been the accessibility of its primary historical sources, for all modern scholars have relied heavily on the chronology and document trail provided in the contemporaneous account of the rebellion and its forceful suppression published under the name of Don Cristóbal Manso de Contreras.[7]

Manso de Contreras was a prominent Spanish resident of Antequera, and as a *regidor* in that city's creole town council, he traveled to Mexico City in late 1660 to voice his fellow settlers' complaints about the surly and impertinent behavior exhibited by Oaxaca natives following the Tehuantepec rebellion, which the *vecinos* felt was encouraged by the failure of the Crown's representatives to respond forcefully and punitively to Avellán's murder. This view of events received a more sympathetic hearing by Alburquerque's successor, the newly installed Viceroy Conde de Baños, who dispatched an important officer of the Audiencia, the *oidor* Don Juan Francisco de Montemayor y Cuenca, to Oaxaca in February of

1661 to gather information and discharge the appropriate penalties. When Montemayor finally entered Tehuantepec in late June, he replaced the former viceroy's appointed *alcalde mayor*, Alonso Ramírez de Espinosa, with Manso de Contreras.

The installation ceremonies for the new *alcalde mayor* held on the outskirts of the province were in fact a clever pretext by which the unsuspecting members of the rebel Tehuantepec *cabildo* were lured to the Chontal town of Tequisistlán, where Montemayor could arrest them without stirring reaction from their absent supporters. It was part of a complicated stratagem Montemayor had been concocting for many months that would allow him to quash the insurrection and punish its perpetrators without recourse to the kind of large-scale militia force that might only have escalated the rebellion. In the end, nine people were sentenced to death by the *oidor*, four in absentia and the majority from the Isthmus village of La Mixtequilla. Only one member of the insurgent Tehuantepec *cabildo* was among those executed, the *regidor* Gerónimo Flores; the others were included in the list of twenty-eight men and women receiving one hundred lashes of the whip and variable sentences of exile and forced labor in the mines and sweatshops of New Spain. By comparison with the lenient manner in which later rebellions were dealt with in the colony, Montemayor's sentences were exceptionally severe, particularly so in light of the king's admonition that the Tehuantepec natives be treated with kindness and without imposing harsh punishment and by "trying to pacify them more than to conquer and make war on them."[8]

The modern Isthmus poet and historian Víctor de la Cruz notes with considerable irony how Manso de Contreras referred to the death of Avellán as an "atrocity," while praising the judgments rendered by Montemayor for their prudence, kindliness, and piety. As Cruz observes, "And so it is that white becomes black and black white, according to their self interest."[9] Although few might today disagree with Cruz's sympathy toward the Tehuantepec rebels, what is particularly striking about this *relación* is the extent to which it demonstrates how sympathetic many seventeenth-century observers were to the native population and its plight. That sentiment and the grounds on which it was based emerge despite Manso's attempt to use these observers' own words to discredit positions he finds naive or weak. Individuals and groups with different interests are represented in Manso's account through transcripts of letters written by such notable participants as the outgoing viceroy, the Duke of

Alburquerque; the Bishop of Oaxaca, Fr. Alonso de Cuevas Dávalos; the post-Avellán *alcalde mayor,* Alonso Ramírez de Espinosa; Montemayor himself; and even the members of the Tehuantepec *cabildo*. The appearance of so many voices offering different perspectives has given this *relación* an unusual multivocality from which modern scholars have been able to derive readings of these events far different from those of the author himself.

What has often gone unrecognized, however, is the prospect that Manso's chronicle selected from a much broader documentary record just those letters that could be construed to build support for the particular interpretation he wished to communicate. As the author states in the book's dedication to the viceroy, it was his intention to provide for his superior a permanent record of the grand and heroic actions which the Conde de Baños, unlike his vacillating predecessor, initiated in order to quell this dangerous mutiny, restore peace, and make an example to nearby groups who might be tempted to imitate the rebellion.[10] What benefits might also accrue to Manso personally by recording his services in these events is left unstated, as is the implicit benefit to the more immediate hero of the account, the *oidor* Don Juan Francisco de Montemayor y Cuenca.

Montemayor as author and protagonist

Indeed, Montemayor's unspoken role in bringing this story to light must be gleaned from other sources, since he apparently thought it prudent to act behind the scenes in helping to create this public and permanent version of the Tehuantepec affair. That he was the actual author of both Manso de Contrera's account and the 1662 *relación* of Juan de Torres Castillo describing related uprisings in three other Oaxaca provinces was abundantly clear to at least some individuals at the time. Indeed it is a remarkable coincidence that two otherwise obscure provincial functionaries would have both the means and the connections to see their works in print, especially since secular chronicles such as these were rarely published in Mexico during the early colonial period.[11] In a lengthy and bitter complaint about Montemayor's conduct in Oaxaca sent to the king in December 1662, a group of caciques and *principales* from different valley towns accused him of advancing his cronies, Manso de Contreras and Torres Castillo, as *alcaldes mayores* in Tehuantepec and Nexapa and penning in their names false accounts intended for his personal aggrandizement:

> Because your viceroy removed Captain Alonso Ramírez de Espinosa from the office of *alcalde mayor* of Tehuantepec, which he had governed with enthusiasm, peace, and quietude, and they were alarmed that he had been taken from them and that Don Cristóbal Manso de Contreras, *regidor* of Oaxaca, was appointed in his place, in whose name your *oidor* later published an account of the pacifications; and the role [of *alcalde mayor*] of Nexapa [was given] to Don Juan de Torres Castillo, the other supposed author of the second account which this *oidor* brought to light concerning those pacifications. He granted himself the office of Ixtepexi as well and not that of Villa Alta of San Ildefonso because, although this *oidor* wanted to show that there had also been uprisings and riots [in Villa Alta], it was always well known [what had happened] and that the stories given in one of those *relaciones* were made and fabricated in the files of this *oidor*.[12]

Montemayor must have had strong political reasons to disguise his own role in the publication of these two books, for a modest reluctance to see his work and name in print was otherwise not an aspect of Montemayor's personality. Palau Dulcet lists fifteen books and pamphlets published in Spain and Mexico with Montemayor's name in his *Manual del librero hispanoamericano*, an extraordinary number only slightly inflated by the inclusion of second editions, translations of his own manuscripts from Latin to Spanish, and the infamous Manso de Contreras *relación* in this list. A graduate in law of the Universidad de Huesca, Montemayor's published works ranged widely from legal issues to political philosophy to religious matters. He was considered by the great early twentieth-century Chilean bibliographer José Toribio Medina to be one of the most notable men of the colonies.[13]

In the past Montemayor had not disdained advancing his own political career through his literary skills, as can be seen in the very first book he published after arriving in Mexico, his 1658 *Discurso político-histórico jurídico del derecho y repartimiento de presas y desposos aprehendidos en justa guerra, premios y castigos de los soldados*. Dedicated to the Duke of Alburquerque, whose viceregal favors the compliment evidently failed to win, this work has a self-justifying subtext which emerges clearly behind the legalistic exposition regarding the taking of prisoners and spoils of war that Medina later praised as one of the few works on human rights published in colonial Spanish America.[14] As the very first chapter of the book states, Montemayor felt compelled to write this scholarly essay, in which he searched through the Bible, Roman and Spanish history, and the works of St. Thomas, Nicolao Bello, and Machiavelli for legal and moral precedents, precisely because his own actions regarding prisoner rights and the disposition of spoils of war had come under public criticism and were even the object of a formal inquiry.

The manuscript was drafted in Santo Domingo in 1654, a year after Montemayor had successfully ordered the routing of French squatters and brigands from the island of Tortuga, during his own brief spell as acting governor of Hispaniola. In this work Montemayor defended both his assumption of the captaincy general of Hispaniola, which he claimed as the most senior *oidor* following the sudden death of the governor, and his rash assault on the French settlers, after which he appropriated a significant premium for the successful mission—one-fifth of the value of spoils taken in slaves, hides, tobacco, money, and other goods after the Crown's royal fifth and other expenses had been accounted for. When the 1,000-peso prize, which the soldiers were said to have bestowed upon their nonparticipating captain general, is added to this sum, Montemayor cleared well over 12,000 pesos from the venture, as well as gaining an appointment to be *oidor* for the Audiencia of Mexico, an appointment stalled for three years while he waited in Santo Domingo for the outcome of his *residencia*.[15] His reputation as a military strategist appears to have been well earned, for Montemayor was credited with leading a successful defense of Santo Domingo during this interval, gathering a militia of two thousand men to face what could have been an overwhelming force of English soldiers sent by Oliver Cromwell to capture the island.[16]

Montemayor's transfer to Mexico in 1657 appears not to have offered him many immediate political advantages. Despite his attempts to ingratiate himself with the Duke of Alburquerque, the viceroy remained distant from Montemayor personally and from the Audiencia in general, if the *oidores*' collective frustration over Alburquerque's failure to consult formally with them regarding the Tehuantepec rebellion is typical of the viceroy's handling of political matters.[17] Montemayor was far more successful with Alburquerque's successor, using the spokesman's role he assumed in the Audiencia to gain the Conde de Baños's ear. Over the course of the next several months, Montemayor moved from his public position of condemning the abuses inflicted on native communities by profiteering *alcaldes mayores*, whose appointment from the personal entourage of the viceroys was a practice the *oidores* wished to halt, to one which had greater resonance with the new viceroy, which was the quelling of the perceived threat to the Crown's sovereignty. Ultimately it was Montemayor who profited, however briefly, from this chain of events, receiving from the viceroy an annual salary of over 21,000 pesos, a reward which was financed by the *oidor* increasing the tribute burden paid by all native communities in Oaxaca.[18]

The documentary record provides some telling glimpses of the close relationship Montemayor courted with the count, who appointed the *oidor* to resolve these matters in place of a more likely official investigator from the Sala de Crimen. Montemayor just happened to be in the viceroy's company in late December when word came that three natives from Tehuantepec had arrived in Mexico seeking the Audiencia's confirmation of recent *cabildo* elections. Brought to the viceroy's chambers, the three men exhibited understandable nervousness, which the two Spaniards took to be evidence of the guilty role that one of these men, the unfortunate Gerónimo Flores, had played in masterminding the rebellion and murdering Avellán. Attempting to enlist Crown support for what would be a rash departure from his predecessor's efforts to contain unrest through peaceful means, the viceroy reported this incident to the Council of the Indies in late December 1660, along with rumors then floating around in Mexico that the rebel governor, Don Marcos de Figueroa, was referred to as king by the Indians of Tehuantepec.

Rebellion or Insurrection? The Tehuantepec Rebellion in Comparative Perspective

> Don Marcos who today governs is [the one] whom they refer to and hold as their king, naming him such and making him sit in the church in the seat and post which should be occupied by the *alcalde mayor*, along with other circumstances of rebellion and bad spirit.[19]

It was a suggested offense that immediately focused the attention of the Council members, who read and underlined the above passage in the viceroy's letter.[20] For subjects of the monarch to have proclaimed by such words their rejection of the king's sovereignty was the gravest of crimes, second only to the crime of heresy, and its penalties were inherited from generation to generation by all descendants of those convicted of even the smallest infraction of the loyalty due the monarch, as the Council reiterated in May 1661.[21]

Did the events that took place in Tehuantepec in fact constitute a rejection of royal authority by the participants, as alleged by Baños when he referred to them in his letter as the "mutiny and riot" ("el motín y alboroto")? In characterizing the Tehuantepec natives as mutinous, the new viceroy was strongly influenced by the alarmist claims made by several prominent Spaniards *vecinos* of Oaxaca, including Manso de Contreras, who insisted that the bishopric's Indians were all "amotinados." From the outset the Audiencia had been more circumspect, using the term "*alboroto*" or "riot" to express its sense of the gravity of native unrest in Tehuantepec and other places in New Spain and its frustration with the Duke of Alburquerque's inaction in resolving both immediate and underlying problems. The outgoing viceroy, on the other hand, characterized the matter as an "ordinary dispute" ("una pendencia ordinaria"), and placed blame on the murdered Avellán for his imprudence in leaving the security of the Casas Reales when it was obvious that his appearance on the plaza would only escalate the violence, given the history of violent protest in the town.[22]

Spaniards such as Don Juan de Virgil de Quiñones, ecclesiastical vicar of Tehuantepec, who was personally familiar with the events surrounding Avellán's death and sympathetic to the native plight, later downplayed their gravity as well, referring to the "altercation" as the last recourse for an abused population and calling attention to the province's peaceful obedience toward the replacement administrator.[23] Meanwhile the rebel-installed Tehuantepec *cabildo* officers proclaimed steadfastly that they were loyal vassals of the king ("fieles vasallos de Su Magestad," "fieles y seguros vasallos de Su Magestad") in an explicit effort to convince both viceroys that their grievance against the murdered *alcalde mayor* did not represent a rejection of colonial authority.

The words employed by these contemporary observers and participants reflected far more than personal style or terminological nuance, for they conveyed very different understandings of the scope and intent of the rebellion. Such understandings, if persuasive, would provoke diametrically different responses from the Spanish Crown, as the Council of the Indies acknowledged when it called upon the viceroy to present sworn affidavits to confirm the rumors he reported in late 1660. At the heart of the issue lies a distinction widely recognized among modern historians and political scientists who have examined rural rebellions elsewhere in modern Europe and its colonial realm, a distinction made between those popular movements that represented an explicit challenge to the established social and political order and those that sought more narrowly to amend corrupt practices. E. J. Hobsbawm, in his classic study of "primitive" or kin-based societies in rebellion in nineteenth- and early twentieth-century Europe, labeled this a distinction between "revolutionaries" and "reformers": "Reformists accept the general framework of an institution or social arrangement, but consider it capable of improvement or, where abuses have crept in, reform; revolutionaries insist that it must be fundamentally transformed or replaced."[24] While Hobsbawn considered both reformist and revolutionary tendencies to be inherent in all social movements, the truly revolutionary rural movements in pre-Marx Europe had an explicit millenarian ideology, an ideology that articulated a utopian social vision, whether it be messianic in nature or anarchistic. What distinguishes such "primitive" revolutionary movements from their more "modern" replacements, in Hobsbawn's view, is the lack of a coherent plan by which the utopian transition will be effected.

Similarly concerned with the impact of capitalism and the modern nation-state on traditional agricultural societies, James Scott examined the widespread peasant rebellions that swept through colonial Southeast Asia in the 1930s.[25] Although Hobsbawm portrayed European peasants as quixotic and prepolitical in their social agitation, Scott perceived in the Southeast Asian data a rational and generalizable axiom that subsistence farmers employ worldwide in assessing the fairness of an economic system and its tolerability. Although the specific calculus will vary by cultural and historical context, the underlying premise of the "moral economy" in peasant society (employing a term coined by E. P. Thompson) is one that both maintains the peasant household's right to eke out a subsistence and simultaneously binds the "haves" and "have-nots" through cultural norms of reciprocity. Where the intrusion of the capitalist state has not completely dismantled the traditional structures by which the moral economy functions, peasant reactions have been largely reformist, in Scott's analysis. Where the removal of corrupt officials is not enough or the restoration of bonds of reciprocity is no longer possible, peasant movements take on revolutionary attributes, as they seek to drive out the representatives of the colonial state and reestablish an autonomous community.[26]

Although religious millenarianism seems not to have been an important inspiration for revolutionary peasant movements in colonial Southeast Asia, where the messianic references of Judeo-Christianity were not widely shared, it did play a central role in many of the indigenous rebellions that took place throughout Spain's colonial domain. Whether nativistic or neo-Christian in inspiration, revelations of a divinely ordained utopia that would replace the present unjust system were common elements in popular native resistance movements, from the sixteenth-century Taki Onqoi in highland Peru to the late colonial Maya revitalization movements in Chiapas and the Yucatán.[27] It seems that the messianic ideology of Christianity struck a responsive chord in many Native American minds and souls, already predisposed as they were to viewing the world in terms of historical prophecy and cyclical cataclysm. In her comparative study of indigenous "socioreligious movements," Alicia Barabas documented forty such millenarian movements for colonial Mexico alone. As she points out, whatever the specific spiritual message may have been, their frequency underscores the fact that religion can function as an important cohesive force for subordinated peoples, giving concrete expression to the utopian dreams of liberation.[28] Because religious revelations carry a spiritual authority that may appeal beyond the boundaries of the social community in which they arise, millenarian movements seem to enjoy a higher rate of success than do more secularly inspired visions in mobilizing rural populations otherwise fragmented into competing village units.

Despite the high visibility of millenarian movements in indigenous Latin America, they in fact constitute only a small percentage of the much more numerous instances of violent resistance to colonial authority. Essentially reformist in their objectives, the vast majority of the 142 native uprisings that Taylor documented for the central and southern Mexican highlands conforms to the geographically restricted type of movement he refers to as "rebellions," in which the violent outburst of a single town or just a few communities has the limited objective of reestablishing what was the normal social order.[29] Only a handful succeeded in becoming revolutionary social movements or "insurrections" in Taylor's terminology (i.e., more broadly based political actions, regional in scope), that have the explicit aim of reorganizing the way communities relate to powerful outsiders:

> Those exceptional movements that did submerge purely local interests in an abortive or temporarily successful regional union followed patterns familiar to peasant insurrections at other places and times. They developed as millenarian movements or formed around nonvillage leaders with whom the peasants shared a common enemy. In both cases, they were fragile movements centered on loyalty to particular leaders rather than to principles based on an identity of conditions and desires.[30]

According to Taylor, easily provoked fears of regional native revolt among Spaniards were usually unwarranted, unless the movement had a millenarian leader, a charismatic individual who could articulate a vision of a perfect social order that transcended the parochial concerns of a single community or a single ethnic group. More secularly based attempts at creating a regional movement against Spanish authority seldom succeeded in inspiring the necessary groundswell of resistance among otherwise unconnected villages and social groups.[31]

How might these generalizations about peasant rebellions apply to the Tehuantepec uprising of 1660? Portraying the murder of Avellán and the installation of a rebel *cabildo* as the planned inception of an organized revolutionary movement intended to drive out Spanish authority was clearly the intent of Montemayor and his crony, Manso de Contreras, for only the threat of an advancing native insurrection would justify the harsh response they meted out. Thus the account of these events provided in their *Relación cierta* alleges a number of incriminating facts: that the rebels had been plotting long before the spontaneous actions of the crowd precipitated the actual uprising; that the rebel *gobernador* was referred to as king by the townspeople; that the Tehuantepec *cabildo* wrote letters to villages near and far urging the populace to confront their local Spanish authorities; that "haremos Tehuantepec" ("we will make a Tehuantepec") had become a rallying cry; and that natives throughout the diocese were acting belligerently toward Spaniards.[32]

Despite the paucity of evidence presented in the *relación* to support these claims, most modern scholars as well as modern Isthmian social activists have accepted Montemayor's portrait of the Tehuantepec rebellion as a Zapotec-led insurrection against Spanish rule. It is a portrait compatible both with local ethnic pride and with the model of native resistance that has replaced earlier views of indigenous people as passive victims of colonial abuse. Based on the nativistic message reported to be circulating among Mixe groups in a related uprising in nearby Nexapa, Barabas has even suggested that the Tehuantepec rebellion had a socioreligious quality that was responsible for its broad regional appeal, although explicitly millenarian ideas were not mentioned in the Manso de Contreras account.[33]

Characterizing the uprising as a regional insurrection or revolt against Spanish domination was not, however, a conclusion that the Council of the Indies judged to be warranted by then current standards of legal evidence. For despite repeated admonitions to the viceroy and his *oidor* that they supply the Council with sworn depositions supporting these charges, the Conte de Baños and Montemayor were either unable or unwilling to do so.[34] No letters from the rebel *cabildo* inciting other communities were intercepted and submitted as part of the vast file of documentation sent to Spain. A single eyewitness to the pacification mission of Bishop Alonso Cuevas Dávalos, Don Miguel de Mediano, owner of a silver mine outside of Nexapa, was responsible for reporting the "haremos Tehuantepec" epithet and for characterizing Tehuantepec's populace as surly toward Spaniards in the aftermath of the uprising.[35] That the rebellious atmosphere had permeated as far as the Valley of Oaxaca was asserted by several Antequera witnesses, but they all cited the same single incident as a concrete example. A certain Juan Ramírez de Aguilar, the Spanish manager of a large sheepfold belonging to Don Diego de Cepeda, *alguacil mayor* of Antequera, had been accosted by an Indian *principal* of Teotitlán del Valle, Don Diego de Velasco, when he strayed onto village lands while bringing the herd to other pastures. In Aguilar's version of this encounter, the *principal* threatened to kill Aguilar if he and Cepeda were claiming these lands as their own:

> If they were his lands or those of the *alguacil mayor*, then he should vacate them right away or they would kill this witness and do with him what those of Tehuantepec had done with their *alcalde mayor*, because until now the Indians have been subjects of the Spaniards and now this time had passed and the Spaniards have to be subjects of the Indians, all of which he said with much anger and a tone of superiority, and the same with the others.[36]

Whether or not the Teotitlán incident actually unfolded as Aguilar reported, the prominence of this single antagonistic encounter as exemplar of prevailing native attitudes and intentions tells us more about the hysteria spreading among Spanish residents of Oaxaca than it does about the supposed contagion of revolutionary fever sweeping through the Oaxaca countryside. Indeed, John Chance has looked at Montemayor's claims for a native insurrection in the largely Zapotec-speaking region around Villa Alta and found them unsupported by the evidence. Serious unrest, he concluded, seems to have been focused on the contiguous Tehuantepec and Nexapa provinces, giving the rebellion a narrower geographic spread.[37]

Similarly, in their December 1662 letter to the king protesting the harsh burdens placed on the bishopric by Montemayor, the group of ten Oaxaca *caciques* and *principales* called allegations of insurrection in Villa Alta "fantástico y soñado" (fantastic, the product of dreams), for the natives of that province were always peaceful, quiet, and obedient to their *alcalde mayor*; Montemayor's suggestion that the province of Ixtepexi was in a state of unrest was also "imaginado" (imagined). The *oidor*'s motivation for concocting such allegations, they claimed, was his desire for both the personal glory reaped from quelling such a dangerous, widespread conflagration and the political and pecuniary benefits to be gained from replacing the existing provincial administrators with men beholden to him. Only in Villa Alta were these efforts unsuccessful, for it was well known at the time that Montemayor's accounts of these incidents were fabrications, according to the Oaxaca nobles.[38] The fact that the viceroy was reserving the position of *corregidor* in this lucrative province for one of his sons may have been a more decisive factor in forestalling an administrative change in Villa Alta, than any particular allegiance the Conde de Baños may have had to truth.[39]

The Oaxaca nobles contended that both the Nexapa and Tehuantepec uprisings were limited in scope. In Nexapa native anger was directed solely at the *mestizo* interpreter, Bartolomé Ximénez, though the *alcalde mayor* and other Spaniards panicked and summoned Oaxaca soldiers from their convent retreat, thus escalating the crisis without justification. In Tehuantepec, the nobles maintained, it was only the evil Avellán, "a man of inhuman, terrible, and bloodthirsty character, who treated the Indians with cruelties never before seen," and the duplicitous native *cabildo* against whom the riot was directed, not Spanish authority or the Spanish race. As evidence they cited the fact that neither Avellán's family nor any other Spaniard was harmed beyond those killed along with the *alcalde mayor*; shops in the town belonging to Spaniards were not robbed nor were the many mule trains passing through the province interfered with in any way.[40]

Marcello Carmagnani has come to a similar conclusion about the revolutionary intent of the Tehuantepec rebellion and its connection to any other Oaxaca uprisings. Rather than being "anti-colonial," Carmagnani argues that the purpose of the rebellion was one of redefining the political space between the Spanish and Indian spheres, first within the town of Tehuantepec and secondarily within the province as a whole. After the death of Avellán, Tehuantepec's elite native leaders sought to reduce the economic and political intrusion of the *alcalde mayor* into their communities by reasserting their rights under colonial law to freely elect their own political officers and by refusing to accede to onerous (and illegal) *repartimiento* demands.[41] Indeed, Alburquerque, the outgoing viceroy, implicitly acknowledged this redefined political space when he chose Alonso Ramírez de Espinosa as Avellán's replacement, for here was a man who met all his requirements for a new administrator in the troubled province: creole by birth, mature in years, experienced in dealing with the natives and understanding of their nature, one who had served in many offices in New Spain without complaint from any quarter.[42] By all accounts, including Ramírez's own, the arrangement had been successful, for the province continued to be peaceful from the time of his installation until Montemayor replaced him with Cristóbal Manso de Contreras less than a year later.

If the Montemayor faction's biases and political motivations are taken into consideration, the weight of opposing testimony from the outgoing viceroy, the Bishop of Oaxaca, Spanish residents of Tehuantepec, and the rebel *cabildo* would appear to best support a reformist view of the uprising. Rather than challenging the religious and political premises of the colonial state, the leadership of the native rebellion sought to restore an acceptable equilibrium between Spanish authority and community autonomy. Concurring with Carmagnani on this point, Héctor Díaz-Polanco and Consuelo Sánchez argue that the 1660 revolt was not a rebellion against the colonial system, but against the local representatives of government and those who had been complicit in the indigenous population's abuse: "what was violently rejected was not [colonial] domination, but *the relatively brusque change of previously accepted (or supposedly accepted) rules* [authors' emphasis], that provincial authorities violated with these excessive tributary burdens and *repartimientos*, or with the distortion of traditional forms of government."[43] Characterizing the 1660 rebellion as reformist, however, is not to deny the existence of voices that may have proclaimed their hatred for all Spaniards, that may have rejected the institutional apparatus of colonial rule, or that may have longed for the reestablishment of a pre-Christian social order. As Hobsbawm reminds us, all social movements exhibit a pull between reformist and revolutionary tendencies, tendencies revealed in the opinions and actions of individuals.

The pull, I would argue, moved more forcefully in the direction of social revolution in Tehuantepec as time passed and the rebellion's historical reputation itself assumed utopian dimensions. Ironically, it was a reputation built at least in part on the actions of Montemayor, who, temporarily successful in decapitating the reform leadership and terrorizing the native population of the area, also succeeded in elevating the more modest accomplishments of the Tehuantepec rebels to insurrectionary heights undreamed of by most participants. By creating a dangerous mutiny out of the events of 1660, events not much different in nature than earlier incidents in the town, Montemayor justified the horrific punishments inflicted on the reformists and transformed justifiable unrest into a tragic insurrection. Public whipping, hanging, beheading, dismembering, and perpetual exile were all elements of his theatrical subordination of indigenous will and restoration of an autocratic system deemed corrupt and unjust by the indigenous populace.

How hollow must Montemayor's issuing yet another proclamation outlawing the egregious abuses committed by Avellán have sounded in the context of this brutal repression. Whether the men and women who received these harsh sentences were regarded as martyrs by their fellows we do not know. Surely the weight of their sacrifice was further impressed upon the native population's collective memory by Montemayor's concluding pageant, which featured Masses and candlelight ceremonies, the installation of a patriotic tableau in front of the Casas Reales, and the swearing of allegiance by all twenty-eight native governors of the province.[44] For despite Montemayor's admonition that the "mutiny" and its aftermath were never to be spoken or written about again, they were long remembered: "placing as I place from now on perpetual silence on all that has resulted and will result concerning this mutiny and deaths and their aftermath, so that nothing more will be spoken of about it, neither in writing nor in word, as if it had never happened."[45]

His modest protestations notwithstanding, remembrance was the intended outcome of the *oidor*'s own behind-the-scenes role in publishing the *Relación cierta*. The book appears to have been read and discussed among literate Spaniards and natives alike in contemporary New Spain, if we may judge from the references to it made by the Oaxaca nobles in their 1662 letter to the king. Whether that original printing was enough to keep the rebellion's reputation alive in Mexico until the book was rediscovered and reprinted in the twentieth century is less certain. Fr. José Antonio Gay cited Manso de Contreras in his 1881 *Historia de Oaxaca*, but appears to have relied on other accounts to construct a somewhat confused chronology for the rebellion.[46]

Whatever the wider literary fate of this work in late colonial times may have been, the oral history of the 1660 rebellion kept its lessons alive in the Tehuantepec province for generations. We cannot often see these acts of retelling directly in the historical record, but they lurk just under the surface of numerous later conflicts between Isthmus communities and the colonial state, providing a blueprint, sometimes explicitly so, for how the people of Tehuantepec might resist the intrusion of outsiders into their own political space. To understand what that insurrectionary model was, it is necessary to define the parameters of the social and political equilibrium the 1660 rebels sought to restore.

Restoring Justice in 1660

The Tehuantepec rebellion's leaders were explicit about the source of their desperation under Avellán. They charged that he failed to administer justice as the king ordered to ensure the peace and well-being of the province and its inhabitants; that he exacted enormous *repartimientos* from the natives worth more than 20,000 pesos, compelling each household to sell whatever goods they had at low value to avoid the *alcalde mayor*'s violent punishment, because he regularly whipped or threw into jail cacique and commoner alike for any shortages; and that a recently instituted *repartimiento* of 1,500 *mantas* (homespun cloth measuring a yard in width and five and a half yards in length) was an impossible quota.[47]

The common practice among New Spain's *alcaldes mayores* of extorting the forced purchase of unwanted goods by the local Indian population was, of course, well established in Tehuantepec long before 1660, as was seen earlier in Fr. Moreno's condemnation of this abused prerogative. The excesses committed by the hated Avellán, however, went beyond all previously tolerated demands, as the resident priest, Don Juan de Virgil, explained. Communities had to purchase mules they did not need (and could not use because they were too young) at excessive prices. Whereas previous *alcaldes mayores* were accustomed to making three *repartimientos* of manufactured clothing during the course of their two years in office, Avellán required the populace to buy clothing from him every two months at inflated quantities and prices. Such was the burden of these payments that many people had to sell their own clothing to find the cash to comply with the *repartimiento* demands. Virtually the entire province was kept busy meeting diverse labor demands for Avellán's gain: salt-making, fishing, preparing deer hides, hunting and collecting rabbit wool for hats. He forced communities to sell him vanilla, which at least was produced locally, but paid them only half the going price. Worst of all, however, was the cotton cloth quota, which no other *alcalde mayor* had attempted to institute in recent memory. Since cotton was not produced locally at this time, people had to journey all the way to Chiapas to buy the fiber before they could even begin to weave the extra large *mantas* he required. Where Avellán paid 1 peso for each cloth at the beginning of his term, at the end he paid just half a peso in cash and the other half in kind, inflating the value of useless merchandise he passed out in payment.[48]

The burden of cloth production

Because the tributary count for the province as a whole in this year would have numbered around 2,500, it seems that only certain communities were required to produce the 1,500 *mantas* demanded each month, while others were engaged in meeting different production demands. The *manta*-producing villages included La Mixtequilla and Tequisistlán, and the vehemence of the Tehuantepec leaders' complaint suggests that the much more populous *cabecera* was enlisted as well. The population of these three communities was sufficient to supply the estimated one thousand households involved in cloth production, a figure extrapolated from the rough average of one and a half *mantas* per couple implied in the quota of 110 *mantas* cited by the rebels for one unnamed village of seventy households.

Within each cloth-producing community, we can only guess at the likely impact of this *repartimiento* on the labor resources of a typical native household, particularly on the labor of its female members, who traditionally practiced this type of weaving in Mesoamerica. Frederic Hicks has combed ethnographic and ethnohistorical data in an analysis of the economic role of cloth in late prehispanic Central Mexico and provides some useful household production figures for comparison. In an efficient domestic production strategy, he calculates that native women might weave about four square yards of plain cotton cloth in a week, using the help of children for odd tasks and interspersing cloth-making among other household chores.[49] By this precolumbian standard, the burden on an individual household to produce just under eight square yards of cloth each month for Avellán does not appear to be an impossible target, although the two weeks out of every four it consumed in labor is much higher than the third of a year Hicks estimates was invested by prehispanic households in meeting their cloth tribute demands to the Aztec rulers. Tribute, of course, involved unrecompensed goods and services, whether given to indigenous lords before 1521 or to the colonial bureaucracy thereafter. Its distinction from colonial *repartimientos* may not have been very meaningful to native producers, however, burdened as they were by a Spanish administrator who paid little for finished cloth at a time when the cost of raw materials was high.

What was feasible in the abstract was no longer tolerable in the specific social and economic context of colonial Tehuantepec. *Mantas* maintained their precolumbian role in the early colonial tribute system of Tehuantepec, where we see them represented pictographically in the 1553 complaint made against Don Juan Cortés, but much had changed by the mid-seventeenth century. Once a major source of cotton for highland Mesoamerica, the province no longer produced its own fiber. Tribute assessments in cotton and cotton cloth, like all tribute in kind, had been phased out in Tehuantepec late in Don Juan Cortés's lifetime, and cloth's utility as a *repartimiento* product in this province appears to have been overlooked by most of Avellán's predecessors. Although it seems likely that Isthmus women continued to practice traditional arts of spinning and weaving to meet their own family's clothing needs, it may be that familiar grades and lengths of cloth were unlike those demanded by Avellán, whose irritation at products that were too loosely woven or not the requisite size was notorious.

More important, we cannot assume that the structure of household labor in seventeenth-century Tehuantepec could have easily incorporated the persistent attention to cloth production that Avellán's quota represented. That Isthmus Zapotec women may have already been occupied in the kinds of artisan and marketing activities for which they are presently well known is an intriguing speculation, but one for which we have no direct evidence. Nearly thirty years before the Tehuantepec rebellion, the Oaxaca *provincial*, Fr. Gerónimo Moreno, reproached those colonial administrators whose demands for cloth interfered with the economic and domestic activities in which native women normally engaged: "the Indian women have their own enterprises apart and different from those of their husbands, from which they get money to pay their tribute, and they have to spin and weave to clothe themselves and their sons, daughters, and husbands, and make meals and do other things which are their responsibility."[50] Whatever may have been the viable female economic activities displaced by this cloth quota in Tehuantepec, it is certain that the family structure that supports weaving as a household craft in native Mesoamerica today had been severely undermined by the cumulative impact of postconquest epidemic disease. In 1660 the Tehuantepec population had barely passed its postconquest demographic nadir, and community population structure would not yet reflect a healthy age pyramid, one in which a large number of young adults and subadults survived the vulnerable years of early childhood. Indeed, Don Juan de Virgil noted that Avellán's *repartimiento* demands came at a time when the population once again was ravaged by disease. Perhaps it was the lingering aftermath of the same epidemic that swept through the province nearly ten years earlier, inflicting such a high mortality that the community had to seek a new tribute census in 1653.[51]

For a household craft that depended upon the contributions of both children and adult women for its efficient operation, the loss of family members to disease and the fragmentation of the extended family unit would have made the quotas particularly hard to bear. In one deplorable incident recounted by the priest, an old and sick woman from La Mixtequilla hanged herself out of fear of the punishment she would receive from Avellán because she was unable to meet the monthly cloth assessment. In cases such as hers, where age and infirmity should have earned a tribute-payer an exemption under colonial law, this Tehuantepec *alcalde mayor* would brook no exceptions from his arbitrary and unrelenting demands.

A crisis in community government

Further social ramifications of Avellán's *repartimientos,* as noted by the priest, included the breakup of many households, as native men fled to other provinces to escape the burdensome demands, leaving their wives and children behind.[52] The dislocation of families affected not just individual households, but the community as a whole, which found its traditional institutions of social support overwhelmed by the level of need presented by the sick and the abandoned. Furthermore it was the native leaders of each community to whom the job of collecting and delivering payments to Avellán fell and from whom a personal accounting was expected for unfilled quotas of cloth and other products or for any shortages in cash payments. Any leniency they showed toward individual cases of hardship created a deficit in their own tallies, which was sure to be met with a violent response from the *alcalde mayor.*

As the rebel *cabildo* members recounted in their letter to the Duke of Alburquerque, the governors and *principales* who delivered these goods were responsible for the slightest shortfall and were subject to being stripped and whipped to the point of death.[53] Their letter specifically mentions the cacique of Tequisistlán, who had died a short time earlier from these whippings, as the reason for their uprising. The vicar said he heard from some of the Dominican friars that two native *regidores* from different villages were whipped so severely for some defect in the *mantas* they delivered that they succumbed to their injuries within a few days.[54]

The mistreatment of the native leaders under Avellán had shocked Bishop Cuevas Dávalos when he journeyed to the province in late April 1660 at the request of Alburquerque. Among the letters and reports he sent the viceroy from Tehuantepec was an emotional portrayal of the venerable caciques of these communities who, having served their people well for thirty or forty years and earned their love and respect, were publicly humiliated by being stripped naked atop the pillory and sentenced to two hundred lashes of the whip with no more judicial process than the whim of the *alcalde mayor* and with no more cause than a finger's shortage in the length of a cloth. Seeing the fresh wounds of these whippings had brought tears to the bishop's eyes.[55]

Very few of the *principales* holding office at the end of Avellán's tenure were the objects of community respect, however. The *alcalde mayor* regularly removed dutifully elected members of the indigenous *cabildos* from their community offices and replaced them with individuals of his own liking, and of the two hundred or so native offices in the province, only those from one or two villages had not been tampered with, according to Cuevas Dávalos. As the bishop noted in his approval of the return to elected government immediately following the uprising, the viceroy himself would be heartened by these actions of the rebels and their sincere concern with proper political procedures:

> Close examination begs one to see the calm and common sense with which this population proceeded in the midst of the fervor of its disorder, as is manifested in having obliged [to assume offices] the most respected Indians, who had been blocked by the particular interests of their *alcalde mayor*, regarding as intrusive and unnatural those who held them without election; it is well known that the former officials, either because of love and affection for the community or for fear of the public, delivered [the staffs of office] right away to the others who, guided by the same fear, received them; and there are so many [of these cases] in the whole province, a little less than two hundred I am told, and only one or two pueblos did not take this action.[56]

Such concern with the institutions of community government and the juridical process imposed under Spanish rule was widely expressed among native groups throughout New Spain, as it had been in the Tehuantepec province since the mid-sixteenth century, when the documentary record first shows the *cabecera* and its subject communities seeking confirmation of elected officers or pursuing juridical redress at all levels of the colonial government. As the rebel Tehuantepec *cabildo* officers explained in their letter to Viceroy Alburquerque, the community archives contained numerous royal decrees which they had obtained over the years forbidding abuses from their *alcaldes mayores* and, they asserted, most of Avellán's predecessors had complied with these orders.[57] When an earlier Tehuantepec *cabildo* complained in its 1653 petition for a new tribute census that Don Antonio Paulo Galçon was unwilling to cease collecting *repartimiento de mercancía* debts owed by those who died in the mid-seventeenth-century epidemic, the *alcalde mayor* seems to have heeded the Audiencia's admonition, for he escaped the fate received by his murdered predecessor, Don Diego de Fajardo.

Not only was Avellán unwilling to comply with previous viceregal orders, but a group of Tehuantepec leaders had been frustrated in its attempts even to get a complaint against him heard by the General Indian Court, despite two separate trips they made to Mexico City. One of the Audiencia's *oidores* sympathetic to the natives' distress noted that, because Avellán had arrived in Mexico in the entourage of the Duke of Alburquerque and had received both the Tehuantepec position and his previous assignment in Teutila as a *criado* of the viceroy, he was protected from juridical review. Fearful of the consequences to their own careers, none of the court's lawyers would even write a petition on their behalf, leaving the men to return home empty-handed and face further retribution from the *alcalde mayor*.[58]

The majority of the *oidores* agreed that this failure of the judicial system and the chaos it had led to, not just in Tehuantepec but in other parts of Oaxaca, Tlaxcala, and New Mexico, were symptomatic of a broader problem. In September 1660 the Audiencia petitioned the incoming viceroy to refrain from placing relatives and other members of his own inner circle in these sensitive posts and to reform the existing *residencia* process so that outgoing *alcaldes mayores* would have reason to fear serious punishment for their illegal and abusive actions in office. But the Conde de Baños declined to relinquish this customary prerogative of appointing his favorites to office, promising only to forward their suggestions concerning juridical review to the royal council for further study.[59] In fact the count had little interest in reforming the administration of justice, and his short-lived reign as viceroy was known as one of the most oppressive and corrupt in colonial Mexico.[60]

That the Crown, despite persistent complaints about the hardships inflicted on its indigenous subjects, failed to implement any of the thoughtful programs of structural reform it solicited from a succession of archbishops, from Palafox to Osorio de Escobar to Cuevas Dávalos himself, says much about the political bankruptcy of the seventeenth-century Spanish imperial state.[61] As Díaz-Polanco and his collaborators underscore in *El fuego de la inobediencia*, Tehuantepec's mid-century crisis was rooted not in the excesses and greed of a single individual, Juan de Avellán, inappropriately assigned to a position of authority over the native population, but in the vast structural corruption within government at home and abroad. Fueled by the discrepancy between Spain's growing need for capital to support ill-conceived European wars and the declining revenues generated by diminished native tribute-payers and poorly producing American mines, the practice of selling colonial offices from *alcalde mayor* and *corregidor* posts to that of the viceroy itself inevitably produced administrators whose primary goal was making a quick profit with which to repay the backers who had lent them money for the office to begin with.[62]

The people of Tehuantepec could not see all the ill-fitting parts that comprised this colonial state, however, only those components that impinged on their own lives. And while their relationships with provincial Spanish administrators may have been severely troubled for decades, they maintained their allegiance to the distant Spanish king and took hope in the decrees and royal provisions that his representatives in Mexico City would grant them. Indeed, obtaining legal writs of redress was a primary function of the community's political leadership, and the governor, *alcaldes*, and *regidores* were specifically cited as the petitioning party in most responses to native complaints. Failure to obtain such writs against Avellán seems to be a central issue in the discrediting of the prerebellion *cabildo*, although there are two quite different but plausible roles these officers may have played. One is the role intimated by Bishop Cuevas Dávalos: that the rejected officers were colluding with the *alcalde mayor* who had installed them because of his irritation at the efforts of the properly elected officers to stand up for the people. Early letters from the rebel *cabildo* and the vecinos of Tehuantepec are much vaguer about the reasons why the old *cabildo* was considered illegitimate, and that vagueness allows the possibility of another role.

Had they been the ones who sought unsuccessfully to pursue the native cause against Avellán in court, the community might have turned against the old officials because of their failure to obtain formal papers acknowledging the injustices done them and ordering their relief. If so, it would not be the first time in the province that ineffectual, but legitimately elected officers had been summarily deposed. In 1586 the native governor Don Francisco Vásquez was thrown in the community jail by the *alcaldes* and other *principales* who were unhappy with his conduct in office; first among the charges was his allowing the current *alcalde mayor* to make an unaccustomed number of *visitas*, official tours of the community by the administrator and a large entourage generally known to be occasions for extorting extra goods and money from the Indians. Yet Vásquez himself had paid some 400 pesos out of his own salary to make up a tribute deficit incurred during that same period when an epidemic had taken its toll on a large number of tribute payers.[63] In the case of the prerebellion *cabildo* officers, the explanation for their overthrow given by Alburquerque's replacement *alcalde mayor* is the fullest we have to go on: that they had pleased Avellán too much, so the crowd turned on them as they had turned on the murdered *alcalde mayor,* plundering their houses as they had his when the discredited officers hid in the church to save their lives. Only reluctantly did the newly elected officers accept the staffs emblematic of their duties, which they did out of fear of the excesses of the rioters.[64]

The circumstances by which both *cabildos* were selected may remain shadowy, but subsequent events confirm the importance given *cabildo* elections by the people of Tehuantepec. The following December, as Viceroy Conde de Baños informed the king, representatives from the town journeyed all the way to Mexico City to have the results of their recently concluded elections confirmed by the Audiencia. In this unusual gesture, they appear to have bypassed Ramírez, who as *alcalde mayor* would normally have been the representative of the colonial government to validate community elections. The limited documentary information does not indicate whether the community was consciously rejecting the authority of this officer or whether the weight of recent events had made the direct appeal to the Audiencia merely a prudent precaution. Some twenty years later, Tehuantepec *principales* were still complaining about their *alcaldes mayores* meddling in the electoral process and imposing their choices for native officers on the community. So desperate had things become in 1682 that the electors took the unusual measure of assembling surreptitiously in the nearby village of Huilotepec to elect *ca-*

bildo officers for the following year. The governors of Huilotepec and Ixtepec were then dispatched to Mexico to secure the viceroy's direct confirmation of the chosen officers.[65]

The long and costly journey which these native leaders made to Mexico signals the critical institutional role played first by the indigenous *cabildo* as a mediator between its powerless constituents and a powerful agent of the colonial regime and second by the election process as a community check on the actions and allegiances of its officials. At this point in the seventeenth century, both positions as officer and elector were still restricted to members of the elite. The traditional division of the Zapotec elite into the highest nobility and those drawn from the *collaba* or barrio, however, meant that a large number of the electors and some of the lower-ranking *cabildo* officers were themselves barrio headmen, whose involvement in the day-to-day concerns of the commoner household would have made them responsive to the needs of the community as a whole. Thus constituted, the elected Tehuantepec *cabildo* fulfilled exactly the kind of protective role that the moral economy assigns to elites in precapitalist peasant society, according to James Scott's model. As Scott portrays the criteria by which peasants accept the wealth and status accorded these elites, "the only justification for economic inequality is the benign, community-serving use of power; elites, to validate their power, must do their duty."[66]

Surely the elected *cabildo* was not the only institution operating within the Zapotec community that served to protect peasant households. Important organizations that commonly met social insurance needs in colonial native society elsewhere in Mesoamerica included religious confraternities or *cofradías*, but their presence among the Isthmus Zapotec at this time is somewhat doubtful, despite the best efforts of the Dominicans to foster their development. Traditional community lands ("tierras de comunidad") were used to support the church, the widowed, and the infirm, as well as to replace tribute shortfalls among some Zapotec towns as late as the early 1700s.[67] A similar role must have been played by other documented colonial institutions, such as the community chest ("caja de comunidad"), providing a measure of the subsistence security that drives the peasant moral economy, but it is only by chance that they were brought to the attention of the Audiencia. By contrast, the elected *cabildo* appears over and over again in the trail of documents sent to Mexico, precisely because it interfaced so directly and intentionally with the colonial state.

If the *cabildo* was imposed by law in the mid-sixteenth century according to Spanish institutional structures and Spanish concepts of proper polity, is its importance to the colonial Zapotecs a century later merely evidence of the regime's hegemonic co-optation of native values over time? Here the actual interplay of native actors suggests that the people of Tehuantepec continued to invest these offices with political meanings based on indigenous concepts of authority and legitimacy quite apart from the colonial state's intentions. That they would do so is in keeping with what scholars working in other regions of colonial New Spain have uncovered. As a case in point, Robert Haskett found that Nahua communities in Cuernavaca continued throughout the colonial period to confer a wide array of responsibilities on their *cabildo* officials, especially on the office of *gobernador*. Many of these functions were related to precolumbian political duties: "A tlatoani/governor, the mother and father of his community, no longer organized military activities, but he did do battle in the Spanish courts. The broad authority retained by the jurisdiction's governors as chief executives, chief constables, judges, juries, accountants, tax collectors, and advocates for the people (and sometimes their oppressors) owed at least as much to tradition as to colonial innovation."[68]

Tehuantepec's political leadership in 1660

As so often is the case in efforts to screen documentary sources for information on native individuals, the data are sketchy but intriguing for three important men who appear as major players in the events of 1660: Don Pablo de Mendoza, *gobernador* of the discredited Avellán-era *cabildo*; Don Marcos de Figueroa, rebel *gobernador*; and Don Antonio de Vargas, who served as intermediary for Bishop Cuevas Dávalos during his pacification mission to the province.

The honorific title of "don" that all three men bore suggests that they were members of the upper stratum of Tehuantepec's hereditary elite. One hundred years earlier, the title would have implied royal blood, but the details emerging from the 1660 uprising and its aftermath must be scrutinized to be certain that these individuals were similarly regarded. When Bishop Cuevas Dávalos visited the province a month after the riot on his pacification mission, he referred to Don Pablo de Mendoza as one of the principal caciques of the province, a status he accorded Don Pablo's arch rival Don Marcos de Figueroa as well. The bishop also was informed that Don Pablo and Don Marcos were bitter enemies. Such was the resulting mistrust between these men that it threatened the tranquility of the population as a whole, and their complaints against one another placed overwhelming obstacles on the path to peace. The bishop's solution to this interpersonal problem was to issue a proclamation urging these men to put aside their differences and behave as friends toward one another.[69]

Whatever measure of peace had been gained by this act was subverted upon Montemayor's arrival in Tehuantepec the following year, when he put Don Pablo de Mendoza in charge of naming the miscreants who had been leaders of the rebellion and gave the reinstated governor wide latitude to act upon his suppressed hostilities. The sentence Montemayor handed Don Marcos—one hundred lashes of the whip, ten years of labor in the mines, and perpetual exile from the province—was never fully enforced, for the *oidor* feared that the great affection in which he was held by the community might rekindle the uprising. Hearing that the Tehuantepec natives were hatching another plot to reinstate Don Marcos as their head, Montemayor sent the cacique to prison in Mexico City.[70] By August 1664, however, Don Marcos and three leaders from other provinces similarly sentenced by Montemayor had been released by a court more sympathetic to their cause, and not long after, he was rumored to be back in Tehuantepec, despite the instructions of the Audiencia that the former prisoners keep out of the communities from which they were exiled.

Who was this Don Marcos de Figueroa and what was the basis for a public esteem and affection that had impressed even the overbearing and contemptuous Montemayor? Montemayor referred to him as an "indio cacique" in a 1665 letter urging the Audiencia to rearrest Don Marcos before he incited more unrest, and it seems that the man's cacique ancestry underlaid reports that he had been called "rey" or "king" during the rebellion. *Coqui*, the Zapotec word that Córdova glossed for "rey" a hundred years before in his *Vocabulario*, was an appellation reserved for members of the hereditary cacique class. Although the data are admittedly sparse, one likely conclusion is that Don Marcos was himself a descendant of Don Juan Cortés, the last precolumbian ruler of Tehuantepec.

Spanish law recognized only the issue of his late marriage to Doña Magdalena de Zúñiga as the legitimate heirs to Don Juan's patrimony, but there were adult children of the ruler's polygamous unions present in the early decades of Spanish rule. One of these "illegitimate" descendants was a son, Don Francisco de Figueroa, who had gone to Mexico on Doña Magdalena's behalf a number of times after his father's death in 1563, and was an extremely well-connected individual when, as discussed previously, he petitioned for a ranching *merced* in Chihuitán in 1598. Other *estancia* petitions from the late 1590s refer to a ranch owned by Don Marcos de Figueroa, the same individual whom the barrio members of Santa Cruz Tagolaba accused of improperly taking salt from properties they rented from Doña Magdalena when he served as *alcalde* in 1590. As later disputes over these *salinas* illustrate, only members of the Tehuantepec royal lineage would have assumed rightful access to this valuable part of the *cacicazgo* patrimony.

Surnames are a problematic basis for tracing lineages during this early colonial period, when the Zapotecs often adopted baptismal names completely independently of family ties, but the circumstantial evidence suggests that Don Marcos, governor of the rebel *cabildo*, was indeed a member of this royal lineage. If he was not the same Don Marcos de Figueroa identified above as an important Tehuantepec *principal* at the close of the sixteenth century, an identity which would make the rebel governor quite an elderly man (in his eighties at least), then he may have been his son or nephew. Despite the difficulty of pinning down the genealogical details, it seems clear that Don Marcos de Figueroa had a strong claim to cacique status in 1660. However much personal charisma or his position as a respected elder may have added to his public esteem, it was his link to the Tehuantepec royal family that secured Don Marcos's authority within the community.

It was an authority feared not only by Montemayor, who wrote numerous letters to the viceroy and even to the queen between 1665 and 1666 seeking to prevent the cacique's release from his sentence or to have him reincarcerated, but by the Avellán-era *cabildo* as well. In November 1663, Don Pablo de Mendoza and two *alcaldes*, Hipólito de Santiago and Don Juan de Tapia, sent a letter to Juan Feliz de Galves, who was *alcalde mayor* at the time, asking him to bar any communication between Don Marcos and the natives of the province. Through the *mulato* courier, they had intercepted a letter sent from Mexico by the rebel governor to an associate of his in Tehuantepec, which they submitted as evidence that Don Marcos was attempting to stir up his faction and cause trouble again.[71]

The benign contents of this letter belie the overtly political worries of the governor and raise other issues regarding the colonial *cacicazgo* that can only be speculated about with current documentation. These documents include a handful of references to Don Pablo de Mendoza outside of the 1660 rebellion. In 1655, well before Juan de Avellán assumed the office of *alcalde mayor*, Mendoza was already serving as *gobernador* of Tehuantepec, and among the responsibilities he bore was the adjudication of a long-simmering boundary dispute between the community of Huilotepec and the Tehuantepec barrio of San Pedro Bixana.[72] A possible earlier reference dates to 1635, when charges were brought against the vicar of Zanatepec for exacting excessive fees for Masses and other religious observations, in which it was claimed that the cleric had also withheld the inheritance of the deceased cacique's son, Don Pablo de Mendoza.[73] If this is the same individual as the pre- and postrebellion governor, then Don Pablo might well have been a cacique, as Bishop Cuevas Dávalos insisted, but his position in the *cabecera* of Tehuantepec requires some further explanation.

Zanatepec was known as a Zoque-speaking community, not Zapotec-speaking like the provincial capital, but affixing the ethnicity of its cacique family is difficult for several reasons. One was the common practice of forging politically strategic marriage alliances among prehispanic royalty, a practice which often resulted in marriages between royal families from different ethnic states. The establishment of the Zapotec conquest polity in the Isthmus may have involved both interethnic alliances of this type and a more serious intrusion into the political affairs of non-Zapotec subjugated peoples through tribute collectors appointed by the Tehuantepec ruler, many of whom would have had some kind of extended kinship tie to the royal family.

After the death of Don Juan Cortés, a number of formerly subject communities asserted independence from Tehuantepec and claimed for themselves heritable cacique positions. Zanatepec follows this pattern of creating an independent *cacicazgo* where one had not been acknowledged during the Tehuantepec ruler's lifetime. I suspect that this process of asserting independence involved one of two principles in each case; some non-Zapotec communities might have revitalized an existing heritable lordship that had been suppressed under the Zapotec conquest, while other communities, possibly both Zapotec and non-Zapotec in ethnicity, may have allowed noble families descended from collateral kinsmen of the ruler to elevate themselves to the status of caciques. An example of the latter, a case in which a strong bond of kinship linked a rural *cacicazgo* and the Tehuantepec royal family, is documented among the *estancia* requests made by the province's native nobility a half-century earlier, which was discussed in the previous chapter. Don Fabian de Zárate identified himself as cacique of both Chihuitán and Tehuantepec in some of his ranching petitions and sought permission to raise livestock on lands he had inherited from his uncle, Don Felipe Cortés, who was Don Juan Cortés's son and heir. Whether Don Pablo de Mendoza's cacique status also derived from more distant kinship ties between Zanatepec's *cacicazgo* and the Tehuantepec royal family cannot be determined. What is clear is that this governor had reason to fear Don Marcos de Figueroa's political legitimacy.

In light of this fierce conflict over political authority, the mediating role played by another provincial nobleman is revealing. According to the *Relación cierta*, Don Antonio de Vargas enabled Bishop Cuevas Dávalos's pacification efforts to move forward by successfully persuading the rebel *cabildo* to hand over the goods that had been looted from the Casas Reales during the riot: "Don Antonio de Vargas, cacique of San Francisco de la Mar of this jurisdiction, intervened with the intrusive governor and *alcaldes*, and asked them with words of submission and deference that they reconsider their plans; and with [these words] he achieved what the pious prelate could not for being of the same nature."[74] That Don Antonio was an important leader in San Francisco del Mar (also known as Ixtaltepec del Mar) is attested to by his position as governor of this Huave community's *cabildo* in 1650. He represented San Francisco's interests when the village had transferred to it lands belonging to the abandoned village of Ixhuatán, former *sujeto* of Zanatepec. His name appears again as the elderly *cacique* of San Francisco in 1710, when, no longer active in the daily running of the community, he held the office of *juez veedor* and added his name to the list of *cabildo* officers involved in a dispute with the Dominicans over those same lands.[75] Although the bishop does not mention Don Antonio in his 1660 report to the viceroy, he clearly is the same Hispanicized nobleman ("*indio ladino en lengua castellano*") identified as interpreting Cuevas Dávalos's admonitions to the rebel leaders by Don Miguel de Mediano, the Nexapa miner and lay official in the church who accompanied the bishop on his mission to Tehuantepec.

The influence that Don Antonio had on the rebel *cabildo*, however, did not stem solely from his bilingual skills in Spanish and Zapotec, nor did it derive from his status as yet another seventeenth-century cacique in the province. Rather it was based on the special relationship that obtained between the *cacicazgo* of San Francisco del Mar and the Tehuantepec royal family, perhaps the same kind of relationship that existed between the *cacicazgo* of Chihuitán and the descendants of Don Juan Cortés. In testimony and transcripts of royal decrees that they presented in the early eighteenth century, the San Francisco caciques traced their ownership of the salt beds that had once been part of the Tehuantepec ruler's patrimony to Don Juan Cortés's widow. Unfortunately the documentation cited in these cases leaves a large hole in the genealogy by which this transfer was effected, a critical one hundred–year gap that will be examined more fully in Chapter 7.[76]

In drawing out the slim threads of evidence that link Don Marcos de Figueroa, Don Pablo de Mendoza, and Don Antonio de Vargas to traditional Zapotec precepts of lordly power and responsibility in the case at hand, I do not wish to suggest that the 1660 Tehuantepec rebellion can be reduced to petty factionalism among the once royal lineages of this important polity. That such disputes were part of the undercurrent of native political affairs would be a reasonable assumption, even without direct information on the substantive issues underlying long-held enmities. The precipitating factors behind the riot and the political crisis that ensued were precisely the ones cited by those Spaniards who listened to native complaints: (1) an unsupportable increase in the labor and monetary demands made by a greedy and abusive administrator and (2) a failure of the political institutions of the colonial state to restore an acceptable level of economic burden on the populace. The role of these elite factions emerged only in the aftermath of the riot, when the individual whose blood connection to the Zapotec kings was the clearest or most legitimate in the eyes of the Tehuantepec community assumed the responsibility that kinship conferred on him, a responsibility to restore justice for the community as a whole.

From Riot to Spectacle

Faced with accounting for what caused particular peasant revolts in Southeast Asia, James Scott emphasized that his comparative study was concerned with the "creation of social dynamite rather than with its detonation."[77] Here, with a single peasant rebellion my focus, I will indulge briefly in further probing of the historical record in the effort to find the spark that lit the explosive charge. On the fateful day when Avellán was killed, an unusually large crowd of frustrated peasants and townspeople was drawn to the town center, all members of a volatile native population that had been provoked on other occasions into spontaneous protest. The timing of the riot during Holy Week suggests that the crowd was augmented by marketing or other activities related to what was the most sanctified occasion in the Catholic calendar in New Spain. As others have suggested, one of the province's notorious droughts may have left food reserves seriously depleted by this point in the late dry season, aggravating tensions further on another uncomfortably hot March day in Tehuantepec.[78]

Although there is little evidence to support Montemayor's claim that the revolt had been planned, at least a small core of the assemblage may have been drawn to town in angry protest. Eight of the individuals whom Montemayor ultimately sentenced to punishments ranging from whippings and exile to death were *cabildo* officers and others from the small community of La Mixtequilla. Early reports suggest that the village had sent a small delegation to complain to the *alcalde mayor* about the impending *repartimiento* deadline and the death of an elderly woman that it had caused. The motivation of other actors sentenced for their participation in the riot is less clear. Barrio or community identity is given for just three other individuals sentenced by Montemayor, two of whom lived in the agriculturally oriented urban barrios of Santa Cruz Tagolaba and Santa María Yoloteca. Most active participants punished by Montemayor appear to have been just ordinary native or even mestizo residents of the town center, people whose personalities or beliefs pushed them into more visible roles in the developing melee. Eighteen of the thirty-seven sentences were directed at individuals without either an official title or an affiliation with a named residential community. Among these likely residents of the urban core were five artisans identified by their occupations as chairmaker (*sillero*), woodworker (*tornero*), or musician (*clarinero*).[79]

Another seven were women, all sentenced independently of any crimes their husbands may have committed during the rebellion, including one who sat on the corpse of the murdered *alcalde mayor* and another who started a fire in the horse stalls of the Casas Reales. Such public and expressive political action is a much esteemed tradition among Zapotec women of the Isthmus today, but it was a violation of all that the Spaniard Montemayor held dear about female comportment and virtue.

So, in addition to the severe sentences short of execution he handed to Indian men—typically consisting of one hundred lashes of the whip, several years of labor in the colony's *obrajes*, and perpetual exile from the community—Montemayor imposed further degradations on the women in an effort to mark them visibly as criminals. Their hair was cropped or their bodies mutilated by cutting off an ear, which was nailed to the gallows. In a strangely revealing passage, Montemayor explained that he only rescinded his order to have one hand cut off each of the two women whose abuses of royal authority and property had been most flagrant, because he had neither orders nor the desire to cure their wounds.[80]

Although our modern sensibilities are shocked by the physical cruelty of the whippings and mutilations that formed the public spectacle of these sentences, Montemayor's actions were not exceptional in the seventeenth-century European tradition of jurisprudence to which he claimed such a scholarly attachment. As Michel Foucault pointed out in his path-breaking study of the eighteenth-century reformist movements that sought to replace the physical torture that was at the core of this tradition, the very theatricality of such punishments was part of their supposed efficacy. It was (and is) the "potentially guilty" who were the primary targets of criminal sanctions.

> [T]orture forms part of a ritual. It is an element in the liturgy of punishment and meets two demands. It must mark the victim: it is intended, either by the scar it leaves on the body, or by the spectacle that accompanies it, to brand the victim with infamy; even if its function is to "purge" the crime, torture does not reconcile; it traces around or, rather, on the very body of the condemned man signs that must not be effaced; in any case, men will remember public exhibition, the pillory, torture and pain duly observed. And, from the point of view of the law that imposes it, public torture and execution must be spectacular, it must be seen by all almost as its triumph.[81]

Foucault's dictum that public punishment requires public validation for its legitimacy and effectiveness reminds us of the disparity and inherent tension between power and legitimization in the pluralistic colonial society of New Spain. In the continuously renegotiated space between Spanish and native society in the aftermath of the conquest, actions and objects signified different things for different sectors of the resident population. Those most frequently thrust into situations in which these sectors interacted directly—the clerics who administered to indigenous souls, the caciques and others who worked as cultural brokers for the native community, the ranchers and tradesmen who had dealings with natives—came to a working understanding of these cultural differences in a way that the more isolated members of their own societies did not. While they may have not understood the specific cultural meanings held by their cultural opposites, they were more likely to be able to predict the behavioral responses certain actions and signs triggered.

Supreme strategist and manipulator of political affairs that he may have been, the recently arrived Montemayor had little understanding of the nuances of Indian–Spanish interaction, nor did he encourage or support anything which broached the separation between colonist and colonized. The blurring of these identities that ladinoization represented bothered him greatly, and he complained to the viceroy about natives dressing like Spaniards and carrying swords, for such persons represented a visible leadership caste within communities and undermined his ability to deal with the population as an undifferentiated estate, following the familiar Iberian model.

In one particularly patronizing and duplicitous letter to the rebel *cabildo* of Tehuantepec in April 1661, Montemayor stated that he rejected their gift sent to him in Oaxaca of 110 fish and a jar of *escaveche* because it was illegal for ministers in his position to receive any kind of gift. Perhaps it was simply a gift of too little value, for the gesture seems an empty one from a man who came to be well known for his extortion of goods and gold.[82] How odd the gift's rejection must have appeared to the Tehuantepec leaders, accustomed as they were to providing local products as "gifts" on demand to visiting administrators in their own communities or on delegations to the Audiencia, where a measure of cochineal or vanilla was thought to secure the official's attention to their case. In this case the rejection of the gift, offered in anticipation of the justice that the *oidor* promised to restore for the people of Tehuantepec, might appropriately have been read as a rejection of their cause. For Montemayor, it may have represented a personal connection between himself and the rebels that he was loathe to establish.

If Montemayor embodied an extreme position on the Spanish side of the chasm of misunderstanding separating the colonists and the colonized, it is not surprising that the Tehuantepec community had a different reading of the events of 1660 than that which the *oidor*'s dramatic conclusion would have received in Spain. Rather than impressing a chastened populace with the brutal power of the Spanish colonial state to root out those who dared to confront its authority and its laws, Montemayor helped create an epic tale of native resistance that was the obverse of the lesson he intended. For most of the later colonial era, documentary sources only rarely give direct evidence of the story's retelling, but in the structure of continuing conflict and resistance in Tehuantepec, the parallels native actors drew between later events and the 1660 rebellion can still be glimpsed.

CHAPTER SIX

Community Opposition in Late Colonial Times

Two separate instances of conflict between the indigenous towns of the province and Spanish administrators of the early eighteenth century provide a final glimpse of the Zapotec community's perception of its political relationship with the colonial state prior to the Bourbon Reforms. Although neither confrontation was to achieve the notoriety of the 1660 rebellion, the events that precipitated these crises, the structure of native opposition, and the manner of the government's response further illuminate the boundaries that the community struggled to delineate under the colonial political economy. Before discussing each of these events in more detail, however, let us first take a look at the extent to which the Isthmian social landscape had shifted following the Tehuantepec rebellion, when Burgoa's comprehensive cultural geography of Oaxaca provided a contemporaneous overview of native life in the province's towns and villages.

Almost seventy-five years after the 1674 publication of the prelate's *Geográfica descripción*, the Tehuantepec province was featured more briefly in Antonio Villaseñor y Sánchez's mid-eighteenth-century survey of New Spain, *Theatro americano*.[1] By that time the long-standing jurisdictional dispute over Indian souls had created a doctrinal split among the province's native communities, one that established resident clergy in more remote towns with growing populations and separated communities serviced by secular parish priests from those continuing to receive their religious instruction from the Dominicans.[2] Although this unstable ecclesiastical boundary was subject to repeated renegotiation, it fell along natural cleavage lines within the Tehuantepec province that separated communities by ethnicity, ecology, and traditional political alliance.

Villaseñor y Sánchez described separately several head towns or *cabeceras* administered by the Tehuantepec province's *alcalde mayor* or his deputy. The Chontal-speaking pueblo of Tequisistlán on the western edge of the province, created through ecclesiastical *congregaciones* at the end of the sixteenth century, had been ceded by the Dominicans to the secular clergy, as had the lagoon-shore Huave *cabeceras* of San Mateo del Mar and San Francisco del Mar. The two Zoque-speaking villages, Zanatepec (identified as Tanatepec by the author), located on the eastern coastal plain, and Santa María Chimalapa, situated in the cool evergreen forests of the eastern sierra, continued to be serviced by the Dominicans from the convent established at Zanatepec. Two sierra communities, the partly Mixe village of San Juan Guichicovi and Zapotec-speaking Santa María Petapa, were retained under separate Dominican ministries, while those farther west were under the jurisdiction of the Jalapa (Xalapa) convent. Finally, despite the early eighteenth-century campaign by Fr. Angel Maldonado, reformist bishop of Oaxaca, to have an independent jurisdiction created for the Río de los Perros communities, the remaining Zapotec communities of the Isthmus coastal plain were still controlled by the Dominicans at Tehuantepec, the *cabecera principal* for the province as a whole.[3]

Villaseñor y Sánchez's brief and highly impressionistic portrait of the province in the 1740s suggests that, with few exceptions, the indigenous economy was little changed from that which had been established earlier in the colonial period. The cultivation of maize and other grains and fruits supported most families, although the Huave villages raised a large number of cattle, like their Zoque neighbors in Zanatepec, in addition to fishing in the shallow coastal lagoons. Most nonnatives reportedly made their living from trade in locally produced salt, grains, and cochineal, but Villaseñor y Sánchez also mentions livestock production, lumber cut from the Chimalapa forests, and sugar production in the well-watered lands near Guichicovi as significant Spanish enterprises.

Underlying this placid impression of the province was a legacy of struggle and strife that the dramatic events of 1660 had not resolved. Political interference by the Spanish *alcalde mayor* and factionalism within the native communities continued to brew and boil over on occasion. As noted earlier, Tehuantepec leaders were compelled to move to neighboring Huilotepec in 1683 to hold *cabildo* elections away from the *alcalde mayor*'s manipulation. Three years later, when the Crown *fiscal* passed through the Isthmus (which he referred to as "the throat of the realms of Mexico and Guatemala"), the province was still in a state of unrest. Less well-acquainted with the internal politics of the region, the *fiscal* attributed its agitation to the persistent threat posed by pirates known to be stalking the Pacific coastal waters.

When Tehuantepec actually was attacked by pirates in 1687, the townspeople fled to the countryside for safety, only to find on returning a week later that their fields and houses had been ransacked; their stored grain, pigs, and poultry carted off; and their livestock butchered for meat by the enemy. A silver cross and other religious objects were taken from the church, and fifteen houses were burned to the ground, as were the Casas Reales, the community house, and the guest house for travelers. Malnutrition and disease followed the pirates' departure. About one-third (971) of the town's native households received an exemption from tribute payments for the next two years, while the town rebuilt itself physically and economically.[4]

Unsettling as this calamity surely was, the chronic drain on native labor and resources perpetuated by a corrupt colonial bureaucracy took its own harsh toll on families and exasperated community efforts to demarcate a sphere of political autonomy. Although tensions never quite escalated again to the level of violence that had precipitated the murder of Juan de Avellán, the century that followed the 1660 rebellion was neither one of peaceful accommodation nor one of passive resignation. Two episodes of struggle documented in the historical record of the early eighteenth century illustrate most clearly both the source of Zapotec frustration and the structure of indigenous politics. The first of these developed in 1715 and was largely focused in Tehuantepec itself. The second episode began four years later and, although the underlying grievances were raised by Zapotec communities of the Isthmus sierra, the extensive litigation record provides a rich, if anecdotal, description of life in the *cabecera*. Complementing the latter is an unusual entry in the province's documentary record, the first detailed census record of the native population that is known to have reached the courts in Mexico City. Because of the inclusive view this house-by-house survey provides of the Isthmus Zapotec population, I will first examine the resulting demographic profile for what can be seen of native social organization before turning to the issue of late colonial political confrontation.

Isthmus Zapotec Population and Society in Late Colonial Times

Such was the presence of non-Indians in the province that Villaseñor y Sánchez went so far as to suggest that Tehuantepec itself was dominated by the combined total of Spanish and mestizo (50) and mulatto (115) households, even though there were still some 2,600 indigenous families in the Zapotec-speaking Tehuantepec *doctrina*. The growth of nonnative households in the *villa* is a striking development, and the author's report that these men formed two militia companies that patrolled the Pacific coast fending off pirate invasions may in part explain the economic attraction of the town for mixed-race individuals.[5] But Villaseñor y Sánchez's impression that Tehuantepec had lost its "Indianness" was surely based on the concentration of nonnative households in the town center, while he ignored the predominantly Zapotec barrios aggregated around it.

Just twenty years earlier, when actual census records rather than summaries were brought to Mexico City as part of the lengthy dispute between several Zapotec towns and the Spanish *alcalde mayor,* the town's fifteen late colonial-era barrios were intact, and their 2,926 residents constituted approximately 32 percent of the province's Zapotec-speaking population. With only twenty of the households in these barrios including a non-*indio* spouse (out of twenty-four mixed-race Zapotec families province-wide), Tehuantepec did not look like a town that had lost its Zapotec ethnicity, despite the high profile of nonnative residents.[6] As can be seen from the population distribution summarized in Table 6.1, however, not all of Tehuantepec's barrios were flourishing. The two largest, San Blas Atempa and Santa María Yoloteca, together held almost half the native population of Tehuantepec, while the two smallest, San Pedro Chalco and Santa María Yagabeche, held barely fifty people between them. Regardless of these size disparities, the barrio remained central to late colonial Tehuantepec's social and political organization, as it had been since the prehispanic formation of the city.

Within each barrio, the Catholic church established during one of the ecclesiastical *congregaciones* of the late sixteenth and early seventeenth centuries had long become the nexus of celebrations and institutions around which community life revolved in Tehuantepec. So vital to community identity were the accustomed rituals of Catholic pageantry that one greedy Spanish administrator was able to extort additional sums

TABLE 6.1
Rank Order by Total Population of Zapotec-Speaking Urban Barrios and Rural Communities in 1722

Tehuantepec Barrio		Rural Community	
San Blas Atempa	854	Santa María Petapa	1,290
Santa María Yoloteca	467	San Juan Guichicobi	1,126
San Juan Guichibere	255	Santa María Guienagati	623
San Gerónimo	250	San Vicente Juchitán	554
Santa Cruz Tagolaba	176	Santiago Lachiguiri	468
Laborio	168	Santo Domingo Petapa	457
San Pedro Vixana	161	San Gerónimo Ixtepec	411
San Pedro Guichigui	125	Santa María Magdalena Guelabene	363
San Juan Totonilco	119	Santiago Guevea	270
San Juan de los Cerrillos	103	Santa Catarina Mixtequilla	123
Santa María Jalieza	98	Huilotepec	120
San Jacinto Tapaguichi	50	Santa María Magdalena Tlacotepec	116
Santa Cruz Jalisco	49	Santo Domingo Pixahui Chihuitan	75
San Pedro Chalco	31	Santiago Laollaga	49
Santa María Yagabeche	20	Santa María Ixtaltepec	48
		Santa Cruz Atitlan	36
		San Pedro Martín Comitan	14

SOURCE: Archivo General de la Nación Civil, vol. 619, exp. 2

from the Tehuantepec *principales* by holding hostage the drums that each barrio used to celebrate its patron saint's *fiesta*.[7] How deeply held the theological values represented by the church may have been within the Zapotec community is, of course, much more difficult to assess. In at least one case, fervent Catholic evangelism had been met with so much ridicule by barrio and *cabildo* officials that the native believer, Domingo Martín, felt compelled to petition the viceroy for intercession. Although elected *mayordomo* in the barrio of San Blas in 1672, Domingo found himself constantly interrupted by jeering native officials when he went out onto the streets of the barrio on Saturdays to pray the rosary and teach among the barrio children.[8]

It is presumed that the majority of Tehuantepec's native households based their livelihood on agriculture or trade, but specific occupations are rarely noted in the 1722 census. Court proceedings from the early and mid-eighteenth century occasionally identify native men from different barrios and Isthmus villages by their artisan skills as masons, carpenters, chairmakers, or weavers of coarse cloth. When, nearly one hundred years later, the Tehuantepec barrio of Santa María Yoloteca sought redress in

Mexico City for its acute land shortage, the barrio was well known for its skills in carpentry and leather-working, with saddles and shoes made in Santa María being widely sold throughout the province and beyond. How long those occupations had been established in the barrio is uncertain, but Santa María's *principales* claimed that its citizenry turned to artisanry because the barrio lacked agricultural lands of its own and had to rent them from the excess lands belonging to less populous barrios and neighboring villages.[9]

Why Santa María appeared to be the only Tehuantepec barrio without land more than that sufficient to feed its burgeoning population was a question about which none of the barrio leaders or Spanish officials could do more than speculate. The normal pattern in late colonial Tehuantepec was for each barrio to control its own delimited agricultural zone, actively defending it against encroachments by outsiders, whether they be nonnatives or other indigenous communities, and renting parcels to others when normal inheritance patterns failed to keep these lands under active cultivation. Disputes over land only rarely became so contentious as to find their way to Mexico City for resolution before the latter half of the eighteenth century, but surviving municipal archives in some Isthmus communities surveyed by Michel Oudijk hint at how pervasive and long-standing these matters could be.[10]

In 1682 the *alcalde mayor* Don Luís de Medina attempted to settle a protracted boundary conflict between the Tehuantepec barrio of San Pedro Guichigui and its neighbor, the village of San Pedro Huilotepec. Huilotepec officials complained about the location of boundary markers replacing those destroyed by a flood six years earlier, while the Guichigui *principal* countered that, since their first settlers, the inhabitants of Huilotepec had been trying to move those of his barrio from the lands to which they had just title. In its defense the barrio produced titles it had been granted in 1655 after a similar dispute that also included the Tehuantepec barrio of San Pedro Bixana (also spelled Vixana). These records in turn contained a 1639 *memoria* by a former *principal* of Guichigui, who had inherited the tract of land under dispute and who alleged that Huilotepec had been attempting to claim this land since 1599. Both communities produced *pinturas* (called "venturas" in Zapotec) that showed the validation of their land holdings by the sixteenth-century Tehuantepec kings, although only the *lienzo* known as the Mapa de Huilotepec survives today.[11]

It was the role of barrio and village officials to defend community interests against outside encroachment, as the Huilotepec–San Pedro Guichigui dispute illustrates. The documentary evidence gives few further clues as to how such leaders functioned within the communities they served, other than that they were responsible for the collection of tribute and *repartimiento* obligations. Following prehispanic and early colonial patterns, they presumably organized labor for religious celebrations and other public events and adjudicated disputes within the community as well. On occasion such traditional activities ran into conflict with newly instituted colonial organizations. As was noted in Chapter 4, the governor and other officials of Juchitán, by now the largest of Tehuantepec's former dependencies, claimed in 1736 that the Dominican friars had converted their traditional community lands by force some twenty years before into five *cofradía* haciendas, which were under the convent's direct control. The pueblo no longer could rely on its livestock and small orchards of fruit and cacao trees for funds needed to pay the tribute debts of the ill or to maintain their church expenses.[12]

Although it is not possible to specify all the responsibilities they held, the offices and titles for both barrio and village leaders in late colonial Tehuantepec are reiterated in various documents. Under the Zapotec city-state, there had been no political distinction between rural and urban barrios, but the autonomy that formerly subject villages developed under Spanish law led to their forming separate *cabildo* organizations. Thus Huilotepec and other Zapotec-speaking villages of the province, no matter what their size, elected the *cabildo* officers of *governor, alcalde, regidor, juez* or *alguacil*, and *escrivano*. Whether by birthright or by service to the community, individual villagers could also claim the title of *principal*, which in late colonial times as today in the Isthmus was interchanged with the Zapotec term for "noble," *xuana* (*joana* in sixteenth-century orthography).

Because they remained politically integrated with the town center, Tehuantepec's barrios were without their own colonial *cabildos*, but they did maintain aspects of traditional Zapotec leadership structure in the late seventeenth and eighteenth centuries. Numerous individuals within both large and small barrios were identified by the title of *principal*, but there was also an elected position of barrio headman held by an individual who was known officially as the *xuana principal*. In San Blas Atempa, Tehuantepec's largest barrio, there was at least one additional *xuana* role, head of the fishermen ("xuana de los pescadores"), a title claimed by a witness in one of the cases discussed below; there may have been others as well. Oudijk has suggested that there may have been subdivisions even within smaller barrios like San Pedro Guichigui, which in the late sixteenth and early seventeenth centuries were referred to as *pichi*, each with its own *xuana*.[13] Occasional references to a barrio *tequitlato* in addition to the *xuana principal* indicate that the office of tribute collector (known in sixteenth-century Zapotec as the "collabachiña") had not disappeared.

Data from a four-year period in early eighteenth-century San Blas indicate that the term of office for the *xuana principal*, like that of the town *cabildo* offices, was one year. In several cases then and in the late seventeenth century, according to the litigation record between Huilotepec and San Pedro Guichigui, the same individuals passed back and forth between the *cabildo* offices of governor, *alcalde*, and barrio headman. By the early eighteenth century, Tehuantepec no longer elected five or six *regidores* from among the different barrio *principales* in addition to the lesser offices of *juez* and *escrivano*. Instead, all fifteen barrio *xuanas* were included in the *cabildo*, as may have been the informal practice before, with a single individual among them identified as the *regidor mayor* or *primero principal*. These officers met daily in the community house, going as a group to the Casas Reales when summoned by the *alcalde mayor*.[14]

The early eighteenth-century census record provides the first comprehensive data for Isthmus Zapotec communities outside the urban center. Table 6.1 demonstrates that these communities ranged widely in size, as did the Tehuantepec barrios. Among the nine Zapotec-speaking communities of the coastal plain that once had been dependencies of the Tehuantepec city-state, only Juchitán and Ixtepec had substantial populations of a few hundred or more, and four others were just barely surviving, with fifty or fewer individuals counted in each. None of the Zapotec sierra communities were as small as this, and two of them, Santa María Petapa and San Juan Guichicovi, had native populations well over one thousand. Unfortunately, because previous population figures for the province, including those cited by Balthasar de San Miguel, do not give totals for any of the pueblos subject to the *cabecera* of Tehuantepec, there is no baseline figure against which to compare the 1722 population for individual communities. Earlier Spanish impressions of these villages as uniformly small and inconsequential suggest that at least some of the native communities had made substantial population gains in the last century.

For the province as a whole, the picture is more ambiguous and it appears that the native population had just begun its recovery from the depredations of epidemic disease by which it had been ravaged in the sixteenth and seventeenth centuries. A precise demographic comparison with earlier tribute summaries cannot be made, for, with the exception of Chontal-speaking Tequisistlán, the 1722 census notebooks do not record the non-Zapotec communities of the province. Neither the traditionally small Huave villages nor the two surviving Zoque communities are likely to have boosted the tributary count for the province considerably beyond the 2,327 full-time tributary equivalents recorded that year for the Isthmus Zapotecs. With 2,437 tributaries of all ethnicities registered one hundred years earlier at what appears to have been the colonial era nadir (see Chapter 4), the combined 1722 population may have gained only two or three hundred households. It cannot have grown much beyond the 2,788 Indian tributaries reported less than a half-century earlier in 1687.

Though small, it was the beginning of a more sustained recovery, the full impact of which was felt later in the century, when Villaseñor y Sánchez counted 2,600 Zapotec households in 1743, an increase of almost 12 percent in twenty-one years. An average growth rate of over 0.5 percent per year is exceptionally high for a rural preindustrial population, but a closer examination of the age distribution of the 1722 population shows how a sustained respite from epidemic disease might have allowed this increase to come about.

The age profile of the 1722 census (Fig. 6.1) also reveals some anomalous distributions among the 9,069 Indian men, women, and children who were registered in Zapotec towns. The two youngest groups, representing all children under ten years of age (3,333 individuals), together comprise over one-third of the population (36 percent). At the same time, there is a rapid decrease in the numbers of older individuals, a trend partly anticipated by disease and death patterns typical for premodern rural society, where fewer individuals survived infant and childhood illnesses. The weak representation of individuals aged fifteen to nineteen years in this sample is surprising, however, for it is an anomalous dip in the population curve that would be difficult to attribute to some special life hazards experienced just prior to age fifteen. Very likely this anomaly reflects some earlier epidemic cycle that increased early childhood death rates for this group or lowered the number of their births as a con-

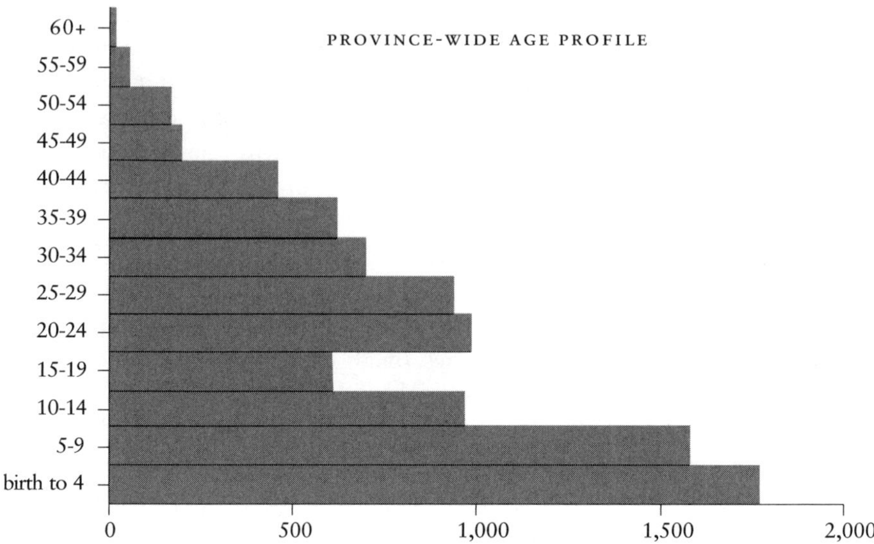

FIG. 6.1. 1722 age distribution in five-year intervals for the Zapotec-speaking population of the Isthmus of Tehuantepec. Source: Archivo General de la Nación Civil, vol. 619, exp. 2.

sequence of increased death rates in their parents' generation. Such episodes continued to stall full demographic recovery in many parts of New Spain long after native populations passed their early seventeenth-century nadir.

Nonetheless, the potential for population growth had improved greatly in the Tehuantepec province in 1722, and its promise can be found in the large cohort of children born after 1712. If this generation were so fortunate as to be spared new epidemics or other natural calamities and a majority survived to be adults and parents in 1743, their contribution to the tributary count alone would account for the demographic spurt registered by Villaseñor y Sánchez. Other trends seen in the 1722 census records suggest that these demographic gains rested on solid foundations. Average family size increased somewhat from that documented in the mid-sixteenth century, when the first comprehensive count of the Isthmus population was reported by Balthasar de San Miguel. Then, not long after the initial waves of epidemic disease, average family size was small, with just 3.2 individuals of all ages for every full tributary equivalent; in 1722 there were 3.9 individuals per tribute-paying household, both in the *villa* of Tehuantepec and among the Isthmus Zapotec as a whole. However modest, the gain is yet another expression of the capacity for population recovery that native society had recouped by late colonial times. Despite further occurrences of measles and other epidemic diseases, the population of Tehuantepec continued to rebound, and by the close of the eighteenth century the number of native tributaries was 50 percent more than that reported by Villaseñor y Sánchez.[15]

The Native Population in Turmoil: Conflict over Political Autonomy in the Early Eighteenth Century

The Isthmus population resurgence during the eighteenth century came at the price of increased levels of social tension. Here as elsewhere in late colonial New Spain, disputes between native communities and between communities and Spanish landowners escalated as scarce *milpa* and pasture lands were needed by swelling native households. More prosperous and stable populations also found themselves newly targeted for economic exploitation under a corrupt system of colonial administration. How the Isthmus Zapotec responded to these assaults on their political and economic vitality can be seen in the details surrounding two particularly contentious confrontations with Spanish administrators. Both crises have been discussed previously by historians, with Laura Machuca and Carlos Manzo among the most recent scholars to examine the lengthy document files pertaining to the cases.[16] While the primary focus of these studies has been the economic burden of *repartimiento* monopolies and their interference with regional trade patterns, the present analysis emphasizes the terms of autonomy that Isthmus communities sought to delineate for themselves within the context of the colonial political economy.

The events of 1715–1716

In September 1715, the people of Tehuantepec were in a riotous state, their anger once again directed at the local Spanish authorities who had abused them and at the native *cabildo* officers regarded as complicit to this injustice. The precipitating event seems to have been an accident, or so it was explained by the province's *alcalde mayor* Don Cosme de Mier y Estrada and his *teniente general* Don Nicolás Gonzales de la Madrid.[17] An unnamed militiaman, posted at the small hilltop fortress overlooking the town plaza, wounded a local man, whom he apparently mistook for a dangerous animal in the dark. Gonzales, who was captain of the militia, was the target of the angry crowds that assembled the next day, forcing the *teniente general* to take refuge in the Dominican convent. Despite receiving a serious injury in the resulting melee, this time the focus of native rage survived his ordeal, unlike the unfortunate Juan de Avellán, *alcalde mayor* of the province a half-century earlier. The underlying issues which created such a reservoir of antipathy toward this Spaniard, however, were much the same as they had been in 1660. Gonzales, the most visible and rapacious representative of the colonial administration, had overstepped the boundary which the community drew around itself economically and politically. What differed this time was the nature of the response made by the colonial authorities.

Gonzales hinted in his own account of these events at the degree to which he attempted to meddle in community affairs. He was able to do so as the responsible Spanish authority under a largely absentee *alcalde mayor,* Don Cosme de Mier y Estrada, who simultaneously held the equivalent position of *justicia mayor* in nearby Jalapa under the authority of the Marquesado del Valle rather than the Crown. For years the Jalapa position had been filled by the lessee of the Marquesado's Tehuantepec haciendas, and Mier y Estrada appears to have been a typical renter-administrator. Preoccupied with his own entrepreneurial activities in the province, the *alcalde mayor* was absent frequently from Tehuantepec and little involved in the province's governance, leaving his lieutenant a free hand to act as he saw fit.

Gonzales imposed two ordinances that he himself suggested contributed to local unrest, though their objective, he maintained, had been only to benefit the native population. The first was an order requiring farmers to plant their *milpas*, a measure that the *teniente* claimed was designed to avoid the extreme shortages in maize production that the province experienced previously, requiring them to buy food at inflated prices from native traders. This ordinance had received the approval of the clerics and the governor of the town council, Don Baltasar de los Reyes, a man whom Gonzales described as very Hispanicized and inclined to good habits and good works. The second ordinance, he maintained, was intended for the health and well-being of the town and applied to Spaniards as well as natives. Whatever its supposed health benefits may have been, this order to clear vegetation and open up the area around all houses and gardens must have been poorly received in the environs of Tehuantepec, where shady respite from the tropical sun has always been welcome.

When the native population of the province formalized its complaints before the General Indian Court in August of the following year, they presented a different list of grievances. Gonzales, a resident of Tehuantepec, who, they noted, had served as *teniente* under previous administrations, had conspired with the town's long-term royal scribe, Felipe Gamboa, to exploit his position for personal gain over the past seven years. The specific offenses they cited were wide-ranging and touched on all sectors of the province's native population, whether urban or rural, coastal or sierra, Zapotec, Huave, or Zoque. The formal complaint was made jointly by the town councils of Tehuantepec, San Juan Guichicovi, Santa María Petapa, Santo Domingo Petapa, Santiago Lachiguiri, Santiago Guevea, Santa María Guienagati, Santa María Magdalena Guelavani, Santa María Huazontlan del Mar, San Mateo del Mar, San Dionisio del Mar, San Francisco del Mar, San Miguel Chimalapa, and Santa María Chimalapa.

The issue at heart in these charges was a familiar one in the province's experience under Spanish rule: Gonzales interfered with the native economy through a monopoly on trade and through compulsory *repartimientos de mercancías*. Only beef from cattle raised on his hacienda could be sold in the Tehuantepec market, which he sought to control in all sectors by removing other middlemen. Gonzales stationed guards on the roads to intercept traders, whose merchandise he then resold at extremely high prices. When the sierra communities of Guichicovi and the Petapas brought maize to Tehuantepec to sell, he extracted one-quarter of the product for himself, leaving the producers with no profit after the cost of mule transport was deducted. He forced the Huave communities to sell him fish and shrimp at reduced price, paying only 4 to 6 *reales* per basket, when the market value in Tehuantepec was four times that price. Like the sierra Zapotec communities that were forced to sell cochineal at below-market values, these villages complained of having to purchase goods they did not need or want at inflated prices from the *teniente*. He sent policemen (*topiles*) out to the villages to enforce his demands, and refusals were met with fines, jailing, and general mistreatment. Such extortions left the native population with insufficient resources to support their families, to pay their tribute, or to support the church.

Gonzales illegally used his official power in other ways as well for his personal profit or that of the *alcalde mayor*. Lumber cut and transported from the mountains, supposedly for use in the Casas Reales, was in fact used to construct Gonzales's own house. The *teniente* obliged native muleteers to carry salt from the *salinas* operations that the *alcalde mayor* was renting. None of these costs or the services of the eleven men and women who worked each day in the Casas Reales were reimbursed by the *teniente*. Native officials who complained about his abuses had their offices taken away from them, only to be replaced by men more agreeable to the demands of the *teniente* and his *alcalde mayor.* When complaints were made to Don Cosme de Mier y Estrada in his capacity as resident judge, the scribe Gamboa kept all the documentation that community officials presented on the pretext of needing to make copies, but refused to return either the documents or the fee of 300 pesos he extracted for the copies. Now the representatives of the province's beleaguered native communities turned to the Audiencia for justice through a fair review of their complaints. They asked that Gonzales and Gamboa be removed from the province so that free testimony could be taken by an unbiased official and that their belongings be sequestered so that restitution eventually could be made to the aggrieved parties.[18]

The pervasiveness of these charges, affecting as they did so many aspects of the economic life of the province, and the wide representation of Isthmus communities contributing their particular grievances made an impression on the court. Concern for the unrest and instability which had spread throughout the province over the last months was the decisive factor. As the *fiscal* noted, the Indians had abandoned their pueblos in order to escape these depredations that had only increased since their charges were made, depriving the king of his tributaries. The court agreed to all the requests, including the immediate appointment of Don Juan Arias Gudiel as the special judge investigating the complaints, rather than deferring an examination of these charges to the normal end-of-office *residencia* of these officials.

When the Tehuantepec community appealed to the Audiencia in October to confirm its elected *cabildo* officers for the incoming year, citing the antipathy of their *alcalde mayor*, who refused to accept them, the viceroy again was sympathetic. As Viceroy Zúñiga noted, the *fiscal* had endorsed the slate of candidates enthusiastically when he reviewed the petition, vouching personally for Don Diego de Velasco, the proposed governor, whom he knew to be "one of the principal caciques of that province, of good judgment and other good qualities."[19] How different was this judicious response to native complaints and the affirmation of native self-government from that made almost a half-century earlier by another newly installed viceroy, the Conde de Baños. In 1660 the viceroy had regarded a similar Tehuantepec delegation seeking confirmation of its elected officers with suspicion, interrogating the Zapotec messengers closely and using their perceived guilty behavior as an excuse to launch Montemayor's vicious attack on the Tehuantepec rebels and their elected *cabildo*.

It was also a decidedly different reading of the natives' plight than that which the local Dominican prior had forwarded a year earlier in his September 1715 appeal to the then Viceroy Duque de Linares for action against the rioters. Fray Alonso de Vargas Machuca, who had given refuge in the Tehuantepec convent to Gonzales and the disgraced native governor and *alcaldes*, sought some strong action from Mexico to put an end to the uprising. Each day that passed, the rebels demanded new concessions from the *alcalde mayor*, who had rushed to the town from Jalapa when he was informed of the riot. In order to calm things, Mier y Estrada had agreed to the removal of the disgraced *cabildo* officers and the impromptu election of new officers, without going through the customary vote by the town's *principales*. Not only did the rioters demand the removal of Gonzales from the office of *teniente general*, but they even wanted to elect his Spanish successor, a demand which the *alcalde mayor* refused on principle, even as he responded to native pressure and selected someone known to be acceptable to them. Fray Alonso dismissed these grievances as insubstantial and suggested that the problems were caused by different factions among the Spaniards residing in the town, each of whom was courting native allegiances to advance his own economic self-interest.[20]

The accounts of the riot offered by the three Spanish officials implicated in these events—Mier y Estrada, Gonzales, and Gamboa—filled in more details about the actors responsible for the rebellion, providing a glimpse of politics within the native community.[21] The riot was instigated by a group from the Tehuantepec barrio of Santa María Yoloteca, but three individuals were singled out as the leaders: a man identified only as "el golaba" (cf. *collaba*, the Zapotec term for barrio; this appears to be a shorthand reference to the Santa María barrio *tequitlato* or *collabachiña*), his companion, and a woman known as "la india Tereza." The person whom the rioters wanted to install as governor was a man named Juan Martín, whom the Spanish officials regarded as incompetent because of his prior record of service in that office during the period when Don Miguel de Munarres was *alcalde mayor*. According to Mier y Estrada and Gonzales, Martín had been jailed for spending all the royal tribute he had collected from the community, and the incarceration had put his barrio in an uproar. His near escape, with the help of several women of the barrio in which he was *principal,* was an event unparalleled since the time Don Luís de Medina served as *alcalde mayor* in the province during the 1680s, when Tehuantepec natives had stormed the jail with axes and machetes to free a man whom they then named governor.

Not only was Juan Martín incompetent in the judgment of these Spaniards, but the men chosen to be his *alcaldes* were considered to be youths of little consequence. None of these men was elected freely by the community elders and *principales,* but because of their fear of the agitated commoners, they acceded to the rebels' choices. The *alcalde mayor* then was obliged to bestow the staffs of office on the insurgents, however unqualified they might be, in order to keep the riot from accelerating. Following a practice that had been used successfully in other situations to quell native insurrection, the *fiscal* recommended that Mier y Estrada find some pretext to lure the three rebel leaders out of town, so they could be taken to Oaxaca or Mexico City for punishment without causing further commotion in Tehuantepec.

The participants in the 1715 events, whether native or Spaniard, made no reference to the 1660 Tehuantepec rebellion that was recorded in these documents, but the structure of the Zapotec community's political activity in the riot and its aftermath is remarkably similar. Once again a native casualty sparked the crisis, but the underlying tensions resulted from the egregious exploitation the native community suffered at the hands of intrusive colonial officials. Once again commoner rage was directed as much at the indigenous *cabildo* that had failed to prevent these abuses as at the Spanish *vecinos* who caused them. Whether these *cabildo* officers had corruptly given Gonzales a free hand or merely been unable to stop him is not clear from the record, but this was not the first time that the governor Baltasar de los Reyes had been a target of popular anger. As a young man he had served as *escrivano* in the loyalist *cabildo* of 1660.

The 1660 rebellion was instigated by individuals representing a fairly broad spectrum of Tehuantepec's urban and rural society, judging from the residential and occupational identities in the *oidor* Montemayor's list of sentences for those whom he and the loyalist *cabildo* deemed most culpable. One of the two urban barrios represented in 1660 was Santa María Yoloteca, again named in the present crisis as the affiliation of the riot's leaders. With a large population and limited agricultural lands available to it, Santa María may have been particularly hard hit by Gonzales's scheme to increase maize production, though there is no direct evidence for what compelled a handful of its residents to play such an active role. Particularly significant is the fact that the primary leader of the insurrection appears to be identified by his Zapotec title as a Santa María barrio leader, providing one of many indicators of the continued strength of Tehuantepec's barrio organization, even as the *cabildo* structure failed in its responsibility to the community.

As was the case in the 1660 rebellion, those who challenged Spanish authority were essentially reformists rather than revolutionaries, seeking to make the existing colonial system of governance more responsive to native needs. With the *teniente* Gonzales the target of local rage, replacing him with a man considered more sympathetic to their plight was a primary demand of the rebels from their *alcalde mayor*, although it appears from the complaints the province's communities raised against all three Spanish authorities the following year that Mier y Estrada's concession was short-lived. The riot leaders did not seek to wrest political control of the native community for themselves either, but rather promoted a new slate of officers. However disliked by the *alcalde mayor* this new *cabildo* may have been, Juan Martín, its chosen *governador*, was considered qualified by his status as barrio *principal* for a position to which he had been elected legitimately before.

The records are silent about the twelve months that intervened between the September 1715 crisis and the petitions brought to the viceroy on behalf of the province's native population a year later. Whether or not the rebel *cabildo* managed to stay in office, as it had in 1660, clearly some group of Zapotec leaders worked diligently during those months to coordinate the province-wide complaint of August 1716. In 1660 the Tehuantepec rebels had been accused of fomenting rebellion by sending letters to surrounding communities enlisting their support, but no intercepted writings were entered in evidence to support these rumors. This later case, however, exhibits the successful results of just such a campaign, whether launched through written messages or personal envoys. With Tehuantepec taking upon itself the task of representing its traditional subjects among the Zapotec-speaking communities of the coastal plain (and presumably their dwindling Zoque neighbors as well), the resulting complaint against the three Spanish officials included charges from all the independent Isthmus sierra Zapotec communities, all the coastal Huave villages, and both sierra Zoque pueblos. The multiethnic nature of this petition was not explicitly needed to persuade the Audiencia, disposed as it was to regard "Indian" as a unified social category of "otherness" and to prioritize the importance of native complaints by the number of pueblos involved as much as the number and seriousness of the charges. However, for the organizers of this petition to have transcended the linguistic and territorial boundaries that divided communities into independent and often hostile corporate entities in late colonial times was a significant political accomplishment.

In 1716 the coordinated list of charges won over an Audiencia already disposed to find some solution to native unrest and official corruption, though there is no direct evidence that the mandated judicial inquiry took place as directed. The natives did not succeed in driving Gonzales and Gamboa from the province, for their names appear among later documents. Don Cosme de Mier y Estrada left office sometime in 1717, but it is unclear whether his departure was the end of his term, the result of criminal findings, or occasioned by his death. Whatever the cause, his cousin was left to collect tributes that were never turned over to the *alcalde mayor* who succeeded him, Don Joseph Rodríguez de Ledesma.[22] The testimony emerging from repeated efforts by the Crown to collect these back tribute payments itself provides a glimpse of the complex financial arrangements that underwrote the profitable administration of native towns in late colonial Oaxaca, but my primary concern here is the impact of these structures on native society in Tehuantepec.[23] To that end I turn next to an examination of the corruption charges levied against Ledesma's successor, Don Pedro de Saravía, whose astonishing excesses generated a detailed criminal examination from which emerges a more nuanced portrait of the workings of native politics.

The events of 1719–1721

Don Pedro de Saravía y Cortés came to Tehuantepec as *alcalde mayor* in early 1719, accompanied by his brother Antonio in the office of *teniente general*. Saravía wasted no time in squeezing what profits could be wrung from the province's native population, demonstrating a greed and brutality so beyond the pale of the typical Spanish administrator that the natives of Santa María Guienagati considered him to have been even crueler than the infamous Juan de Avellan, murdered in the Tehuantepec riot of 1660. "There has been no other example of an *alcalde mayor* like him since they killed Don Pedro [sic] Avellán in the town of Tehuantepec, who although he was bad in his *repartimientos* and tyrannical behavior, this one [Pedro de Saravía y Cortés] and his *teniente* are worse for their cruelties."[24] The *cabildo* officers of Guienagati had been so aggrieved by these abuses and severe *repartimientos* that they joined suit with the Isthmian sierra pueblos of Lachiguiri and Guevea, seeking recompense for the money that had been extorted from their communities. Each of the two years that Saravía had served as *alcalde mayor*, he forced them to accept increasingly arduous *repartimiento* burdens, from mules and burros too young to be of any use to goods from his store sold at inflated prices. The candle wax, machetes, cloth, tobacco, and cacao that were forced upon them might have had some economic use within these villages, but not in the quantities or at the prices imposed by the *alcalde mayor*.[25] When the sierra community of San Juan Guichicovi added its complaints to the charges against the Saravía brothers, its 1719 *repartimiento* of livestock and goods totaling over 1,000 pesos had been increased to more than 1,200 pesos the following year, an annual burden of more than 1 peso for every man, woman, and child in the village.[26]

Cochineal, which was the principal product of the mountain region and the villagers' only source of cash to support their families and meet their tribute and ecclesiastical duties, was a primary target of Saravía's greed. Each year he increased the quantity of *grana*, as the dye-producing insects were known, that each community had to sell him, but the prices Saravía paid were less than one-third the market value. When the local cochineal harvest failed, as it did in 1720, the *alcalde mayor* still demanded the product, forcing villagers to travel as far away as Mixe territory in the Nejapa province to purchase the *grana* they had not been able to grow themselves. Destitute families sold their clothing to meet their share of the *repartimiento* burden, while others abandoned their villages, moving to pueblos outside the grasp of the Saravía brothers or simply disappearing into the bush.[27]

When communities were unable to make their *repartimiento* payments, it was the *cabildo* officers who felt the *alcalde mayor*'s wrath directly. For the slightest shortage or delay in payments, he would incarcerate whatever responsible party he could get his hands on for arbitrary periods that ranged from a couple of days to more than a month. Successive officers from all the litigating communities had been subjected to this abuse. What happened to Diego Ruíz, governor of Santa María Guienagati, is but one example. For ten days he was jailed while the community attempted to find the money to make up its *repartimiento* shortfall.

In desperation his son sold all Diego's livestock—three cows, one bull, and two horses—but the 35 pesos he got for them was not enough, and the *alcalde mayor* kept the governor in jail for fifty-one days more. When his replacement as governor was jailed for twenty-two days the following year for failing to meet yet another round of *repartimiento* debt, the poor man almost starved to death; no one from the community dared to come to town and bring him food, for fear of what the *alcalde mayor* or his brother would do to them.[28]

It was not just the threat of capricious imprisonment that terrorized the province, however, but also the cruel and even life-threatening whippings that inevitably accompanied a prolonged stint in jail. Corporal punishment was a long-practiced penalty inflicted by both bureaucrats and priests in the Spanish colonial world, but the violence of the Saravía brothers exceeded even these harsh norms. In what was a repeated native charge, Diego Ruíz claimed that the *alcalde mayor* had tied him to a pillar in the patio of the Casas Reales and given him fifty lashes, until he begged for his life, pleading that he was just an old man and that he would find a way to pay. But Don Pedro said he didn't care if he died with a thousand devils from the whipping, and the *alcalde mayor* would have continued to beat him had Don Pedro's wife not come out to the patio and told him to untie the man and throw him in jail.[29]

When Don Pedro was away from the *villa*, his brother did not hesitate to follow the same abusive pattern. Knowing that their villages would be unable to meet yet another round of cash payments, the sierra *cabildos* refused initially when Don Antonio ordered new *repartimientos*. Their protest was countered when the *teniente* jailed the village officers, who had come to town to celebrate the fiesta of San Pedro, whipping them until they agreed to take the unwanted goods. So traumatized was one of the men from Santiago Lachiguiri that he had not yet recovered from the attack of *susto* or fright precipitated by the beatings and Don Antonio's threat to have them all sent to prison. The following October, when the Lachiguiri *alcaldes* brought a final installment of the new cochineal *repartimiento* to town, the *teniente* claimed their shipment was short and threw them in jail, ordering that they be given twenty-five lashes each. His rage still unabated, Don Antonio dragged the men out into the patio and had them tied to posts for another round with the whip. This time the sergeant major charged with delivering this punishment refused, saying that he had already beaten the men in the jail, that they were only poor Indians, and that he did not want to run the risk of seriously injuring them.[30] Since one man from the coastal plain town of San Gerónimo Ixtepec was reported to have died from a whipping given him by Don Pedro Saravía, his caution was amply justified.

The *alcalde mayor*'s violent nature got him into serious difficulties with the Audiencia, but not initially for his ill treatment of the native population in his jurisdiction. It was instead his assault on another Spaniard, Don Antonio Sandín de Calderón, *comisario de tributos* for the province, along with his failure to comply with the investigation of tribute irregularities that finally sent him to prison at San Juan de Ulua, Veracruz. Two Zapotec eyewitnesses recounted details of this assault for Don Andrés de Miranda, *justicia mayor* of Jalapa, who, as the nearest administrative official, had been commissioned to investigate the charges originally levied by Sandín in March 1720. They testified that Saravía had become enraged by the tribute commissioner's persistent efforts to question him and, after shouting many insults at Sandín, had begun to punch and strike him against the doors of the Sala de Armas, grabbing the portfolio in which the comissioner carried his papers and hitting him with it until blood flowed from his head and body. A friar visiting the Tehuantepec convent took the badly injured Sandín to Oaxaca to recover.[31]

Don Pedro left Tehuantepec before Miranda arrived in the late spring to investigate Sandín's complaints, provoking the exacerbated Audiencia to levy the extraordinary fine of 1,000 pesos against the *alcalde mayor* and another 200 pesos against his brother, although they attempted to claim a privileged military exemption (*fuero militar*) from civil punishment. Although the twenty-six-year-old Antonio Saravía remained in town—the brothers needed the income provided by *repartimientos* to repay their own creditors, as was the customary practice in New Spain—that choice became untenable once Miranda's investigation was rekindled at the end of the year. By now the charges of abuse from the Lachiguiri, Guevea, and Guienagati communities had been added to the judge's dossier. Finding sufficient cause to their demand for restitution, Miranda put the *teniente* under temporary guard while he inventoried Don Pedro's property in the Casas Reales. Antonio managed to escape from his guards in early January, taking refuge in the convent, where the Dominicans refused to give him up on grounds of ecclesiastical immunity, although they did permit Miranda to interview him there.[32]

Several months later this impasse had still not been breached, and Crown authorities became increasingly concerned about the province's tribute revenues, which the *teniente* claimed had only been partially collected before his incarceration. Meanwhile complaints against the Saravía brothers had been mounting from both native communities and from Spanish *vecinos* of the town. Despite his expressed sympathy for the natives' plight, Miranda attempted unsuccessfully to keep the scope of his investigation limited to the original charges. In June 1721 the Audiencia added the San Juan Guichicovi petition to his commission, and it appears that the stress of these obligations finally was too great for the beleaguered judge, who was desperate to return to his obligations as *justicia mayor* of Jalapa and lessee of the Tehuantepec Haciendas Marquesanas. By December Miranda had died, and the former commissioner of tributes, Don Antonio Sandín de Calderon, assumed his responsibilities in February 1722, an act which required the recertification of all the documents in Miranda's files. Whatever result Sandín's investigation may have yielded, as late as November 1724 the sierra communities were still seeking the financial restitution they had been granted by the court, four years after their initial petitions had been brought before the Audiencia.

And what was the position of the native *cabildo* of Tehuantepec in these protracted proceedings? Although the issues they raised were overshadowed by the extensive record of abuse and extortion perpetrated by the Saravía brothers on the sierra Zapotec communities, Tehuantepec's political leaders also registered their complaints against the *alcalde mayor* and his *teniente* not long after Miranda was first dispatched to the Isthmus to investigate the matter with the tribute collector. In August 1720, a letter was sent directly to the viceroy and signed by Tehuantepec's remaining *alcalde*, Joseph de Zúñiga of the barrio of San Blas, along with the *cabildo* notary and the fifteen *principales* who constituted the headmen of the town's barrios. They complained of a series of offenses committed by Don Pedro de Saravía and his brother, the *teniente*, a list that began with the *alcalde mayor*'s refusal in January to accept their duly elected governor, Francisco Cortés of the barrio of Santa María. Don Pedro ripped up the election results and insisted that they hold a new election and install his choice, Ambrosio de los Angeles, who had been serving as his interpreter. Out of fear of the *alcalde mayor*, the electors did as they had been ordered, only to find themselves now serving a governor who was little more than a conduit for Don Pedro's impossible demands.[33]

Principal among the Tehuantepec *cabildo*'s grievances was Saravía's heavy-handed interference with regional trade, for the *alcalde mayor* was determined to divert all commercial exchanges to his own store, which he began constructing immediately upon assuming his position. At his orders and without consulting the *cabildo*, the intrusive native governor had the town's only inn torn down, a building that was said to have been built by Hernán Cortés himself, leaving the community with no place to house travelers and merchants, who now were permitted to stay in town only two days. Although Saravía claimed that this last measure was only a response to complaints about the merchants from Spanish *vecinos* of the town, the *principales* were certain that was not the case, for both Spaniard and Indian suffered from the lack of merchants who might sell goods at lower prices than the town's stores, including that belonging to the *alcalde mayor,* and from the lack of buyers for the chickens, eggs, tortillas, produce, salt, and clothing which the native population had to sell. Particularly frustrating was the length to which Saravía went to monopolize all trade in salt, with guards established on all the roads into the province to divert native traders who came to buy salt, so that they would be forced to deal with him alone. And in a last sad and dangerous defacement of the town's physical amenities, Saravía ordered a huge *guanacaste* tree in the central plaza that was at least eighty years old cut down to its base, just so that the vendors who normally sold goods in its shade would be forced to move to the flimsy stalls he had built in view of the Casas Reales.[34]

Both the violation of electoral autonomy and the monopolization of commerce were familiar grievances that Tehuantepec community charged against corrupt Spanish administrators, even if Saravía seems to have found novel ways to enforce his desires. Indeed, the specificity of native officials' complaints regarding his interference with interregional trade underscores a central point made by Manzo regarding trade's long-standing economic importance to the Isthmus Zapotec and its role in fueling a persistent tradition of antistate politics.[35] Moreover, the frustration they expressed at the extreme measures the *alcalde mayor* took to eliminate his merchant competitors calls into question the premise of Jeremy Baskes's thesis that "peasants participated in the *repartimiento* voluntarily because through the system they obtained valued goods and needed income, unobtainable from other sources."[36] Whether or not some Isthmus communities, like other late colonial Oaxaca villages cited by Baskes, did find the regular cash advances officials offered for cochineal production or the goods they sold on credit an important economic resource under better circumstances, the Saravía brothers' mode of doing business shows the dark underbelly of a fundamentally flawed economic institution.

The pervasiveness of the brothers' abusive and coercive tactics is revealed in other charges listed in the Tehuantepec *principales*' petition. They complained that the *alcalde mayor* required them to collect tribute payments from barrio households on a weekly basis rather than three times a year, as the Crown required. If someone was sick and unable to make payment of the 1 real due that week, the *principal* would be thrown in jail. Further intruding on custom and practice in the Zapotec town, Saravía collected the ceremonial drums which each barrio used to celebrate its fiestas. To use their own instruments, which were an integral part of such festivities, barrio officials had to pay the *alcalde mayor* 1 peso and return them to his custody at the conclusion of the celebration. So extreme were these hardships and so hopeless did the *principales* feel in the face of the Saravía brothers' cruelty and arrogant assertions of privilege under the *fuero militar*, that the *principales* feared that the town and the province would be ruined and that the villages would riot because of the strenuous *repartimientos* the *alcalde mayor* had imposed on them. These hardships only continued to mount under his brother, the *teniente*.[37]

> For these justified complaints of ours, Your Highness must be served by ordering a royal decree for the remedy of all that we have brought before you, and because we fear that this *teniente* will not obey any such royal dispatch, because he has said publicly that he is just as powerful as his brother who can do much in Your Highness's interest, because if he stays longer he will finish destroying the town and the jurisdiction with the terror that all of us are experiencing and because we fear that there might be a revolt in the villages as a result of the burdens that [the *alcalde mayor*] has placed on them and that this *teniente* continues to increase to this day.[38]

Elsewhere in the extensive case against the Saravía brothers, more details emerged about their capricious treatment of native officials and residents of Tehuantepec, as witnesses were called upon to collaborate the abuses charged by the sierra villages. It became apparent that the forced election of the interpreter Ambrosio de los Angeles was not the only occasion when the *alcalde mayor* had interfered with the town's native *cabildo*. In 1719 he had taken away the staffs of office from the governor, Pasqual de los Reyes, and one of the *alcaldes*, Sebastián Antonio, replacing him with Clemente Vásquez of the barrio of San Blas. Irritated at the *topil* Lucas Martín's failure to do his bidding quickly enough—in this case bringing the *cabildo* of San Juan Guichicovi to jail for their failure to deliver surplus maize for sale in the *villa*—Don Pedro removed him from office that same year, much to the consternation of the Tehuantepec *cabildo*.

What Saravía demanded was officials who would do precisely what he wanted. The Hispanicized Ambrosio de los Angeles was well suited for this role, dispatching *topiles* to sierra villages like Guichicovi at the whim of the *alcalde mayor* or his *teniente* to collect *repartimiento* arrears, to demand that maize be sent to the Saravía's fishing station on the lagoons, or to order that lumber be sent for various carpentry projects in the Casas Reales. When the Spaniard was displeased with the results of these demands, Ambrosio de los Angeles on at least one occasion dispensed the odious whippings that inevitably accompanied Saravía's displeasure. When the *alcalde* Joseph de Zúñiga learned that Ambrosio was the one who had ordered the Guichicovi *cabildo* to be whipped, Zúñiga and all the *principales* were extremely angry at the idea that their governor had been levying punishments for *repartimiento* debts on the officials of other villages. Zúñiga reported that they summoned the governor to a *cabildo* meeting and chastised him for his actions: "And when the governor arrived, [we] *principales* said to him 'we did not elect you to be governor so that you could go to the palace to mete out punishments, but so that you would pay attention to the governing of the town's affairs,' and he responded that he had not been able to excuse himself because the *teniente* ordered him to do it."[39]

Through a campaign of terror and brutality, Don Pedro Saravía and his brother Antonio held the native population of the Tehuantepec province hostage to their greedy extortions for the better part of two years. Why widespread revolt, which had so worried the Tehuantepec *principales*, did not materialize is not the question normally posed for this or any particular historical context. Because at least some members of the Isthmus Zapotec population saw revolt as a likely outcome under conditions that still others equated with those precipitated by the infamous Juan de Avellán, it is tempting to speculate about the factors missing in this situation but present in either the 1660 Tehuantepec rebellion or the truncated revolt of 1715.

In all three instances, complaints about colonial officials concerned their crossing a fragile boundary to intrude into the political and economic life of the Zapotec community. This intrusion involved cooption of *cabildo* elections and interference with the ability of communities to govern themselves, onerous *repartimiento* demands that burdened the economic well-being of households, and the control of commerce, hindering the movement of useful goods in and out of the province. Only the Saravía case provides extensive documentation of the details of these abuses, so it is not possible to rank the three administrations by the degree of suffering they caused. It does appear that this last *alcalde mayor* selectively targeted populations far removed from the *cabecera* for the heaviest *repartimiento* burden, but whether it was to minimize local resistance or, as Machuca suggests, to exploit economic resources and growing populations unique to the sierra, is uncertain.[40] Whatever the reason, the litigation record points to a likely geographic disparity in the degree to which the *alcalde* mayor exploited Isthmus communities. Although Miranda's investigation report did not itemize *repartimiento* amounts from Saravía's store for all twenty-eight of the communities with such accounts, it did include the eight villages and one individual that still owed him money. Four sierra villages had debts greater than 100 pesos, while all three coastal plain communities in this summary owed half or less that amount.[41]

Even if Tehuantepec and its barrios were exempt from more onerous *repartimiento* demands, there were still sufficient economic hardships listed in the *principales*' complaints to have created a climate of hostility and resentment that might kindle a riot. What the Saravía case appears to have lacked was the dramatic precipitating event that had triggered mass revolt in the two previous situations: the shooting of a man from one of Tehuantepec's barrios in 1715 and the whipping death of the Tequisistlán cacique in 1660. Saravía's abuse was certainly capable of causing death, and there were rumors of a man dying in the village of Ixtepec, but the vague reports of the latter seem to have been muted by the routine nature of this administration's embrace of the whip and the terror it caused among the townspeople.

Perhaps another factor that quelled more active insurrection was the visibility of the Audiencia's prosecution of Saravía. In the case of Avellán, Tehuantepec officials had been stymied in their efforts to seek legal protection in Mexico City by the *alcalde mayor*'s close association with the viceroy. But now, less than a year after he took office, the Audiencia had already begun proceedings against Saravía for other matters. The physical presence of the sympathetic Miranda in the role of *juez comisario* and the departure of the hated Don Pedro validated the native community's belief that they would receive justice from the colonial administration, even if the *teniente* was briefly still in power and the sought-for restitution never came.

It may also have been the Audiencia's tangible efforts to restore justice that kept the *villa*'s native political leaders from instigating a province-wide, multiethnic alliance of aggrieved communities, as they were reported to have done in 1660 and as they evidenced in their petition of 1716. Throughout the Saravía case, only the three sierra communities of Guevea, Lachiguiri, and Guienagati pleaded their grievances together. This small group may have formed because of the villages' physical proximity to one another (although one village normally linked to Guevea, Santo Domingo Petapa, is absent) or because they were jointly served by the Dominican convent in Jalapa. Whatever the basis of their coalition, the Tehuantepec officials and *principales* appear never to have involved themselves directly in the substance of the sierra communities' complaints, even when, as they testified, they had direct knowledge of the abuse inflicted by Saravía.

Of the three conflicts I have described, this last case produced the most detailed native testimony on the day-to-day politics of community life in Tehuantepec. The fact that it stalled well before a province-wide coalition emerged leaves little direct evidence for exactly how such intercommunity alliances were forged. Doubtlessly a vital agent in this process would have been effective political leadership, as it appears to have been in the previous two incidents. Whether or not any of the individuals prominent in the Tehuantepec *cabildo* organization during Saravía's tenure might have possessed the appropriate personal qualities for such an extraordinary role is difficult to say; their temerity in the face of the *alcalde mayor*'s brutality suggests that they did not. There was at least one individual whose personality and familiarity with the Spanish world ought to have made him an ideal cultural broker, one whose claims to be a descendant of the ancient kings of Tehuantepec should have enhanced his political authority within the native world. That he did not automatically play this leadership role suggests how much Isthmus Zapotec society had changed by late colonial times.

CHAPTER SEVEN

Historical Memory and Political Authority

Among those whom Don Pedro de Saravía consigned to the Tehuantepec jail was a native of the province named Don Fernando de Zúñiga y Cortés. Cacique of the village of San Francisco del Mar, Don Fernando grew up in the town of Tehuantepec, his principal residence, but was married outside the province to a woman from the village of Chiapa. In 1720, at the age of thirty-six, he appeared before Don Andrés de Miranda to testify about his knowledge of the *alcalde mayor*'s abuses. Don Fernando spoke freely without aid of an interpreter, an intermediary that none of the other native witnesses had been willing to relinquish, no matter how Hispanicized they appeared to the judge. According to his testimony, Saravía had held Don Fernando in jail for two months on allegations made by his cousin, Don Pedro de Zúñiga y Cortés, concerning some missing loads of salt. Although Don Fernando challenged these charges, he ultimately paid for the value of the contested goods in order to avoid suffering the whipping and forced labor the *alcalde mayor* had threatened would be his sentence:

> The *alcalde mayor* said that, on account of the [disputed] salt, he would first have to give him a set of nine whippings and then he would have to send him to an *obraje* for four years, and since the witness was at the time in jail and saw the punishments that he was giving to the natives from other villages for smaller things, and how it went with Diego Ruíz, who was the current governor of Santa María Guienagati of this jurisdiction, and with other Indians who were in the jail, he was afraid of the *alcalde mayor*'s violence. For that reason he found it less inconvenient to pay him for the salt (which he did not owe) so as not to receive the injury that had been promised, and that in addition to that sum he was fined six pesos.[1]

The long-simmering dispute between the Zúñiga Cortés cousins had erupted three years earlier, when Don Pedro sued for sole ownership of certain salt beds along the lagoon shore between Tehuantepec and Juchitán that he claimed to have inherited from his father, Don Fernando de Zúñiga y Cortés. The ownership issue was not formally resolved until 1729, after Don Pedro's widow, Doña María de Meléndez, lost her four-year effort to pursue her late husband's claims on behalf of their daughters, Doña Barbara and Doña Nicolasa. Countering Don Pedro's assertion that the *salinas* were an entailed property that he alone had inherited as the eldest son of an eldest son, Don Fernando maintained on behalf of his own two brothers and sister and Don Pedro's three sisters that the salt beds were the joint property of all the family heirs.[2] In 1742, when Don Fernando was once again called upon to defend the family's property rights, this time in a boundary dispute between the communities of San Francisco del Mar and San Dionisio del Mar, he produced 158 folios of documentation in support of their titles. Among these documents were three from 1563, 1567, and 1568 confirming the possession of the *salinas* by Doña Magdalena de Zúñiga, widow of Don Juan Cortés, cacique of Tehuantepec.[3]

The production of salt, an important comestible trade item for the southern Isthmus since precolumbian times, had grown in export value under colonialism due to its industrial role in the extraction of gold and silver.[4] According to figures compiled by Laura Machuca, the Crown's expropriation of eleven Isthmus *salinas* in 1779 yielded an average net income of over 5,600 pesos annually to the royal treasury in the decade that followed.[5] The salt trade's lucrative potential had driven successive *alcaldes mayores* in earlier administrations to use their *repartimiento* privileges to buy salt from Huave communities or to lease mining rights from private owners, primarily the Zúñiga Cortés family. With so much at stake, rights to salt production easily became a focus of contention for these *alcaldes mayores*, both with native communities and native elites and with other Spanish administrator-entrepreneurs. Doña María de Meléndez's assertion that a previous administrator of Tehuantepec, Don Joseph Rodríguez de Ledesma, took salt from her husband's *salinas* without permission resulted in an embargo of the 1,241 loads in dispute and the Spaniard's consequent inability to pay back the 5,017 pesos he owed in tribute revenues.[6] Whether or not, as Rodríguez insinuated, subsequent officials were colluding to gain control of the salt for themselves, the in-

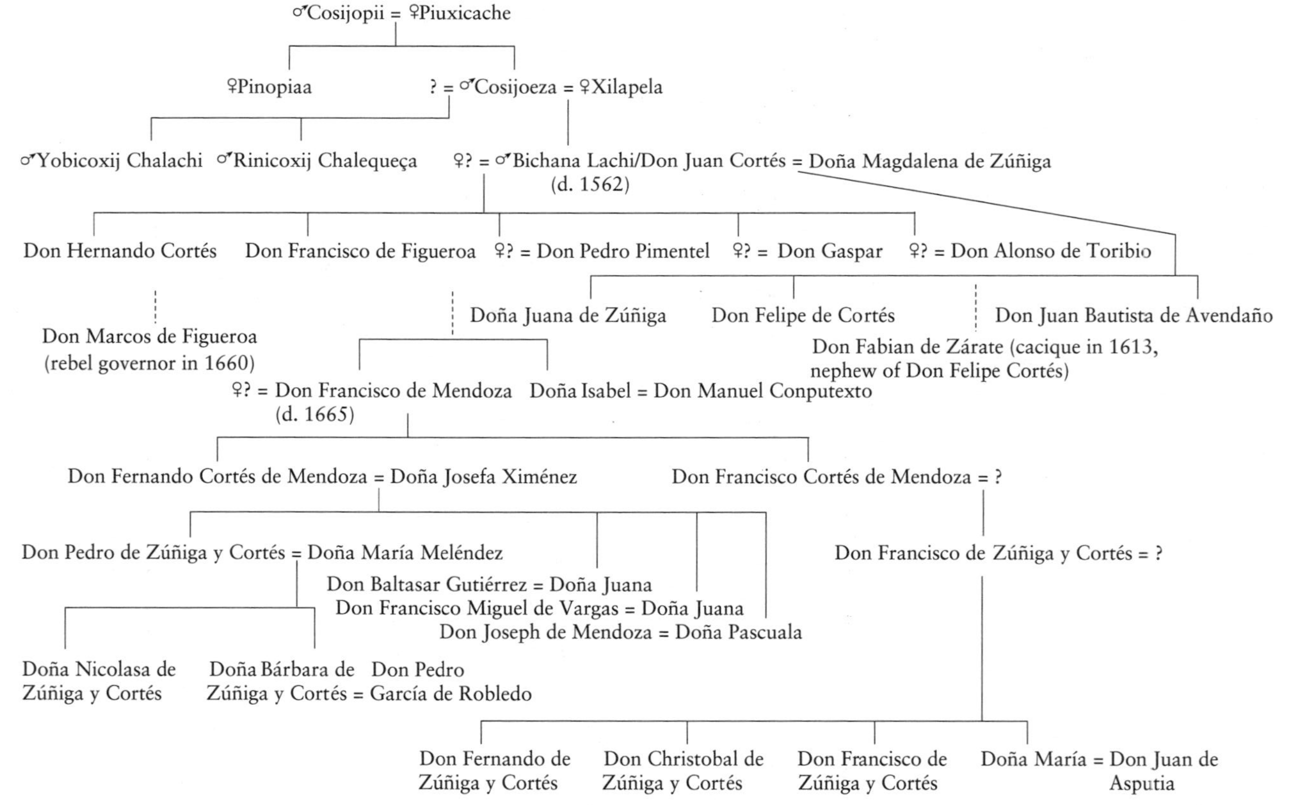

FIG. 7.1. Tehuantepec/San Francisco del Mar *cacicazgo* genealogies.

cident underscores the economic importance of this commodity and its susceptibility to political manipulation by both Spaniards and natives.

The complex web of financial arrangements surrounding salt production is a topic beyond the scope of the present study of Isthmus Zapotec ethnohistory. As the most visible late colonial remnant of the royal family's patrimonial properties, however, the Tehuantepec *salinas* offer a window onto the *cacicazgo*'s fate and what, if any, place the traditional authority of Zapotec kings might continue to hold in native politics. That these key assets were now in the hands of individuals whose primary identification was with a Huave community requires some initial genealogical reconstruction. An incomplete documentary trail leaves some critical holes in this effort to link the early eighteenth-century Zúñiga Cortés family with the last precolumbian king, Don Juan Cortés and his wife, Doña Magdalena de Zúñiga, but it does expose some fundamental questions concerning ethnicity and political legitimacy within Isthmus Zapotec society. In an attempt to answer them, I will revisit several of the indigenous histories from the late colonial period referred to at the beginning of the book, as well as introduce some genealogical reconstructions offered by nineteenth-century historians. At the heart of this discussion is the role that historical memory has played in maintaining community identity and autonomy in native society.

Royal Genealogy, Ethnicity, and Political Legitimacy in Late Colonial Tehuantepec

Three generations of men from the Zúñiga Cortés family were identified in colonial records as caciques of San Francisco del Mar, the Huave community also known as Ixtaltepec del Mar, where they on occasion served in high-ranking *cabildo* offices. Because different groups of descendants emphasized different surnames before finally settling on Zúñiga y Cortés, it would be difficult to trace their genealogy without the additional information about family relationships entered into the judicial record in support of the eighteenth-century *salinas* disputes. As early as 1650, Don Francisco de Mendoza y Cortés, grandfather of the litigious eighteenth-century cousins, was serving as *regidor* of San Francisco when the community formally received lands belonging to the abandoned Zoque pueblo of Ixhuatán; he was elected governor of the pueblo in 1661.[7] Viceregal confirmation of their possession of the *salinas* in question as part of an inherited *cacicazgo* was conferred on Don Francisco and his brothers in 1655. In 1669 his son Don Fernando Cortés, acting on behalf of himself and his brother Don Francisco Cortés, sought confirmation of this possession after the death of their father, a possession which was reasserted in 1672 against the intrusions of their deceased aunt's husband and again in 1679 against the encroachment of the community of Juchitán. It was the sons and daughters of these two men whose disagreement about whether or not the *cacicazgo* properties were entailed or shared equally among all heirs that formed the basis of the Zúñiga Cortés family dispute in the early eighteenth century.[8]

Sadly missing from this litigation record is the genealogical link between Don Francisco de Mendoza, the San Francisco cacique active politically as early as 1650, and Doña Magdalena de Zúñiga, widow of Don Juan Cortés, the last precolumbian ruler of Tehuantepec. Yet in 1742 the Zúñiga Cortés family had in its possession the three viceregal decrees obtained by Doña Magdalena granting her and her heirs possession of the salt beds and fishing territories, summaries of which were entered into the record. From the extensive litigation file associated with Doña Magdalena, who battled to preserve ownership of the *salinas* in the face of the royal *fiscal*'s claims on behalf of the Crown, it is clear that she pursued her case not in her own name, but in the name of her three minor children as heirs to the Tehuantepec *cacicazgo*.[9] These children, Don Felipe Cortés, Don Juan Bautista de Avendaño, and Doña Juana de Zúñíga, all survived into adulthood, with Don Felipe recognized as his father's successor in the late sixteenth-century native *pintura*, the Mapa de Huilotepec. Don Felipe's ownership of the *salinas* as part of his inheritance was acknowledged by the Spanish administrator in his 1580 Relación Geográfica for the province.

Few details are known of what became of older children from the cacique's previous marriage and polygamous alliances. As noted previously, these individuals include three unnamed daughters, whose husbands, Don Pedro Pimentel, Don Alonso de Toribio, both of Tehuantepec, and Don Gaspar, cacique of Astatla, were identified as the cacique's sons-in-law in sixteenth-century documents. An illegitimate son (*hijo natural*, in the words of one of the Dominican friars), Don Francisco de Figueroa, attempted to intercede with the Audiencia on behalf of his stepmother's claims in the late 1560s, as did another son, Don Hernando Cortés, whose name appears on two petitions granted by Viceroy Luís de Velasco in 1563.[10] In one, Don Hernando complained of the abuses suffered by commoners in the province; in so doing he assumed the traditional political responsibilities of the province cacique. The second petition was made jointly with Don Felipe, who was at the time about eight years old, regarding the refusal of *terrazgueros* to work on patrimonial lands they had inherited from their father. Don Hernando must have died before his stepmother initiated litigation protecting only her children's patrimonial rights in 1567, for later records do not mention his name. Although the younger children's exclusive rights to the salt beds were not formally contested by other potential heirs, it appears that not all members of the extended royal family were pleased by this turn. In her later suit with the *fiscal*, witnesses for Doña Magdalena testified that the deceased cacique's son-in-law, Don Pedro Pimentel, had maliciously conspired with the *alcalde mayor*, Juan de Salinas, when he was governor of the town in 1563 to deprive her children of rights to these properties.[11]

Don Juan Bautista and his sister Doña Juana may have been the only surviving legitimate children of Don Juan Cortés in 1591, when they sought viceregal help to get new houses built to replace those left to them by their parents that had burned the previous year.[12] Doña Juana, the first-born of the three full siblings, would have been in her late thirties at the time; her brother Don Juan Bautista would have been about twenty-nine years old. There is no information about any offspring of the three children of Doña Magdalena who might have inherited *cacicazgo* properties, in fact it seems there were none and that the adult children may have predeceased their mother. In 1674 Burgoa recalled that Doña Magdalena, whom the friar misidentified as Don Juan's daughter, not his young widow, had given some of the patrimonial properties consisting of orchards and irrigated lands near Laollaga to the Dominicans upon her death. In Chapter 4 it was noted that Don Fabian de Zárate called himself cacique of Tehuantepec in the early seventeenth century, the same individual who had established an *estancia* in 1608 on lands he inherited from his uncle, Don Felipe Cortés. Thus the title of Tehuantepec cacique was perpetuated for some time after the death of Don Juan Cortés, even as the extensive properties associated with the *cacicazgo* were in danger of becoming dispersed.[13]

Alternative genealogies, alternative histories

If the half-century separating the last known direct descendants of the Tehuantepec royal family and the San Francisco caciques cannot readily be bridged with the documents at hand, that does not mean there are no historical explanations for the relationship. Chapter 1 introduced the account of Tehuantepec royal history presented before the Audiencia in 1730 by the man claiming to be Don Antonio de Velasco, cacique of Antequera and descendant of the Zaachila and Tehuantepec royal households. According to this account, title to the disputed *salinas* had passed to the San Francisco caciques illegitimately when Doña Josefa de Chávez, the Huave wife of Don Juan Cortés, the Tehuantepec king, whose baptismal name the claimant erroneously gave as Don Juan de Velasco y Montezuma de Austria, improperly allowed the properties to be taken by her Huave brother upon the death of her husband. Thus the salt beds had been confiscated by the ancestors of Don Fernando de Zúñiga y Cortés, whom the claimant continued to refer to as "the Huave, Don Fernando de Zúñiga," depriving the direct descendants of the Tehuantepec king of their rightful ownership.[14]

The ethnic label and misplaced genealogy were not left unchallenged. In his initiating petition against the so-called Don Antonio de Velasco, whom he insisted was the *mulato libre* pretender Antonio de Aguero, Don Fernando professed to be cacique of the villa of Tehuantepec, a title not asserted in earlier disputes among family members concerning the *salinas*. He sought restitution of certain papers belonging to his great-grandfather, whom Don Fernando named as Don Juan de Zúñiga y Cortés, papers that he alleged Antonio had improperly acquired through a complex chain of events. According to the petition, Don Fernando's close relative, Don Diego de Velasco, cacique of Zaachila, had left these papers in the care of a now-deceased hacienda owner, Antonio Vásquez, whose son refused to return them, despite Don Diego's efforts to have the bishop, Fr. Angel Maldonado, intercede on his behalf. Now the papers were all in disarray, and it was discovered that Antonio de Aguero had sold some of them for the sum of 50 pesos to Joseph de Luna, cacique of the pueblo of Xalatlaco, who would not relinquish them without first being compensated. When the "stolen" papers finally were produced under court order, including those in the possession of the Xalatlaco cacique, it appeared that the documents were all falsifications, lacking the royal seal or proper signatures, according to the petitioner's attorney.[15] Despite the request by Don Fernando that the false documents possessed by Antonio de Aguero be burned, the discredited genealogy resurfaced again in 1796 as the basis of another attempt to lay claim to the Tehuantepec salt beds.[16]

Although few historical details concerning the descendants of Don Juan Cortés were known even to Fr. Francisco de Burgoa, whose penchant for confusing names and relationships pervades his Zapotec chronicles, the illiterate Aguero's genealogy demonstrates the tenor of oral traditions in circulation concerning the Zapotec kings. Different but similarly inventive genealogies appeared in the works of the most prominent nineteenth-century historians of Oaxaca, Juan Bautista Carriedo, José Antonio Gay, and Manuel Martínez Gracida, with Martínez Gracida's *El rey Cosijoeza y su familia* (1888) standing out for its dramatic embellishment of the "historical and legendary" accounts of the last Zapotec kings.[17]

These writers for the most part followed Burgoa's chronological outline, by which Cosijoeza left his young son Cosijopii on the throne in Tehuantepec, while returning to rule himself at Zaachila, where battles with Mixtec enemies forced him to take refuge in the surrounding mountains until the Spanish Conquest and the arrival of Francisco de Orozco's forces put an end to the war. Burgoa's claim that Cosijoeza converted to Christianity and was baptized Don Carlos Cosijoeza prior to his death was, as seen earlier, at odds with the sixteenth-century testimony of Tehuantepec *principales*, many of whom had known Cosijoeza personally and remembered that Cosijoeza died long before the events of 1521, when his son Bichana Lachi was still a young boy. In Martínez Gracida's reconstruction of events, Cosijoeza died in 1529, leaving the Zaachila throne vacant, since his only surviving heir already served as ruler of Tehuantepec. Thus the town's *principales* gave it to Don Juan de Aguilar, a descendant of the ruler of the Mixtec town of Tilantongo and husband of the heroic daughter of Cosijoeza, Donaji. Donaji (probably a variant of the Zapotec title for a noblewoman, *xonàxi*) was baptized as Doña Magdalena, according to Gay, and either Doña Magdalena or Doña Juana, according to Martínez Gracida's own inconsistent account. When Aguilar vacated the title under Spanish pressure, the *cacicazgo* passed to the Zapotec Don Luís de Velasco, claimed by Martínez Gracida to be in the direct line of the Zaachila kings.[18]

In an ambitious five-volume project completed in 1892, but not published in his lifetime, Martínez Gracida assembled a vast number of documents concerning Oaxaca native history to which he had been given access through his many politically important contacts and his strong ties to the Zaachila noble family. Michel Oudijk and Maarten Jansen have recently drawn attention to a purported coat of arms for the *cacicazgo* of Zaachila among these documents, depicted in plate 136 of the collection as a European-style insignia dominated by twin castle towers and the familiar Hapsburg double-headed eagle crest. A scene below the insignia shows five individuals, one man in Spanish dress and four women in colonial-period native attire, presenting themselves before Viceroy Luís de Velasco. The first two figures, presumably husband and wife, are identified in the caption as Don Diego Vásquez de Chávez, cacique of Zaachila and Doña María Magdalena del Espiritu Santo Zúñiga Cortés y Velasco de Vázquez Chávez, daughter of the king of Teozapotlan (Zaachila), Don Gerónimo Zúñiga Cortés y Velasco, and his wife Doña María Ysabel de los Angeles de Austria y León. The three other women's relationships are not specified, but by similarity of surnames should be sisters of the first: Doña Luisa Zúñiga de Austría y León, Doña María de los Angeles Zúñiga y Velasco de Austría y León, and Doña Margarita Zúñiga Velasco de Austría y León. Elsewhere in his commentary, Martínez Gracida constructed an early royal genealogy for Zaachila in which the four sisters and their parents are given Zapotec names as well, but in this version Doña Margarita is identified as the wife of Don Diego instead of Doña Magdalena, although the latter's Zapotec name is said to be Tonaxiaba, a likely variant of Donaji.[19] Given the fashion for creating coats of arms in the nineteenth century—Martínez Gracida claimed that Donaji was the heroine whom the Oaxaca state government chose to commemorate in its 1827 insignia—the reliability of the genealogy associated with the Zaachila heraldic crest is suspect as well. Indeed, the multiplicity of surnames and elaborate titles mimics that found in the discredited earlier genealogy of Antonio de Aguero. Rather than resolve any genealogical questions, the Martínez Gracida coat of arms validates all claims by placing the contested surnames in play during the mid-sixteenth-century government of Viceroy Luís de Velasco; thus individual name combinations include Chávez, Cortés, Vásquez, Velasco, and Zúñiga, as well as the royal-sounding Austría y León.

To clarify some issues that these complex and contradictory genealogies present, it should first be noted that the shallowness of the genealogies probably reflects their basis in oral history, for colonial-period pictorial genealogies from other Oaxaca towns cover many generations. By contrast, oral recollections of kinship relationships seem not to have extended back more than two generations in any of the earlier Tehuantepec documents I have reviewed, from the sixteenth-century testimony provided for the patrimony of Don Juan Cortés to the seventeenth-century property claims found in the Huilotepec boundary dispute. That the Zúñiga Cortés family was apparently unable to reconstruct the specifics of its kinship relationship to the Tehuantepec cacique is consistent with the oral nature of family history and not in itself a blight on the family's claim. Similarly, the complex kin relationships that Aguero as well as Burgoa and the nineteenth-century historians deduced from oral traditions are compressed to just the two generations of the last kings of Zaachila and Tehuantepec, with no detailed connection made to living family members.

As time passed, the thread of kinship that bound the royal ancestor to his presumed heirs became more fragile and in need of additional bolstering, if the remembered relationships were to have juridical credibility under colonial law. Thus the eighteenth-century Zúñiga Cortés caciques as well as their contemporary and later challengers all sought to reinforce their own version of the royal past and their personal or politically favored connections to it through the manipulation of names. It was a manipulation attempted in two directions: through the recasting of family names among the living to better support the linkage to the past, as in the case of the Zúñiga Cortés cousins, and through the reconfiguration of names for the revered ancestors, in order to better support their connection to the present, as in the case of the Oaxaca claimants. How this phenomenon is reflected in later copies of the Lienzo de Guevea is an issue that I will turn to shortly, after first examining what value was placed on this connection to the royal past in the political currency of late colonial Tehuantepec.

Political authority and ethnicity in the late colonial cacicazgos

Among the illustrations Martínez Gracida compiled in 1892 was a portrait of the surviving members of the Zaachila cacique family, the seventy-five-year-old Monica Gabriela Velasco, and her two adult children, Juan Gabriela Velasco and Manuel Luís Velasco. Neither this historian nor any of his predecessors offered specific information linking the Velasco family to the sixteenth-century caciques other than the implied link of surname. Presumably these three individuals were related to the early eighteenth-century Zaachila kinsman of the Zúñiga Cortés family, Don Diego de Velasco, who was also identified on a 1704 baptismal record from the Oaxaca pueblo as the father of a son named Juan, born to Don Diego and his wife María Petrona.[20]

It may be recalled from the previous chapter that, when the abuses suffered under the colonial administration of Tehuantepec brought the town's native population to a state of unrest in 1715, the community chose a certain Don Diego de Velasco to be governor of the reformist *cabildo*, a man whom the *fiscal* himself personally approved in 1716 because he was known to be one of the principal caciques of the province and a person of good judgment.[21] Whether or not this Don Diego can be assumed to be the same person as the Zaachila cacique without more direct evidence, it is telling that yet again the town's *principales* did not select one of the wealthy native residents of Tehuantepec associated with the San Francisco del Mar *cacicazgo* to lead them during a time of crisis. Cosmopolitan men of the Zúñiga Cortés family could sign their names and, in the case of Don Fernando, even compose lengthy documents in Spanish. They might serve as *cabildo* officers in San Francisco, where Don Fernando's brother was governor in 1709. As was the case with another San Francisco cacique before them, Don Antonio de Vargas, whose successful plea in Zapotec enabled the return of items looted from the Casas Reales in the 1660 riot, this facility at brokering between the colonial and native worlds apparently did not translate into political leadership within Tehuantepec itself.

Longtime Spanish residents of the town might recognize the Zúñiga Cortés family as "caciques of the Zapotec nation," as several were to testify in their 1742 boundary dispute with the pueblo of San Dionisio del Mar,[22] but it is more doubtful that they were accorded that authority broadly among the Zapotec public. When the Zúñiga Cortés cousins needed support from Tehuantepec natives in official proceedings, they drew their witnesses from the barrio of San Blas Atempa, a community that continues to this day to have a strong symbolic link to the Huave. Antonio de Aguero's contemptuous reference to his opponent Don Fernando as "the Huave" and his claim that the family had usurped the Zapotec patrimony very likely had some resonance in Tehuantepec itself.

Exactly how important ethnic identification may have been in legitimizing political leaders in Tehuantepec is an impossible question to answer directly with the data at hand, but the broader parameters of ethnicity's role in late colonial times can be delineated. On this point I wish to make it clear that I am concerned for the moment with the dynamic and situational aspects of ethnicity (what anthropologists and sociologists refer to as the "instrumentalist" nature of ethnicity), in which ethnic identity is used by actors to define the boundaries of political groups and control access to economic resources.[23] I am not here addressing the underlying symbolic values of cultural orientation, as emphasized in the "primordialist" view of ethnicity. That there were profound cultural or ethnic differences among the diverse communities of the Isthmian landscape in precolumbian and colonial times is an inescapable conclusion. After all, the three major indigenous groups of the southern Isthmus each brought distinctive historical traditions to their newly forged fifteenth-century coexistence; colonialism inserted into that mix Spanish and African peoples and cultural values.

Participants in these distinctive cultural traditions, nonetheless, were inevitably drawn into contact with individuals from other groups during the course of daily life. Whether it was the indigenous commoner who submitted to the friar's ministrations, the mulatto soldier who answered to his Spanish commander's call, or the Huave governor who delivered his community's tribute to the Zapotec-speaking town, no one lived in total cultural isolation from those who spoke a different language or practiced different customs in the intimacy of their own social groupings. The late colonial historical record for the province is replete with examples of individuals of varying socioeconomic status whose lives bridged the norms of their communities of origin with the values and expectations of another ethnic group with which they interacted daily. What I am particularly concerned with exploring here is the degree to which prominent persons of native ancestry, like the Zúñiga Cortés family, were able to adapt to diverse social settings and, conversely, the constraints that different constituencies placed on their political role because of their presumed ethnicity. In so doing, it is necessary to consider briefly alternative explanations for such constraints that differences of social class or racial mixture might have imposed.

Looking at the position of the Zúñiga Cortés family situationally, it is clear that these individuals were able to negotiate the complex cultural terrain in which they lived with some facility. They were sufficiently well versed in the customs and Huave idiom of their San Francisco del Mar base to serve that community in public roles, yet most of the family members resided in Tehuantepec or Xalapa. Many are known to have spoken Zapotec, including the contentious María de Meléndez, who needed the services of a Zapotec interpreter to plead her case, and it seems fair to assume that Zapotec proficiency would have been necessary for all to get through the daily routine of life in both these towns. Male members of the family were more likely to have some degree of fluency in Spanish as well. That colonial judges would identify the literate, Spanish-speaking Don Fernando de Zúñiga y Cortés as "muy ladino" in dress and behavior raises an alternative possibility that these caciques could be perceived as being too Hispanicized or too non-Indian to represent community interests properly (although that was not the case in San Francisco del Mar). To help understand what role these perceptions may have played in Tehuantepec, some of the broader issues underlying discussions of Indianness in late colonial New Spain must first be clarified.

Throughout Spain's American colonies, many individuals of native ancestry were able to manipulate cultural and linguistic markers appropriate to different contexts. That ability was much reviled by the seventeenth-century suppressor of the Tehuantepec revolt, Don Francisco de Montemayor, because it violated the clear division into social estates that he understood to be the cornerstone of colonial policies, policies that used racially identified statuses to segregate natives legally from even the poorest whites and blacks through the institutions of tribute, *encomienda*, and *repartimiento*. As a newcomer to New Spain, Montemayor must have been perplexed by the ways in which differences of class and socioeconomic mobility among the indigenous population blurred the divisions he thought essential to the maintenance of social order. Within the native community, however, differences of class and social standing were familiar principles of social organization, and the readiness with which members of the elite throughout New Spain adopted Spanish dress and the swords and horses that were the markers of high status did not in themselves connote distance from the social communities in which most remained rooted.

Although Spanish dress and facility with Spanish language may not have discredited an individual's legitimacy as a political leader, issues surrounding racial identity did enter the contested arena of native politics more frequently. Community complaints that an official was of mixed blood remained an effective means of challenging election results in many native towns throughout the colonial era, although they are curiously rare among recorded political disputes in the Tehuantepec province. Since the very notion of race was a foreign idea, one imposed by the colonists, whose concept of "blood purity" arose in the Iberian context of historical interactions among Spaniards, Moors, Jews, and Africans, it is less certain what race would mean within a community that had no precolumbian experience with phenotypically distinctive groups. To the extent that racially mixed individuals were exempted by the colonizer from the socioeconomic strictures surrounding *indios*, however, it seems reasonable that natives would regard social Indianness as a prerequisite for political authority. In this context, Fernando de Zúñiga y Cortés's labeling of Antonio de Aguero as a mulatto was intended to disqualify Aguero's claim of Zapotec royal heritage as much to the native ear as it might to the Spanish court.

Conversely, no one appears to have challenged the Zúñiga Cortés cousins in their many late colonial lawsuits for being non-Indian or mixed-race *mestizos*. Whether this would change for any children born to the marriage between María de Meléndez's daughter Bárbara and the Spaniard, Don Pedro García de Robledo, is not known, but it seems likely that the early eighteenth-century match was not the first that the wealthy family contracted with local Spaniards. Assuming that there were a few mixed marriages in the past in this family or in others among Tehuantepec's native elite, it may be that the biology of racial mixture was not very important in Zapotec political culture, as it appears not to have been among the Nahua. Looking more deeply behind attempts to disqualify *cabildo* candidates in the Cuernavaca region, Robert Haskett found that an accusation of mixed race was never the sole charge against an individual. To the contrary, biological *mestizos* frequently held colonial office in Morelos, including that of governor, and maintained their positions in large part because their connections and political skills were useful in dealing with the Spanish world, as long as they remained rooted in their native communities.[24]

Beyond its biological connotations, the Spanish concept of race also carried with it more subtle notions about ethnicity or "nation" (*nación*), by which Iberians had long identified themselves and others.[25] With its implications of a common racial origin or linguistic heritage, *nación* became the term by which later Spanish chroniclers preferred to describe Mesoamerican peoples and their histories, rather than relying exclusively on the more specific political-territorial designations by which indigenous historians described actors and events (e.g., the Zempoalans or the Huexotzincans). Fr. Juan de Torquemada, writing in the early seventeenth century, exemplified this process of ethnic categorization in his *Monarquía indiana*, which divided the indigenous landscape into separate *naciones*. Thus Torquemada wrote of the *provincia zapoteca*, the *gente tarasca*, the *naciones chichimeca*, even as he described traditional battles between competing city-states. A revealing passage clarifies the Spaniard's ethnic coding criteria when he described the Totonacs not as the Zempoalans, but as "a people different in language from the Mexicans, and they were the ones who received [Hernán Cortés] in Zempoala."[26]

In Oaxaca, as demonstrated earlier, Burgoa also filtered indigenous written and narrative histories through decidedly Iberian lenses. The question most difficult to answer without access to the texts and individuals Burgoa himself consulted is whether there was such a concept as the *nación zapoteca*, with its implication of a broadly based ethnic identity, rooted in common language and historical origins, before the Dominican abstracted one from native sources.[27] The small corpus of late precolumbian or early colonial native documents from Oaxaca that has survived tells a familiar, elite-centered story of rulers and the places they ruled or conquered; it is not a story of the Zapotec "nation" as a whole. Would an ethnographic survey of how ordinary citizens of Zapotec-speaking communities thought about themselves and their neighbors have yielded a different perspective?

The only glimpse of what might have been the broader understanding of ethnicity held by sixteenth-century Zapotecs is provided by semantic clues. In his *Vocabulario*, Fr. Juan de Córdova offered alternative Zapotec terms for *nación*: *chàcuè* and *tòbicue*, both referring to a grouping or a flank or side, and the more descriptive phrase, *tòbi lào peniàti quèche làyoo*, signifying a unit of people associated with a community and its territory. None of these terms conveys the sweeping linguistic or racial overtones implied in the Spanish usage of *nación*. The longer gloss suggests the primary importance of place to Zapotec notions of ethnicity, however much elite histories emphasized lineal descent and exogamous marriage ties among rulers. Fundamentally, the *quèche* or autonomous community was at the heart of one's social identity, for the commoner citizen, the *peniquèche*, was by definition a member of such a community.

The political community or *altepetl* was the modal population unit among the Nahua as well, whether or not that community dominated others through conquest or was in turn subordinate to another more powerful *altepetl*. James Lockhart concludes that the term "ethnic state" best conveys the significance of *altepetl*, with its connotations of a delineated territory, large or small, and a set of named constituent parts or wards governed by a dynastic ruler.[28] Whatever distinctive cultural or linguistic concepts these ethnic states might share more broadly, ethnicity for the Nahua was based in the *altepetl* and not in the larger cultural entity implied by the European concept of nation. Although lacking the Nahua and Zapotec division into residential wards or barrios, the territorially based community unit or *cah* was similarly the focus of political identity for the Maya. Matthew Restall observes that there are just a few written contexts in which the indigenous inhabitants of Yucatán used the label "Maya" in the colonial period to refer to anything but their shared language, a fact that he suggests underscores the similar lack of a wider ethnic consciousness among these native Mesoamericans, Spanish preconceptions notwithstanding.[29]

By contrast, Terraciano finds that the Mixtecs made wide use of the ethnic label "Ñudzahui" ("people of the Rain God") in colonial documents to refer to themselves as a people, to their language, to the region and its flora and fauna, and even to locally produced objects. Noting that preconquest Mixtec codices include a hieroglyphic representation of this term as well, Terraciano suggests that the unusual pan-Mixtec ethnicity was deeply rooted and derived from the multiethnic and multilingual history of the Mixteca region.[30] Although the Mixteca did differ markedly on the eve of the Spanish Conquest from the culturally homogeneous Yucatán region, it would be difficult to draw such a stark contrast with Nahua-speaking areas of Central Mexico, which similarly were home to a variety of other language groups. It may be that distinctive features of Mixtec sociopolitical organization, with its emphasis on bilateral royal inheritance and its late prehispanic pattern of colonizing regions through the resettlement of royal households and their large entourages of dependent families, are more significant contributing factors. Given these two contrasting patterns of Mesoamerican ethnicity, it seems likely that a similarly rich corpus of native language texts for the Zapotecs would follow the pattern indicated by Nahua and Maya practices, giving primacy to the political community as the source of ethnic identity.

As Lockhart and other scholars have noted, the institutions of colonial government tended to reinforce the indigenous political community, despite the fact that many preconquest ethnic states were whittled down to a more compact form through *congregación* and the assertion of autonomy by their more peripheral constituencies. Under these circumstances, the indigenous Zapotec concept of ethnicity, rooted as it was in one's membership within a territorially defined political community, must have been similarly strengthened during the colonial period, even as the focus of that identity narrowed. By the eighteenth century, virtually all of the Tehuantepec province's rural villages could claim political independence through the election of their own town councils, giving former *estancias* and subordinate communities alike the institutional support for a separate corporate identity than that of the *cabecera*'s population. Only the ecclesiastical grouping of communities into *doctrinas*, based in large measure on dialect similarities among villages in order to facilitate religious instruction, would have provided a hint of the historical relationship between the urban center and its rural wards. It may be that the political leaders of the *cabecera* of Tehuantepec persisted in claiming some measure of authority over the town's former dependencies, despite the frequency with which Zapotec communities of the coastal plain represented their own interests before the Spanish courts. That is the conclusion I have drawn from the omission of these coastal plain communities among the signatories to the province-wide petition Tehuantepec officials presented to the Audiencia in 1716.

San Francisco del Mar was one of the four Huave villages that did join the petition, confirming the fact that the Zapotecs of Tehuantepec regarded this community as a separate, autonomous polity. In that context, it seems all the more likely that a failure to pass an important late colonial ethnicity standard was the principal reason that the Zúñiga Cortés family was denied any important leadership role within the town of Tehuantepec, despite its claimed genealogical ties to Zapotec royalty. To the extent that the family was associated historically with the land and community of San Francisco del Mar, its members were politically "other," no matter how well individuals spoke the Zapotec language or no matter how skilled they were at brokering with the Spanish judicial system. At the same time, however, it appears that Don Diego de Velasco, a likely resident of Zaachila, was accorded this prominent political role during a period of crisis. Rather than signaling that a pan-Zapotec ethnicity had emerged in late colonial times, this "anomaly" should be seen as a renewal of the traditional principle of dynastic rulership on which the ethnic state model was based. To demonstrate that principle and its operation at this late date, I will return again to the native sources that provide the best record of changing political symbolism among the Isthmus Zapotecs, the Lienzo de Guevea and its multiple later versions.

Historical Memory in the Lienzo de Guevea

It will be recalled from the discussion in Chapter 1 that the colonial-period native drawing known as the Lienzo de Guevea had both historical-political functions, relating the rulers of the Isthmus sierra town of Santiago Guevea to the kings of Zaachila and their successors at Tehuantepec, and boundary-marking functions, mapping the eighteen toponyms that defined the territorial limits of the Guevea community. Thanks to the exhaustive research efforts of Michel Oudijk, scholars now have a more complete understanding of the four known native versions of this document and the sequence in which they were drawn. To highlight the ways in which the *lienzo* continued to function as a charter of political authority among Isthmus Zapotec communities in late colonial times, I will focus this discussion on the two seventeenth-century copies, Guevea II and Petapa I.[31]

Both of these late versions conveyed the political realities of their time by adding representations of the "brother" communities of Santiago Guevea and Santo Domingo Petapa below the figure of the ruler of Guevea in the original. What is striking, however, are the many differences between them, differences that may reflect idiosyncratic choices of the two artists or disparate expectations of the two communities which authorized the copies, perhaps at different times. Each of the later artists took certain liberties with the representational elements of Guevea I; the Petapa artist employed a more naturalistic rendering of the human body, while the Guevea artist offered a more romanticized landscape. Each artist emphasized somewhat different costume elements. They contrast markedly from one another, however, in the nature and application of their Latin letter glosses.

Guevea II follows the original sixteenth-century document closely with a mix of Nahuatl, Spanish, and Zapotec names for places and for the Tehuantepec kings. Petapa I, on the other hand, avoids almost all non-Zapotec names and adds Zapotec glosses for the hieroglyphic names of the prehispanic rulers of both Zaachila and Guevea, glosses not given in the sixteenth-century original. As discussed in Chapter 1, the Zapotec names of the Zaachila kings correspond to the five individuals whom Burgoa identified as members of the Tehuantepec royal family: the father and son rulers, Cosijoeza and Cosijopii, Cosijopii's sister Pinopiaa, and two unnamed older brothers of Cosijopii, who was said to be the third-born son. The personal names given for the Guevea rulers correspond closely to the images of their hieroglyphic notations, but the names given for the Zaachila kings are unconnected to their calendrical name glyphs.

Oudijk has demonstrated the close relationship between Petapa I and the Probanza de Petapa compiled in 1698. Like other seventeenth-century compilations of the genre known as *títulos primordiales*, the *probanza* includes a number of transcriptions of purportedly early documents that are difficult to accept as authentic. Rather than transparent efforts to dissemble the truth, such documents represent an attempt by native communities to give oral narratives about the past a concreteness and authoritativeness that the written word and the Christian calendar had acquired under colonial rule. Their obvious factual discrepancies may have discredited them in Spanish courts, but, as Stephanie Wood reminds us, the intended audience of the *títulos* was always the local community, and as such the documents provide rare testimony for how historical memory was structured and given meaning within late colonial period indigenous society.[32]

One of the transcribed documents in the Probanza de Petapa, dated April 15, 1540, is presented as the joint testimony of two men, the governor Rigala Guevea and his brother Xoana Logobicha, as they were known prior to their baptism. In it the brothers claim that their grandfather was given the land of their communities by the great lord Cosijoeza for them and all their children in posterity to use and never to sell. They refer to two maps or *pinturas* marking the boundaries of these lands, one given to each brother, and proceed to list the eighteen places that delimit the territory, reciting them in the same order as appears on the Lienzo de Guevea.[33]

The names given for both brothers were among those added to the Petapa I version of the Lienzo de Guevea. There Logobicha is identified as the eighth man in the column opposite the Zaachila-Tehuantepec kings, where he sits directly facing Cosijoeza. Rigala Guevea, which is a title rather than a name, was added in Petapa I to the gloss identifying Pedro Santiago as the sixteenth-century lord of Guevea. Rather than an original, early sixteenth-century document, the April 15, 1540, account appears to be a much later record of a narrative made while interpreting or reading the *lienzo*; perhaps this reading was offered in the names of individuals taken to be the founding brothers of the two, closely affiliated communities. The political realities in place during the *probanza*'s composition had changed markedly from those prevailing during Cosijoeza's lifetime or important at the time that the original *lienzo* was composed, when Santiago Guevea was still known by its Nahuatl name of Nanacatepec (Nanacaltepec). An established polity with its own roots at Zaachila, Nanacatepec may have been subordinate to the Tehuantepec conquest state, as the display of gifts before the two precolumbian kings in the *lienzo* acknowledges, but it had a separate history and political status from that of subject communities formed during the Zapotec colonization of the coastal plain, as I have demonstrated in Chapter 2.

Although Oudijk and Jansen consider the column of eight Guevea lords to be a synchronous representation of an assemblage of nobles from the community receiving rights to land from the Tehuantepec ruler,[34] I suggest that the column mirrors the diachronic presentation of eight Zaachila-Tehuantepec kings and that it was intended to show the historical alliance of Nanacatepec's successive lords with the Zaachila-based royal lineage. Only two of these lords are shown with warrior shields, shields that very likely were status markers honoring the participation of the sixth and seventh lords in the Tehuantepec conquest and other battles during the reigns of Cosijopii and Cosiijohueza. Perhaps because of similarities in their personal names (the hieroglyphs for the final two pairs of Guevea lords repeat "snake" and "eagle" roots), the Guevea I artist originally confused the identity of the warrior lords, outlining shields for the fifth and eighth lords that he attempted to cover up with white paint. The nature of this error was not understood by either the Guevea II or the Petapa I artist, both of whom copied the still visible outlines on Guevea I and painted warrior shields for all four men.

Of broader interest here is what the "copyist errors" reveal about what the artists and their communities knew about the past. As the practice of elite genealogical record-keeping dried up locally, it appears that oral tradition became the principal instrument for conveying historical information among most Isthmus Zapotecs in the seventeenth century.[35] The anthropologist Jack Goody has observed that oral traditions are capable of transmitting long lists of names of the form found in these Zapotec pictorial genealogies, but they do so not simply because of certain groups' exceptional capacity for rote learning. Rather it is because the lists of names fit closely with contemporary social relations and are repeated in other contexts of social interaction, as Goody suggests was the case for the long genealogies transcribed in the opening books of the Bible or for the strings of names recalled by the Sudanese Nuer.[36] The lists themselves are maintained because they help to explain existing political realities.

In the Tehuantepec province, political realities had changed greatly since the original composition of the Lienzo de Guevea. What mattered for the late colonial community of Santo Domingo Petapa as it struggled to uphold its territorial integrity was its ability to link its own legitimacy to that of its "brother" community of Santiago Guevea, not to the complex and now forgotten list of Guevea lords. Thus the eight precolumbian and single early colonial lords were reduced in the *probanza* to the essential two, the two brothers whose sibling relationship symbolized the political reality of the seventeenth-century world that the Petapa community knew. Although the Petapa I artist was able to interpret pictographic names for the other seven individuals, there were no stories left to tell about these men.

There were stories, nevertheless, about the Tehuantepec kings in broad circulation, as Burgoa, the Petapa I artist, and Antonio de Aguero's *cacicazgo* claim all make clear. The stories revolved around three major themes: (1) the establishment of a political-territorial base through conquest, (2) the resistance against enemies from a mountain redoubt, and (3) a marital alliance with the ruler of a powerful enemy state. Burgoa presents a fourth theme as well, that of the royal family's abiding connection to the supernatural realm. His sources for this theme, however, appear to have been earlier idolatry discoveries by his Dominican predecessors, and thus the stories of Penopiia's mountaintop altar or the baptized Don Juan's heresy may not have been widely repeated among late colonial native communities that had incorporated a folk Catholicism into the fabric of daily life. The more politically oriented themes, by contrast, were safer topics for retelling, and one can only imagine the dramatic pleasure that both narrator and listener savored in the story of Cosijoeza withstanding Aztec forces at Guiengola. As foundation myths for the communities they represented, the stories played an even more significant role in explaining their current structural realities. By providing an account of the Zaachila origins of the conquest state, they confirmed the legitimacy of the Tehuantepec polity. By recounting tales of military resistance followed by peaceful alliance with a powerful enemy, the stories provided a heroic parallel for the familiar circumstances of Spanish subjugation.

If the covert purpose of retelling these stories was to explain the circumstances of the moment, then perhaps it is not so surprising that the late colonial versions so easily muddled the names of the principals. The Guevea I artist's initial mistake about the identity of the similarly named warrior-lords of Guevea underscores how confusing these details might be, even when elaborate genealogical records were part of the recent cultural tradition. That the later Zaachila-Tehuantepec kings might be similarly misidentified is understandable as well, particularly when the personal name Cosijoeza was associated with both the Zaachila king 11 Water and his Tehuantepec descendant, the father of Don Juan Cortés. Perhaps it was this first Cosijoeza, rather than the king of Tehuantepec, whose retreat from Zaachila before Mixtec warriors and eventual rescue through marriage alliance, this time of his daughter to a Mixtec lord, was recounted in the confusing late colonial narratives of Zaachila. For the mythic purposes these historical anecdotes served, the specific actors were not as important as their structural role. Although neither of these individuals would have been alive when the Spaniards entered Oaxaca, such chronological details did not compromise the role the hero Cosijoeza played in legitimizing the transition to colonial reality.

Observations on the Demise of the Tehuantepec *cacicazgo*

With the data at hand I cannot definitively specify the reasons that the once powerful *cacicazgo* of Tehuantepec fell into political decline, even as much of its economic base in the patrimonial *salinas* was preserved until the mid-eighteenth century. Leadership disputes between the loyalist and rebel governments in the notorious 1660 rebellion suggest that the death of the last broadly recognized cacique, Don Felipe Cortés, left the *cacicazgo* without a direct heir, and that several elite factions contended with one another for a legitimacy linked to their presumed royal blood. As far as can be determined, none of these factions emerged from this conflict with the kind of legitimizing document that an elite genealogy represents, which further confirms the weak political authority accorded the Tehuantepec *cacicazgo* in late colonial times.

Early eighteenth-century documents suggest that the weight of community politics shifted gradually in Tehuantepec from its traditional control by the highest-ranking members of the native aristocracy to the authority of influential barrio leaders. Few of the town's *cabildo* officials named in the disputes discussed in Chapter 6 bore the honorific title of "don," although titled individuals had dominated higher levels of town government through the mid-seventeenth century. Men identified as barrio *principales* were elected to the office of governor in several instances in the early 1700s, and while such men had always been accorded the Zapotec title of *joana*, sixteenth-century usage patterns would have limited their status to that of the minor elite and precluded them from achieving the rank of governor. At least two such individuals had been *principal* of the populous barrio of Santa María Yoloteca, the same barrio whose charismatic leaders and activists figured importantly in late colonial uprisings. Although the traditional aristocracy no longer controlled the practical politics of late colonial life, moments of crisis might compel Tehuantepec's electors to return to the stabilizing leadership that the authority vested in its founding dynasty could confer.

When community leaders sought to restore legitimacy to its disgraced *cabildo* in the early eighteenth century, cacique status was one important qualification for the man they chose as governor. It appears that the now tenuous genealogical ties claimed by the Zúñiga Cortés family were insufficient and that their long association with San Francisco del Mar compromised their attachment to the town in which they lived, thereby disqualifying them as leaders of the Tehuantepec people, the *tòbi lào peniàti quèche làyoo*. If, as suggested here, the electors went farther outside the physical territory of Tehuantepec to propose the cacique of Zaachila, Don Diego de Velasco, as governor, I would argue that this choice was based not on some far-reaching idea of the Zapotec nation. Rather it was the broadly shared historical memory that named Zaachila specifically as the ultimate origin of the Tehuantepec community and its leaders. Like the royal genealogies of the sixteenth century that based political legitimacy on the blood tie of its kings to Zaachila, the oral traditions of the late colonial period continued to replicate this foundation narrative, even after its genealogical premise no longer figured in the normal running of community affairs.

John Chance has offered a comparative framework for evaluating the political and economic position of late colonial caciques and other elites, according to which he discerns three major Mesoamerican variants. In northern Yucatán, a weakly developed colonial economy permitted indigenous caciques and *principales* to monopolize political offices introduced under Spanish rule without much outside interference. In the Sierra Zapoteca of northern Oaxaca, dispersed and isolated communities saw their traditional caciques lose wealth and status, while new elites proliferated in response to the economic and political alliances they forged with Spanish administrators. In the Oaxaca Valley and the Mixteca Alta, a third variant is seen in the prosperous late colonial cacique families that, while often having lost their struggle to maintain political control of their communities, took advantage of the new economic opportunities that their landed *cacicazgos* permitted.[37] His own study of colonial elites in the eastern Puebla community of Tecali has pointed to an important variant of the second pattern, in which the numbers of individuals claiming elite status increased substantially in late colonial times, even as the economic profile of the hereditary nobles became more heterogeneous. Unlike the Sierra Zapoteca case, however, these new elites were basing their status on a revitalized assertion of precolumbian ideas about the noble house rather than on any appeal to powerful Spaniards.[38]

Situating the southern Isthmus within Chance's typology, I would have to conclude that native elites had a mixed experience in this culturally and economically diverse landscape. They played an important political and economic role in some communities, like San Francisco del Mar, where the Zúñiga Cortés family was but the most prominent of several families that claimed cacique status, filled *cabildo* offices, and enjoyed sufficient wealth to help launch community *cofradía* enterprises, much as was the case with Yucatán's caciques and *principales*. Whether or not elite titles were proliferating in the eighteenth century cannot be documented with the records at hand for San Francisco or any other Isthmus community, but my impression is that the percentage of elites within the native population was not substantially changed anywhere in the province over the course of the colonial period. For Tehuantepec itself, as discussed earlier, individuals who might claim cacique status no longer retained significant political authority by the eighteenth century, much as was the case in the Oaxaca Valley, yet *principales* continued to be actively involved in community affairs, a role surely bolstered by the stability of Tehuantepec's barrio organization. Whether or not any of these individuals also attained the kind of economic status that the Zúñiga Cortés family based on its inherited salt beds is less certain, but ownership of productive irrigated farmlands as well as the new opportunities afforded by ranching and long-distance mule trade were among the economic means available to these *principales*.

If local caciques no longer actively shaped politics in Tehuantepec by the eighteenth century, it is all the more remarkable how ideas about the role of the dynastic ruler continued to mold Zapotec conceptions of the ethnic state, to apply Lockhart's term. Chance has suggested that the reconstitution of the Tecali noble house similarly was based upon an appeal to indigenous traditions, even as the nature of elite status had altered to fit the colonial context. Although the venues in which these traditions were kept alive in the colonial period are seldom visible in the historical record, the Tehuantepec case provides an important example. Here the very act of remembering the past reinforced the fundamental dynastic principles by which the political community asserted its legitimacy.

CHAPTER EIGHT

Isthmus Zapotec Politics and the Trajectory of Colonial Change

Founded fewer than one hundred years prior to the entrance of Hernán Cortés on the Mesoamerican cultural stage, the Tehuantepec conquest state presents an extreme version of the power of Zapotec kings. Its distance from the entrenched political disputes and territorial compromises that had plagued leaders of the Late Postclassic Oaxaca Valley towns allowed the war leader Cosijopii and his son Cosijoeza to create the Zapotec state anew based on principles that reinforced royal power. Partitioning conquered lands and peoples among their confederates according to the military valor and zeal each had shown was an effective means of cementing elite loyalty. Allotments of agricultural lands to squadrons of soldier colonists similarly bound the constituent communities of the newly formed polity to the ruler, further reinforcing the king's traditional role as custodian of the city-state's supernatural fate. As Enrique Florescano has argued for the Aztecs after the military defeat of Azcapotzalco, warfare and colonization appear to have shifted the balance of political prominence heavily toward rulers and elite-centered institutions and away from the barrio or *calpolli* (*collaba* among the Zapotecs) organizations that constituted the polity's core.[1]

The relatively brief period of time in which these arrangements flourished in Tehuantepec would have inhibited any counter trends bolstering the power of existing barrio institutions among the Zapotec colonists. Yet elite loyalties could be fragile, as revealed after the death of the ruler Cosijoeza, when the contested succession of his young son, Bichana Lachi, led to insurrection at the margins of the conquest state. Had Cortés's arrival and Pedro de Alvarado's suppression of the Xalapa revolt not occurred when they did, the Tehuantepec ruler would have faced a difficult military and political crisis in the years ahead. To consolidate its economic and political position for the longer term, the polity may have required more developed bureaucratic institutions than those now visible in the ethnohistorical record.

As events actually unfolded, the cataclysm occasioned by Spain's conquest spelled the end of Tehuantepec's autonomy and the erosion of kingly sovereignty on the Isthmus. Distance from the primary seat of Spanish rule and inclusion in the Marquesado del Valle forestalled the immediacy of this political demise for a time, an outcome not easily predicted from the tumultuous first decades of Spanish rule in Tehuantepec, when the imposition of Nahua overlords in the province brought further misery and dislocation. After the Zapotec king was finally restored to his rightful position as *señor natural* by the Marqués's administrator, he resumed his former powers in a diminished state. A smaller version of the territory once controlled by the king was returned to his supervision, tribute and public works obligations of commoners recommenced, if at a reduced scale, and the labor service duties of *terrazgueros* on royal estates were reinstated. However compromised it may have been by the escalating mortality of its people and by the unyielding power of Spanish administrators and clergy, native rulership in Tehuantepec survived until Don Juan Cortés's death in 1562 and the reversion of the province the following year to direct control by the Spanish Crown.

The principle of royal inheritance continued to retain some political force in Tehuantepec in the years immediately following the death of Don Juan. The representation of Don Felipe Cortés as successor to Tehuantepec's kings in the Mapa de Huilotepec illustrates how royal authority could still be invoked in the late sixteenth century to legitimize private property rights, just as it had been used at mid-century by the Lienzo de Guevea artist to defend the autonomous but subordinate position of the Guevea polity. Nonetheless, the cacique's leadership role was abridged in practice by the community's growing familiarity with the *cabildo* form of colonial government and by the apparent failure of later royal descendants to resolve their conflicting claims to genealogical legitimacy. Disputes over dynastic succession were not new to the Zapotecs, but the imposition of Spanish colonial rule removed from the public arena the kind of symbolic performance that had in the past sanctioned the successful royal claimant. Without the public investiture of the king, without the ceremonial dances in which the jewels and other physical symbols of the polity's foundation were displayed, without the continued ritual performances in which the new king's ability to invoke the supernatural was affirmed, there would be no formal and public assumption of royal succession.[2] Cacique titles might remain in circulation until late colonial times, along with some of the patrimonial properties on which royal wealth was based, but Tehuantepec was like many other communities in eighteenth-century New Spain that saw its highest-ranking traditional elites increasingly disengaged from the political interests of the community as a whole.

As the role of the *cacicazgo* diminished, Tehuantepec's prehispanic barrio structures assumed an increasing importance in the political organization of the colonial period town, filling the void of community identity and cohesion left by the loss of the ruler's centralized authority. Florescano notes that the imposed *cabildo* offices in New Spain's *repúblicas de indios* were readily molded to fit the existing structural arrangements within each community, and the Tehuantepec case amply illustrates his point. Although the number of urban barrios was reduced under *congregación* to just fifteen by late colonial times, their internal organization largely mirrored traditional practice, as barrio headmen and tribute collectors continued to play important leadership roles and parish churches with their own hierarchy of lay officials assumed the central place in the community's social and spiritual life once held by the barrio temple. Tehuantepec's *cabildo* may not have officially accommodated all these barrio leaders prior to the eighteenth century, but the five or six *regidor* positions rotated among the larger, unofficial assembly of barrio headmen that regularly consulted on matters of concern to the town as a whole for most of the seventeenth century. Both in adapting the new *cabildo* forms to meet traditional organizational principles and in exploiting their advantages under Spanish law, the Isthmus Zapotec exhibited patterns amply documented elsewhere in colonial Mesoamerica. Where they differed is in the particulars of that restructuring, based as it was on a more centralized kingly authority prevailing in precolumbian times than in many of the Nahua communities described by ethnohistorians, and suffering a greater erosion of aristocratic political power under Spanish rule than was the case among the Yucatec Maya.[3]

In Tehuantepec local structures of *cabildo* inclusion helped to diminish any centrifugal tendencies that might have fragmented the town along barrio cleavage lines until the late nineteenth century, when San Blas Atempa became independent in the wake of political and ideological divisions. No such institutions were capable of bridging the physical distance between the town and its subject rural communities, however, and

Tehuantepec's villages and hamlets began asserting their political autonomy not long after the death of Don Juan Cortés. Whether they had enjoyed the same structural relationship to king and polity as Tehuantepec's urban barrios or whether they were formed initially as communities of *terrazguero* laborers, the province's rural pueblos sought to be recognized as their own autonomous *repúblicas de indios*, a status many achieved by the beginning of the seventeenth century in the southern Isthmus, a little earlier than the separation of subject communities in many other parts of New Spain.[4]

If the institutional demise of royal authority was accelerated in Tehuantepec by inheritance disputes that the loss of public ritual left unresolved, it should also be acknowledged that colonialism provided abundant ceremonial space for the assertion of barrio and community identity in the ensuing political void. The demands of the Catholic ritual calendar, the adoption of patron saints for the community church, the pageantry of public religious parades and celebrations all were powerful reinforcements of social solidarity that became as important to the colonial Zapotec community as their precolumbian precursors once had been. Large sums of money might be lavished on candles, fireworks, and adornments for the parish churches; bribes were paid grudgingly to the *alcalde mayor* in order to secure use of the drums and other instruments considered necessary for the proper celebration of the saints; corrupt priests were paid for Masses to ensure that the community's ritual obligations were observed. Yet despite the manifest public celebrations of Catholic piety in Tehuantepec and other parts of Oaxaca, the meanings they invoked for the celebrants differed from that expressed in Catholic doctrine. Priestly sanctions suppressed the maintenance of most traditional Zapotec observance, but the fundamental understandings of the world and its spiritual needs undoubtedly remained distinct.

No late colonial idolatry accusations for Tehuantepec provide a comparison with that uncovered in 1653 by the parish priest of San Miguel Sola; there are no reports of calendrical books regularly consulted for private prognostications, like those Bishop Maldonado's investigations revealed a half century later in the Villa Alta region or those ethnographers found still in use in Mitla as recently as the early twentieth century. The more public ritual observations at new year and patron saint festivities that were discovered in a large percentage of Sierra Zapotec villages would have been difficult to support under the watchful gaze of Tehuantepec's resident Dominicans, as Don Juan Cortés's tragic exposure a century earlier demonstrates. For Tehuantepec officials to maintain into late colonial times what Tavárez refers to as the "dual system of public religious practices" operative in some isolated Villa Alta villages would require a better combination of stealth and good fortune than the documentary record of political strife in this populous town suggests was the case.[5]

Nonetheless, the Isthmus Zapotec world continues to be populated to this day with supernatural spirits and powers that survived the colonial years by catering to the more private needs of individuals and their families. Were these powers celebrated ritually on behalf of the community as a whole at sacred places in the Isthmus landscape, as Marcello Carmagnani has argued was part of a widespread late colonial spiritual revitalization in Oaxaca?[6] Unfortunately, this question cannot be answered directly from documentary evidence alone. Related data for the Isthmus include archaeological traces of the continued colonial-period use of mountaintop shrines and the contemporary survival of Catholic celebrations focused at Tehuantepec landmarks, from the periodic observances at the modern chapel atop Cerro del Tigre to the Holy Week processions from the town to the nearby cave at Cerro de Lieza. As was the case elsewhere in Oaxaca, the landscape continued to be viewed as an embodiment of the sacred in Tehuantepec during the late colonial period. The degree to which the rituals that celebrated its sacred quality commingled traditional Zapotec precepts with Catholic images and ritual objects may be a secondary matter.

If Carmagnani's thesis that there was a late colonial period reclamation of the sacred landscape by Oaxaca's native communities is difficult to support with time-specific data for the Isthmus, nonetheless his observations concerning the multifaceted role played by the native political hierarchy in the life of the community resonate well with what I have noted for Tehuantepec. As discussed before, barrio representation through rotation of the position of *regidor* and through the informal *cabildo* assembly forestalled the fragmentation of Tehuantepec's urban core. Furthermore, the privileged election of the hereditary elite during most of the colonial period to the major offices of governor, *alcalde*, and *regidor* carried with it responsibilities that obliged these men to safeguard the community's sphere of autonomy within the colonial system.[7] Failure to protect community resources and boundaries, failure to shelter a sustainable economic base from excessively onerous tribute and *repartimiento* demands, failure to defend community customs and traditions—these derelictions of communal responsibility were grounds for removal from office from the late sixteenth through the eighteenth centuries. Removal could be effected through the regular electoral process, through grievances lodged with the colonial authorities, or through violence at the hands of an angry mob.

Most of the time annual *cabildo* elections proceeded smoothly through internal processes seen dimly in the historical record for Tehuantepec. Whatever the specific mechanisms of election may have been, whatever the formal rituals entailed in the transferal of office from the last year's *cabildo* members to the newly elected, the documentary record signals only the final stage of political transition, the conferring of the *varas* or staffs of office. This action alone required the formal participation of the colonial administrator, whose penchant both for manipulating the electoral process and for asserting his ability to do so positioned more than one *alcalde mayor* in hostile confrontation with the people of Tehuantepec. So potent were these symbols of office to the recipients and so vital the electoral process to the community's political constitution that the direct approval of the viceroy himself would be sought if the local administrator would not or could not validate the election results.

Accustomed to a political system in which the patronage of powerful benefactors and the purchase of lucrative offices had become structural necessities, the Spaniards who administered the colony's native provinces cannot have fathomed the significance a mid-sixteenth-century transplanted town government form would have for the communities upon which it had been imposed. When a Tehuantepec *alcalde mayor* offered what might be considered to be legitimate grounds for rejecting the community's choice for governor, alleging that the candidate had mismanaged tribute collections in a previous term, a near-revolt ensued. Such incidents illustrate both the community's disavowal of the administrator's right to interfere in its political process and the distinctive values and meanings given to these offices that conditioned an individual's suitability, even if the historical documents seldom comment on the pedigree of particular native officials or the explicit selection criteria. In a large, socially and economically diverse native population like that of Tehuantepec, one might expect that missing testimony would offer similarly diverse opinions about the personal qualifications of individuals or the most important attributes of political leaders. As David Kertzer points out, political rituals like those surrounding these native elections do not necessarily require a uniformity of belief or meaning, for "the strength of political organizations comes less from any homogeneity of their members' beliefs than from the continuing expressions of allegiance through ritual."[8]

It is during episodes of extreme political crisis in Tehuantepec, episodes in which the degree of native discontent with both the colonial administration and the Indian *cabildos* that failed to protect them threatened to undermine Spanish hegemony, that hints surface of a surprisingly persistent symbol of political authority in Tehuantepec, that of royal blood. Marcos de Figueroa, chosen as rebel *gobernador* in 1660, was a descendant of the Tehuantepec rulers, as confirmed by reports that he was addressed by the Zapotec title *coqui*. Diego de Velasco, who was elected Tehuantepec's *gobernador* in 1715, was, I propose, the same person acknowledged widely to be the descendant of the Zaachila kings. A personal legitimacy based on blood ties to the revered prehispanic kings enabled each man to transcend the current political quandary by linking the polity symbolically to its primordial past. Carmagnani may be correct in his conclusion that late colonial Oaxaca communities were engaged in a "progressive transformation of a political system founded on inheritance into a political system founded on the electoral process."[9] In the case of Tehuantepec, however, invoking the strength of ancient inheritance-based structures remained a powerful tool for reinforcing community political values during times of crisis.[10]

The past was kept alive in the southern Isthmus through many forms, among which its retelling in the painted medium of the Lienzo de Guevea *pinturas* is the one most celebrated by outsiders. Strong parallels among multiple late colonial recorded versions of Tehuantepec's royal history suggest that there may have been a variety of more public occasions for retelling that past. As discussed previously, the "facts" of these later stories are not precisely those that were familiar to individuals who themselves knew the old kings or were witnesses to the Spanish invasion. Far from discrediting the late colonial narrative, the newer elements and their structural patterns highlight the moral lessons that narrative history was intended to offer contemporary audiences. The remembered past was used to legitimize community origins and territorial rights while it provided heroic tales to compensate for present realities, countering Spanish hegemony with an earlier rejection of Aztec imperial domination. Such narrations, like others that have remained hidden from the historical record, continually reinforced community solidarity and identity in colonial Tehuantepec. That they were part of a living historical memory that incorporated struggles with the colonial state as well is evidenced by an eighteenth-century native witness's reference to Avellán and by the prominence the 1660 Tehuantepec rebellion has been accorded by twentieth-century Isthmus Zapotec artists and intellectuals. Tehuantepec's geographic situation and resulting economic patterns may help explain the region's estrangement from the national agenda, but it is the culture of resistance that historical memory fostered among successive generations of Isthmus Zapotecs that underlies people's readiness for political confrontation.

The remembered past and its lessons of autonomy and resistance also provide important clues to the paradox of "acculturation" among the Isthmus Zapotecs. Archaeological remains and architectural data offer pervasive material evidence for native accommodation to Hispanic cultural patterns. The proliferation of early seventeenth-century churches surrounded by streets of closely aligned houses with Spanish-style doors and windows represented not just an external conformity of Tehuantepec's barrios to imposed norms. The archaeological data suggest how widespread the demand for European household items might have been, from metal tools that replaced highland obsidian to imported Mexico City majolica. Native communities might complain about stray cattle or *repartimientos* of mules sold them by the *alcalde mayor*, but they quickly learned the principles of animal husbandry and assimilated domestic animals and nonnative plants into their subsistence strategies. Mule teams allowed some to become successful long-distance traders; both archaeological and historical data point to a gradual increase in the role of markets in the Isthmus economy. Expanding populations of late eighteenth-century Tehuantepec show more evidence of economic specialization, from the documented saddle-making skills of the Santa María barrio residents to the widespread presence of local pottery manufactured by skilled artisans on the introduced potter's wheel.

Like their modern descendants, whose fascination with commerce and new technologies is apparent in the bustling streets of every Isthmus town, members of colonial Zapotec communities incorporated these novel goods and practices into a mode of living that persistently defined itself as culturally unique and autonomous. Neither the archaeological nor the historical records can tell exactly what meanings were given to these objects and institutions by the colonial participants. Nonetheless, it is clear that the structural bases of community organization and the symbolic ties to the sacred landscape forged in prehistory provided a remarkably resilient frame with which successive generations might contest the impositions of outsiders.

Notes

The following abbreviations are used in the Notes:

AGI Archivo General de las Indias (Seville, Spain)
AGN Archivo General de la Nación (Mexico City, Mexico)

Chapter 1

1. "Todos los naturales de esta provincia fue gente advenediza y eran naturales del valle de Oaxaca y vinieron a conquistar a los naturales que aquí havía de lengua Guazonteca, a los quales los abuellos y antepasados del dicho Don Juan conquistaron y echaron de aquí y destruyeron de manera que quedó todo a su lado. Y el abuello y antepasado del dicho Don Juan Cortés, viendo como la tierra quedó despoblada de los naturales que la poseían, la pobló toda esta provincia y hizo asiento en ella con su gente." 1571 testimony of Don Alonso de Toribio, witness for plaintiff, Doña Magdalena de Zúñiga vs. *fiscal* over ownership of salt beds and *estancias* in the Tehuantepec province. AGI Escribanía de Cámara, 160 b, f. 248.

2. Burgoa, *Geográfica descripción*, 2, pp. 340–42.

3. Accounts of Mixtec incursions into the Oaxaca Valley through a series of thirteenth-century marriage alliances between Mixtec and Zapotec ruling families are given by Fray Agustín de Salazar, "Relación de Cuilapa" [1581] and Fray Juan de Mata, "Relación de Teozapotlan" [1580]. Acuña included both reports in his recent edition, *Relaciones geográficas del siglo XVI: Antequera*. Although these sixteenth-century accounts suggest that the scale of Mixtec immigration was small, archaeological data recovered by the Oaxaca Valley Settlement Pattern Survey indicate a much more significant Late Postclassic colonization. At that time the largest of the dispersed Mixtec settlements stretched between Cuilapan and the lower slopes of Monte Albán and is estimated to have housed a population of more than 13,000, according to Blanton et al., *Monte Albán's Hinterland*, p. 121.

4. Sixteenth-century Zapotec terms are found in the *Vocabulario en lengua zapoteca* compiled by Fr. Juan de Córdova in 1570.

5. Elsa Redmond has made a detailed study of late Zapotec militarism, focusing on its organizational and strategic aspects, in her monograph, *A Fuego y Sangre*. Although the Relaciones Geográficas compiled under the mandate of Phillip II illuminate some tributary relationships among the Oaxaca Valley towns (see Acuña, *Relaciones geográficas*), most of Redmond's information comes from Burgoa's *Geográfica descripción*, with its scattered seventeenth-century references to the Tehuantepec conquest.

6. Boone, *Stories in Red and Black*, identifies these traits typical of Aztec histories. Sousa and Terraciano, "The Original Conquest," compare colonial-period historical genres among the Nahuas and Mixtecs and observe that the latter group did not begin its foundation narratives with migration stories, but rather claimed to have lived in a particular locale since the beginning of time. Such persistent cultural contrasts in narrative structure (the examples studied by Sousa and Terraciano date to the late seventeenth century) are important cautionary notes to the archaeologists' impulse to treat these documents as straightforward historical texts. In the case of the Tehuantepec foundation narrative, the archaeological record, discussed below, supports the basic narrative outline of events.

7. Miguel Tini, an eighty-year-old commoner from one of Tehuantepec's barrios, testified in 1570 that he had seen these ceremonial dances as a child, when Don Juan Cortés's father was lord of the province. Marveling at the rich attire of the lord and his *principales*, he was told their significance by his own father. 1570–72 Doña Magdalena de Zúñiga vs. *fiscal*, AGI Escribanía de Cámara, 160 b, f. 215.

8. See Marcus, *Mesoamerican Writing Systems*, pp. 69–75, for a discussion of colonial period Zapotec texts and the sixteenth-century terminology for books and writing. Some twenty-five distinct pictorial manuscripts and eight maps drawn for the 1579–85 Relaciones Geográficas could be securely ascribed to Zapotec-speaking areas of Oaxaca at the time that Glass concluded his "Survey of Native Middle American Pictorial Manuscripts," table 25. Since then a newly identified Oaxaca Valley manuscript was published in 1990 by Whitecotton, *Zapotec Elite Ethnohistory*. An additional mid-sixteenth-century *pintura* and three fragments of the longer tribute strip accompanying it were published by Zeitlin and Thomas in "Spanish Justice and the Indian Cacique," figs. 2–5. As discussed below, Michel Oudijk came across a fourth version of one of the inventoried Zapotec manuscripts, the Lienzo de Guevea, as recently as 1997, giving hope to the potential recovery of further pictorial documents from community archives.

9. AGI Escribanía de Cámara, 160 b, f. 400v; Burgoa, *Geográfica descripción*, 2, p. 345.

10. Hernán Cortés mentions Tehuantepec briefly in his third and fourth *Cartas de Relación*. Pedro de Alvarado was the first Spaniard to spend any length of time in the province, where he was well received and resupplied with food and warriors before setting off to conquer Soconusco and Guatemala. Although Pedro de Alvarado sent descriptions of his exploits to Mexico from Tehuantepec

and Soconusco, only the two letters sent later from Guatemala and published in 1525 as an appendix to Cortés's Fourth Letter have survived, according to Sedley Mackie in his edition, *An Account of the Conquest of Guatemala in 1524 by Pedro de Alvarado.*

11. Durán, *Historia de las indias de Nueva España*; Dávila Padilla, *Historia de la fundación*; Ojea, *Libro tercero.*

12. Ulloa, *Los predicadores dividos*, pp. 97–140.

13. Ricard, *The Spiritual Conquest of Mexico*, p. 210; Gonzalbo Aizpuru, *Historia de la educación en la época colonial*, pp. 135–51.

14. "nombrado en su idioma i jentilida Gosigoesa, que signifíca Rallo de Asero, el qual salió de dicha cabesera de Teosapotlan i fue a fundar la nasión sapoteca en dicha billa de Teguantepeque, lli es así quel emperador Montesuma desta corte con las noticias que tubo del rumbo lli entrada del Rei sapoteco en Teguantepeque, pretendió el desalojarlo, en qual contienda salió bencido dicho emperador, por quella causa tubo por buen acuerdo tratar medios de pas con el Rei sapoteco, la principal fue que este casase con una hija del emperador, llamada por su belda, Copo de Algodón. Y puesto en Tehuantepec dicho rey Gosigoesa, de quella conjunta ubieron y proquraron a Gosigopi, que significa Rallo del Viento, así llamado en su idioma y gentilidad, el cual, hallandose agto destado, y Gobi [se] quedó en dicha billa de Teguantepeque, biviendose su [padre] a su Reino de Teosapotlan. Casó dicho Cosijopi con una mujer de los Huaves llamada en su gentilidad Billosicahi y estando en este estado, estos dos reyes, vino a dar a esta tierra . . . Don Fernando Cortés del Castillo." Testimony of defendant, Don Antonio de Velasco; 1730 Fernando de Zúñiga y Cortés, cacique of Tehuantepec, petition concerning the exhibition of documents pertaining to his cacicazgo, AGN Tierras, vol. 493, exp. 6.

15. Burgoa, *Geográfica descripción,* 2, p. 338, begins his chapter on Tehuantepec with the following apology: "Grande Provincia empredemos, es ya común adagio de explicar los casi imposibles de una dificultosa empresa y la que contiene el haber de reducir a compendio y breve método lo espacioso y circunstancias de esta Provincia célebre, cuando conduce a dilatados escritos, escrupulea el juicio, el pautarle sus excelentes propiedades, en lo ceñido de este capítulo, mereciéndose toda una historia, pero esta que tengo entre manos, se ocupa con la descripción de todo lo restante de varias naciones, y llega fatigado el pulso a las postrimerías de esta molesta fatiga, atareada por mi mesma mano, sin que una letra haya interpuesto otra extraña, cuando los años de once seises afanados de achaques, y zozobrados cuidados a mi fragilidad, se ha expuesto ésta a los repartidos yerros, que reconozco en este asunto y confieso de presente por el que se ofrece de tantas y varias materias, como han sucedido, en este pueblo de Tehuantepeque."

16. *Ibid.*, pp. 328, 338–45.

17. "Nada he podido hallar respecto á este Pueblo como corte de la Nación Zapoteca, y así no se tenga a defecto del que escribe, pues debería hablar del Palacio Real, sus cortesanos, Gobierno etc. Si no lo hace es porque no han quedado documentos ni vestigios." Murguia y Galardi, *Extracto general*, p. 4.

18. Carriedo, *Estudios históricos y estadísticos,* 1, chapters 2, 3, 19, and 20.

19. Gay, *Historia de Oaxaca*; Martínez Gracida, *El rey Cocijoeza y su familia.*

20. Oaxaca scholars continue to find Gay's reconstruction of the Zaachila-Tehuantepec royal dynasty useful, for example, Joyce Marcus, "The Reconstructed Chronology of the Later Zapotec Rulers, A.D. 1415–1563." Modern efforts to weave a single linear historical chronology out of the disparate sources of Central Mexican preconquest ethnohistory are exemplified by the work of Burr Cartwright Brundage (see *A Rain of Darts*), but Brundage's criteria for choosing among discrepant versions of the native past are not discussed. A more explicit critique of ethnohistorical sources was given by the eminent Andeanist John Rowe. Surveying sixteenth- and seventeenth-century works on Inca history in the 1940s, Rowe's "Inca Culture" dismissed native chroniclers as "confused" or "unreliable," in favor of those Spaniards like Bernabé Cobo, whose works he found "clear in its phrasing and scientific in its approach."

21. Although far from a complete list, the specific examples I am referring to here are such works as Adorno, *Guaman Poma*; Gillespie, *The Aztec Kings*; Bricker, *The Indian Christ, The Indian King*; and Gruzinski, *Man-Gods in the Mexican Highlands.*

22. Originally appearing in *Zeitschrift fur Ethnologie* in 1906, "Das Dorfbuch von Santiago Guevea" was reprinted by Eduard Seler in his collected works, *Gesammelte Abhandlungen.* Later commentaries and reproductions of the Lienzo de Guevea manuscripts are provided by Paddock, *Lord 5 Flower's Family*; Whitecotton, *Zapotec Elite Ethnohistory*; and Oudijk, *Historiography of the Bènizàa.*

23. See J. Zeitlin, "Recordando a los reyes," for a more detailed comparison of three versions of the *lienzo* and their chronological placement.

24. Seler, "Das Dorfbuch"; Marcus, "Zapotec Writing."

25. A separate, earlier migration of Zapotec-speakers from the Oaxaca Valley to the Isthmus *sierra* would account for the strong dialectical differences between Guevea and other mountain communities on the one hand and the Zapotec-speaking towns of the coastal plain.

26. Oudijk, *Historiography of the Bènizàa*, p. 97.

27. Burgoa, *Geográfica descripción*, 2, p. 330.

28. Seler, "Das Dorfbuch," pp. 188–92; Oudijk, *Historiography of the Bènizàa*, p. 70. Seler ignored the female identity of Burgoa's Pinopia and instead assumed that this was the same individual who served as cacique of Zaachila under the baptismal name of Don Juan de Aguilar.

29. My reading of these glyphs agrees with that reached by Jansen, "El viaje al otro mundo," and Oudijk, *Historiography of the Bènizàa.* Paddock offered a slightly different interpretation in *Lord 5 Flower's Family*, pp. 24–26, finding some kind of bird represented in the glyph for the fifth Zaachila king (although the teeth-like element would seem to rule out an avian correspondent), and Rain and Wind, respectively, for the first and second Tehuantepec kings.

30. Jansen, "El viaje al otro mundo"; Paddock, *Lord 5 Flower's Family*, p. 73. Although Paddock thought that 5 Flower should precede 3 Serpent in this sequence and did not only because of a scribal error, Oudijk, *Historiography of the*

Bènizàa, pp. 100f., argues persuasively that the Nuttall depicts an individual tied by marriage to Mixtec royalty, who died before inheriting the Zaachila throne. Jansen explores the Mixtec toponyms in greater depth in "Monte Albán y Zaachila en los codices mixtecos."

31. Seler, "Das Dorfbuch," briefly noted the similarities between the Lienzo de Guevea rulers' headdresses with those attributed in Aztec pictorials to the god Xipe, and both Alfonso Caso, "The Lords of Yanhuitlan," and Paddock, *Lord 5 Flower's Family*, pp. 63–73, explore the occurrences of Xipe representations among the ruling families of Late Postclassic Oaxaca in some detail. Because none of the Lienzo de Guevea copyists were completely faithful to the symbolism of costume elements whose meanings they did not understand, the strength of the "Xipe dynasty" connection is much more apparent when the García version figures are compared.

32. Alvarado Tezózomoc, *Crónica mexicana*, p. 373.

33. Oudijk, *Historiography of the Bènizàa*, pp. 102–7.

34. Paddock, *Lord 5 Flower's Family*, pp. 83–97.

35. Whitecotton, *Zapotec Elite Ethnohistory*, p. 119. Burgoa, *Geográfica descripción*, 2.

36. Over five hundred folio pages are preserved in this case, "Autos seguidos por Doña María de Zúñiga, mujer que fue de Don Juan Cortés casique . . . contra el fiscal de Su Magestad sobre la posesión de los indios y otras varias estancias," AGI Escribanía de Cámara, 160 b, 1567–72.

37. I am indebted to Pedro Carrasco, who himself read this document many years ago while conducting other research at the Archivo General de las Indias, for his help in sorting out possible Nahuatl etymologies. The derivation of the Tehuantepec rulers' names is discussed in detail in J. Zeitlin, "Recordando a los reyes."

38. While Córdova translated "hazedor" as *huesa*, leading some scholars to read Cosijoeza as "Lightning or Rain Maker," the sixteenth-century linguist also included the Zapotec root *-quesa* in glosses for various Spanish words for knife. Clearly he refers specifically to obsidian or flint in the term he gives for "black stone from which knives are obtained" (*piedra negra de donde sacan navajas*; Zapotec *piogo quesa*, with *piogo* meaning "dark stone").

39. Coyolicatzin may have been a nineteenth-century Nahuatl invention of José Antonio Gay (pp. 107–8), for she is unnamed in Durán's *Historia de las indias de Nueva España*, 2: 421–22, or in the *Codex Telleriano-Remensis*, two early sources on Aztec history in which this marriage is mentioned.

40. Oudijk, *Historiography of the Bènizàa*, p. 123.

41. See Karttunen, *An Analytical Dictionary of Nahuatl*, p. 76.

42. This identification is substantiated by several Tehuantepec witnesses, who knew Don Juan as Coquilachi or Bichana Lachi. AGI Escribanía de Cámara, 160 b, various. Whitecotton, *Zapotec Elite Ethnohistory*, p. 119, reports seeing a sketch made by Heinrich Berlin of a document in the Brasseur de Bourbourg papers in Guatemala, which shows four figures above a temple glossed as "Zachijla"; they are in order "Cociopiy," "Cocijueza," "Don Jo [Juan] Laczi," and "Don Felipe Cortes."

43. 1554 testimony of Luís Netela, principal of Tehuantepec, Don Juan, cacique of Nanacatepeque, and others, AGI Escribanía de Cámara, 160 b.

44. 1730 Fernando de Zúñiga y Cortés, cacique of Tehuantepec, concerning the exhibition of documents pertaining to his *cacicazgo*, AGN Tierras, vol. 493, exp. 6.

45. Various native witnesses testifying on behalf of Don Juan Cortés in 1554 stated that Yecaquiahuitl conquered the Tehuantepec province in a war against the Guasontecas or Huaves. AGI Escribanía de Cámara, 160 b.

46. It may be, as Oudijk, *Historiography of the Bènizàa*, p. 123, has suggested, that the prominence of the Zaachila ruler 11 Water Cosijohueza, whose second wife was named Xilapela, just like the wife of the Tehuantepec ruler Cosijohueza, added to this apparent confusion among later colonial sources. Although Oudijk proposes that the practice of adopting personal names associated with distinguished ancestors was an intentional assertion of power and legitimacy, it appears to have been a postmortem recognition for Don Juan Cortés, since his contemporaries did not refer to him by this name.

47. Don Juan's son-in-law, Alonso de Toribio, testified particularly clearly on these events in 1571, as the quotation at the beginning of this chapter illustrates, but several earlier witnesses also verified the thoroughness of the Zapotec rout of the province's indigenous inhabitants. According to Luís Netela, *principal* of Tehuantepec, "they [the Guazontecas] went fleeing" (*se avían ido huyendo*). AGI Escribanía de Cámara, 160 b.

48. "Ytzquiahuitl [sic] vino a esta provincia con solo seisciento hombres del valle de guaxaca y conquistaron esta provincia que la poseyan yndios de lengua guaconteca e conquistada toda la tierra e a su lado el dicho Ytzquiahuitl [sic] repartió la tierra entre los yndios soldados que traya y ansí entre los pueblos e lugares que repartió y dió fueron los dichos barrios e pueblos y estancias de Totonilco, Tlacotepeque, Chiltepec y Suchitlan y Amatitlan y en ellos dexaron los dichos yndios guacontecas huertas de capotes y otros arboles e frutales y las dichas huertas e frutales gozaron siempre el dicho Don Juan y sus padres y que acabo de ciertos dichos yndios el dicho Ytzquiahuitl al valle de Guaxaca de donde heran naturales a dar aviso de la tierra que avía conquistado e que les rogava a los señores de la que les enbiasen gente con que poblasen la tierra y ansí le enbiaron trezientos hombres con los quales acabo de poblar esta provincia." 1571 testimony of Don Baltasar García, AGI Escribanía de Cámara, 160 b, f. 254v–255.

49. Dates for the Early–Late Postclassic transition are only approximate, since the 1972 excavations and surface survey Robert Zeitlin and I conducted along the Río de los Perros produced no radiocarbon determinations for this period. See J. Zeitlin, "Changing Patterns" for a report on prehistoric settlement patterns in the study area. Full details of the archaeological investigation from which these conclusions are drawn are found in J. Zeitlin, "Community Distribution."

50. Thomas, *Linguistic, Geographic, and Demographic Position*; Kaufman, "Mixe-Zoque Subgroups."

51. Changes in pottery styles during the Postclassic are discussed in detail in

J. Zeitlin, "Community Distribution," pp. 87–98 and appendix A. R. Zeitlin's spectrochemical analysis of obsidian samples from these and other Río de los Perros sites is summarized in his article, "Toward a More Comprehensive Model."

52. According to Burgoa, *Geográfica descripción*, 2, p. 398, "la nación de estos indios huabes habían venido de tierras muy lejanas de allá de la costa del Sur, más cerca de la eclíptica vecindad del Perú." Later in that passage the Dominican attributes the Zapotec conquest to their irritation at Huave accommodations to Moctezuma, to whom "le franquearon el paso a sus ejércitos, para proseguir con sus conquistas a otros reinos." Navarrete, *El sistema prehispánico*, reports that one of the two routes linking Tehuantepec with the Aztec's favored cacao-supplying area of Soconusco was the network of estuaries extending from the Laguna Superior to the Río Suchiate. Robert Zeitlin and I have suggested that these lagoon-shore communities may have obtained their obsidian in payment for services rendered as boatmen for the Aztec *pochteca*, "Arqueología y época prehispánica," p. 435.

53. Burgoa, *Geográfica descripción*, 2, p. 378, mistaking Don Juan Cortés's widow, Doña Magdalena, for his daughter, describes in enthusiastic detail the half-league of orchards near the Río de los Perros village of Laollaga that she donated to the Dominican convent. Witnesses called by Doña Magdalena in her suit with the Crown *fiscal* to have her husband's patrimonial estates returned to her children testified that the Indians working these estates were serfs or *terrazgueros*. Her opponents claimed that the cacique had only small numbers of slaves residing on these estates until after the Spanish Conquest, when commoners from other villages were persuaded to relocate there. AGI Escribanía de Cámara, 160 b.

54. Burgoa, *Geográfica descripción*, 2, pp. 342–43.

55. Nineteenth-century reports on Guiengola begin with the 1806 visit to the site by the Mexican army officer Guillermo Dupaix, later published in French and appearing in the modern Spanish version as *Expediciones*. More detailed descriptions followed in the works of Estrada, *Las ruinas del Cerro Guiengola*; Seler, "Die Ruinen auf dem Guie-Ngola"; Acosta and Moedano Koer, "Los juegos de pelota"; Covarrubias, *Mexico South*. The Institute of Oaxaca Studies mapping project is reported on by Peterson and MacDougall, *Guiengola* and by Peterson in "Guiengola: fortaleza zapoteca."

56. Peterson, "Guiengola: fortaleza zapoteca," fig. 22, illustrates a particularly fine example of a polychrome funerary vessel in a private Tehuantepec collection. During an archaeological reconnaissance in the southern Isthmus in 1990, I viewed several such private collections among Tehuantepec residents, although in these cases the predominant pottery was the ubiquitous fine gray ware. Matadamas, "Recorrido," reports on the rapid destruction of visible archaeological features in a four-month period between Instituto Nacional de Antropoligía e Historia site inspections in 1982 under the direction of Roberto Zárate.

57. Archaeological fieldwork at this and other sites during the spring of 1990 was generously sponsored by a grant to the author from the Wenner Gren Foundation for Anthropological Research. A summary of investigations at the Santa Cruz Tagolaba site, known locally as the Panteón Antiguo, is presented in J. Zeitlin, "Precolumbian Barrio Organization."

58. Late prehispanic settlement patterns and population projections for the Oaxaca Valley's principal subregions are detailed by Stephen Kowalewski et al. in *Monte Alban's Hinterland, Part II.*

59. Sixteenth-century depopulation rates for different subregions of the Oaxaca Valley based on archaeological estimates and Spanish censuses are compared with high and low estimates for Tehuantepec in J. Zeitlin, "Precolumbian Barrio Organization," which concludes that most of Tehuantepec's residents were migrants from the Tlacolula arm of the Oaxaca Valley.

60. 1554 interrogatory of Don Juan Cortés, AGI Escribanía de Cámara, 160 b, f. 143. An early fifteenth-century conquest of Tehuantepec by Cosijopii would be hard to reconcile with the Codex Nuttall's genealogy for Cuilapan-Zaachila, whose ruler 6 Water reigned at the time the manuscript was painted around 1438, according to Caso, *Reyes y reinos de la Mixteca,* vol. 1, p. 18. The Lienzo de Guevea places Cosijopii a generation apart from his ancestor 6 Water.

Chapter 2

1. Pagden, *Hernán Cortés*, p. 444.

2. "porque aquellos pueblos o poblaciones son fechos a barrios, como son las poblaciones en los valles de algunas provincias de España, en Vizcaya y Guipúzcoa y en las Montañas; y todo les parescería, a este clérigo y a los otros, que era un pueblo, non obstante que, sin eso, hay grandes poblaciones juntas." Oviedo, *Historia general,* 2, p. 257.

3. J. Zeitlin, "Precolumbian Barrio Organization," p. 289.

4. Carrasco, "Estratificación social indígena"; see also his article, "The Joint Family in Ancient Mexico."

5. Paso y Troncoso, "Relación de la visita que hizo Baltasar de San Miguel."

6. 1553 criminal complaint against Don Juan Cortés, *gobernador* of Tehuantepec, AGN Hospital de Jesús, leg. 450, exp. 1.

7. *Ibid.*

8. 1555 proclamation of commoner tribute obligations to Don Juan Cortés by Viceroy Don Luís de Velasco, AGN Mercedes, vol. 4, f. 142. In that year tribute payments were set at 4 *tomines* of gold and a half *fanega* of maize per married tributary. Native tribute documents from the colonial era often followed precolumbian practice in specifying the amount of tribute owed quarterly ("cada ochenta días"), and this schedule was specified for monetary tribute in Viceroy Velasco's proclamation as well.

9. Leander, *Códice de Otlazpan*; Horn, *Postconquest Coyoacan*, pp. 132–34.

10. J. Zeitlin, "Precolumbian Barrio Organization," p. 292.

11. As was noted in the previous chapter, the Mexican governor of Xalapa, Don Baltasar García, testified that the conqueror (whom he often confused with Don Juan's father rather than his grandfather) went back to the "valle de Guaxaca de donde heran naturales a dar aviso de la tierra que avía conquistado e que les rogava a los señores de la que les enviasen gente con que poblasen la tierra." AGI Escribanía de Cámara, 160 b, f. 255.

12. According to Horn, *Postconquest Coyoacan*, p. 140, *tecpantlaca* or

"palace people" in early colonial Coyoacan were responsible for cultivating palace lands and maintaining the palace, but paid no tribute.

13. AGI Escribanía de Cámara, 160 b. The barrios represented by Tehuantepec witnesses are Atempa, Coyonacalco, Diego Goma, Nautecpa/Nahuitelpa, Moscaltepeque, Tecpantlacatl, Tecpanquiahuat, Tecolapa, Teozapotlan/Tequehzapotlan, Tixava, Totoncalco,Totonilco/Atotonica, Xalisco, Yeteca, Yolotecatl/Yoloteca, and Yzquiapa. I am grateful to Dr. Pedro Carrasco for his help in translating the Nahuatl place names.

14. Chance, "Barrios of Colonial Tecali."

15. Details of this kind of work project emerged in another complaint filed against the cacique Don Juan Cortés during the *residencia secreta* that produced the charges of excessive tribute demands by the four Zapotec commoners, AGN Hospital de Jesús, leg. 450, exp. 1.

16. The complaints of fifteen Tehuantepec barrio *principales* against the actions of the province's *alcalde mayor* were included in the 1720 suit of the Indians of Lachiguiri, Guevea, and Guienagati against Don Pedro de Saravía Cortés, AGN Civil, vol. 599, exp. 4–5.

17. That is the conclusion drawn in earlier assessments of late prehispanic Zapotec social organization; cf. Spores, "The Zapotec and Mixtec at Spanish Contact"; Whitecotton, *The Zapotecs*, p. 144. Several witnesses in the suit by Doña Magdalena attempted to distinguish the cacique's hold on patrimonial barrios and *estancias* from the obligations of ordinary communities and the appointment of *tequitlatos* was noted in particular by Diego Ruíz, *tequitlato* of the Tecolapa (Tagolaba) barrio. AGI Escribanía de Cámara, 160 b.

18. 1554 testimony of Pedro Lache, Tomás Guelo, Pedro Nuñez and others, AGI Escribanía de Cámara, 160 b.

19. "Con todos los yndios e naturales que en las dichas estancias biven, gozandolas e desfrutandolas, y gozando los tributos de ellas como tal señor propincuo e natural." 1554 petition to Alonso de Buyca, juez de comisión, by Don Juan Cortés, AGI Escribanía de Cámara, 160 b, f. 45v.

20. *El libro de las tasaciones,* pp. 372–77.

21. "e ansí truxó algunos vezes mantielos e otras cosas de poco valor al este testigo [Alcala] diziendole que aquello hera lo que las dichas estancias davan por tributo e que desde a poco tiempo fue por visitador a contar la dicha provincia de Teguantepeque Diego Ramírez por merced del Sr. Virrey don Antonio de Mendoza y el dicho visitador tornó todas al dicho Don Juan las estancias y no sabe este testigo por que causa se las bolbió e dió." 1571 testimony of Pedro de Alcala, AGI Escribanía de Cámara, 160 b, fs. 340v–41.

22. 1555 viceregal decrees mandated by Dr. Quesada, former *oidor* of the Audiencia, concerning Tehuantepec and the Marquesado, AGN Mercedes, vol. 4, fs. 138–44v.

23. AGI Escribanía de Cámara, 160 b, various.

24. 1554 testimony of Sebastian Niza, AGI Escribanía de Cámara, 160 b, f. 110 v.

25. "por razón de los muchos tributos que los españoles les pedían e por otras causas e después el dicho Don Juan Cortés como sus vasallos e de su patri-

monio los avía buscado e fue a buscar a los pueblos comarcanos y les habló e dixó que pues los avía tenido por hijos y ellos a el por su padre y señor que les rogava que se bolviesen a sus estancias donde las tierras que cultivasen e labrasen como los solían antes hazer y desde entonces le comenzaron a tributar de nuevo como antes lo solían hazer y que tan solamente le tributavan al dicho Don Juan Cortés e no al Marqués y que las dichas estancias e tierras de lo siempre fueron de los aguellos e padres del dicho Don Juan e después de sus días del dicho Don Juan de su patrimonio." 1570 testimony of Fr. Bernardo de Santa María, AGI Escribanía de Cámara, 160 b, f. 391v.

26. Córdova, *Vocabulario*. Not all hired laborers were permanent residents of the city, however. According to the "Relación de Iztepexi," people from that town went to Tehuantepec and the provinces of Soconusco and Guatemala to obtain gold and green feathers for tribute payments to their Mixtec and Aztec overlords, which they earned by hiring themselves out for six months to a year carrying goods for merchants or cultivating lands, or whatever the lords and caciques of these towns desired. Paso y Troncoso, ed., "Relaciones Geográficas de la diócesis de Oaxaca," p. 17.

In an earlier paper I explored the possibility that the term *penicozaaca*, which Córdova gives for foreigner, might refer to serf-like status within ancient Zapotec society because it is glossed as well for "renter who lives on my lands" ("rentero que vive en mis tierras"), with the explanatory note that this term is appropriate because "commonly they are strangers" ("comunmente son estranjeros"); see J. Zeitlin, "Colonialism and the Political Transformation." Although the occupation of rented lands may indeed signify a special social status among the Zapotec, it now seems to me likely that it is distinct from the social status held by the class of dependent people described in the testimony regarding Don Juan Cortés's patrimonial estates.

27. Terraciano, *Mixtecs of Colonial Oaxaca*, pp. 140–45, uses a rich corpus of colonial-period native language sources to explore the status and social obligations of dependent laborers within Mixtec society. His data suggest that the composition of this social class and its obligations to Mixtec lords may have been more fluid than what is portrayed for the Isthmus Zapotec in this early colonial assertion of royal authority.

28. 1571 testimony of Don Francisco Vásquez de Coronado, AGI Escribanía de Cámara, 160 b, f. 388. Horn, *Postconquest Coyoacan*, pp. 140–41, provides some comparative figures on *terrazguero* claims by Coyoacan elites in a 1553 *visita* to that Nahua town. The cacique and other high-ranking nobles might have large numbers of patrimonial serfs (208 for the cacique and 62 for another titled noble), but half of the twenty-five nobles claiming *terrazgueros* had fewer than ten.

29. Haskett, for example, *Indigenous Rulers*, p. 135, observes a similar pattern in Cuernavaca, where the title was bestowed mainly on individuals of the Nahua *tlatoani* and *teuctli* rank, who held only the highest offices on the colonial town council. Restall, *The Maya World*, p. 46, notes that the Yucatec Maya maintained their restricted application of the title to members of the highest nobility throughout the colonial period, even when its usage had become more flex-

ible in both Spanish and Nahua communities. Terraciano, *Mixtecs of Colonial Oaxaca*, p. 156, finds a similarly persistent pattern of restricted usage of the Spanish honorific within Mixtec society, in which not all noble men and women were eligible for the title.

30. Córdova, *Vocabulario*, f. 246.

31. Kartunnen, *An Analytical Dictionary of Nahuatl*, p. 217.

32. Some of this discussion is drawn from an earlier exploration of Zapotec concepts of political authority in Zeitlin and Thomas, "Spanish Justice." In addition to consulting Córdova's *Vocabulario* directly, I have made use of Joseph W. Whitecotton and Judith Bradley Whitecotton's helpful Zapotec-Spanish vocabulary derived from Córdova's original, *Vocabulario zapoteco-castellano*.

33. 1571 testimony of Don Francisco Vásquez de Coronado, AGI Escribanía de Cámara, leg. 160 b, f. 388.

34. 1553 criminal complaint against Don Juan Cortés, AGN Hospital de Jesús, leg. 450, exp. 1. Aspects of Zapotec sociopolitical organization evidenced in this case are discussed in Zeitlin and Thomas, "Spanish Justice."

35. Oudijk, *Historiography of the Bènizàa*, pp. 79–99. I am grateful to Michel Oudijk for his generously making available to me photographs of the Mapa de Huilotepec and for sharing many ideas and documents concerning our mutual research interests. References to the council of royal advisors in the 1553 complaint against Don Juan Cortés are discussed in Zeitlin and Thomas, "Spanish Justice."

36. Oudijk, *Historiography of the Bènizàa*, p. 87, notes that this example of mirror-writing is a unique occurrence in the pictorial record. Because mirror-writing is not a pattern associated with cognitive or learning disabilities among modern writers, it seems most likely that the Mapa de Huilotepec artist simply inverted the letter forms by mistake when copying another text, perhaps as he viewed the painted text through the reverse side of the cloth.

37. See J. Zeitlin, "Ranchers and Indians." At least ten *principales* requested permission to establish twenty-four *estancias de ganado menor* within the limits of the villa of Tehuantepec before the end of the ranching boom in the early seventeenth century, and many of the *estancias* requested in other communities were by members of the Tehuantepec nobility.

38. 1571 testimony of Don Baltasar García, AGI Escribanía de Cámara, 160 b, f. 254v.

39. Peterson and MacDougall, *Guiengola*.

40. Paso y Troncoso, ed., "Relaciones Geográficas de la diócesis de Oaxaca," p. 221.

41. Terraciano, *Mixtecs of Colonial Oaxaca*, pp. 77–81; León-Portilla, "Nahuatl Literature." Tavárez, *Invisible Wars*, pp. 422–35, finds that a large sample of Sierra Zapotec songs recovered in late colonial anti-idolatry campaigns are based in part on compositions that sixteenth-century priests made for purposes of spreading Catholic doctrine.

42. Caso, ed., "Relación de Tehuantepec," p. 170.

43. Urcid, *Zapotec Hieroglyphic Writing*, presents a systematic comparison of scholarly attempts to decipher this calendrical system with data recorded by

colonial period sources. Urcid's comments (personal communication 1998) have helped me unravel some knots of my own making in this endeavor, and I defer to his published explication in much of the summary presented here.

44. Citations from Córdova's discussion of the calendar are from the somewhat differently titled, Nicolás León edition, *Arte del idioma zapoteca*, pp. 201–12.

45. "Y dezian los indios que estos quatro planetas causavan todas las cosas en la tierra y assi tenianlos por dioses, y llamavanlos, cocijos, o pitaos. Que quiere dezir grandes, y a estos offrecian sus sacrificios, y su sangre sacandosela de diversas partes de su cuerpos, como de las orejas, del pico de la lengua, de los muslos y de otras partes. Y el orden que tenian era que mientras corrian los 65 del un planeta sacrificavan aquel y cumplidos al otro, que entrava por aquel modo, y assi por su orden, hasta que tornava entrar el primero &c. Y a estos les pedian todo lo que avian menester para sus sustento." *Ibid.*, p. 202.

46. Caso and Bernal, *Urnas de Oaxaca*. Marcus summarizes ethnographic stories about the elements associated with these jars in her article "Zapotec Religion." See Thompson, *Maya History and Religion*, pp. 251–70, for a compilation of archaeological, ethnohistorical, and ethnographic data on Maya Rain God concepts.

47. Smith Stark, "Dioses, sacerdotes y sacrificio"; Alcina Franch, *Calendario y religión entre los zapotecos*, see especially figures 7–26; Urcid, *Zapotec Hieroglyphic Writing*, pp. 84–102.

48. Marcus, "Zapotec Religion."

49. Córdova, *Arte del idioma*, pp. 202–3.

50. Córdova, *Vocabulario*.

51. Marcus, "Zapotec Religion."

52. Córdova tells us that "solo el entrava en sus sancta sanctorum donde estavan los ydolos a offrecer sacrificio," *Vocabulario*, p. 299 v.

53. Burgoa, *Geográfica descripción*, 2, pp. 350, 355. Dávila Padilla, *Historia de la fundación*, p. 635.

54. Marcus and Flannery, "Ancient Zapotec Ritual and Religion." See also their extended discussion of the emergence of this temple form in *Zapotec Civilization*, pp. 181–88.

55. Peterson and MacDougall, *Guiengola*.

56. Marcus and Flannery, *Zapotec Civilization*, pp. 186–88.

57. Burgoa, *Geográfica descripción*, 2, pp. 329–30.

58. Delgado, *Archaeological Reconnaissance* illustrates one such site at the summit of the hill Dani Guiati between Ixtepec and Ixtaltepec. While conducting archaeological reconnaissance on the Isthmus in 1972, Robert Zeitlin and I were taken to another rock shelter with petroglyphs and pottery offerings in the foothills of the Sierra Atravesada near Tlacotepec; Zeitlin, "Community Distribution," p. 180. Some of the figures at Dani Guiati evidence a postconquest use of the site, which may have been the case with the Tlacotepec rock shelter as well, given the continuation of late Postclassic ceramics into the late sixteenth century.

59. Burgoa, *Geográfica descripción*, 2, p. 351.

60. *Ibid.*, p. 400.

61. Romero Frizzi, "Indigenous Mentality." Oudijk, *Historiography of the Bènizàa*, pp. 164–66, notes that these bundles contained relics associated with the sacred power and legitimacy of elite lineages and that they continued to be objects of worship and sacrifice in Sierra Zapotec communities into the early eighteenth century, when several were discovered and opened in anti-idolatry campaigns.

62. Marcus, "Zapotec Religion," pp. 348–49.

63. Urcid (personal communication 1998) observes that there is yet no archaeological or osteological evidence in support of the practice of entombing sacrificial victims with the deceased lord or lady as reported by Córdova, largely because the major known Zapotec tombs were emptied in antiquity and ritually sealed. He suggests that the veneration of royal ancestors led to the removal of all skeletal remains to create mortuary bundles more accessible for ritual propitiation.

64. Burgoa, *Geográfica descripción*, 2, p. 331.

65. Oudijk, *Historiography of the Bènizàa*, pp. 227–29.

66. One Spanish *vecino* of Tehuantepec, who testified on behalf of the *fiscal* against Doña Magdalena (even though he was her children's godfather), said that he heard from Don Baltasar García, governor of Xalapa, as well as from other Indians in the province, that at least one of the disputed patrimonial *estancias* had formerly been subject to Xalapa and not Tehuantepec. 1571 testimony of Juan Ximenes, AGI Escribanía de Cámara, 160 b, f. 241v. Such a fact would imply some preexisting political autonomy for Xalapa. Burgoa, however, reported that Xalapa's "señores y caciques" had all been placed there by the king of Zaachila, though none of their lineal descendants were still alive in the mid-seventeenth century. Burgoa, *Geográfica descripción*, 2, p. 338. Such important political appointments were distributed only among trusted royal kin, but of course we do not know to which of the royal factions the Xalapa rulers belonged.

67. Ramírez, *Proceso de residencia,* pp. 6–7; the Xalapa incident is described in items 14 and 15 of the interrogatory.

68. *Ibid.*, pp. 75f.

69. Modern scholarly assessments of the market and other aspects of the Aztec economy are found in Smith, *The Aztecs*; Hodge and Smith, *Economies and Polities in the Aztec Realm*; and Hassig, *Trade, Tribute, and Transportation.*

70. 1555 ordinances decreed by Viceroy Don Luís de Velasco following the Tehuantepec *visita* of the *oidor* Dr. Quesada, AGN Mercedes, vol. 4, fs. 138–48.

71. Paso y Troncoso, ed. "Relaciones Geográficas de la diócesis de Oaxaca."

72. "e tenía sus mayordomos que tenían cuidado de guardarse las dichas salinas e recoger la sal de ellas e venderla y este testigo vió algunos vezes e le tomó a ver el dicho Vizquihuitl que los dichos mayordomos le trayan hachuelas y oro e piedras e mantas e cueros de tigre que hera resgate de la sal que vendían y le acudían con todo ello como Señor de las dichas salinas lo qual este testigo le vió tener e poseer al susodicho hasta que faleció sin contradición alguna e de ninguna persona." 1554 testimony of Don Alonso of Xalapa, AGI Escribanía de Cámara, 160 b, f. 50v.

73. Acosta, *Historia natural*, p. 351.

74. Mexican sources attributing Tehuantepec's conquest to Ahuitzotl include Durán, Tezózomoc, Torquemada, and the *Codex Mendoza*. Sahagún lists Izcoatlan, Xochtlan, Amaxtlan, and Xoconochco among Ahuitzotl's victories, but does not mention Tehuantepec.

75. Durán, *Historia de las indias*, 2, pp. 357–62; Alvarado Tezozmoc, *Crónica mexicana*, pp. 355–75.

76. Durán, *Historia de las indias*, 2, p. 357. The inferior things which the Aztecs were said to have brought in trade included several food specialties prepared from Lake Texcoco's algae and insect life, which the Spaniards found particularly distasteful, as well as elaborate manufactured goods.

77. *Ibid.*, p. 361. Alvarado Tezózomoc, *Crónica mexicana*, p. 373, says the tribute included gold-bedecked weapons and other military equipment, the jewel-covered mitre which was the symbol of Tehuantepec's *señorío*, cloaks of black and white feathers called *yhuitlmaxtli,* and many rich things, especially lots of "tiger" skins, since Tehuantepec was the land of more wild cats than any place else in New Spain. While reference is made to the Tehuantepec *principales* in this account, unlike Durán, Tezózomoc does not mention its ruler. He claims five coastal towns, Tehuantepec, Izhuatlan, Xochitecas, Chiltepec, and Amaxtlan, paid tribute to the Triple Alliance.

78. Durán and Tezózomoc both tell of Tehuantepec's reluctance to offer allegiance to the new ruler of Tenochtitlan, but of these two only Durán, *Historia de las indias*, 2, pp. 421–22, relates the story of Cosijoeza's marriage to an unnamed Aztec princess and her loyalty to her husband in the face of her father's treachery. The annotator of the 1540s Codex Telleriano-Remensis, however, mentions the bride and her role in thwarting an Aztec military victory in Tehuantepec; see Quiñones-Keber, *Codex*, p. 85.

79. Burgoa, *Geográfica descripción*, 2, pp. 341–45. As was noted earlier, testimony presented in 1554 on behalf of Don Juan's patrimonial claims gave the name of Cosijoeza/Itzquiahuitl's wife as Pelaxilla or Xilabela/Quetzalcoatl, not Cotton Puff, and claimed that she was the sister of Motecuhzoma, not his daughter. AGI Escribanía de Cámara, 160 b.

80. Evidence for the Aztec presence in Soconusco has been discussed recently in Voorhies, *Ancient Trade and Tribute*.

81. Durán, *Historia de las indias,* p. 388.

82. This practice is discussed by Gibson, "Structure of the Aztec Empire," p. 390.

83. Xochitlan, Amaxtlan, and Tehuantepec are listed as conquests during the reign of Ahuitzotl on folio 13 of the *Codex Mendoza*, but there is no tribute page for the province. All three Isthmus towns and the coastal provinces to the west and east of Tehuantepec are included in the Memorial de Tlacopan, listing towns paying tribute to the Triple Alliance. Paso y Troncoso, "Memorial de los pueblos sujetos," pp. 118–22. In his exhaustive study, *The Tenochca Empire of Ancient Mexico,* Carrasco, p. 241, compares these two documents at length and concludes that military services may have been the primary obligation of places like Tehuantepec that were omitted from the *Codex Mendoza*.

84. "en donde asimismo fueron destrozados y perdieron mucho de su fama y

reputación, y mostró Diós su castigo y zaña que contra el tenía por los muchos sacrificios que habían hecho, y no paró aquí sino que les envió otros castigos como se verá adelante. El siguiente de noventa y siete sojuzgaron otras dos provincias, las de Amaxtlán y Xochitlán." Alva Ixtlilxóchitl, *Obras históricas,* 2, p. 283.

85. *Ibid.*, pp. 289–318.

86. Sahagún, *Florentine Codex*, Book 8, p. 2.

87. August 21, 1567, *real provisión* on behalf of the *fiscal*, Dr. Cespedes de Cardenas, against Doña Magdalena de Zúñiga, AGI Escribanía de Cámara, 160 b.

Chapter 3

1. Restall, *Maya Conquistador*. The role played by the Tlaxcaltecans in the conquest of Tenochtitlan is well known, but the complex array of indigenous reactions to the Spaniards in other parts of Mesoamerica has been less often noted. Romero, *El sol y la cruz*, pp. 76–86, makes a similar point, drawing upon examples from Oaxaca.

2. Ramírez, *Proceso de residencia*, pp. 6-7.

3. Pagden, *Hernán Cortés*, p. 276.

4. *Ibid.*, p. 270. Burgoa, *Geográfica descripción*, 2, pp. 351–52, related the Zapotec story that the coming of the Spaniards and the defeat of the Aztecs had been foretold to the young Tehuantepec king in an oracular message from the sacred idol, Corazón del Reino, and that it was this prognostication which persuaded him to submit at once to the Spaniards. This account, like the Aztec story of Cortés's identification with Ce Acatl Topiltzin Quetzalcoatl and the evil omens which preceded the Spanish *entrada,* may be best understood as a post hoc rationalization of a calamity that required anticipation in Mesoamerican ideology.

5. Testimony on behalf of Doña Magdalena de Zúñiga, AGI Escribanía de Cámara, 160 b, fs. 185v, 274, and 400v. Alvarado, however, did not consider the Tehuantepecas' assistance worth mentioning in his official reports; see Alvarado, *An Account of the Conquest of Guatemala*. But neither did the vanquished Maya acknowledge the Mexican and Zapotec warriors who accompanied the ill-named "Tonatiuh" or Sun, as the blond lieutenant was called, in their version of this campaign; Recinos and Goetz, *Annals of the Cakchiquels.*

6. Transcription of 1554 testimony by Don Juan of Nanacatepec, Alonso de Chila of Amatlan, and Luís Netela of Tehuantepec, AGI Escribanía de Cámara, 160 b, fs. 54v, 114, and 99.

7. "El dicho Marcos de Aguilar como justicia mayor para ello me dió poderes bastantes mandandome que hiziese ciertos navios para cumplimiento del mandado de Su Magestad por las quales dichas provisiones me mandó tomar la gente donde quiera que la hallase e yo por virtud de lo sobredicho fue a las villas de Medellyn e Villa Rica tomé gentes e adereços en que gostenía muchos dyneros e vine a este pueblo de Teguantepeque con todo ello en donde a llegado hallé que todos los pueblos comarcanos estavan de guerra a cuya causa me fue fecho de entender en conquistarlos e pasyficarlos lo qual hize con la ayuda de Diós e con my

persona e de los que comigo yvan en lo qual gasté mucha cantidad de pesos de oro e después yo puso por obra de hazerlos navios que a my me eran mandados para el servicio de Su Magestad." 1529 petition by Francisco Maldonado in 1533–42 suit of Martín López vs. Francisco Maldonado, AGN Hospital de Jesús, leg. 300, exp. 107.

8. "porque toda la mas de la gente que ayudavan hazer los dichos navios se fueron a Chiapa con Don Juan e otros muchos a Guatimala e no quedaron en este pueblo de todos ellos mas de dos maestros y un herrero y cladenero." Transcript of 1529 report by Martín López, included in the suit of Martín López against Francisco Maldonado over the administration of Indians in the province of Tehuantepec, 1533–42, AGN Hospital de Jesús, leg. 300, exp. 107.

9. 1571 testimony by both Mexican Indians who had been part of this original group of settlers, Baltasar García of Xalapa and Juan García of Tehuantepec, and unfriendly Zapotecs like Don Hernando Peres, principal of Chihuitán, recounted the handing over of tribute-collecting and governing authority to the Mexicans by Cortés, AGI Escribanía de Cámara, 160 b, fs. 327–27v, 331, and 329.

10. "Quando el dicho Marqués se fue de la dicha villa dexó por principales e tlacateotl [sic] de ella a un Luís Mexicano y a dicho Diego y el dicho Don Juan quedó sin cargo de señor ni governador y que este testigo después de ydo el dicho marqués que quedava a su cargo de mantener y proveer doze o treze quadrillos de esclavos con sus mineros e mayordomos españoles y alcalde de minas y el astillero de sus navios con Fernando Cortés carpintero de ribera y otros muchos españoles y gente que sustentar y cosas muchas que proveer este testigo viniendo a su noticia como el dicho Don Juan Cortés era señor natural de la dicha villa e provincia le nombró por tal y le mandó se encargase del govierno de ella y del cuidado de recoger los tributos y gente de servicio para las dichas minas y bastimientos para ellas y el dicho astillero y quitó al dicho Luís Mexicano que el dicho marqués le avía puesto antes y este testigo comunicando lo con el dicho marqués por carta lo tuvió por bien y ansí se quedó desde entonces por señor." 1571 testimony of Juan de Toledo, AGI Escribanía de Cámara, 160 b, fs. 244v–45.

11. "al tiempo que por mandado del dicho Don Hernando Cortés se conquistó e pacificó esta dicha provincia los naturales de las dichas estancias como otros de la propria cabecera e otras partes de la provincia se huyeron e ausentaron muchos de ellos de miedo de los españoles y se derramaron por los pueblos de la comarca donde mas seguros pudiesen bivir e después que se acabó de apazificar la dicha provincia el dicho Don Juan Cortés los buscó e hizo traer e recoger las proprias estancias donde solían bivir que heran de su patrimonio como yndios suyos e de su patrimonio." 1571 testimony of Diego Ruíz, AGI Escribanía de Cámara, 160 b, fs. 382v–83.

12. *El libro de las tasaciones de pueblos*, pp. 372–77.

13. *Ibid.*

14. 1556 wage receipts of Juan Ximénez, alcalde mayor for Tehuantepec, AGN Hospital de Jesús, leg. 160 bis. Machuca Gallegos, *Tehuantepec en el siglo XVI*, p. 112, notes that this labor draft involved almost 90 percent of the province's tributary population.

15. 1529 report of Martín López, AGN Hospital de Jesús, leg. 300, exp. 107. While López's antipathy to Cortés was clear, it appears that he based his complaints about Maldonado's administration on interviews with the province's inhabitants and with the Spanish shipbuilders.

16. 1556 wage receipts of Juan Ximénez, alcalde mayor for Tehuantepec, AGN Hospital de Jesús, leg. 160 bis. Some of this information is discussed in J. Zeitlin, "Ranchers and Indians," pp. 44f. For the Huave account, see Burgoa, *Geográfica descripción*, 2, p. 400.

17. 1572 testimony of various Zapotec witnesses on behalf of Doña Magdalena, AGI Escribanía de Cámara, 160 b, fs. 417–23v.

18. 1543 *residencia* of the administration of Juan de Toledo, *alcalde mayor* of Tehuantepec, AGN Hospital de Jesús, leg. 160 bis.

19. 1571 testimony of Pedro de Alcala, AGI Escribanía de Cámara, 160 b, fs. 340v–41.

20. 1554 testimony of Marcos Lecal, AGI Escribanía de Cámara, 160 b, fs. 51v–52.

21. The record of the Tehuantepec court proceedings was forwarded to the Marquesado's administrator. 1553 criminal complaint against Don Juan Cortés, AGN Hospital de Jesús, leg. 450, exp. 1. See the analysis of this case in Zeitlin and Thomas, "Spanish Justice."

22. Zeitlin and Thomas, "Spanish Justice."

23. "e le dexen libremente usar su officio y juntarse en su casa pública como en lo demás principales y officiales de la república de los yndios y hordenar y disponer lo que entre ellos biere que conbiene al servicio de nuestro señor y bien de los naturales y execución de la justicia y castigos de pecados públicos y bienes y propios y quentas de su consejo syn que nadie se meta en ellos ni en parte alguna dellos segun y como lo han hecho en tiempos pasados y como lo hacen los demás pueblos desta Nueva España de la Real Corona de Su Magestad y los dexen nombrar officiales y personas que conbengan al bien de la república de los yndios y execución de las hordenanças de la real Audiencia y las demas que en su poder quedan." 1555 edict by Viceroy Luís de Velasco ordering the *naturales* of Tehuantepec to obey Don Juan Cortés as their cacique and governor, AGN Mercedes, vol. 4, f. 138v.

24. *Ibid.*

25. Mullen, *Dominican Architecture*, pp. 38, 138. Burgoa, *Geográfica descripción*, 2, p. 378.

26. Burgoa, *Geográfica descripción*, 2, p. 349.

27. 1529 report to the Audiencia by Martín López, AGN Hospital de Jesús, leg. 300, exp. 107. Lopéz reported removing Minaya from the monastery in Tehuantepec because he was by himself, when the order's regulations required at least two friars to staff each convent. Burgoa's chronicle of the Oaxaca province, *Palestra historial*, f. 2v–6v, discusses the arduous labors of the first Dominican missionaries, but does not mention Minaya's work in Tehuantepec.

28. Cortés's Tehuantepec letters are cited by Moorehead, "Hernán Cortés and the Tehuantepec Passage." Motives for the trip are given by López de Gómara, *Cortés: The Life of the Conqueror*, pp. 397–99.

29. Motolinía, *Motolinía's History of the Indians of New Spain*, pp. 253–55.

30. Velasco Pérez summarizes the history of the Dominican chapter and bishopric in his commemorative treatise for the 450th anniversary of Oaxaca, *La conquista armada y espirtitual.* Although Burgoa provides the names of the early vicars of Tehuantepec in his *Geográfica descripción*, 2, pp. 379–81, he gives no date for the founding of the religious house there. Father Gay claimed that the Tehuantepec mission was established in 1538, *Historia de Oaxaca*, p. 182, but I have found no such date in his primary source for this section of evangelical history, Burgoa's *Palestra historial.*

31. The open chapel at Teposcolula, which at midcentury was the richest and most populous town in the Mixteca Alta because of its successful silk and cochineal industries, is described by Perry, *Mexico's Fortress Monasteries*, p. 197, as "one of the great masterworks of Spanish colonial architecture." The similarities between the Teposcolula and Tehuantepec open chapels was noted by McAndrew, *Open-Air Churches*, pp. 558f. Mullen, *Dominican Architecture*, p. 151, n. 10, suggests that Albuquerque provided the link between the two chapel designs.

32. Paso y Troncoso, "Relación de la visita," p. 312.

33. Gay, *Historia de Oaxaca,* p. 182, stated that Beteta wrote a Zapotec-language *doctrina,* but it is unmentioned in the list of Dominican authors compiled by the Domincan chronicler Dávila Padilla in his history of the Dominican mission in New Spain, *Historia de la fundación.*

34. "Son los indios gente flemática, y con la continuación del trabajo salen con muchas obras dignas de estimación. Si les quieren dar priessa, y sacarlos de su passo, sin cobrar el que les dan, pierden el que tenían, y no hazen cosa de importancia." Dávila Padilla, *Historia de la fundación*, p. 256.

35. *Ibid.*, pp. 256–57.

36. Feria, *La doctrina christiana*, f. 4v.

37. *Ibid.*, fs. 20v–23.

38. *Ibid.*, f. 62.

39. *Ibid.*, fs. 64–64v.

40. *Ibid.*, fs. 77–77v, 14v.

41. 1555 confirmation by Viceroy Don Luís de Velasco of the rulings made by Dr. Quesada, *oidor* for Tehuantepec and the Marquesado, AGN Mercedes, vol. 4, fs. 138–48.

42. 1572 testimony on behalf of Doña Magdalena de Zúñiga, AGI Escribanía de Cámara, 160 b, fs. 414v–23.

43. Tavárez, *Invisible Wars*, pp. 131–40.

44. Burgoa, *Geográfica descripción*, 2, pp. 353–55.

45. *Ibid.*, pp. 357–59.

46. 1567 petition by Dr. Cespedes de Cárdenas for the return of the Tehuantepec salinas to the Crown, AGI Escribanía de Cámara, 160 b, f. 1v.

47. Burgoa, *Geográfica descripción*, 2, p. 356.

48. Tavárez, *Invisible Wars*, p. 490.

49. Dávila Padilla, *História de la fundación*, p. 79; Tavárez, *Invisible Wars*, pp. 426–35; Burgoa, *Geográfica descripción,* 2, p. 390.

50. Tavárez, *Invisible Wars*, pp. 37f.

Chapter 4

1. Lockhart, *Nahuas and Spaniards*, pp. 2–22; *The Nahuas After the Conquest*, pp. 429–42; Kartunnen and Lockhart, *Nahuatl in the Middle Years*.

2. Restall, "A History of the New Philology and the New Philology in History," reviews the contributions that native text-based studies have made to a deeper understanding of indigenous Mesoamerican society during the colonial period. The known corpus of Zapotec language alphabetic texts, though small in comparison to Nahuatl and Maya documentation, is growing. Michel Oudijk, who has conducted the most exhaustive research in this area, reports that some seven hundred Zapotec texts are encompassed in a transcription and translation project he is conducting with Ángeles Romero Frizzi (personnel communication, 2003).

3. According to Fr. Francisco de Burgoa, Don Juan ordered that the fishing barrio of San Blas Atempa provide the convent's eight friars and their attendants with fresh fish daily, since these observant men did not eat meat; *Geográfica descripción*, 2, p. 378. Apparently other "gifts" were requested of the cacique as well. At the heart of the Zapotec commoners' complaint in Don Juan's *residencia secreta* was a large sum of expropriated cacao beans, which their *tequitlato* testified was used to purchase cochineal demanded by the church *fiscal*. 1553 criminal complaint against Don Juan Cortés, governor of Tehuantepec, AGN Hospital de Jesús, leg. 450, exp. 1.

4. 1555 viceregal decree concerning the obligations of the Marqués del Valle towards the Dominican houses of Tehuantepec and Xalapa, AGN Mercedes, vol. 4, fs. 138–44.

5. 1543 *residencia* of Juan de Toledo, *alcalde mayor* for the Tehuantepec province, AGN Hospital de Jesús, leg. 160 bis.

6. Burgoa, *Geográfica descripción*, 2, p. 378.

7. 1643 petition from Tehuantepec landowners to the *alcalde mayor*, Don Gerónimo de Loaisa, transcribed from the original and included as evidence in the 1752 suit by the natives of Ixtaltepec against Don Juan de Cartas Luzurriaga over land ownership rights, AGN Tierras, vol. 760, exp. 2.

8. Taylor, *Landlord and Peasant*, p. 179.

9. Burgoa, *Geográfica descripción*, 2, p. 408.

10. Paso y Troncoso, "Relación de la visita," pp. 312–14. Borah and Cook, *The Population of Central Mexico in 1548*, p. 18. In the case of the Tehuantepec census, however, Borah and Cook's assumption that serfs were not counted does not hold, for those who paid their tribute directly to Don Juan Cortés were explicitly included in this count.

11. García Pimentel, "Descripción del obispado de Antequera." The Tehuantepec Relación Geográfica was first published by Alfonso Caso as "Descripción de Tehuantepec."

12. Dávila Padilla, *História de la fundación*, pp. 100–101.

13. Scholes and Adams, *Moderación de doctrinas*; 1653 *cedula real* ordering a new tributary count for Tehuantepec, AGN Tierras, vol. 2971, exp. 67; 1687 viceregal decree exempting Tehuantepec and its barrios from tribute payments for a period of 2 years, AGN Indios, vol. 30, exp. 109.

14. Martin, *Rural Society*, pp. 56–59, has been able to document this demographic pattern more fully in her study of native population trends in Morelos.

15. "Los indígenas, por ser de natural bajo e imperfecto, han de ser regidos y gobernados mas por temor que por amor." Quoted by Llaguno, *La personalidad jurídica del indio*, p. 57.

16. "juntado a esta cabecera e a los demás pue[bl]os sujetos a ella," Acuña, *Relaciones geográficas*, p. 116.

17. J. Zeitlin, "Community Distribution," p. 194.

18. Zeitlin and Thomas, "Indian Consumers."

19. Cline, "Civil Congregations of the Indians."

20. The impact of these late sixteenth-century *congregaciones* is clear from a comparison of settlement locations on the indigenous map accompanying the 1580 Relación Geográfica with later maps of the province, although few documentary records have been located. Machuca Gallegos, *Tehuantepec*, p. 86, notes that the Río de los Perros communities of Xochitlan and Ixtaltepec were initially congregated together with Ixtepec, but that they successfully reclaimed their original community lands in 1604. The 1583 reference to the former Tlapanatepec settlement location was made in AGN Tierras, vol. 2737, exp. 25, f. 29.

21. Burgoa, *Palestra historial*, f. 80.

22. A summary of this conflict is provided by García in *Don Juan Palafox y Mendoza.*

23. Palma y Freites, *Por las religiones.*

24. Ybañes, *El juez conservador de los religiosos.*

25. 1590 petition of the community of Ixtaltepec, AGN Indios, vol. 3, exp. 71, f. 17v.

26. 1635 charge to the Dominican provincial of Oaxaca regarding damages received by the community of Zanatepec from their vicar, Fr. Francisco Esteván, AGN Indios, vol. 12, exp. 196.

27. Enthusiastic approvals for the book's publication were provided by such notable figures as Don Lope Diez de Armendaríz, Marqués de Cadereyta and viceroy of New Spain; Fr. Bartholomé Ladrón de Guevara, vicar general of the Archishopric of Mexico; Fr. Juan Noval, commissioner of the Holy Office of the Inquisition; and Fr. Alonso del Castillo, provincial of the Oaxaca convent. Though granted a ten-year license for publication in December 1636, the book was quickly printed the following year; Moreno, *Reglas ciertas.*

28. "De manera que ay leyes humanas, puestas por los Principes Seglares, que obligan en consciencia: y dexadas a parte opiniones que ay a cerca de determinar de donde tiene la ley humana fuerça para obligar a culpa mortal, y remitiendo esto al lector a 1a I, 2 de Sancto Thomas q. 96, con sus interpretes, digo, que la obligación de la ley a culpa mortal, no nace tanto de las palabras del mandato, ó prohibición quanto de la gravedad de la materia que se manda ó prohibe en la ley." *Ibid.*, f. 21.

29. *Ibid.*, fs. 45–50.

30. The use and abuse of *repartimientos de efectos* throughout New Spain has been widely documented from Central Mexico to Chiapas; see, for example, Gibson, *Aztecs Under Spanish Rule*; Pastor, *Campesinos y reformas*; Wasser-

strom, *Class and Society*; Patch, *Maya and Spaniard*, among others. Knight, *Mexico: The Colonial Era*, pp. 154f., n. 584, finds that the practice was particularly abusive in the south, where it was used to extract such valuable commodities as silk, cochineal, cacao, cotton textiles, and wax from native producers. He rejects the revisionist thesis promoted by such scholars as Baskes, *Indians, Merchants and Markets*, which maintains that *repartimiento* practices benefited native communities economically by providing them with access to credit under imperfect and risky market conditions. Although Baskes's supporting data from late colonial period Oaxaca are outside the time frame of my study, I will address the substance of his argument in a later chapter.

31. Moreno, *Reglas ciertas*, fs. 34–35.

32. 1653 *real cedula* prohibiting the collection of *repartimiento* debts from Tehuantepec community funds, AGN Tierras, vol. 2971, exp. 68.

33. Moreno, *Reglas ciertas*, fs. 35v–36.

34. Transcription of 1529 testimony of Francisco Maldonado, AGN Hospital de Jesús, leg. 300, exp. 107, fs. 53–60.

35. 1543 *residencia* of Juan de Toledo, *alcalde mayor* for the Marques del Valle, AGN Hospital de Jesús, leg. 160 bis, fs. 38–39.

36. Paso y Troncoso, "Relación de lo que valieron las rentas."

37. 1574 inventory of the Tehuantepec estancias belonging to the Marqués del Valle by his *mayordomo*, Juan Ximénez, AGN Hospital de Jesús, leg. 160 bis, papeles sueltos.

38. This period of hacienda expansion is well documented by Brockington, *The Leverage of Labor*, pp. 36–70.

39. I have discussed the parameters of this ranching boom and its impact on the province's native communities elsewhere; J. Zeitlin, "Ranchers and Indians."

40. Martin, *Rural Society*, pp. 29–31; Taylor, *Landlord and Peasant*, pp. 119–33, Appendix D.

41. Simpson, *Exploitation of Land.*

42. Vásquez de Espinosa, "Cartas del P. Bernabé Cobo," p. 200.

43. Reported by Taylor, *Landlord and Peasant*, p. 174.

44. 1592 proceedings regarding a request by the Convent of Santo Domingo to cull and slaughter 1,000 head of cattle, AGN Tierras, vol. 2737, exp. 24.

45. 1580 description of Tehuantepec made by its *alcalde mayor*, Juan de Torres, Benson Latin American Collection, Libraries of the University of Texas, Austin. Transcriptions of the original manuscript have been published several times, but are often incomplete (e.g., Caso's "Relación de Tehuantepec"). See Acuña, *Relaciones geográficas*, for an updated edition of the Oaxaca region documents, including the accompanying maps and illustrations. Documents of this type were produced by provincial administrators throughout Spain's overseas empire in response to a fifty-point questionnaire promulgated under the authority of Felipe II.

46. The governor, *principales*, and other natives of the Tehuantepec province complained to Dr. Quesada during his 1554 *visita* that the Marqués-appointed *alcalde mayor* was giving out *estancias* and *caballerías*, causing great damage and injury to the indigenous population. The viceroy's order that he cease doing so

and that the land be restored to the Indians may not have been effective, for the Buenavista property is just one of several later *estancias* unaccounted for in the Mercedes records. 1555 orders from Viceroy Velasco concerning the Tehuantepec province, AGN Mercedes, vol. 4, fs. 138–48.

47. Diego Ruíz de Andrada's long career in the Tehuantepec province is documented by several sources. His account records as *mayordomo* are found in AGN Hospital de Jesús, leg. 160 bis, loose papers from 1554; the 1567 *merced* and 1595 petition are recorded respectively in AGN Mercedes, vol. 9, f. 49 and vol. 20, f. 58v.; a 1779 transcription of the Buenavista sale record is found in AGN Hospital de Jesús, leg. 287, exp. 4.

48. Brockington, *Leverage of Labor*, pp. 42–43.

49. The history of the Zopiloapa hacienda is recorded in various transcripts of earlier documents included as evidence in the 1752 suit against Don Juan de Cartas Luzurriaga by the Indians of Ixtaltepec, AGN Tierras, vol. 760, exp. 2.

50. Brockington, *Leverage of Labor*, pp. 34–84.

51. *Ibid.*, Tables 2 and 3.

52. "Las estancias y ganado mayor y menor y tierras de sembra maíz que allí en esta provincia de Tehuantepeque y de la manera que las poseen y tienen los dueños el día de hoy." 1643 record of Tehuantepec's private landowners and their holdings, as transcribed in 1752 suit against Don Juan de Cartas Luzurriaga by the Indians of Ixtaltepec, AGN Tierras, vol. 760, exp. 2, fs. 92v–101v.

53. Brockington, *Leverage of Labor*, pp. 69–78.

54. Burgoa, *Geográfica descripción*, 2, pp. 395f.

55. *Ibid.*, p. 389. Burgoa's description of the Tehuantepec economy follows on the same page.

56. 1580 description of Tehuantepec made by its *alcalde mayor*, Juan de Torres, Benson Latin American Collection, Libraries of the University of Texas, Austin

57. "dichas dos lagunas son de Don Felipe Cortés, cacique natural de esta provincia e hijo legítimo de Don Juan Cortés señor que fue antiguamente de ella e las tiene e posee por suyas y tiene executoria real de su magestad." *Ibid.*, fs. 12v–13.

58. 1563 viceregal order concerning the patrimonial *terrazgueros* claimed by the descendants of Don Juan Cortés, AGN Mercedes, vol. 5–6, 2a parte, fs. 415v–19v; 1571–72 suit by Doña Magdalena de Zúñiga against the royal *fiscal* over the possession of Indians and other diverse *estancias*, AGI Escribanía de Cámara, 160b.

59. 1571 testimony of Don Francisco Vasquez de Coronado on behalf of Doña Magdalena de Zúñiga, AGI Escribanía de Cámara, 160b, f. 388v.

60. Taylor, *Landlord and Peasant*, pp. 41–43.

61. Gibson, *Aztecs Under Spanish Rule*, p. 154.

62. 1556 account records from Juan Ximénez, Tehuantepec alcalde mayor, AGN Hospital de Jesús, leg. 160 bis., loose papers.

63. Native *estancia* requests, like those made by Spaniards, are largely found scattered through different volumes of AGN Mercedes, though some petitions and authorizations are also found in AGN Tierras, various.

64. Taylor, *Landlord and Peasant*, p. 40 and note 20, p. 235.

65. This is a point I have made earlier in reference to the large number of community requests for sheep and goat estancias, but I believe it is relevant to elite preferences as well. See J. Zeitlin, "Ranchers and Indians," p. 48.

66. 1643 dispute between the Indians of Guazontlán and Ocelotlán and Mateo López, cacique of Ocelotlán, over damage to crops, AGN Tierras, vol. 2727, exp. 1.

67. 1589 *ganado menor* petition by Don Francisco Vásquez, AGN Mercedes, vol. 14, f. 375; 1590 *ganado menor* petition by Don Francisco Vásquez, AGN Mercedes, vol. 15, f. 158; 1589 *ganado mayor* grant to Don Juan Bautista de Avendaño, AGN Mercedes, vol. 15, f. 40.

68. 1598 proceedings of Gaspar de Vargas, *alcalde mayor* of the province of Tehuantepec, regarding the *sitio de ganado menor* request of Francisco de Figueroa, Indian of Chihuitán, AGN Tierras, vol. 2764, exp. 26, f. 291.

69. Don Fabián de Zárate's many *estancia* requests and grants are found in the following volumes of AGN Mercedes: (1601) vol. 23, f. 166; (1608) vol. 26, f. 90v; (1613) three separate requests found in vol. 28, f. 61; (1614) vol. 28, f. 388; (1614), vol. 28, f. 388v.

70. Haskett, *Indigenous Rulers*, pp. 9–26, illustrates how complex this realignment of traditional political organizations was in the Cuernavaca region, where Spanish colonial restructuring efforts did not always erase traditional bonds between a subject community and the head town or *altepetl* with which it was affiliated.

71. 1568 salary list for the governor, *alcaldes, regidores* and other officials of the pueblo of Ixtaltepec, AGN Indios, vol. 1, exp. 153, f. 56–56v.

72. 1590 *sitio de ganado menor* granted to Don Martín López, cacique of Ixtaltepec, AGN Mercedes, vol. 16, f. 70; 1591 viceregal order that Don Martín, cacique and principal of Ixtaltepec, be given an *indio* and *india* for service, AGN Indios, vol. 3, exp. 398.

73. These tendencies were, of course, not unique to the Isthmus. Horn, *Postconquest Coyoacan*, pp. 31–38, notes how "calpolli micro-patriotism" surfaced in the Basin of Mexico as external pressures that initially reinforced *altepetl* loyalties waned and communities sought to establish independence based on new criteria of political autonomy.

74. These mercedes were granted or sought in 1584, AGN Mercedes, vol. 13, f. 100v; 1585, AGN Mercedes, vol. 13, f. 147v; and 1590, AGN Mercedes, vol. 15, f. 252.

75. Romero, *El sol y la cruz*, pp. 154–59, discusses the pervasive role of community sheep and goat *estancias* among Oaxaca's native communities. She notes that in 1563 the Mixtec community of Teposcolula contracted with a Spanish resident of the town to manage its sheep and goat ranch, with more than eight thousand animals; terms of this contract spelled out in detail how the wool, meat, and hides were to be split in addition to payment in kind and services that the community would provide the *mayordomo* in return for his management and apprenticeship of the native shepherds assigned to help him. A similarly active engagement with Spaniards to learn the business of livestock management must

underlie the inception of native ranching in the Isthmus, although it cannot be documented at present.

76. Taylor, *Landlord and Peasant*, p. 80, table 7.

77. The alleged sale of this community *estancia* was a critical matter of contention in the 1752 dispute between the community of Ixtaltepec and the current owner of the Hacienda Zopiloapa, AGN Tierras, vol. 760, exp. 2. The facts of the sale of the Tehuantepec *sitio de ganado menor* were presented in Juan del Moral's 1636 petition regarding a boundary dispute with the community of Tehuantepec, AGN Mercedes, vol. 40, f. 86v–87.

78. 1712 community of San Francisco del Mar vs. the Dominican convent of San Hipólito Martir over the possession of lands, AGN Tierras, vol. 287, exp. 3.

79. 1736 request by the Indians of San Vicente Juchitán and its barrios to have community lands restored, AGN Tierras, vol. 578, exp. 6.

80. 1609–11 account records of Gerónimo de Espinosa, *mayordomo* of the Tehuantepec *estancias*, AGN Hospital de Jesús, leg. 272, exp. 12–14.

81. The original 1801 *merced* was kindly shown me by Sr. Fernando Lavín Mier of Ixtepec, whose father had owned the Rancho Santa Cruz when he was a small boy and located the document hidden among the ranch house rafters. In response to the formulaic question of whether the proposed sugar refinery would harm any Indian households, the document asserted that "earlier there had been a village but it disappeared some time ago" ("antes había un pueblo pero hace tiempo que se desapareció"). A summary report on the archaeological findings at Rancho Santa Cruz can be found in Zeitlin and Thomas, "Indian Consumers."

82. Analysis of the Rancho Santa Cruz faunal collection was completed by Elizabeth Terese Newman at Yale University. The collection was initially sorted and identified by Abaco Robinson under the supervision of Elizabeth Wing at the Florida Museum of Natural History.

83. Spores, *Mixtecs*, p. 127, reports that an Indian principal of the Mixtec community of Teposcolula and his son-in-law operated a blacksmith shop in that community during the mid- to late sixteenth century, where they produced a variety of hand-forged iron implements like these for sale to Spaniards and, we might presume, natives as well. He duplicates an illustration from the colonial period Mixtec text, the Codice Sierra, in which nails and cotter pins like those recovered in the Rancho Santa Cruz excavations are shown.

84. Lister and Lister, *Andalusian Ceramics*; Goggin, *Spanish Majolica*; Seifert, *Archaeological Majolicas*; Charleton, *Post-Conquest Developments*.

85. Spores, *Stratigraphic Excavations*, recovered European-introduced ceramics in early colonial archaeological deposits at Yanhuitlán. Terraciano's analysis of early colonial Mixtec-language testaments shows that nobles possessed an array of introduced European items that indicate a change in dining customs among the elite, including cups, plates, glasses, jars, silverware, candles, tables, chairs, and tablecloths; *Mixtecs of Colonial Oaxaca*, p. 203. Gasco, *Cacao*, recovered relatively high percentages of majolica, though much of it was produced by Guatemalan *obrajes*, in her excavations at the Soconusco site of Ocelocalco, where the distribution patterns suggest a broader access to imported goods.

86. Spores, *Mixtecs*, p. 135.

87. Gasco, *Cacao*, pp. 290f.

88. Problems with Marquesado cattle in the Tehuantepec province are attested to in several 1554–55 viceregal edicts found in AGN Mercedes, vol. 4, fs. 27–27v, fs. 138–48, and f. 249.

89. Burgoa, *Geográfica descripción*, 2, pp. 409f.

90. 1583–86 community of Tlapanatepec challenges a *merced* requested by Juan Díaz Roldán, AGN Tierras, vol. 2737, exp. 25; 1589 *ganado menor* grant to Don Estevan Cortés, indio *principal* of the pueblo of Tlapanatepec, AGN Mercedes, vol. 15, f. 7.

91. 1619 viceregal order concerning the removal from office and payment of crop damages by the *teniente* Alonso López, AGN Indios, vol. 7, exp. 410; 1626 order that Alonso López show title to the *estancia de ganado mayor* on which he keeps an excessive number of cattle, AGN Mercedes, vol. 37, f. 35.

92. Transcript of 1650 transfer of rights to populate the community of Ixhuatán, AGN Tierras, vol. 2971, exp. 67–68.

93. Brockington, *Leverage of Labor*, pp. 99–125. Further details are found in the 1609 account records of Gerónimo de Espinosa, *mayordomo* of the Tehuantepec Haciendas Marquesanas, AGN Hospital de Jesús, leg. 272, exp. 12.

94. 1611 account records of Gerónimo de Espinosa, *mayordomo* of the Tehuantepec Haciendas Marquesanas, AGN Hospital de Jesús, leg. 272, exp. 14.

95. Aspects of these issues have been explored by Taylor, "Landed Society"; Osborne, "Indian Land Retention"; Farriss, *Maya Society*; Restall, *The Maya World*, and Spores, *Mixtecs*, among others. My own earlier attempt to distinguish indigenous sociocultural and ecological variables that affected community survival in the Tehuantepec province is found in J. Zeitlin, "Indians and Ranchers."

96. Douglas and Isherwood, *World of Goods*.

97. Comaroff and Comaroff, *Of Revelation and Revolution*, p. 5.

Chapter 5

1. "de las mas grandes provincias de este reino, de gente belicosa, de esforzadas naturalezas y condiciones, ladinos en lengua castellana, muchos de ellos ejercitados en las armas de fuego por ser dados á la caza y contratación de sus pieles con especial aplicación; en tal manera, que se ha hecho cómputo que á poca diligencia se hallaran con más de diez mil hombres fáciles de llegar á este paraje desde las sierras de su cercanía, osados por la constelación de la tierra, como lo dicen los atroces sucesos que se han visto, más en esta sola provincia, que en todas las demás que hay en este reino; y tan cautelosos, que he oído y sabido de ellos cosas en este negocio, que de capitanes muy ejercitados no suelen celebrarse." Letter from bishop to viceroy quoted by Manso de Contreras in his chronicle of the Tehuantepec rebellion, *Relación cierta*. Several modern editions of this work have been published, the first by Genaro García in his edited volume, *Tumultos y rebeliones*, pp. 109–229. A recent edition with a foreword by the Isthmus poet and historian Víctor de la Cruz was published with the title *La Rebelión de Tehuantepec* by the municipal government of Juchitán.

2. Most of the events summarized here were recounted by Manso de Contr-

eras in his *Relación cierta*, but many additional details are found among the *autos* and *memorias* included in the massive file compiled by the Consejo de Indias between 1642 and 1678 documenting the need for administrative reform in the system of *alcaldes mayores*, AGI México 600. I am grateful to Carlos Manzo and Héctor Díaz-Polanco for directing my attention to this important document. Díaz-Polanco has included a transcription of an important early section of this file pertaining to the rebellion in his edited volume, *El fuego de la inobediencia.*

3. Taylor, *Drinking, Homicide and Rebellion*, pp. 113–51.

4. Slightly different details of these events are presented in a October 21, 1660, *consulta* from the Audiencia to the incoming viceroy, Conde de Baños, AGI México 600, f. 115v and a November 6, 1660, *memoria* given to the new viceroy by his predecessor, the Duke of Alburquerque, AGI México 600, f. 126. In the case of Fajardo's murder, however, an investigation of the case determined that the principal instigator of the violence was another Spaniard, the *alguacil mayor* Don Nicolás de la Pena, according to an opinion written to the Duke of Alburquerque by the *fiscal*, Don Luís de Mendoza on March 31, 1660. AGI México 600, f. 195v.

5. For example, the *juchiteco* poet and journalist Macario Matus points to the 1660 rebellion in Tehuantepec as the time when "the seed was planted, the seed of protest against injustice and the iniquities of man and religion," in his essay "Juchitán political moments," reprinted in Campbell et al., *Zapotec Struggles,* p. 126.

6. Among more recent studies that deal with the 1660 rebellion at some length are those by Tutino, "Indian Rebellion"; Barabas, "Rebeliones e insurrecciones"; Carmagnani, "Un movimiento político indio"; and Díaz-Polanco, *El fuego de la inobediencia.*

7. See note 1.

8. "que tratasen de pacificar a los indios con toda blandura sin molestarlos con castigos asperos y sin preceder dar quenta con aquella advertencia de que lo procurasen consequir, tratando mas de pacificar que de conquistar y guerrear." The king was reminded of this earlier charge to the viceroy and Audiencia of New Spain in an August 1662 letter from the Council of the Indies. AGI México 600, f. 543v. The Council suggested, perhaps ironically, since it was already unhappy with Montemayor's accounting of these events, that this admonition had simply not been received in time, or surely the *oidor* would have exercised more leniency. Among the cases he studied, Taylor found that Spanish authorities normally responded to native communities in revolt with restraint, desiring as much as the villagers themselves a rapid return to normalcy. Exceptions came during the 1767–69 local rebellions in Michoacán and San Luís Potosí, when similarly harsh verdicts to those dealt by Montemayor were meted out by the *visitador* José de Gálvez, whom Taylor identifies as "a leading peninsular reformer who had little understanding of the delicate divide-and-rule policies that had governed the Mexican countryside for two centuries," *Drinking, Homicide and Rebellion,* pp. 121–22.

9. Cruz, "Introducción," *La Rebelión*, p. 8.

10. *Ibid.*, pp. 11f.

11. In an analysis of Toribio Medina's bibliographic survey, *La imprenta en México, 1539–1821*, I found that fewer than twenty similar *relaciones* or secular chronicles had been published in New Spain prior to the editions attributed to Manso de Contreras and Juan de Torres Castillo; this figure represents less than 3 percent of the 765 books and pamphlets published before 1661.

12. "porque vuestro virrey quitó el oficio de alcalde mayor de Tehuantepec al dicho Capitan Alonso Ramírez de Espinsoa, que le estaba governando con todo gusto, paz, y quietud, y sintieron gravemente que se le quitassen, y le proveyó en su lugar don Christóbal Manso de Contrera, regidor de Oaxaca, en cuyo nombre después imprimió el dicho vuestro oidor de lo hecho en aquellas pacificaciones; y el oficio de Nexapa en Don Juan de Torres Castillo el otro autor supuesto de la segunda relación que sacó a luz el dicho vuestro oidor de lo hecho en aquellas pacificaciones. Proveiose también el oficio de Yxtepexi y no el de la Villa Alta de San Ildefonso, porque aunque el dicho vuestro oidor quiso introducir que también havía levantamientos y alborotos, fue siempre notorio que los hubo y los que se quentan en una de las dichas relaciones son hechos y fabricados en los autos de vuestro oidor." December 1, 1662, letter to the king from the Indians of Oaxaca, AGI México 600, fs. 675–83.

13. Palau Dulcet, *Manual*; Toribio Medina, *La imprenta,* vol. 2, p. 401.

14. Montemayor de Cuenca, *Discurso*; Toribio Medina, *La imprenta*, vol. 2, pp. 339f.

15. Montemayor de Cuenca, *Discurso.*

16. Díaz-Polanco and Sánchez, "El vigor de la espada restauradora," p. 60.

17. September 27, 1660, report to Viceroy Conde de Baños from the Audiencia, AGI México 600, fs. 115–17v.

18. The figure of 21,000 pesos is cited in their December 1, 1662, letter to the king by the caciques and *principales* of Oaxaca Valley towns, AGI México 600, f. 680. In 1663 the *contador* of Mexico, Valerio Martínez de Vidaorreta, confirmed that more than 20,000 pesos were deducted from the Oaxaca tributes for salaries and costs associated with his commission there. Such a deduction did not diminish the revenues flowing to the Crown, however, for Montemayor used parish registers to increase the count of what he claimed were previously underrepresented tributaries appearing on the bishopric's tribute lists. 1663 report of Valerio Martínez concerning new taxations for Tehuantepec. AGI Patronato, 230B, ramo 19.

19. "Don Marcos que hoy gobierna a quién apelidaban y tenían por su rey, nombrandole assí y haciendole a sentar en la iglesia en silla y en el puesto que solía ocupar el alcalde mayor, con otras circunstancias de rebeldía y mal ánimo." December 28, 1660, letter to the king from Viceroy Conde de Baños, AGI México 600, fs. 154–55.

20. *Ibid.*

21. "Siendo este punto el mas sagrado que fuera del de la heresía y apostasía se puede cometer contra la suprema Magestad, cuyas penas pasan a los descendientes, condenando la ley hasta la imaginación quando llega a acto exterior por pequeño que sea." May 17, 1661, letter from the Council of the Indies to the king, AGI México 600, f. 388v.

22. September 27, 1660, report to Viceroy Conde de Baños from the Audiencia, AGI México 600, fs. 115–17v.

23. November 1660 testimony of Don Juan Virgil de Quiñones taken by Bishop Alonso Cuevas Dávalos, AGI México 600, fs. 412v–13v. Apparently the secular priest's perspective on these events had calmed considerably over the several months elapsed since the day of the uprising, when he drafted a letter sent by seven *vecinos* notifying the viceroy of the murders and proclaiming that the town was in grave danger ("notable riesgo"). Manso, *Relación cierta,* f. 8v.

24. Hobsbawn, *Primitive Rebels*, note, p. 10.

25. Scott, *Moral Economy.*

26. *Ibid.*, p. 191.

27. See, for example, Stern, *Peru's Indian Peoples*; Bricker, *Indian Christ*; Gosner, "Religion and Rebellion"; Patch, "Culture, Community, and 'Rebellion.'"

28. Barabas, *Utopías indias*, p. 4.

29. Taylor, *Drinking, Homicide and Rebellion*, p. 114.

30. *Ibid.*, p. 124.

31. *Ibid.*, p. 125.

32. Manso de Contreras, *Relación cierta*, various.

33. Barabas, *Utopías indias*, pp. 133–37, "Rebeliones e insurrecciones," pp. 237–40.

34. May 17, 1661, letter from the Council of the Indies to the king, AGI México 600, fs. 382–89.

35. April 1, 1661, testimony of Don Miguel de Mediano, AGI México 600, fs. 510v–16v.

36. "si eran suyas aquellas tierras o del dicho alguacil mayor que lo sacasse luego o lo matarían y harían con este testigo lo que ha habían hecho los de Tehuantepec con su alcalde mayor porque hasta ahora habían estado los indios sujetos a los españoles y ya se había pasado este tiempo y los españoles habían de estar sujetos a los indios, lo qual decía con mucha cólera y sobervia, y los demás lo mismo." April 2, 1661, testimony of Juan Ramírez de Aguilar, AGI México 600, f. 517.

37. Chance, "La dinámica étnica."

38. December 1, 1662, letter to the king from the caciques and principales of Oaxaca, AGI México 600, fs. 645v–46.

39. 1663 letter from Bishop Cuevas Dávalos quoted in Israel, *Race, Class and Politics*, p. 261.

40. "un hombre de inhumana, terrible y sangrienta condición y que trató a los indios con nunca vistas crueldades." December 1, 1662, letter to the king from the caciques and *principales* of Oaxaca, AGI México 600, f. 645v.

41. Carmagnani, "Un movimiento."

42. October 4, 1660, report from the Duke of Alburquerque to his successor, the Conde de Baños, AGI México 600, f. 130.

43. Díaz-Polanco and Sánchez, "El vigor de la espada restauradora," p. 64.

44. Manso de Contreras, *Relación cierta*, pp. 30–35v.

45. "poniendo como pongo desde luego en todo lo que a resultado y resultaré tocante al dicho motín y muertes, y sus dependencias perpetuo silencio, para que no se trate mas dello, por escrito, ni de palabra, como si no uviera sucedido." *Ibid.*, p. 34v.

46. Gay, *Historia de Oaxaca*, pp. 363–65, 381.

47. Letter from the rebel cabildo to Viceroy Alburquerque, quoted in Manso de Contreras, *Relación cierta*, f. 9v.

48. November 15, 1660, testimony of Don Juan de Virgil before Bishop Alonso Cuevas Dávalos, AGI México 600, fs. 412v–13.

49. Hicks, "Cloth."

50. "las Indias tengan sus grangerías a parte, y diferentes de las de sus maridos, de que sacan dineros para pagar sus tributos, y ayan de hilar y tejer para vestirse así, y a sus hijos, hijas, y maridos, hazer de comer, y otras cosas que estan a cargo dellas." Moreno, *Reglas ciertas*, f. 10v.

51. 1653 petition to the Audiencia for a new tribute count, AGN Tierras, vol. 2971, exp. 67–68.

52. "por el rigor del dicho Don Juan de Avellán se havían ausentado muchos de los naturales a otras provincias, desamparando sus casas, y dejandolas desiertas con sus mujeres e hijos." November 15, 1660, testimony of Don Juan de Virgil before Bishop Alonso Cuevas Dávalos, AGI México 600, f. 413.

53. "si faltaba algún tanto de la medida, los desnudaba y principalmente á los gobernadores y principales que las traían, y les daba tantos azotes hasta que quedaban casi muertos." Manso de Contreras, *Relación cierta*, f. 9v.

54. November 15, 1660, testimony of Don Juan de Virgil before Bishop Alonso Cuevas Dávalos, AGI México 600, f. 413.

55. April 22, 1660, letter to Viceroy Alburquerque from Bishop Alonso Cuevas Dávalos, AGI México 600, f. 203v.

56. "Grande atención pide ver el sosiego y seso con que esta plebe procedió en medio del fervor de su desorden, como se manifiesta en haber obligado á los indios de su mayor estimación á que se les había puesto impedimento por particulares afecciones de su Alcalde Mayor, tendiendo por intrusos y violentos á los otros que sin estar elegidos la tenían, de los cuales se ha reconocido que por amor á lo común de su causa y sentimiento, ó por temor á plebe, las entregaron luego á los otros que, regidos del mismo temor, las recibieron; y son en tanto número en toda la Provincia, que soy informado son poco menos de doscientos, y sólo se reservaron de esta acción uno ó dos pueblos." April 22, 1660, letter to Viceroy Alburquerque from Bishop Alonso Cuevas Dávalos, quoted in Manso de Contreras, *Relación cierta*, f. 11v.

57. March 1660 letter from the rebel *cabildo* to Viceroy Alburquerque, quoted in Manso de Contreras, *Relación cierta*, f. 9v. Several such early seventeenth-century complaints reaching the General Indian Court are documented in AGN Indios, vol. 7, exp. 304, vol. 9, exp. 103 (both from 1618), and AGN Indios, vol. 13, exp. 114 and 116 (both from 1641).

58. "Buscaronle [el remedio] por dos vezes, caminando ciento y cinquenta leguas a esta real audiencia; y la atención de criado del Señor Duque de Albur-

querque, impidió la obligación de impartirles su auxilio y defensa, a los porteros, procuradores, y abogados, sin hallar quién le hiziera ni firmara una petición. Considerese su desamparo, el desconsuelo con que volvieron sin esperanza de ayuda, donde tan segura deve ser la de los oprimidos, recibidos en sus casas con nuevos y rigurosos castigos en manos de la desperación." September 27, 1660, summary of debate within the Audiencia concerning the Tehuantepec rebellion, AGI México 600, f. 107v.

59. September 27, 1660, *consulta* of the Audiencia and October 3, 1660 response of Viceroy Baños, AGI México 600, fs. 115–18v.

60. Israel, *Race, Class, and Politics*, pp. 260–66.

61. Letters from all three religious leaders are interspersed throughout the massive file or *legajo* I have been drawing from for this account of the Tehuantepec rebellion, AGI México 600. The council's purpose of creating this file, which includes many transcripts and original documents dated between 1642 and 1678, was to investigate the administration of justice by the *alcaldes mayores* and the need for reform as urged by Palafox when he was *visitador* for New Spain and as occasioned by the uprisings in the Oaxaca provinces.

62. See, for example, Díaz-Polanco and Burguete, "Sociedad colonial y rebelión indígena," pp. 23–28.

63. 1586 complaint by the alcaldes and naturales of Tehuantepec regarding their governor, Don Francisco Vásquez, AGN Tierras, vol. 2969, exp. 6, f. 40; 1590 petition from Don Francisco Vásquez for restitution of 400 pesos, AGN Indios, vol. 4, exp. 382.

64. "antes el governador y alcaldes que al presente lo eran corrieron el riesgo que su alcalde mayor, porque queriendolo favorecer, la pleve y tumulto se volvieron contra ellos, quieriendolos assí mismo matar como lo hicieran, si no huvieran retraido a la iglesia. Y visto se les havían escapado el governador y alcaldes, fueron a su casa y se la robaron y saquearon como havían hecho a la alcalde mayor. Y estando retraidos algunos días los dichos governadores y alcaldes, el pleve y tumulto nombraron otros en su lugar a quienes por fuerza hicieron tomar las varas, temiendo los rigores del dicho tumulto." September 14, 1660, letter from Alonso Ramírez de Espinosa to Viceroy, AGI México 600, f. 137.

65. 1683 *autos* concerning elections in Tehuantepec, AGN Indios, vol. 27, exps. 276, 283, and 317.

66. Scott, *Moral Economy*, p. 52.

67. 1790 account of *cofradías* in Tehuantepec, AGN Historia, vol. 313, exp. 1, n. 13, fs. 68–72v; 1736–37 appeal by the community of San Vicente Juchitán to have its communal properties restored, AGN Tierras, vol. 578, exp. 6, fs. 1–53v.

68. Haskett, *Indigenous Rulers*, p. 104.

69. April 1660 report from Tehuantepec from Bishop Alonso Cuevas Dávalos, AGI México 600, fs. 228–29.

70. 1665–66 letters of the Viceroy Marqués de Mancera concerning an *indio cacique* of Tehuantepec, AGI México, vol.41, n. 44.

71. *Ibid.*

72. A transcript of the 1655 boundary dispute is included among the docu-

ments forming the Archivo Histórico de San Pedro Huilotepec, fs. 14r–17v. The archive was transcribed in 1995 by Michel Oudijk, who generously made a copy available to me.

73. 1635 complaint against the vicar of Zanatepec, AGN Indios, vol. 12, exp. 196.

74. "Don Antonio de Vargas, cacique de San Francisco de la Mar desta jurisdición, que se interpuso con el Governador, y Alcaldes intrusos, y les pidió con palabras de sumición y rendimiento pospusiesen sus intentos, con que alcançó dellos por ser de su misma naturaleça lo que no pudo su piadoso Prelado." Manso de Contreras, *Relación cierta*, f. 13v.

75. A transcript of this 1650 land transfer is included in the documentation for the later 1710–12 suit by the community of San Francisco del Mar against the Dominican owners of the Hacienda Zanatepec, AGN Tierras, vol. 287, exp. 3.

76. Transcripts of earlier documents concerning the San Francisco cacicazgo and rights to the salt-making operations are found in the 1726–29 case of Don Fernando de Zúñiga y Cortés vs. Doña María de Meléndez concerning rights to Salinas, AGN Tierras, vol. 450, exp. 1. The results of 1660–61 elections in the village were confirmed in 1660 and 1661 by Montemayor himself, and transcribed into the record of the 1710–12 suit against the Dominican owners of the Hacienda Zanatepec, AGN Tierras, vol. 287, exp. 3.

77. Scott, *Moral Economy*, p. 4.

78. Díaz-Polanco and Sánchez, "El vigor de la espada restauradora," p. 72.

79. Manso de Contreras, *Relación cierta*, fs. 27–35.

80. "Y en quanto a las dichas Magdalena María y Gracia María se han de executar sus sentencias menos en quanto á cortarles las manos, porque en esto se hubo piadosamente el Señor Oidor, por no haver orden, ni disposición para curarlas." *Ibid.*, f. 28v.

81. Foucault, *Discipline and Punish*, p. 34.

82. March 25, 1661, report of Montemayor to Viceroy Conde de Baños, AGI México 600, fs. 467–68v; April 9, 1661, letter from Montemayor to the Tehuantepec *cabildo*, AGI México 600, fs. 462v–63.

Chapter 6

1. Villaseñor y Sánchez, *Theatro americano*, pp. 184–86.

2. Canterla and Tovar, *La iglesia de Oaxaca.*

3. Villaseñor y Sánchez, *Theatro americano*; Canterla and Tovar, *La iglesia de Oaxaca*, pp. 53–84.

4. 1687 request by the native population of Tehuantepec and its barrios for tribute exemption, AGN Indios, vol. 30, exp. 109.

5. Villaseñor y Sánchez, *Theatro americano*, p. 184.

6. 1722 census records for the Tehuantepec province, AGN Civil, vol. 619, exp. 2.

7. 1720 complaint of the *alcalde* and *principales* of Tehuantepec against Don Pedro de Saravía, their *alcalde mayor*, AGN Civil, vol. 599, exp. 4.

8. 1672 viceregal order that the governor and officials of Tehuantepec cease

interfering with Domingo Martín, *mayordomo* of San Blas, AGN Indios, vol. 24, exp. 440.

9. 1819 petition from the Tehuantepec barrio of Santa María Yoloteca for agricultural lands, AGN Tierras, vol. 1423, exp. 9.

10. Oudijk, *Historiography*. I am grateful to Dr. Oudijk for generously sharing with me a prepublication draft of his thesis and his transcription of the Huilotepec historical archive (Archivo Histórico de Huilotepec).

11. 1682 land dispute between the village of Huilotepec and the Tehuantepec barrio of San Pedro Guichigui, Archivo Histórico de Huilotepec, fs. 6–28v.

12. 1736 request by the village of San Vicente Juchitán to have its community lands restored, AGN Tierras, vol. 578, exp. 6. Haskett, *Indigenous Rulers*, made use of a larger sample of Nahuatl and Spanish documents to reconstruct the functions of native *cabildo* offices in the Cuernavaca region, functions which, for the most part, are compatible with what can be discerned for Tehuantepec. His central point, p. 123, that a "characteristically indigenous interpretation of corporate service," shaped the structuring of Nahua *cabildo* office duties early on and persisted well into the late colonial period, can be applied to Tehuantepec as well.

13. Oudijk, *Historiography*, p. 92.

14. Data concerning late colonial political organization in Tehuantepec and its barrios are based primarily upon the 1682 Huilotepec land dispute, Archivo Histórico de Huilotepec, fs. 6–28v, and the extensive litigation record stemming from the 1720 complaints against Don Pedro de Saravía and his brother discussed at length below, AGN Civil, vols. 570, 599, and 600 in particular.

15. Machuca Gallegos, *Los pueblos indios*, table 3, p. 36.

16. *Ibid.*; Manzo, *Asimilación y resistencia* and "Comericio y rebelión."

17. 1715 notice of unrest among the Tehuantepec Indians by the *alcalde mayor* and his *teniente general*, AGN Indios, vol. 39, exp. 169.

18. 1716 complaint of abuses by the Spanish officials of Tehuantepec registered by the province's *repúblicas de indios*, AGN Indios, vol. 40, exp. 59.

19. 1716 viceregal approval of Tehuantepec elections, AGN Indios, vol. 40, exp. 64.

20. 1715 viceregal response to petition concerning the riots in Tehuantepec by Fray Alonso de Vargas Machuca, AGN Indios, vol. 39, exp. 167.

21. Gamboa's account was referred to in the viceroy's 1715 response to Fray Alonso's petition, AGN Indios, vol. 39, exp. 167. Mier y Estrada and Gonzales gave their version of the riot in AGN Indios, vol. 39, exp. 168.

22. 1726 petition by Don Joseph Rodríguez de Ledesma, former *alcalde mayor* of Tehuantepec, concerning the embargo of a certain quantity of salt, AGN Tierras, vol. 450, exp. 2.

23. The complex financial arrangements associated with Tehuantepec's late colonial administrators is explored in Machuca Gallegos, *Los pueblos indios*, which also analyzes the 1715 and 1720 conflicts with Spanish administrators.

24. "no hay exemplar de otro ninguno alcalde mayor desde que mataran en villa de Tehuantepec a Don Pedro [sic] Avellan que, aunque aquí fue malo en los repartimientos y tiranías, es mucho por este y su teniente por los crueles." 1720

letter to Don Domingo García from the *cabildo* officers of Santa María Guienagati, AGN Civil, vol. 599, exp. 4.

25. 1720 proceedings initiated by the pueblos of Lachiguiri, Guevea, Guienagati, all of the Tehuantepec jurisdiction, against Don Pedro de Saravía, *alcalde mayor*, and Don Antonio de Saravía, his *teniente*, AGN Civil, vol. 570, exp. 4.

26. 1720 petition from the governor and other officers of the pueblo of San Juan Guichicovi presented to Don Andrés de Miranda, *juez comisario* in the proceedings against the Saravía Cortés brothers, AGN Civil, vol. 600, exp. 1.

27. 1720 pueblos of Lachiguiri, Guevea, Guienagati vs. Don Pedro de Saravía, *alcalde mayor*, and Don Antonio de Saravía, his *teniente*, AGN Civil, vol. 570, exp. 4.

28. *Ibid.*, fs. 46v–48.

29. *Ibid.*

30. *Ibid.*, fs. 17v–18.

31. 1721 actions taken at the request of Don Antonio Sandín Calderon against Don Pedro Saravía, *alcalde mayor* of Tehuantepec, AGN Civil, vol. 600, cuaderno 4.

32. 1720 pueblos of Lachiguiri, Guevea, Guienagati vs. Don Pedro de Saravía, *alcalde mayor*, and Don Antonio de Saravía, his *teniente*, AGN Civil, vol. 570, exp. 4.

33. 1720 petition to the viceroy by the *alcalde* and *principales* of Tehuantepec, AGN Civil, vol. 599, exp. 4.

34. *Ibid.*

35. Manzo, "Comercio y rebelión," p. 112.

36. Baskes, *Indians, Merchants, and Markets*, p. 2.

37. 1720 petition to the viceroy by the *alcalde* and *principales* of Tehuantepec, AGN Civil, vol. 599, exp. 4.

38. "En estas de nuestras justificadas querellas se ha de servir Vuestra Alteza de mandar sobre real producción para el remedio de todo lo que llevamos a representar y porque nos tememos que este teniente no ha de obedecer dicho real despacho por tan absoluto como su hermano puede haver dicho publicamente no hay decir porque su hermano puede mucho por lo que se ha de servir V. S. dicho teniente porque si durase ha de acabar de destruir la villa y su jurisdicción por las temeridades que todos estamos experimentando y porque estamos temiendo no haya algun alboroto en los pueblos por los rigores con que se les ha cobrado y actualmente esta cobrando cresciendo mas en esa día de este teniente." *Ibid.*

39. "y quando el dicho governador llegó a el le dijeron los principales no pusimos a Usted por governador para que vaia a palacio a hazer justicia sino para que acuda al govierno de las cosas de la villa y que respondió no se havía podido escusar por haverselo mandado el teniente." 1721 testimony of Joseph de Zúñiga, AGN Civil, vol. 600, fs. 41v–42v.

40. Machuca Gallegos, *Los pueblos indios*, sees the Tehuantepec *repartimientos* of the eighteenth century following an economic and ecological pattern, in which the production targets were based on the productive potential of the community and the size of its population, with demands exceeding these capa-

bilities leading to native revolt. However well that model may fit the sierra communities, it is difficult to see why notorious Spanish administrators like Saravía avoided the potential of the large urban population of Tehuantepec to produce some salable commodity under *repartimiento* unless it was too risky politically.

41. 1720 inventory of property belonging to Don Pedro Saravía, AGN Civil, vol. 570, exp. 4, fs. 90v–98.

Chapter 7

1. "le dijó dicho alcalde mayor que por dicha sal le havía de dar primero un novenario de azotes y lo havía de embiar a un obraje por quatro años y como el declarante estaba en la carcel viendo los castigos que estava haziendo con los naturales de otros pueblos por cosas mas pequeñas, y como succedió con Diego Ruíz, quien era gobernador actual del pueblo de Santa María Guienagati de esta jurisdicción, y otros indios que estaban en dicha carcel, temió la violencia de dicho alcalde mayor por lo qual tuvo por menos inconveniente pagarle la dicha sal (que no devía) por no recebir el agravio que le havía prometido, y que fuera de lo referido lo multó en seis pesos." 1720 testimony of Don Fernando de Zúñiga y Cortés, AGN Civil, vol. 599, exp. 5.

2. 1726–29 Don Fernando de Zúñiga y Cortés vs. Doña María de Meléndez, AGN Tierras, vol. 450, exp. 1.

3. 1738–47 Don Fernando de Zúñiga y Cortés vs. natives of the pueblos of San Francisco del Mar and San Dionisio del Mar over the ownership of lands and salt beds, AGN Tierras, vol. 588, exp. 6.

4. Ewald, *Mexican Salt Industry*; Machuca Gallegos, *Los pueblos indios*, pp. 100–104.

5. Machuca Gallegos, *Los pueblos indios*, table 6, p. 102.

6. 1726 Don Joseph Rodríguez de Ledesma concerning the embargo of a certain quantity of salt, AGN Tierras, vol. 450, exp. 2.

7. Transcripts of these documents are provided in AGN Tierras, vol. 287, exp. 3.

8. Transcripts of these decrees are included in AGN Tierras, vol. 450, exp. 1.

9. 1571 Doña Magdalena de Zúñiga vs. the royal fiscal, AGI Escribanía de Cámara, 160 b, exp. 1.

10. 1563 complaint by Don Hernando Cortés regarding abuses by Spaniards, AGN Mercedes, vol. 5–6, part 2, f. 416; 1563 petition by Don Felipe and Don Hernando Cortés regarding labor services from *terrazgueros* and commoners, AGN Mercedes, vol. 5–6, fs. 417v–18.

11. 1571 testimony of Juan de Aguilar, AGI Escribanía de Cámara, 160b, f. 250v.

12. 1591 petition by Don Juan Bautista de Avendaño and his sister Doña Juana de Zúñiga regarding the construction of new houses, AGN Indios, vol. 6, part 2, exp. 223.

13. Burgoa, *Geográfica descripción*, 2, p. 378; 1608 *estancia* request by

Fabian de Zárate, AGN Mercedes, vol. 26, f. 90v; 1613 *estancia* request by Fabian de Zárate, cacique of the villa of Tehuantepec, AGN Mercedes, vol. 28, f. 61.

14. 1730 petition by Fernando de Zúñiga y Cortés concerning the exhibition of documents belonging to his cacicazgo, AGN Tierras, vol. 493, exp. 6.

15. *Ibid.*

16. 1796 claims made by Don Antonio Velasco Moctezuma concerning titles to lands and *salinas* in the villa of Guadalcazar, AGN Tierras, vol. 2783, exp. 12.

17. Carriedo, *Estudios históricos*; Gay, *História de Oaxaca*; Martínez Gracida, *El rey Cosijoeza*.

18. Martínez Gracida, *El rey Cosijoeza*, pp. 130–31.

19. Martínez Gracida, *Los indios oaxaqueños*. My summary of the Zaachila genealogy from this work is based on Oudijk and Jansen, "Changing History," pp. 313–14.

20. 1791 certification of baptismal record by the curate of Zaachila, presented in AGN Tierras, vol. 2783, exp. 12.

21. 1716 approval of Tehuantepec elections, AGN Indios, vol. 40, exp. 64.

22. 1738–47 Don Fernando de Zúñiga y Cortés vs. natives of the pueblos of San Francisco del Mar and San Dionisio del Mar over the ownership of lands and salt beds, AGN Tierras, vol. 588, exp. 6.

23. This approach is strongly identified in anthropology with the work of Frederic Barth, *Ethnic Groups*. For a detailed discussion of the theoretical differences among the "instrumentalists" and the "primordialists" see Jones, *Archaeology of Ethnicity*.

24. Haskett, *Indigenous Rulers*, pp. 47–48.

25. Pagden, *Spanish Imperialism*, p. 98.

26. Torquemada, *Monarquía indiana*, 1, p. 278.

27. Burgoa, *Geográfica descripción*, 1, pp. 410–17.

28. Lockhart, *Nahuas After the Conquest*, pp. 14f.

29. Restall, *The Maya World*, pp. 13–19.

30. Terracano, *Mixtecs of Colonial Oaxaca*, pp. 318–31.

31. Oudijk, *Historiography of the Bènizàa*; Oudijk and Jansen, "Changing History." Oudijk feels that both Guevea II and Petapa I may derive from yet a fifth, now-lost version of Guevea I. My discussion contrasts the two with the sixteenth-century original and is based on my earlier analysis in "Recordando a los reyes," where I present stylistic grounds for an early seventeenth-century date for Guevea II.

32. Lockhart, *Nahuas After the Conquest*, pp. 410–18; Gruzinski, *Conquest of Mexico*, pp. 98–145; Wood, *Transcending Conquest*, pp. 107–35.

33. Oudijk, *Historiography of the Bènizàa*, pp. 257–59.

34. Oudijk and Jansen, "Changing History," p. 310.

35. Scattered Zapotec communities in other parts of Oaxaca continued to compile elite genealogical records as late as the beginning of the eighteenth century (cf. the Genealogy of Quialoo, also known as the Yale Genealogy, analyzed by Whitecotton, *Zapotec Elite Ethnohistory*, and Oudijk, *Historiography of the*

Bènizàa). That this tradition appears to have died out earlier on the Isthmus may be a reflection of the contested nature of the Tehuantepec *cacicazgo*.

36. Goody, *Interface*, p. 175.

37. Chance, "Indian Elites."

38. Chance, "Caciques of Tecali."

Chapter 8

1. Florescano, *Etnia, estado y nación*, pp. 133–34.

2. Terraciano, "Colonial Mixtec Community," pp. 16–20, has shown how rituals surrounding possession of the royal palace in colonial Mixtec towns helped to link the new cacique symbolically to the sacred ancestors of the past. The loss of Tehuantepec's royal houses to fire at the end of the sixteenth century, by contrast, removed this important public means of ritually transferring cacique authority during a period when royal inheritance became contested.

3. Compare the rotation of the precolumbian *tlatoani* position among constituent sociopolitical divisions in Morelos, as described by Haskett, *Indigenous Rulers*, p. 10, and the Maya aristocracy's stronghold on the colonial office of governor, which Restall, *The Maya World*, pp. 63–67, notes might be retained by a single individual without reelection for twenty years or more. Tehuantepec's early colonial experience might be closer to that of the Mixteca communities studied by Terraciano, *Mixtecs of Colonial Oaxaca*, pp. 158–97, although there the independent political power vested in female *cacicas* was an early casualty of the patriarchal Spanish governmental forms.

4. Lockhart, *Nahuas After the Conquest*, pp. 54–56, sees this process of community fragmentation into separate *repúblicas* taking place in Central Mexico primarily during his third stage of colonial adaptation, between about 1640 and 1800.

5. Berlin, "Las antiguas creencias"; Alcina Franch, *Calendario*; Parsons, *Mitla*. Tavárez, *Invisible Wars*, p. 441.

6. Carmagnani, *El regreso de los dioses*, p. 50. Carmagnani's elegant model draws from the many late seventeenth-century discoveries of native idolatry in Oaxaca, as occurred elsewhere in New Spain and Peru. It is difficult, however, to discount the role that a reformist clergy of the period, eager to root out lingering pagan practice, contributed to the discovery process. Was idolatry more common or were the priests and friars looking for it more deeply? Tavárez's detailed examination of this issue leads him to conclude that there was an increase in the incidents of idolatry in late colonial times, an increase he attributes to sociocultural pressures within the native community attributable to expanding populations following the seventeenth-century demographic recovery; *Invisible Wars*, p. 489.

7. Carmagnani, *El regreso de los dioses*, pp. 180–223.

8. Kertzer, *Ritual*, pp. 68–69.

9. Carmagnani, *El regreso de los dioses*, pp. 190–91.

10. This apparent paradox between the disengagement of most caciques from community affairs in Tehuantepec while the concept of rulership retained a powerful political authority may not be unique to the Isthmus Zapotecs. Terraciano,

Mixtecs of Colonial Oaxaca, pp. 195–97, finds that the erosion of cacique political authority in the Mixteca was largely complete by the eighteenth century, despite the retention of titles and economic privileges by some. Yet Monaghan et al., "Transformations of the Indigenous Cacicazgo," illustrate some important nineteenth-century exceptions to this pattern in the Mixteca and suggest that the symbolic role of the cacicazgo in legitimizing community political autonomy lay behind this political authority.

Bibliography

Acosta, Jorge and Hugo Moedano Koer. "Los juegos de pelota." In Jorge A. Vivó, ed., *México prehispánico*, pp. 365–84. Mexico: Editorial Emma Hurtado, 1946.

Acosta, Fr. Joseph de. *Historia natural y moral de las Indias* [1590]. Rev. ed. by Edmundo O'Gorman. Mexico: Fondo de Cultura Económica, 1962.

Acuña, René, ed. *Relaciones geográficas del siglo XVI: Antequera,* 2 vols. Mexico: Universidad Autónoma de México, 1984.

Adorno, Rolena. *Guaman Poma: Writing and Resistance in Colonial Peru.* Austin: University of Texas Press, 1986.

Alcina Franch, José. *Calendario y religión entre los zapotecos.* Mexico: Universidad Nacional Autónoma de México, 1993.

Alva Ixtlilxóchitl, Don Fernando de. *Obras históricas,* edited by Alfredo Chavero. Mexico: Editora Nacional, 1952.

Alvarado, Pedro de. *An Account of the Conquest of Guatemala in 1524 by Pedro de Alvarado*, edited by Sedley Mackie. New York: Cortes Society, 1924.

Alvarado Tezózomoc, Hernando. *Crónica mexicana* [1598]. Mexico: Editorial Leyenda, 1944.

Barabas, Alicia M. "Rebeliones e insurrecciones indígenas en Oaxaca: La trayectoria histórica de la resisténcia étnica." In Alicia M. Barabas and Miguel A. Bartolomé, eds., *Etnicidad y pluralismo cultural: La dinámica étnica en Oaxaca*, pp. 213–56. Mexico: Instituto Nacional de Antropología, 1986.

———. *Utopías indias: movimientos sociorreligiosos en México.* Mexico: Editorial Grijalbo, 1989.

Barlow, Robert H. "The Extent of the Empire of the Culhua Mexica." *Ibero-Americana* 28. Berkeley: University of California Press, 1949.

———. "The Mapa de Huilotepec." *Tlalocan* 1, no. 2 (1943): 155–57.

Barth, Frederic. *Ethnic Groups and Boundaries.* Boston: Little, Brown, 1969.

Baskes, Jeremy. *Indians, Merchants, and Markets. A Reinterpretation of the Repartimiento and Spanish-Indian Economic Relations in Colonial Oaxaca, 1750–1821.* Stanford, Calif.: Stanford University Press, 2000.

Berlin, Heinrich. "Las antiguas creencias en San Miguel Sola, Oaxaca, México." Reprinted in *Idolatría y superstición entre los indios de Oaxaca*, pp. 7–89. Mexico: Ediciones Toledo, 1988.

Blanton, Richard, Stephen Kowalewski, Gary Feinman, and Jill Appel. *Monte Albán's Hinterland, Part I: Prehispanic Settlement Patterns of the Central and Southern Parts of the Valley of Oaxaca, Mexico.* Memoirs of the Museum of Anthropology, University of Michigan, no. 15. Ann Arbor, Mich.: Museum of Anthropology, 1982.

Boone, Elizabeth Hill. *Stories in Red and Black: Pictorial Histories of the Aztec and Mixtec.* Austin: University of Texas Press, 2000.

Borah, Woodrow and Shelburne F. Cook. The Population of Central Mexico in 1548: An Analysis of the "Suma de visitas de pueblos." *Ibero-Americana* 43. Berkeley and Los Angeles: University of California Press, 1960.

Bourdieu, Pierre. *The Logic of Practice.* Stanford, Calif.: Stanford University Press, 1990.

Bricker, Victoria Reifler. *The Indian Christ, The Indian King: The Historical Substrate of Maya Myth and Ritual.* Austin: University of Texas Press, 1981.

Brockington, Lolita Gutiérrez. *The Leverage of Labor: Managing the Cortés Haciendas in Tehuantepec, 1588–1688.* Durham, N.C.: Duke University Press, 1989.

Brundage, Burr Cartwright. *A Rain of Darts: The Mexica Aztecs.* Austin: University of Texas Press, 1972.

Burgoa, Fr. Francisco de. *Geográfica descripción* [1674], 2 vols. Mexico: Editorial Porrua, 1989.

———. *Palestra historial.* Mexico: Juan Ruiz, 1670.

Campbell, Howard, Leigh Binford, Miguel Bartolomé, and Alicia Barabas, eds. *Zapotec Struggles: Histories, Politics and Representations from Juchitán, Oaxaca.* Washington, D.C.: Smithsonian Institution Press, 1993.

Canterla, Francisco and Martín de Tovar. *La iglesia de Oaxaca en el siglo XVIII.* Seville: Escuela de Estudios Hispano-Americanos, 1982.

Carmagnani, Marcello. "Un movimiento político indio: La 'rebelión' de Tehuantepec, 1660–1661." In Jaime E. Rodríguez O., ed., *Patterns of Contention in Mexican History*, pp. 17–35. Wilmington, Del.: S. R. Books, 1992.

———. *El regreso de los dioses: El proceso de reconstitución de la identidad étnica en Oaxaca. Siglos XVII y XVIII.* Mexico: Fondo de Cultura Económica, 1988.

Carrasco, Pedro. "Estratificación social indígena en Morelos durante el siglo XVI." In Pedro Carrasco and Johanna Broda, eds. *Estratificación social en la Mesoamérica prehispánica*, pp. 102–77. Mexico:Instituto Nacional de Antropoligía e Historia, 1976.

———. "The Joint Family in Ancient Mexico: The Case of Molotla." In Hugo Nutini, Pedro Carrasco, and James M. Taggett, eds., *Essays on Mexican Kinship*, pp. 45–64. Pittsburgh: University of Pittsburgh Press, 1976.

———. *The Tenochca Empire of Ancient Mexico: The Triple Alliance of Tenochtitlan, Tetzcoco, and Tlacopan.* Norman, Okla.: University of Oklahoma Press, 1999.

Carriedo, Juan Bautista. *Estudios históricos y estadísticos del estado libre de Oajaca*, vol. 1. Oaxaca, Mexico: private printing, 1847.

Caso, Alfonso. "The Lords of Yanhuitlan." In John Paddock, ed., *Ancient Oaxaca,* pp. 313–35. Stanford, Calif.: Stanford University Press, 1966.

———. "Zapotec Writing and Calendar." In Gordon R. Willey, ed., *Handbook of Middle American Indians*, vol. 3, The Archaeology of Southern Mesoamerica, pp. 931–47. Austin: University of Texas Press, 1965.

———, ed. "Relación de Tehuantepec." *Revista mexicana de estudios históricos* 2, no. 5 (Sept.–Oct. 1928): appendix.

Caso, Alfonso and Ignacio Bernal. *Urnas de Oaxaca*. Mexico: Instituto Nacional de Antropología e Historia, 1952.

———. *Reyes y reinos de la Mixteca,* vol. I. Mexico: Fondo de Cultura Económica, 1977.

Chance, John K. "The Barrios of Colonial Tecali: Patronage, Kinship, and Territorial Relations in a Central Mexican Community." *Ethnology* 35, no. 2 (1996): 107–39.

———. "The Caciques of Tecali: Class and Ethnic Identity in Late Colonial Mexico." *Hispanic American Historical Review* 76, no. 3 (1996): 475–502.

———. "La dinámica étnica en Oaxaca colonial." In Alicia M. Barabas and Miguel A. Bartolomé, eds., *Etnicidad y pluralismo cultural. La dinámica étnica en Oaxaca,* pp. 143–72. Mexico: Instituto Nacional de Antropología e Historia, 1986.

———. "Indian Elites in Late Colonial Mesoamerica." In Joyce Marcus and Judith Francis Zeitlin, eds., *Caciques and Their People*, pp. 45–65. Anthropological Papers, Museum of Anthropology, no. 89. Ann Arbor, Mich.: Museum of Anthropology, University of Michigan, 1994.

Charleton, Thomas H. *Post-Conquest Developments in the Teotihuacán Valley, Mexico. Part 1, Excavations*. Iowa City, Iowa: Office of the State Archaeologist, 1972.

Cline, Howard F. "Civil Congregations of the Indians in New Spain, 1598–1606." *Hispanic American Historical Review* 29, no. 3 (1949): 349–69.

Codex Mendoza. James Cooper Clark, ed. London: Waterlow and Sons, Ltd., 1938.

Comaroff, Jean and John Comaroff. *Of Revelation and Revolution: Christianity, Colonialism, and Consciousness in South Africa*. Chicago: University of Chicago Press, 1991.

Córdova, Fr. Juan de. *Arte del idioma zapoteca por el P. Fr. Juan de Cordoba*. Nicolás León, editor. Morelia: Imprenta del Gobierno, 1886.

———. *Arte en lengua zapoteco*. Mexico: Pedro Balli, 1578.

———. *Vocabulario en lengua zapoteca* [1570]. Mexico: Ediciones Toledo, 1989.

Cortés, Hernán. *Cartas de Relación*. Mexico: Editorial Concepto, 1983.

Covarrubias, Miguel. *Mexico South*. New York: Alfred Knopf, 1947.

Cruz, Victor de la, ed. *La Rebelión de Tehuantepec*. México: Publicaciones del H. Ayuntamiento Popular de Juchitán, Oaxaca, 1983.

Dávila Padilla, Fr. Agustín. *Historia de la fundación y discurso de la provincia de Santiago de Mexico de la Orden de Predicadores por las vidas de sus varones insignes y casos notables de Nueva España* [1596]. Brussels: Juan de Meerbeque, 1625.

Delgado, Agustín. *Archaeological Reconnaissance in the Region of Tehuantepec, Mexico*. Papers of the New World Archaeological Foundation, no. 18. Provo, Utah: New World Archaeological Foundation, Brigham Young University, 1965.

Díaz-Polanco, Héctor, ed. *El fuego de la inobediencia. Autonomía y rebelión india en el Obispado de Oaxaca*. Mexico: Centro de Investigaciones y Estudios Superiores en Antropología Social, 1992.

Díaz-Polanco, Héctor and Araceli Burguete. "Sociedad colonial y rebelión indígena en el Obispado de Oaxaca (1660)." In Héctor Díaz-Polanco, ed., *El fuego de la inobediencia. Autonomía y rebelión india en el Obispado de Oaxaca*, pp. 17–52. Mexico: Centro de Investigaciones y Estudios Superiores en Antropología Social, 1992.

Díaz-Polanco, Héctor and Consuelo Sánchez. "El vigor de la espada restauradora. La represión de las rebeliones indias en Oaxaca (1660–1661)." In Héctor Díaz-Polanco, ed., *El fuego de la inobediencia. Autonomía y rebelión india en el Obispado de Oaxaca*, pp. 53–80. Mexico: Centro de Investigaciones y Estudios Superiores en Antropología Social, 1992.

Douglas, Mary and Baron Isherwood. *The World of Goods*. New York: Basic Books, 1974.

Dupaix, Guillermo. *Expediciones acerca de los antiguos monumentos de la Nueva España, 1805–1808*. José Alcina Franch, editor. 2 vols. Madrid: Ediciones José Porrúa Turanzas, 1969.

Durán, Fr. Diego. *Historia de las indias de Nueva España e islas de la tierra firme* [1570, 1579] 2 vols. Mexico: Editorial Porrua, 1967.

Estrada, Aureliano. *Las ruinas del Cerro Guiengola. Memorias de la Sociedad Científica Antonio Alzate* 6 (Mexico,1892).

Ewald, Ursula. *The Mexican Salt Industry, 1560–1980: A Study in Change*. Stuttgart: Gustav Fischer Verlag, 1985.

Farriss, Nancy M. *Maya Society Under Colonial Rule*. Princeton, N.J.: Princeton University Press, 1984.

Feria, Fr. Pedro de. *La doctrina christiana en lengua castellana y çapoteca*. Mexico: Pedro Ocharte, 1567.

Florescano, Enrique. *Etnia, estado y nación: Ensayo sobre las identidades colectivas en México*. Mexico: Aguilar, 1996.

Foucault, Michel. *Discipline and Punish: The Birth of the Prison*. New York: Random House, 1979.

García, Genaro. *Don Juan Palafox y Mendoza, obispo de Puebla y Osma, visitador y virrey de la Nueva España*. Mexico: Librería de la Vda. de Ch. Bouret, 1918.

———, ed. *Tumultos y rebeliones acaecidos en México*. Documentos inéditos o muy raros para la historia de México, vol. 10. Mexico: Librería de la Vda. de Ch. Bouret, 1907.

García Pimentel, Luís, ed. "Descripción del obispado de Antequera de la Nueva España hecha per el obispo del dicho obispado." *Relación de los obispados de*

Tlaxcala, Michoacan, Oaxaca y otros lugares en el siglo XVI. Documentos históricos de Méjico, vol. 2, pp. 59–154. Mexico: private printing, 1904.

Garrido Cardona, Martha Lis. *Monumentos coloniales religiosos del istmo de Tehuantepec*. Mexico: Instituto Nacional de Antropología e Historia, 1995.

Gasco, Janine. *Cacao and the Economic Integration of Native Society in Colonial Soconusco, New Spain*. Ph.D. dissertation, University of California Santa Barbara, 1987.

———. "Economic History of Ocelocalco, a Colonial Soconusco Town." In Barbara Voorhies, ed., *Ancient Trade and Tribute: Economies of the Soconusco Region of Mesoamerica*, pp. 305–25. Salt Lake City, Utah: University of Utah Press, 1989.

———. "Socioeconomic Change Within Native Society in Colonial Soconusco." In J. D. Rogers and S. M. Wilson, eds., *Ethnohistory and Archaeology: Approaches to Postcontact Change in the Americas*, pp. 163–80. New York: Plenum Press, 1993.

Gay, José Antonio. *Historia de Oaxaca* [1881]. Mexico: Editorial Porrúa, 1990.

Gibson, Charles. *The Aztecs Under Spanish Rule*. Stanford, Calif.: Stanford University Press, 1964.

———. "Structure of the Aztec Empire." In Gordon Ekholm and Ignacio Bernal, vol. eds., *Handbook of Middle American Indians*, vol. 10. Archaeology of Northern Mesoamerica, part I, pp. 376–94. Austin: University of Texas Press, 1971.

Gillespie, Susan D. *The Aztec Kings: The Construction of Rulership in Mexica History*. Tucson, Ariz.: University of Arizona Press, 1989.

Glass, John. "A Survey of Native Middle American Pictorial Manuscripts." In Howard F. Cline, vol. ed., *Handbook of Middle American Indians*, vol. 14, Guide to Ethnohistorical Sources, Part 3, pp. 3–80. Austin: University of Texas Press, 1975.

Goggin, John M. *Spanish Majolica in the New World: Types of the Sixteenth to Eighteenth Centuries*. New Haven, Conn.: Yale University Press, 1968.

Gonzalbo Aizpuru, Pilar. *Historia de la educación en la época colonial: El mundo indígena*. Mexico: El Colegio de México, 1990.

Goody, Jack. *The Interface Between the Written and the Oral*. Cambridge: Cambridge University Press, 1987.

Gosner, Kevin. "Religion and Rebellion in Colonial Chiapas." In Susan Schroeder, ed., *Native Resistance and the Pax Colonial in New Spain*, pp. 47–66. Lincoln, Nebr.: University of Nebraska Press, 1998.

Gruzinski, Serge. *The Conquest of Mexico: The Incorporation of Indian Societies into the Western World, Sixteenth to Eighteenth Centuries*. Cambridge: Polity Press, 1993.

———. *Man-Gods in the Mexican Highlands: Indian Power and Colonial Society, 1520–1800*, Stanford, Calif.: Stanford University Press, 1989.

Hamnett, Brian. *Politics and Trade in Southern Mexico, 1750–1821*. Cambridge: Cambridge University Press, 1971.

Haskett, Robert. *Indigenous Rulers: An Ethnohistory of Town Government in Colonial Cuernavaca*. Albuquerque: University of New Mexico Press, 1991.

Hassig, Ross. *Aztec Warfare: Imperial Expansion and Political Control*. Norman, Okla.: University of Oklahoma Press.

———. *Trade, Tribute, and Transportation: The Sixteenth Century Political Economy of the Valley of Mexico*. Norman, Okla.: University of Oklahoma Press.

Hicks, Frederic. "Cloth in the Political Economy of the Aztec State." In Mary G. Hodge and Michael E. Smith, eds., *Economies and Polities in the Aztec Realm*, pp. 89–111. Albany, N.Y.: Institute for Mesoamerican Studies, State University of New York, 1994.

Hobsbawn, E. J. *Primitive Rebels*. New York: W. W. Norton, 1965.

Hodge, Mary G. and Michael E. Smith, eds. *Economies and Polities in the Aztec Realm*. Albany, N.Y.: Institute for Mesoamerican Studies, State University of New York at Albany, 1994.

Horn, Rebecca. *Postconquest Coyoacan: Nahua-Spanish Relations in Central Mexico, 1519–1650*. Stanford, Calif.: Stanford University Press, 1997.

Israel, J. I. *Race, Class and Politics in Colonial Mexico, 1610–1670*. Oxford: Oxford University Press, 1975.

Jansen, Maarten. "Monte Albán y Zaachila en los codices mixtecos." In Maarten Jansen, Peter Kröfges, and Michel R. Oudijk, *The Shadow of Monte Albán: Politics and Historiography in Postclassic Oaxaca, Mexico*, pp. 67–122. Leiden: Research School CNWS, 1998.

———. "El viaje al otro mundo: La Tumba 1 de Zaachila." In Maarten Jansen and T. Leyenaar, eds., *Los indígenas de México en la época prehispánica y en la actualidad*, pp. 87–118. Leiden: Rutgers, 1982.

Jones, Siân. *The Archaeology of Ethnicity: Constructing Identities in the Past and the Present*. London: Routledge, 1997.

Karttunen, Frances. *An Analytical Dictionary of Nahuatl*. Austin: University of Texas Press, 1983.

Karttunen, Frances, and James Lockhart. *Nahuatl in the Middle Years: Language Contact Phenomena in Texts of the Colonial Period*. University of California Publications in Linguistics, no. 85. Berkeley and Los Angeles: University of California Press, 1976.

Kaufman, Terrence. "Mixe-Zoque Subgroups and the Position of Tapachulteco." *XXXV Congreso Internacional de Americanistas* (Mexico) 35 (1964): 403–11.

Kertzer, David I. *Ritual, Politics, and Power*. New Haven, Conn.: Yale University Press, 1988.

Knight, Alan. *Mexico: The Colonial Era*. Cambridge: Cambridge University Press, 2000.

Kowalewski, Stephen, Gary M. Feinman, Laura Finsten, Richard E. Blanton, and Linda M. Nicolas. *Monte Alban's Hinterland, Part II: Prehispanic Settlement Patterns in Tlacolula, Etla, and Ocotlán, the Valley of Oaxaca, Mexico*. Memoirs of the Museum of Anthropology, University of Michigan, no. 23. 2 vols. Ann Arbor, Mich.: Museum of Anthropology, University of Michigan, 1989.

Leander, Birgitta. *Códice de Otlazpan*. Mexico: Instituto Nacional de Antropología e Historia, Serie Investigaciones, no. 13, 1967.

León-Portilla, Miguel. "Nahuatl Literature." In Munro S. Edmonson, vol. ed., *Supplement to the Handbook of Middle American Indians*, vol. 3, Literatures, pp. 7–43. Austin: University of Texas Press, 1985.

El libro de las tasaciones de pueblos de la Nueva España, siglo XVI. Mexico: Archivo General de la Nación, 1952.

Lister, Florence C. and Robert H. Lister. *Andalusian Ceramics in New Spain: A Cultural Register from the Third Century B.C. to 1700*. Tucson, Ariz.: University of Arizona Press, 1987.

Llaguno, José A., S.J. *La personalidad jurídica del indio y el III Concilio Provincial Mexicano*. Mexico: Editorial Porrua, 1963.

Lockhart, James. *The Nahuas After the Conquest*. Stanford, Calif.: Stanford University Press, 1992.

———. *Nahuas and Spaniards: Postconquest Central Mexican History and Philology*. Stanford, Calif.: Stanford University Press and UCLA Latin American Center Publications, 1991.

López de Gómara, Francisco. *Cortés: The Life of the Conqueror by his Secretary*. Lesley Byrd Simpson, trans. and ed. Berkeley: University of California Press, 1966.

Machuca Gallegos, Laura Olivia. *Los pueblos indios de Tehuantepec y el repartimiento de mercancias durante el siglo XVIII*. Maestria de Filosofía y Letras thesis. Universidad Nacional Autónoma de México, 1999.

———. *Tehuantepec en el siglo XVI*. Licenciado en Historia thesis. Universidad Nacional Autónoma de México, 1996.

Manso de Contreras, Christoval. *Relación cierta, y verdadera de lo que sucedió en esta villa de Guadalcaçar provincia de Tehuantepeque desde los 22 de Março de 1660. Hasta los quatro de Iulio de 1661. Cerca de que los Naturales Indios destas Provincias, Tumultados, y amotinados mataron á Iuan de Avellan, su Alcalde mayor y Theniente de Capitan General; y á tres Criados suyos, procediendo á otros gravissimos delictos hasta aclamar Rey de su Naturaleça; y las diligencias, averiguación, castigo, y perdon que con ellos se á seguido*. Mexico: Iuan Ruyz, 1661.

Manzo, Carlos. *Asimilación y resistencia. Raices coloniales de la autonomía regional en el sur del Istmo de Tehuantepec*. Maestría en Economía thesis. Universidad Nacional Autónoma de México, 1993.

———. "Comercio y rebelión en el Obispado de Oaxaca. Tehuantepec y Nexapa, 1660–1661." In Héctor Díaz-Polanco, ed., *El fuego de la inobediencia. Autonomía y rebelión india en el Obispado de Oaxaca*, pp. 103–32. Mexico: Centro de Investigaciones y Estudios Superiores en Antropología Social, 1992.

Marcus, Joyce. *Mesoamerican Writing Systems: Propaganda, Myth, and History in Four Ancient Civilizations*. Princeton, N.J.: Princeton University Press, 1992.

———. "The Reconstructed Chronology of the Later Zapotec Rulers, A.D. 1415–1563." In Kent V. Flannery and Joyce Marcus, eds., *The Cloud People*, pp. 301–8. New York: Academic Press, 1983.

———. "Zapotec Religion." In Kent V. Flannery and Joyce Marcus, eds., *The Cloud People*, pp. 345–51. New York: Academic Press, 1983.

———. "Zapotec Writing." *Scientific American* 242, no. 2 (1980): 50–64.

Marcus, Joyce and Kent V. Flannery. "Ancient Zapotec Ritual and Religion: An Application of the Direct Historical Approach." In Colin Renfrew and Ezra B.W. Zubrow, eds., *The Ancient Mind: Elements of Cognitive Archaeology*, pp. 55–74. Cambridge: Cambridge University Press, 1994.

———. *Zapotec Civilization: How Urban Society Evolved in Mexico's Oaxaca Valley*. London: Thames and Hudson, 1996.

Martin, Cheryl English. *Rural Society in Colonial Morelos*. Albuquerque, N.M.: University of New Mexico Press, 1985.

Martínez Gracida, Manuel. *Los indios oaxaqueños y sus monumentos arqueológicos* [1892]. Oaxaca: Gobierno del Estado de Oaxaca, 1986.

———. *El rey Cocijoeza y su familia: Reseña histórica y legendaria de los últimos soberanos de Zaachila*. Mexico: Ofic. Tip. de la Secretaría de Fomento, 1888.

Matadamas Díaz, Raul. "Recorrido en el sitio Cerro Padre López de la ciudad de Tehuantepec, Oaxaca." Ms. on file at the offices of the Centro Regional de Oaxaca, Instituto Nacional de Antropología e Historia, Oaxaca, Mexico, 1983.

McAndrew, John. *The Open-Air Churches of Sixteenth-Century Mexico*. Cambridge, Mass.: Harvard University Press, 1965.

Monaghan, John, Arthur Joyce, and Ronald Spores. "Transformations of the Indigenous Cacicazgo in the Nineteenth Century." *Ethnohistory* 50, no. 1 (2003): 131–50.

Montemayor de Cuenca, Juan Francisco. *Discurso politico-historico juridico del derecho y Repartimiento de presas y despojos apprehendidos en justa guerra. Premios y castigos de los soldados*. Mexico: Juan Ruíz, 1658.

Moorehead, Max L. "Hernán Cortés and the Tehuantepec Passage." *Hispanic American Historical Review* 29, no. 3 (1949): 370–79.

Moreno, Fr. Geronymo, O.P. *Reglas ciertas y precisamente necessarias para juezes, y ministros de justicia de las Indias, y para sus Confessores*. Mexico: Emprenta de Francisco Salbago, Ministro del Sancto Officio, 1637.

Motolinía, Fr. Toribio de Benavente. *Motolinia's History of the Indians of New Spain*. Richmond, Va.: Publications of the Academy of American Franciscan History, 1951.

Mullen, Robert J. *Dominican Architecture in Sixteenth-Century Oaxaca*. Tempe, Ariz.: Arizona State University Press, 1975.

Murguia y Galardi, José María. *Extracto general que abraza la Estadística toda en su 1a y 2a parte del Estado de Guaxaca, y ha reunido de Orden del Supremo Gobierno el intendente de Provincia en clase de los cesantes José María Murguia y Galardi*. Ms. Benson Latin American Collection, University of Texas, Austin, 1827.

Navarrete, Carlos. *El sistema prehispánico de comunicaciones entre Chiapas y Tabasco*. Anales de antropología, no. 10. Mexico: Universidad Nacional Autónima de México, 1973.

Ojea, Fr. Fernando. *Libro tercero de la historia religiosa de la provincia de México de la Orden de Santo Domingo* [composed in 1608], edited by José María de Agreda y Sánchez. Mexico: Museo Nacional de México, 1897.

Olivera, Mercedes and María de los Angeles Romero Frizzi. "La estructura política de Oaxaca en el siglo XVI." *Revista mexicana de sociología* 35, no. 2 (1973). Reprinted in María de los Angeles Romero Frizzi, ed., *Lecturas históricas del estado de Oaxaca*, vol. II, pp. 65–78. Mexico: Instituto Nacional de Antropología e Historia/Gobierno del Estado de Oaxaca.

Osborne,Wayne S. "Indian Land Retention in Colonial Metztitlán." *Hispanic American Historical Review* 53, no. 2 (1973): 103–15.

Oudijk, Michel. "The Genealogy of Zaachila: Four Weddings and a Dynastic Struggle." In Maarten Jansen, Peter Kröfges, and Michel R. Oudijk, eds., *The Shadow of Monte Albán: Politics and Historiography in Postclassic Oaxaca, Mexico*, pp. 13–36. Leiden: Research School CNWS, Leiden University, 1998.

———. *Historiography of the Bènizàa: The Postclassic and Early Colonial Periods (1000–1600 A.D.)*. Leiden: Research School CNWS, Leiden University, 2000.

Oudijk, Michel and Maarten Jansen. "Changing History in the Lienzos de Guevea and Santo Domingo Petapa." *Ethnohistory* 47, no. 2 (2000): 281–331.

Oviedo, Gonzalo Fernández de. *Historia general y natural de las indias* [1544]. Madrid: Biblioteca de Autores Españoles, 1959.

Paddock, John. *Lord 5 Flower's Family: Rulers of Zaachila and Cuilapan*. Vanderbilt University Publications in Anthropology, no. 29. Nashville, Tenn.: Department of Anthropology, Vanderbilt University, 1983.

Pagden, Anthony, trans. and ed. *Hernán Cortés: Letters from Mexico*. New Haven, Conn.: Yale University Press, 1986.

———. *Spanish Imperialism and the Political Imagination*. New Haven, Conn.: Yale University Press, 1990.

Palau Dulcet, Antonio. *Manual del librero hispanoamericano*, vol. 10. Oxford and Barcelona: Dolphin Book Co., 1957.

Palma y Freites, Luís de la. *Por las religiones de Santo Domingo, San Francisco y San Agustin de las Provincias de la Nueva España. En defensa de las doctrinas de que fueron removidos de hecho sus Religiosos Doctrineros: por el Ilustrissimo señor Don Juan de Palafox y Mendoza, Obispo de Tlaxcala, del Consejo de su Magestad*. Madrid: La Imprenta Real, 1644.

Parsons, Elsie Clews. *Mitla, Town of the Souls, and Other Zapotec-Speaking Pueblos of Oaxaca, Mexico*. Chicago: University of Chicago Press, 1936.

Paso y Troncoso, Francisco del, ed. "Memorial de los pueblos sujetos al señorío de Tlacupan, y de los que tributaban a México, Tezcuco y Tlacupan." *Epistolario de Nueva España,* vol. 14, pp. 118–22. Mexico: Antigua Librería Robredo de José Porrua e Hijos, 1940.

———, ed. "Relación de lo que valieron las rentas del Marqués del Valle en los años de 1568 y 1569." *Epistolario de Nueva España*, vol. 11, pp. 5–60. Mexico: Antigua Librería Robredo de José Porrúa e Hijos, 1940.

———, ed. "Relación de la visita que hizo Baltasar de San Miguel del pueblo de Tecoantepeque y probincia." *Papeles de Nueva España, segunda serie: geografía y estadística*, vol. 1, pp. 312–14. Madrid: Establecimiento Tip. "Sucesores de Rivadeneyra," 1905.

———, ed. "Relaciones Geográficas de la diócesis de Oaxaca." *Papeles de Nueva*

España, segunda serie: geografía y estadística. Vol. 4. Madrid: Establecimiento Tip. "Sucesores de Rivadeneyra," 1905.

Pastor, Rodolfo, *Campesinos y reformas: La Mixteca, 1700–1856*. Mexico: El Colegio de México, 1987.

Patch, Robert W. "Culture, Community, and 'Rebellion' in the Yucatec Maya Uprising of 1761." In Susan Schroeder, ed., *Native Resistance and the Pax Colonial in New Spain*, pp. 67–83. Lincoln, Nebr.: University of Nebraska Press, 1998.

———. *Maya and Spaniard in Yucatán*. Stanford, Calif.: Stanford University Press, 1993.

Perry, Richard. *Mexico's Fortress Monasteries*. Santa Barbara, Calif.: Espadaña Press, 1992.

Peterson, David. "Guiengola: fortaleza zapoteca en el Istmo de Tehuantepec." In Marcus C. Winter, ed., *Lecturas históricas del estado de Oaxaca,* vol. I, Epoca prehispánica, pp. 455–88. Mexico: Instituto Nacional de Antropología e Historia, 1990.

Peterson, David and Thomas MacDougall. *Guiengola: A Fortified Site in the Isthmus of Tehuantepec*. Vanderbilt University Publications in Anthropology, no. 10. Nashville: Department of Anthropology, Vanderbilt University, 1974.

Quiñones-Keber, Eloise. *Codex Telleriano-Remensis: Ritual, Divination, and History in a Pictorial Aztec Manuscript.* Austin: University of Texas Press, 1995.

Ramírez, José Fernando, ed. *Proceso de residencia contra Pedro de Alvarado.* Ignacio Rayon, transcriber. Mexico: Valdes y Redondas, 1847.

Recinos, Adrián and Delia Goetz, trans. *The Annals of the Cakchiquels.* Norman, Okla.: University of Oklahoma Press, 1953.

Redmond. Elsa M. *A Fuego y Sangre: Early Zapotec Imperialism in the Cuicatlán Cañada, Oaxaca.* Memoirs of the Museum of Anthropology, University of Michigan, no. 16. Ann Arbor, Mich.: Museum of Anthropology, University of Michigan, 1983.

Restall, Matthew. "A History of the New Philology and the New Philology in History." *Latin American Research Review* 38, no. 1 (2003): 113–33.

———. *Maya Conquistador*. Boston: Beacon Press, 1998.

———. *The Maya World: Yucatec Culture and Society, 1550–1850*. Stanford, Calif.: Stanford University Press, 1997.

Ricard, Robert. *The Spiritual Conquest of Mexico*. Berkeley: University of California Press, 1966.

Romero Frizzi, María de los Angeles. *Economía y vida de los españoles en la Mixteca Alta: 1519–1720*. Mexico: Instituto Nacional de Antropología e Historia, 1990.

———. "Indigenous Mentality and Spanish Power: The Conquest in Oaxaca." In Joyce Marcus and Judith Francis Zeitlin, eds., *Caciques and Their People: A Volume in Honor of Ronald Spores*. Anthropological Papers, Museum of Anthropology, University of Michigan, no. 89, pp. 227–44. Ann Arbor, Mich.: Museum of Anthropology, University of Michigan, 1994.

———. *El sol y la cruz: Los pueblos indios de Oaxaca colonial.* Mexico: Centro

de Investigaciones y Estudios Superiores en Antropología Social/Instituto Nacional Indigenista, 1996.
Rowe, John H. "Inca Culture at the Time of the Spanish Conquest." In Julian Steward, ed., *Handbook of South American Indians*, vol. 2, pp. 183–330. Washington, D.C.: Smithsonian Institution, Bureau of American Ethnology, Bulletin 143, 1944.
Sahagún, Fr. Bernardino de. *Florentine Codex: General History of the Things of New Spain*. Charles E. Dibble and Arthur J.O. Anderson, trans. Santa Fe, N.M.: School of American Research, 1954.
Scott, James C. *The Moral Economy of the Peasant: Rebellion and Subsistence in Southeast Asia*. New Haven, Conn.: Yale University Press, 1976.
Seifert, Donna J. *Archaeological Majolicas of the Rural Teotihuacan Valley, Mexico*. Ph.D. dissertation, University of Iowa, 1977.
Seler, Eduard. "Das Dorfbuch von Santiago Guevea." In *Gesammelte Abhandlungen zur amerikanische Sprach- und Altertumskunde*, vol. 3, pp. 157–93. Berlin: A. Ascher, 1908.
———. "Die Ruinen auf dem Guie-Ngola." In *Gesammelte Abhandlungen zur amerikanischen Sprach- und Alterthumskunde*, vol. 2, pp. 184–99. Berlin: Ascher, 1904.
Scholes, France V. and Eleanor B. Adams. *Moderación de doctrinas de la Real Corona administradas por las Ordenes Mendicantes, 1623*. Mexico: J. Porrúa, 1959.
Simpson, Lesley Bird. *Exploitation of Land in Central Mexico in the 16th Century*. Berkeley: University of California Press, 1952.
Smith, Michael E. *The Aztecs*. Malden, Mass. and London: Blackwell, 1996.
Smith Stark, Thomas C. "Dioses, sacerdotes y sacrificio: Una mirada a la religión zapoteca a través del *Vocabulario en Lengua Çapoteca* (1578) de Juan de Córdoba." In Victor de la Cruz and Marcus Winter, eds., *La religión de los binnigula'sa'*, pp. 89–195. Oaxaca, Mexico: Fondo Editorial, IEEPO, 2001.
Sousa, Lisa and Kevin Terraciano. "The 'Original Conquest' of Oaxaca: Nahua and Mixtec Accounts of the Spanish Conquest." *Ethnohistory* 50, no. 2 (2003): 349–400.
Spores, Ronald. *The Mixtecs in Ancient and Colonial Times*. Norman, Okla.: University of Oklahoma Press, 1984.
———. *Stratigraphic Excavations in the Nochixtlan Valley, Oaxaca, Mexico*. Vanderbilt University Publications in Anthropology no. 11. Nashville, Tenn.: Department of Anthropology, Vanderbilt University, 1974.
———. "The Zapotec and Mixtec at Spanish Contact." In Gordon Willey, ed., *Handbook of Middle American Indians*, vol. 3, Archaeology of Southern Mesoamerica, pt. 2, pp. 962–87. Austin: University of Texas Press, 1965.
Stern, Steve J. *Peru's Indian Peoples and the Challenge of Spanish Conquest: Huamanga to 1640*. Madison, Wisc.: University of Wisconsin Press, 1982.
Tavárez, Davíd. *Invisible Wars: Idolatry Extirpation Projects and Native Responses in Nahua and Zapotec Commuinities, 1536–1728*. Ph.D. dissertation, University of Chicago, 2000.

Taylor, William B. *Drinking, Homicide and Rebellion in Colonial Mexican Villages*. Stanford, Calif.: Stanford University Press, 1979.

———. "Landed Society in New Spain: A View from the South." *Hispanic American Historical Review* 54, no. 3 (1974): 387–413.

———. *Landlord and Peasant in Colonial Oaxaca*. Stanford, Calif.: Stanford University Press, 1972.

Terraciano, Kevin. "The Colonial Mixtec Community." *Hispanic American Historical Review* 80, no. 1 (2000): 1–42.

———. *The Mixtecs of Colonial Oaxaca: Ñudzahui History, Sixteenth Through Eighteenth Centuries*. Stanford, Calif.: Stanford University Press, 2001.

Thomas, Norman D. *The Linguistic, Geographic, and Demographic Position of the Zoque of Southern Mexico*. Papers of the New World Archaeological Foundation, no. 36. Provo, Utah: New World Archaeological Foundation, Brigham Young University, 1974.

Thompson, J. Eric S. *Maya History and Religion*. Norman, Okla.: University of Oklahoma Press, 1970.

Toribio Medina, José. *La imprenta en México, 1539–1821*. Amsterdam: N. Israel, 1965 [1912].

Torquemada, Fr. Juan de. *Monarquía indiana* . 3 vols. Mexico: Editorial Porrua, 1975 [1615].

Turner, Victor. *Dramas, Fields, and Metaphors: Symbolic Action in Human Society*. Ithaca, N.Y.: Cornell University Press, 1974.

Tutino, John. "Indian Rebellion in the Isthmus of Tehuantepec: A Sociohistorical Perspective." *Proceedings of the 42nd International Congress of Americanists* 7, no. 3 (1978): 197–214.

Ulloa H., Daniel. *Los predicadores dividos: Los dominicos en Nueva España, siglo XVI* . Mexico: El Colegio de México, 1977.

Urcid Serrano, Javier. *Zapotec Hieroglyphic Writing*. Studies in Pre-Columbian Art and Archaeology, no. 34. Washington, D.C.: Dumbarton Oaks Research Library and Collection, 2001.

Vásquez de Espinosa, Antonio. "Cartas del P. Bernabé Cobo, de la Compañia de Jesús, escritas a un compañero suyo residente en el Perú." In Mariano Cuevas, ed., *Descripción de la Nueva España en el siglo XVII*. Mexico: Editorial Patria, S.A., 1944.

Velasco Pérez, Carlos. *La conquista armada y espititual de la Nueva Antequera*. Mexico: Impr. Bellini, 1982.

Villaseñor y Sánchez, Antonio. *Theatro americano: descripción general de los reynos y provincias de la Nueva España y sus jurisdicciones,* [1746–48]. 2 vols. Facsimile edition. Mexico: Juan Cortina Portilla, 1986.

Voorhies, Barbara, ed. *Ancient Trade and Tribute: Economies of the Soconusco Region of Mesoamerica*. Salt Lake City, Utah: University of Utah Press, 1989.

Wasserstrom, Robert. *Class and Society in Central Chiapas*. Berkeley: University of California Press, 1983.

Whitecotton, Joseph. *Zapotec Elite Ethnohistory: Pictorial Genealogies from Eastern Oaxaca*. Vanderbilt University Publications in Anthropology, no. 39. Nashville, Tenn.: Department of Anthropology, Vanderbilt University, 1990.

———. *The Zapotecs: Princes, Priests, and Peasants*. Norman, Okla.: University of Oklahoma Press, 1977.

Whitecotton, Joseph W. and Judith Bradley Whitecotton, comps. *Vocabulario zapoteco-castellano*. Vanderbilt University Publications in Anthropology no. 45. Nashville, Tenn.: Department of Anthropology,Vanderbilt University, 1993.

Wood, Stephanie. *Transcending Conquest: Nahua Views of Spanish Colonial Mexico*. Norman, Okla.: University of Oklahoma Press, 2003.

Ybañes, Fr. Diego. *El juez conservador de los religiosos de Santo Domingo del Provincia de Guaxaca. En defensa de la jurisdicción que se niega el Obispo de aquel Obispado*. Mexico: ca. 1631.

Zeitlin, Judith Francis. "Changing Patterns of Resource Exploitation, Settlement Distribution, and Demography on the Southern Isthmus of Tehuantepec, Mexico." In Barbara L. Stark and Barbara Voorhies, eds., *Prehistoric Coastal Adaptations: The Economy and Ecology of Maritime Middle America*, pp. 151–77. New York: Academic Press, 1978.

———. "Colonialism and the Political Transformation of Isthmus Zapotec Society." In Ronald Spores and Ross Hassig, eds., *Law and Government in Central Mexico: Pre-Columbian Times to the Present*. Vanderbilt University Publications in Anthropology, no. 30, pp. 65–85. Nashville, Tenn.: Department of Anthropology, Vanderbilt University, 1984.

———. *Community Distribution and Local Economy on the Southern Isthmus of Tehuantepec: An Archaeological and Ethnohistorical Investigation*. Ph.D. dissertation, Yale University, 1978.

———. "Precolumbian Barrio Organization in Tehuantepec, Mexico." In Joyce Marcus and Judith Francis Zeitlin, eds., *Caciques and Their People: A Volume in Honor of Ronald Spores*, pp. 275–300. Anthropological Papers, Museum of Anthropology, University of Michigan, no. 89. Ann Arbor, Mich.: Museum of Anthropology, University of Michigan, 1994.

———. "Ranchers and Indians on the Southern Isthmus of Tehuantepec: Economic Change and Indigenous Survival in Colonial Mexico." *Hispanic American Historical Review* 69, no. 1 (1989): 23–60.

———. "Recordando a los reyes: El lienzo de Guevea y el discurso histórico de la época colonial." In Ma. Angeles Romero Frizzi, ed. *Escritura zapoteca: 2,500 años de historia*, pp. 265–304. Mexico: Centro de Investigaciones y Estudios Superiores en Antropología Social/Instituto Nacional de Antropología, 2003.

Zeitlin, Judith Francis and Lillian Thomas. "Indian Consumers on the Periphery of the Colonial Market System: Tracing Domestic Economic Behavior in a Tehuantepec Hamlet." In Janine Gasco, Greg Charles Smith, and Patricia Fournier-García, eds., *Approaches to the Historical Archaeology of Middle, Central and South America*, pp. 5–16. Los Angeles: Institute of Archaeology, University of California, 1997.

———. "Spanish Justice and the Indian Cacique: Disjunctive Political Systems in Sixteenth-Century Tehuantepec." *Ethnohistory* 39, no. 3 (Summer 1992): 285–315.

Zeitlin, Judith Francis and Robert Zeitlin. "Arqueología y época prehispánica en el sur del istmo de Tehuantepec." In Marcus C. Winter, ed. *Lecturas históricas del estado de Oaxaca,* vol. I, Epoca prehispánica, pp. 393–454. Mexico: Instituto Nacional de Antropología e Historia, 1990.

Zeitlin, Robert N. "Toward a More Comprehensive Model of Interregional Commodity Distribution: Political Variables and Prehistoric Obsidian Procurement in Mesoamerica." *American Antiquity* 47 (1982): 260–75.

Index

In this index an "f" after a number indicates a separate reference on the next page, and an "ff" indicates separate references on the next two pages. A continuous discussion over two or more pages is indicated by a span of page numbers, e.g., "57–59."*Passim* is used for a cluster of references in close but not consecutive sequence.